Intimc

OFC.

Intimate Violence:
Interdisciplinary Perspectives

Edited by

Emilio C. Viano
The American University, Washington, DC

Taylor & Francis
Publishers since 1798

INTIMATE VIOLENCE: Interdisciplinary Perspectives

3 4 5 6 7 8 9 0   E B E B   9 8 7 6 5

This book was set in Times Roman by Hemisphere Publishing Corporation. The editor was Amy Lyles Wilson; the production supervisor was Peggy M. Rote; and the typesetter was Anahid Alvandian. Printing and binding by Edwards Brothers, Inc.
Cover design by Michelle Fleitz.

A CIP catalog record for this book is available from the British Library.
 ∞ The paper in this publication meets the requirements of the ANSI Standard Z39.48-1984(Permanence of Paper)

Library of Congress Cataloging-in-Publication Data

Intimate violence : interdisciplinary perspectives / edited by Emilio C.
  Viano
    p.   cm.
  Includes bibliographical references and index.

  1. Family violence.   2. Wife abuse.   I. Viano, Emilio.
HQ809.I58   1992
362.82'92—dc20   92-49
                                                                             CIP

ISBN 1-56032-244-6

To my parents, Teresa and Giuseppe, and to the parents of all the contributors of this volume, hoping that we will be able to pass their love, dedication, and generosity to future generations.

Contents

PART III
WOMEN WHO KILL

PART IV
VIOLENCE IN DATING RELATIONSHIPS

PART V
THE MALE BATTERER

PART VI
APPROACHES AND INTERVENTIONS

Contributors

Cheryl Benard, Boltzmann Institute, Vienna, AUSTRIA

Noel A. Cazenave, Department of Sociology, The University of Connecticut, Storrs, Connecticut, USA

Youn-gyu Cho, School of Medicine, Hanyang University, Seoul, KOREA

Joan Crowley, Department of Criminal Justice, New Mexico State University, Las Cruces, New Mexico, USA

Liane V. Davis, School of Social Welfare, The University of Kansas, Lawrence, Kansas, USA

Alfred DeMaris, Bowling Green State University, Department of Sociology, Bowling Green, Ohio, USA

Annette Ehrlich, Department of Psychology, California State University, Los Angeles, California, USA

Barbara L. Ellington, Westview Press, Boulder, Colorado, USA

Desmond Ellis, Department of Sociology, York University, Downsview, Ontario, CANADA

Russell K. Endo, Ethnic Studies/Anthropology, University of Colorado, Boulder, Colorado, USA

Diane R. Follingstad, Department of Psychology, University of South Carolina, Columbia, South Carolina, USA

Susan E. Hanks, California School of Psychology, Berkeley, California, USA

Suzanne E. Hatty, University of New South Wales, AUSTRALIA

James E. Hendricks, Criminal Justice Department, Ball State University, Muncie, Indiana, USA

Ida M. Johnson, Department of Criminal Justice, University of Alabama, Tuscaloosa, Alabama, USA

Kwang-iel Kim, School of Medicine, Hanyang University, Seoul, KOREA

Rosemary A. Knight, A.C.T. Board of Health, Canberra, A.C.T., AUSTRALIA

Irma MacKay, Health Sciences Centre, Social Work Department, Winnipeg, Manitoba, CANADA

Coramae Richey Mann, Department of Criminal Justice, Indiana University, Bloomington, Indiana, USA

Kay McNeill-Harkins, Berkeley County Mental Health Center, South Carolina, USA

Komanduri S. Murty, Department of Criminal Justice, Clark-Atlanta University, Atlanta, Georgia, USA

Philip G. Ney, Faculty of Medicine, University of British Columbia, Victoria, B.C., CANADA

Joyce McCarl Nielsen, Department of Sociology, University of Colorado, Boulder, Colorado, USA

Maureen A. Pirog-Good, School of Public and Environmental Affairs, Indiana University, Bloomington, Indiana, USA

Darlene S. Polek, Veterans Administration Medical Center, Augusta, Georgia, USA

Nancy R. Rhodes, Private Practice, Pasadena, California, USA

Julian B. Roebuck, Criminal Justice Department, Clark-Atlanta University, Atlanta, Georgia, USA

Larry L. Rutledge, North Fulton Hospital, Atlanta, Georgia, USA

Edith Schlaffer, Boltzmann Institute, Vienna, AUSTRIA

Ishrat Shamim, Department of Sociology, University of Dhaka, Dhaka, BANGLADESH

Robert T. Sigler, Department of Criminal Justice, University of Alabama, Tuscaloosa, Alabama, USA

Robert M. Theodore, Counseling Center, Northwest Missouri State University, Maryville, Missouri, USA

Renata Vaselle-Augenstein, Private Practice, Los Angeles, California, USA

Emilio C. Viano, School of Public Affairs, The American University, Washington, DC, USA

Margaret A. Zahn, Department of Sociology, The University of North Carolina, Charlotte, North Carolina, USA

Preface

During the past two decades, victimology, a discipline that is concerned primarily with the victims of crime, the dynamics, and the aftermath of victimization, has developed rapidly. Its growth can be easily documented and has been reflected in the number of conferences, symposia, books, and journals that have been offered in recent years. The national victimization surveys and other outstanding research efforts that have been successfully undertaken during the last 20 years in various countries of the world also demonstrate the vigor and impact of victimology. Although academics and scholars working in victimology have different backgrounds, sociologists and psychologists represent a majority among them and have played a prominent role in its development.

Initially, victimology concerned itself principally with sexual assault. Although it was not easy to convince society of the need and importance to take the victim into account and to respond to his or her needs, it was even more difficult for society to refuse to consider this type of victimization, particularly in the case of women attacked violently and unexpectedly by complete strangers.

Opening up the area of domestic violence for consideration and intervention was quite arduous. The prevailing view was, and in some quarters still is, that this type of violence is a family affair, a private matter and therefore not a legitimate concern or reason justifying the interference or intervention of the law, the police, and the public.

However, concerned researchers, professionals, and advocates questioned why society normally does intervene and firmly punish violence between strangers but not among intimates. Because the victims of domestic violence are most often women—wives, mothers, daughters, girlfriends, and cohabitees—and the attackers most often men—husbands, sons, fathers, brothers, and boyfriends—society's inaction has been seen as an expression of strong patriarchal values that support the oppression and exploitation of women and encourage woman-hating or misogyny.

In defense of society's practices, some have stressed the private nature of this type of violence. It happens most often behind closed doors, out of public sight and scrutiny. This, it is said, should explain the apparent inability of society to respond appropriately. However, is it inability or unwillingness? For example, it is known and also experimentally demonstrated that violence between a man and a woman, even in public, rarely elicits the same type of concerned response and intervention that violence between strangers does.

Thus, it appears that society is blind to the needs of women while it is very deferential to the liberty rights of men, even though women constitute in many countries more than 50% of the population and the overwhelming majority of victims of sexual assault, murder, and intimate violence. The political dynamics and processes leading to and justifying this concerted ignorance of the needs and demands of female victims have been and still are well worth studying and addressing. Their end result is not only that women's needs and interests are ignored but that women are blamed for their victimization by police, lawyers, judges, and society in general.

Women's responses to this situation vary and can complicate the situation greatly. Some women suffer in silence and keep living with the same violent man. Cultural, religious, or financial considerations justify this course of action. Some women try to escape from the situation. Other women fight back and occasionally kill the attacker while defending themselves, their mother, or their children. In the latter case, who is the victim and who is the offender can be easily confused and misunderstood, causing severe legal and social problems for women. Because the concept and the law of self-defense are based on males' views and approaches to a threatening situation, women's ways of going about defending themselves have often been excluded from this disculpatory category. This basic flaw has been recognized by some state governors in the United States who have been persuaded recently to pardon women convicted of killing their spouses or cohabitees.

Domestic violence is a powerful problem that forces scholars and practitioners and society in general to reassess the roots and application of certain laws. In the past, for example, the predominant approach to the analysis of law utilized by those challenging society's status quo was a leftist or Marxian one that regularly elicited a response from the right supporting the existing values and rules. The intellectual, political, and practical struggles surrounding the issue of domestic violence have brought forth and sharpened a different vision of the *formulation and application* of the law stressing that they are also, and at times exclusively, mediated by sex and gender considerations. In other words, one can and should analyze women's treatment by the law and the justice system solely or substantially because they are women, regardless of race, class, or social status. Being a woman leads to certain types of reactions, treatment, risk, and victimization that are not significantly affected or mitigated by other variables often considered as paramount in this type of analysis, such as race and class. In other words, patriarchalism is pervasive and reaches and influences the higher strata of society just as it does the lowest. Privacy and the availability of remedies and alternatives are intervening variables that may make a difference in society's perception and awareness of the problem.

Another related dimension is the tendency of the law to address the public sphere and to neglect the private one that characterizes relationships and exchanges within marriage and the family. Because women have generally been confined to the private sphere and excluded from the public one through various limitations on outside employment and careers, the law has traditionally ignored their concerns and left them unprotected, along with children. The superior status of the male in the relationship and in the family, and the well-established dependence of women on men, have justified delegating to men the control and the administration of justice in the private sphere, leaving women dispossessed and unprotected. The irony, danger, and difficulty of a situation when their supposed protector is instead their attacker are clear and inescapable.

Although it is imperative that we develop a unified and all-encompassing victimology that takes into account all segments of society, a gender-related theoretical framework for research and analysis is needed at this time so that we can lay the groundwork for a realistic and more objective victimology. This book has been conceived and designed to contribute to this process and to facilitate the development of victimology as a serious, useful, and relevant approach to the investigation and solution of centuries-old and intractable social problems.

ORGANIZATION OF THE BOOK

The main purpose of this book is to bring together under one cover, and to arrange coherently, current and representative contributions in research, approaches, and interventions. The chapters for this volume were especially selected because their authors were able to present their ideas, research, or practical knowledge in a cogent and interesting way, and because they addressed some of the more current and representative issues in the field of spouse abuse today.

The book opens with a substantial introduction and has been divided into six parts: I. Introduction; II. The Problem; III. Women Who Kill; IV. Violence in Dating Relationships; V. The Male Batterer; VI. Approaches and Interventions; and VII. Comparative Perspectives.

The book has been designed to provide a balance between practical and theoretical issues and concerns and to offer a sample of international perspectives and approaches. This way, the book will constitute a truly positive contribution to the development of the field.

The study of marital and family interaction and the ensuing conflict cuts across disciplinary boundaries. Researchers work in various fields, including sociology, psychology, psychiatry, criminology, social work, nursing, and public health. Each discipline approaches the study of family interaction and violence somewhat differently. Some of these differences stem from the weight that each of them assigns to various levels of analysis from which a study of the family can proceed (Fitzpatrick & Wamboldt, 1990); some derive from the quantitative versus qualitative fault line that splits many researchers and many academic departments. This volume has attempted to keep this fault line from becoming a chasm. It includes both qualitative and quantitative works, it addresses both scholarly and practical questions, and it attempts to translate theory into practice.

The Problem

In Chapter 2, "Transgenerational Triangles of Abuse: A Model of Family Violence," Philip G. Ney attempts to explain why humanity's unhappy history, in particular family violence, repeats itself. He proposes a model that requires the participation of perpetrator, victim, and offender. He stresses that his research has shown that family violence is transmitted intergenerationally. In Chapter 3, "The Assessment of Spousal Abuse: An Alternative to the Conflict Tactics Scale," Nancy R. Rhodes states that research in domestic violence has been impeded by a lack of an instrument capable of measuring frequencies and intensities of violent behavior. She critiques in particular Straus's Conflict Tactics Scale and then describes her approach toward the creation of a more effective instrument. In Chapter 4, "The Relationship Between Locus of Control and Level of Violence in Married Couples," Robert M. Theodore reports on his study of that particular topic. In Chapter 5, "Social Isolation and Wife Abuse," Joyce McCarl Nielsen and her coauthors present quantitative data showing that social isolation and wife abuse are related and then discuss the isolation-abuse relation. Chapter 6, "An Analysis of Crisis Calls by Battered Women in the City of Atlanta" by Komanduri S. Murty and Julian B. Roebuck, is a quantitative analysis of almost 10,000 crisis calls of battered women to the Atlanta Council of Battered Women. The study focused on incidence and volume, victims' sociodemographic characteristics, the battery situation, and services rendered by the council.

Women Who Kill

In Chapter 7, "Female Murderers and Their Motives: A Tale of Two Cities," Coramae Richey Mann reviews police department homicide files in Chicago and Houston, concluding that the primary cause of homicides committed by women is an argument or fight. In Chapter 8, "Women, Murder, and Male Domination: Police Reports of Domestic Violence in Chicago and Philadelphia," Noel A. Cazenave and Margaret A. Zahn analyze 83 homicide cases involving men and women in intimate relationships in Chicago and Philadelphia to determine if there were gender-related patterns of homicide. They found that many of these murders were gender specific.

Violence in Dating Relationships

In Chapter 9, "Sexual Abuse in Dating Relationships," Maureen A. Pirog-Good examines factors that influence women inflicting and sustaining sexual abuse in dating relationships. What is the impact of women's past experiences, self-esteem, and dating habits? In Chapter 10, "Male Versus Female Initiation of Aggression: The Case of Courtship Violence," Alfred DeMaris addresses empirically the commonly held assumption that female violence in relationships is primarily a response, either defensive or retaliatory, to prior aggression on the part of the male. In Chapter 11, "Factors Related to Physical Violence in Dating Relationships," Diane R. Follingstad and her coauthors report the findings of a study on dating violence based on the responses of 210 college women. One of the outcomes of their work was the development of a scale that distinguishes reliably between abused and nonabused females in dating relationships.

The Male Batterer

In Chapter 12, "Male Batterers: Evidence for Psychopathology," Renata Vaselle-Augenstein and Annette Ehrlich review clinical and empirical data on the personality characteristics of male batterers, address the issue of whether or not there is psychopathology in many men who batter, and discuss implications for treatment.

Approaches and Interventions

In Chapter 13, "Translating Theory into Practice: A Conceptual Framework for Clinical Assessment, Differential Diagnosis, and Multi-Modal Treatment of Maritally Violent Individuals, Couples, and Families," Susan E. Hanks argues that psychological, sociological, sociocultural, feminist theories, and empirical research regarding the causes and consequences of marital violence must be bridged in integrating psychotherapeutic interventions with other modes of interventions. She then presents a conceptual framework upon which multi-modal clinical services for maritally violent families can be based. In Chapter 14, "Woman Abuse Among Separated and Divorced Women: The Relevance of Social Support," Desmond Ellis notes that these women vary in the amount and seriousness of violence directed against them by men with whom they lived. These variations, he states, are a function of dependency, availability, and deterrence. Ida M. Johnson and her coauthors report in Chapter 15, "Agency Response to Domestic Violence: Services Provided to Battered Women," on their research about the role of shelters in intervening in cases of domestic violence. In Chapter 16, "Educating the Professional to Aid Abuse Victims in Achieving Human Rights," Irma MacKay examines the education of professionals to enable them to assist in the empowerment process of domestic violence victims and argues that some professional groups, like the clergy, need to make a major value shift. She also provides an overview of curricula and programs. A survey of domestic violence legislation in the United States, with particular focus on probable-cause, warrantless arrests, is offered in Chapter 17, "Domestic Violence Legislation in the United States: A Survey of the States," authored by James E. Hendricks.

Comparative Perspectives

In Chapter 18, "Attitudes Toward Wife Abuse in a Cross-Cultural Context: A Comparison of Colombian and American Human Service Students," Liane V. Davis presents data from a small-scale study that compares attitudes toward abused women among Colombian and American students preparing for careers in human services. In Chapter 19, "Domestic Violence in Austria: The Institutional Response," Cheryl Benard and Edit Schlaffer review the response of the justice system to the problem of domestic violence in Austria using several data sets. In Chapter 20, "Violence Against Women in Australia's Capital City," Rosemary A. Knight and Suzanne E. Hatty examine the main features of intersexual violence as reported by 120 women in Australia's capital. In Chapter 21, "Dowry and Women's Status: A Study of Court Cases in Dhaka and Delhi," Ishrat Shamin analyzes the dynamics of the dowry phenomenon in India and Bangladesh and its negative impact on women's position and status. In Chapter 22, "Epidemiological Survey of Spousal Violence in Korea," Kwang-iel Kim and Youn-gyu Cho present nationwide epidemiological findings of spousal violence in Korea and then discuss possible explanations for the rates uncovered by the study.

Emilio C. Viano

Acknowledgments

This volume would not have been possible without the contributions of the authors. They have certainly earned the gratitude of the editor and of the readers for their willingness to share their work and to contribute to the development of victimology through the publication of this anthology. A special thanks is also warmly extended to Ron Wilder, Acquisitions Editor at Hemisphere Publishing Corporation, for his continued support of publications in the field of victimology, and to Amy Lyles Wilson, Heather Jefferson, and John Rowan for shepherding this volume through the publication process.

PART I

INTRODUCTION

1

Violence Among Intimates: Major Issues and Approaches

Emilio C. Viano
School of Public Affairs, The American University,
Washington, DC

Violence and aggression have been pervasive throughout human history and have been chronicled conspicuously from the scriptures to today's tabloids. Aggression is preser ~~~ basic and in the most complex forms of life. Many of the approac ~~~ counting of the human personality stress the aggr ~~~

L ~~~ of humanity. Inextrica ~~~ ctim pertair ~~~

sic ~~~ nd aggression
ar ~~~ tereotyping
l ~~~ ce with the
a ~~~ y. Prejudice
i ~~~ se practicing
~~~ espected and
~~~ e.

~~~ ion of violent
~~~ act as violent,
~~~ rfacing in the
~~~ Whether or not
~~~ opriate or inap-
~~~ t of the violence
is, and the ueg ~~~

When it comes to the agg ~~~ itimate, then the violent act will also be regarded as such. For ~~~ edged that certain people in society have the right to use force to compel ou~~~ behave in certain ways. Governments, police, the military, multinational corporations, medical personnel, teachers, spouses, and parents are often included in these categories of legitimate agents of violence. In different ways, they have power over the very existence, future, and destiny of other human beings. In many nations of the world, laws have been enacted to control and neutralize the use of these positions against those whose

---

Emilio C. Viano is Professor, Department of Justice, Law and Society, The American University in Washington, D.C., and Editor-in-Chief of *Victimology: An International Journal*. He has been active in the field of victimology and victim/witness services since the early 1970s.

3

lives can be easily impacted by the more powerful. Regrettably, laws are often ignored or not enforced. Transgressions are overlooked or lightly sanctioned, if at all. The resulting harm is similar to behavior that would clearly be considered criminal if it were engaged in by anyone other than those in control of the victims.

Examples of these victimizations are plentiful: unlawful human experimentation, hostage-taking, apartheid, slavery, torture, serfdom, and forced prostitution. Many of the victims are at times targeted for mistreatment and abuse because of their membership in a certain group, like the poor, women, children, minorities, the homeless, political dissenters, religious minorities, and the elderly. Recent research clearly shows that violence and aggression are often used in marriage and family situations to enforce the will of the more powerful, usually a male or an adult, over the weaker, generally a female or a child (Viano, 1990, pp. xiv–xvii).

Who the victim is, is also decisive in determining whether or not violence is appropriate. Generally, throughout the ages and across cultures, the higher someone's status, the less tolerated has been any violence against him or her and, conversely, the more legitimate his or her use of force toward lower ranking people. In many societies, gender is one of the measures of status with maleness being the superior category.

The situation in which violence takes place also colors society's perception of its legitimacy. Self-defense is a clear case in point. The degree of harm inflicted on the victim is another variable to consider when evaluating violence. One variable that affects the way violence is perceived in society, as appropriate or inappropriate, is its visibility or lack of it—a factor taken well into account by perpetrators—and the likelihood of its coming to the attention of others like doctors, teachers, and neighbors. Marriage and family ensure a good cover for the violence that takes place within them, thus making it easy to justify it and explain it away.

Thus, ultimately, personal and social values shape our concept of the victim. The victim is actually a social construct used as a means of social control by those in power. A victim is considered "legitimate" and therefore entitled to social intervention and protection only when the powerful see no threat to their freedom of action, privileges, and position in such a declaration or they are forced to accept such a designation by overwhelming social changes. History is replete with examples of these dynamics that are still taking place in our times.

WIDESPREAD CULTURAL VALUES

Pervasive cultural values that create a climate that is permissive or conducive to victimization should be identified, examined, and targeted for change. Violent acts reflect environments of violence. At the foundation of many patterns of abuse of the "weak"—children, women, the elderly, the mentally retarded—is the overwhelming acceptance of violence in our society as the legitimate and necessary means of enforcing compliance and of solving conflicts at the personal, national, and international levels. These concepts of dominance-submission, controller-controlled, and stronger-weaker pervade parenting, relations between the genders and the ages, and marital patterns.

Every society identifies certain groups as appropriate objects of hostility. These groups must be clearly different and discrete. Status is often used as a indicator of such dissimilarity. Violence often occurs between persons whose social status is not the same, one being superior and the other inferior. Thus, the family, as we know it in our society, bestows upon the male power over the female, thus strengthening the

which it is a part

subordinate status of the wife. This, in turn, raises the probability of her becoming the target of abuse.

Women as a Minority

One of the major ways in which people can be labeled as subordinate is to consider them a minority. The classical definition of a minority, by Louis Wirth (1945, p. 347), describes it as "a group of people who, because of their physical or cultural characteristics, are singled out from others in the society in which they live for differential and unequal treatment and who therefore regard themselves as objects of collective discrimination." The fundamental and most salient dimension that distinguishes a minority from the master group is that of power, the ability to control one's own destiny and, to a certain degree, that of other people as well. Historically, in many societies, women have not had and still do not have much "power."

Professionally, occupationally, educationally, and economically (income-wise) women have had little access to careers that embody the concept of power and authority. Those who did enter such careers were and are treated differently, the equivalent of being discriminated against. Even today, when more women are pursuing ambitious career paths, they are still stopped at a certain point by the so-called "glass ceiling," an invisible barrier that stands between them and those positions of power and authority that are almost within their reach. Recent data show that in the United States in 1990 women held only 175 out of 6,502 corporate officers' positions, that is less than 3% of top jobs (Ball, 1991).

The importance of having access to meaningful careers and positions of power and authority stems from the fact that the concept of self is directly related to the roles that one plays in the status that one occupies. Robert E. Park (1955), a well-known sociologist of the Chicago School and a major proponent of this approach, states that an individual becomes a person only when recognized by the community in which he or she lives. This recognition is bestowed very much according to one's status and power. This, in turn, is crucial in influencing the type of self-concept that a person will develop. In the case of women, their lack of recognition and their being viewed as basically submissive, compliant, nurturing and as sex objects to be conquered justify their being dominated and overpowered by men, be it a stranger, lover, or husband; their existing to serve and please men (the reward for the best ones to do so being marriage); and their subordinate status in society. Other contrasting stereotypes depicting women as sexually seductive, untrustworthy, and emotionally unstable are also used to justify the oppression and subjugation of women.

For example, sexual coercion, the act of being forced, tricked, or pressured to engage in a sexual act or acts, is relatively commonplace in American society. For some women, the experience is a well-known and continuous one, starting in early childhood and continuing into adulthood. Sexual coercion can take different forms that are, however, similar and connected in many ways. As one scholar writes, "The basic common character underlying the many different forms of violence is the abuse, intimidation, coercion, intrusion, threat, and force men use to control women" (Kelly, 1988, p. 76). Leidig (1981) states that all acts of sexual violence are underreported; unidirectional, that is perpetrated by males against females; trivialized by society; involve victim blaming; and serve to control women's lives.

These values and perceptions, when internalized by women, make them accept their situation and their victimization as legitimate, "natural," and deserved. Sexual assault of women, including date rape and rape in marriage, sexual harassment, sexual mutilation, and physical and emotional violence against women are all expressions, in different degrees, of the subordinate roles and of the low status of women in society.

Compulsive Masculinity

As a minority, women have often been the target of enmity and dislike. Although it is true that violence in general is on the increase in the United States, crimes against women, like sexual assault, date rape, domestic violence, and murder are among the crimes that are increasing noticeably. This increase may be due in part to the growing status and independence of women in contemporary society, which elicit the violent reaction of men who see these changes as a direct threat to their superior position. There are those who consider "compulsive masculinity," the anxious need that some men feel to distance themselves from their mother and thus from anything that is female, as leading to a very strong rejection of women and of what they do as having no value or importance and as a powerful justification for using force to establish the superiority of maleness at any cost. Thus, the aggression of men against women, be it physical or mental, is instrumental, intentional, and meant to make it possible for the aggressor to emerge in a stronger position relative to the other party in the interaction.

Cross-cultural Data

The violent and oppressing behavior of men versus women is reinforced in societies in which social norms condone the use of force to settle disputes. In a study of 95 societies, Sanday (1981) classified 47% as rape free and 18% as rape prone. A common characteristic of the rape-free societies was the fairly equal balance between the sexes. These societies respected and valued the contributions of women, especially their functions connected with reproduction, growth, and social continuity. The incidence of rape was instead found by Sanday to be positively correlated with the ideology of machismo and the intensity of interpersonal violence, elements missing in rape-free societies.

Levinson (1989) conducted a worldwide comparative study of 90 small-scale and peasant societies selected from the Human Relations Area Files' Probability Sample Files. This archive is a cross-indexed, cross-referenced collection of mostly primary ethnographic reports describing the ways of life of people in some 330 different cultural and ethnic groups from all regions of the world. He found that there are many different types of family violence in the world, from wife beating to painful initiation ceremonies, particularly for girls, to more rare types, like raiding for wives, and the sacrifice of children. However, wife beating takes place in more societies around the world than any other type of family violence.

Levinson identifies three different types of wife beating existing around the world, based on why people believe the beating occurs (Levinson, 1989, pp. 33–35). The first type takes place principally to "punish a woman" for real or suspected adultery and unfaithfulness. Levinson calls the second type "beating for cause." For example, the wife's failure to fulfill her duties or to treat her husband respectfully as he sees it may "cause" a beating. The third type of wife abuse is "wife beating at will," which takes place in those societies in which it is believed that a husband has the right to beat his wife for any reason or no reason at all.

Levinson also found that, although alcohol plays little or no role at all in family violence events in most societies around the world, there are a few societies in which alcohol consumption is a key factor in the chain of events that leads to wife battering. The supposed disinhibiting effect of alcohol is used to excuse behavior that otherwise would not be accepted by the wife, her family, and the community (Levinson, 1989, p. 36).

Subtle Victimization

Although society at large and most of the research in the field focus on the more sensational, violent, or evident forms of victimization and on the more obviously distorted values, rationalizations, and beliefs that support them, there are in our society actually more insidious, pervasive, and widespread expressions of them, although less visible and objectionable.

The violent and victimizing behaviors that are condemned and abhorred are often only the bolder and exaggerated expressions of values and beliefs actually rooted and widespread in the larger culture. For example, the diffused pedophilia that exudes from advertisements that portray grown-up women as children and vice versa with an unequivocal sexual undertone; the widespread exploitation of the female body in commercials and advertisements, no matter what item is offered for sale; the violence and sexploitation depicted in detail in many television programs, films, and now "adult-content" software; and the atmosphere of ageism and sexism that pervades much of what society does, all create and manifest a climate in which victimizers express in blunt, overt, and intensified manners what society at large believes and practices in a more subtle or carefully camouflaged manner.

DEFINITIONS AND THEORIES

Following Siann (1985, pp. 1–14), aggression involves the intent to inflict hurt or emerge superior to others; does not necessarily involve physical injury; and is not always negatively sanctioned but more likely to be punished when one of the participants does not enter willingly into the interaction. To label a person aggressive in a negative sense depends very much on the subjective judgment of the labeler, influenced both by his or her value system and by his or her perception of whether or not the aggressive behavior is unprovoked and unacceptable or reactive, defensive, or retaliatory, within the range of acceptability.

Violence involves the use of considerable physical force that is often driven by aggressive motivation. Although violence tends to be negatively sanctioned, the recourse to physical force is often legitimized, depending on the values of those evaluating the situation and on the extent to which the use of force is considered provocative or defensive. Although the emphasis in these definitions is traditionally on physical force, presently many point out that emotional and psychological aspects should also be included in the definitions of aggression and violence.

There are several types of family violence: spouse abuse, including both the wife and the husband as possible victims; child abuse; sibling abuse; incest; marital rape; homicide; and abuse of the elderly. Only spouse abuse will be covered in this volume.

Several theories have been advanced to explain family violence (Levinson, 1989, pp. 15–20). The most important ones are outlined briefly here.

The *exchange theory* is summarized by Gelles (1983, p. 157) this way: "People hit and abuse other family members because they can." It is based on the concept of cost-benefit analysis. Members of the family will resort to violence to obtain their goals for as long as what is to be gained outweighs the cost. The privacy of family life and society's refusal to intervene effectively make it "inexpensive" and safe to be violent within the family. This is particularly true when, as in American society, the preferred type of family, the nuclear family, isolates the marital partners from the scrutiny and support of others.

The *culture of violence theory* was originally developed by Wolfgang and Ferracuti (1967). It maintains that within large and pluralistic societies, like the United States, certain subcultural groups develop norms and values that stress and justify the use of physical force to a higher level than thought acceptable in the predominant, larger culture. This theory today has been expanded to compare different societies as well.

The *resource theory* stresses the idea that decisionmaking power in the family stems largely from the aggregate value of the resources (money, property, contacts, prestige) that each partner contributes initially and on a continuous basis to the relationship (Blood and Wolfe, 1960; Warner, Lee, and Lee, 1986). Because men hold the majority of high-paying, prestigious jobs and positions in society, it follows that they also command higher power in the marital and family relationships and that women are in a subordinate and vulnerable position.

The *patriarchal theory* has been advanced mainly by feminists. This theory sees society, in the past and in the present, as dominated by males with women in a subordinate position, considered and treated mostly as men's possessions. This approach has been translated into laws and customs that legitimize this differential status of men and women. Violence is then used by men to enforce those laws and customs, control women, and suppress any rebellion (Martin, 1976; Dobash and Dobash, 1979).

The *ecological theory* connects violence in the family to the larger social values and order. Thus, for example, Garbarino (1977) identifies two predictors of child abuse: the isolation of the family from social support networks, which is characteristic of contemporary advanced societies, and a value system predominant in society that legitimizes violence against children.

The *social learning theory* stresses nurture versus nature. It maintains that aggression and violence are learned and manifest themselves within a social context. Family violence, for example, can be precipitated by a combination of contextual and situational factors (O'Leary, 1988). The first includes individual, couple, and societal characteristics that create an environment in which violence may happen. Examples are violence in the family of origin, stress, and an aggressive personality. The second leads to family violence when the right contextual situation exists. Examples are alcohol or drug use and abuse, financial problems, and strife in the relationship.

The social learning theory has received the most attention when it has proposed that there is an intergenerational transmission of family violence. This means that people who have seen or suffered family violence when growing up have a higher probability of living in a violent marital situation later on. The impact is most pronounced on men as aggressors (Straus, Gelles, and Steinmetz, 1980; Ulbricht and Huber, 1981; Pagelow, 1981; Arias, 1984; Kalmuss, 1984). Research has also suggested that sexual abuse is often found in the background of men who become child sexual abusers (Groth, 1983; Davis and Leitenberg, 1987; Ballard et al., 1990). There are also indications of an intergenerational transmission of child physical abuse (Fraiberg, Adelson, and Shapiro, 1975; Kaufman and Zigler, 1987; Egeland, Jacobritz, and Sroufe, 1988).

The *evolutionary theory* has been advanced mostly by anthropologists who hypothesize that change over time in human societies moves from the simple to the complex. As a consequence, one can also predict changes in social organization, the structure and size of the family, and social and family relations and interactions. Child rearing practices are also affected. In simpler and less technologically advanced societies, independence and self-reliance are encouraged in youngsters. This also means less adult supervision, more individual freedom, and therefore less demand for obedience and submission and fewer occasions for punishment. Instead, in complex, advanced, and hierarchical societies, compliance and obedience are the preferred traits. One has only to think of an industrial assembly line or of a large legal firm working on an important case to realize the pressure toward unquestioning acceptance of assignments and directions along rank lines. This in turn means that violence will be used in those societies during the socialization process to ensure that youngsters become efficient members of society and to maintain the desired patterns of behavior, particularly in the family setting (Barry, Child, and Bacon, 1967; Lenski and Lenski, 1970; Naroll, 1970; Rohner, 1975; Pryor, 1977; Berreman, 1978; Levinson and Malone, 1980).

The *sociobiological theory* is applicable particularly to child abuse and to infanticide. It is based on the inclusive fitness theory, which postulates that individuals will behave in such a manner as to increase the probability that their genes will be transmitted to future generations. Consequently, child abuse can be predicted in cases of paternal uncertainty; against children who do not have high reproductive value because of handicaps or stepchild status; and in poor families when the allocation of limited resources requires the ranking of the offspring and of other members of the family and leads to the abuse, neglect, or infanticide of females, last born, and the handicapped, and to considering all females and the elderly as highly expendable. In these societies, for example, females, regardless of age, are often required to eat last, after serving the males, and must subsist on a poor diet of leftovers. This means that they are often undernourished, smaller, and weigh considerably less than males, experience failure to thrive, have weaker immune systems for resisting illnesses and infections, and experience a higher death rate. Some of these factors make it quite difficult for women to effectively resist male physical violence (Alexander, 1974; Lennington, 1981; Daly and Wilson, 1981; Lightcap, Kurland, and Burgess, 1982; Gray, 1985).

The *social conflict theory* has been advanced recently by Retzinger (1991), who attempts to integrate findings from various approaches to large-scale conflicts, marital disputes, and communication processes. Social bonds are deemed to be vital to community as well as to individual relationships. Conflict is analyzed here in regard to threatened or broken bonds. Retzinger suggests that the emotion of shame plays a particularly important role in the structure and process of bonding, and therefore in conflict. A new theory of escalation is described: escalation of conflict occurs when there is alienation, and shame is evoked but not acknowledged. The theory stresses the role of unacknowledged alienation and shame in the generation of anger, rage, and violence, that is, pathological conflict. Normal conflict can be instructive and positive, reestablishing boundaries that lead to effective problem solving. The dynamics of resolution or repairing of the bond actually involve processes opposite those that cause damage to bonds in the first place.

The *general systems theory* has been advanced by Straus (1978), who hypothesizes that family violence will be better understood and controlled if it is seen as the outcome of a social system propelled by positive feedback and encompassing the individual, family, and societal spheres. Many of the factors highlighted by other theories are included in this model. Sets of these factors interact with each other to maintain the system at the needed level of violence and to generate the positive feedback that ultimately keeps the system going. Examples of these sets are the high level of conflict inherent in the family; the violence that is integrated into personality and behavioral scripts; cultural norms that legitimize violence between family members; and the sexist organization of the society and of its family system.

CONCLUSION

The ultimate goal of all work in criminology, victimology, and related sciences is the establishment of a caring, fair, and just society. A society without violence, oppression, and suffering should be the ultimate goal of the process of social change, generated by our concern for victims of crime. The family, which for centuries has been the basic cell of society and the best known vehicle for raising each successive generation, is buffeted by powerful forces and is in crisis. It needs our renewed attention and efforts to truly make it the cornerstone of a society without fear, violence, and oppression.

The various facets of intimate victimization are but variations on the same general theme: a fundamental lack of understanding and appreciation of the commonality of our humanity, of what truly makes us human, of the bonds that support and nourish us. Patriarchy, sexism, machismo, ageism, and racism are different attempts to establish hierarchies; to inflate and exploit superficial differences; to mask one's weaknesses by denigrating and oppressing others; to deny our interdependence and mutual linkages; and to subdue, oppress, and take advantage of those considered to be inferior (Viano, 1989, pp. 3–14).

It is because of the courage and dedication of reformers, scholars, researchers, and victims themselves that the victims are beginning to be heard. They certainly deserve to be. The work completed to date in various areas has already had considerable impact and borne promising fruit. It is essential that we maintain the momentum, strengthening the collaboration between scholars, researchers, and those active in legal reform, policymaking, and programmatic interventions. It is particularly important that we keep in mind that the ultimate goal is to develop a unified theory of victimization and a comprehensive approach to assisting *all* victims. Work and research in specific areas of victimology, like sexual assault or domestic violence, should be clearly considered as building blocks for the construction of an overall theory and practice addressing disparate problems that all have a common root. This is a major challenge that people working in the field are facing now. It has to be addressed successfully if the discipline is to grow, flourish, and genuinely help make our society a more just and equitable one.

BIBLIOGRAPHY

Alexander, R. D. (1974). The evolution of social behavior. *Annual Review of Ecology and Systematics, 5,* 325–383.

Arias, I. (1984). A social theory explication of the intergenerational transmission of physical aggression in intimate heterosexual relationships. Ph.D. dissertation, State University of New York at Stony Brook.

Ball, K. (1991, August 26). Study finds few women hold top executive jobs. *The Washington Post,* A-11.

Ballard, D. T., Blair, G. D., Devereaux, S., Valentine, L. K., Horton, A. L., and Johnson, B. L. (1990). A contemporary profile of the incest perpetrator: Background characteristics, abuse history, and use of social skills. In A. L. Norton, B. L. Johnson, L. M. Roundy, & D. Williams (Eds.), *The incest perpetrator: A family member no one wants to treat* (pp. 54–64). Newbury Park, CA: Sage.

Barry, H. III, Child, I. L., & Bacon, M. K. (1967). Relation of child training to subsistence economy. In C. S. Ford (Ed.), *Cross-cultural approaches* (pp. 146–158). New Haven, CT: HRAF.

Berreman, G. D. (1978). Scale and social relations. *Current Anthropology, 19,* 225–237.

Blood, R. O., & Wolfe, D M. (1960). *Husbands and wives: The dynamics of married living.* Glencoe, IL: The Free Press.

Daly, M., & Wilson, M. I. (1981). Abuse and neglect of children in evolutionary perspective. In R. Alexander and D. Tinkle (Eds.), *Natural selection and social behavior: Recent research and new theory* (pp. 405–416). New York: Chiron.

Davis, G. E., & Leitenberg, H. (1987). Adolescent sex offenders. *Psychological Bulletin, 101,* 417–427.

Dobash, R. E., & Dobash, R. P. (1979). *Violence against wives.* New York: Free Press.

Egeland, B., Jacobvtz, D., & Sroufe, A. L. (1988). Breaking the cycle of abuse. *Child Development, 59,* 1080–1088.

Fitzpatrick, M. A., & Wamboldt, F. (1990). Where all is said and done: Toward an integration of intrapersonal and interpersonal models of marital and family communication. *Communications Research, 17,* 421–431.

Fraiberg, S., Adelson, E., & Shapiro, V. (1975). Ghosts in the nursery: A psychoanalytic approach to the problems of impaired mother-child relationships. *Journal of the American Association of Child Psychiatry, 14,* 387–421.

Garbarino, J. (1977). The human ecology of child maltreatment; A conceptual model for research. *Journal of Marriage and the Family, 39,* 721–735.

Gelles, R. J. (1983). An exchange social theory. In D. Finkelhor, R. J. Gelles, G. T. Hotaling, and M. A. Straus (Eds.), *The dark side of families: Current family violence research* (pp. 151–165). Beverly Hills, CA: Sage.

Gray, J. P. (1985). *Primate sociobiology.* New Haven, CT: HRAF.

Groth, A. N. (1983). Treatment of the sexual offender in a correctional institution. In J. G. Greer & I. R. Stuart (Eds.), *The sexual aggressor: Current perspectives in treatment* (pp. 160–176). New York: Van Nostrand Reinhold.

Kalmuss, D. S. (1984). The intergenerational transmission of marital aggression. *Journal of Marriage & the Family, 46,* 11–19.

Kaufman, J., & Zigler, E. (1987). Do abused children become abusive parents? *American Journal of Orthopsychiatry, 57,* 316–331.

Kelly, L. (1988). *Surviving sexual violence.* Minneapolis, MN: University of Minnesota Press.

Leidig, M. (1981). Violence against women: A feminist-psychological analysis. In S. Cox (Ed.), *Female psychology* (pp. 190–205). New York: St. Martin's Press.

Lennington, S. (1981). Child abuse: The limits of sociobiology. *Ethology and Sociobiology, 2,* 17–29.

Lenski, G., & Lenski, J. (1970). *Human societies: An introduction to macrosociology.* New York: McGraw-Hill.

Levinson, D. (1979). Population density in cross-cultural perspective. *American Ethnologist, 6,* 742–751.

Levinson, D. (1989). *Family violence in cross-cultural perspective.* Newbury Park, CA: Sage.

Levinson, D., & Malone, M. (1980). *Toward explaining human culture.* New Haven, CT: HRAF.

Lightcap, J. L., Kurland, J. A., & Burgess, R. L. (1982). Child abuse: A test of some predictions from evolutionary theory. *Ethology and Sociobiology, 3,* 61–67.

Martin, D. (1976). *Battered wives.* San Francisco, CA: Glide.

Naroll, R. (1970). What have we learned from cross-cultural surveys? *American Anthropologist, 72,* 1227–1288.

O'Leary, D. K. (1988). Physical aggression between spouses: A social learning theory perspective. In V. B. Van Hasselt (Ed.), *Handbook of family violence* (pp. 31–55). New York: Plenum.

Pagelow, M. D. (1981). *Women-battering: Victims and their experiences.* Beverly Hills, CA: Sage.

Park, R. E. (1955). *Society.* New York: Free Press.

Pryor, F. L. (1977). *The origins of the economy.* New York: Academic Press.

Retzinger, S. M. (1991). *Violent emotions: Shame and rage in marital quarrels.* Newbury Park, CA: Sage.

Rohner, R. P. (1975). *They love me, they love me not: A worldwide study of the effects of parental acceptance and rejection.* New Haven, CT: HRAF.

Sanday, P. R. (1981). The socio-cultural context of a rape: A cross-cultural study. *Journal of Social Issues, 37,* 5–27.

Siann, G. (1985). *Accounting for aggression: Perspectives on aggression and violence.* Boston: Allen & Unwin.

Straus, M. (1978). Wife beating: How common and why? *Victimology, 2*(3, 4), 443–459.

Straus, M. A., Gelles, R. J., & Steinmetz, S. K. (1980). *Behind closed doors: Violence in the American family.* New York: Anchor.

Ulbrich, P., & Huber, J. (1981). Observing parental violence: Distribution and effects. *Journal of Marriage and the Family, 43,* 623–631.

Viano, E. (1989). *Crime and its victims: International research and public policy issues.* New York: Hemisphere.

Viano, E. (1990). *The victimology handbook: Research findings, treatment, and public policy.* New York: Garland.

Warner, R. L., Lee, G. R., & Lee, J. (1986). Social organization, spousal resources, and marital power: A cross-cultural study. *Journal of Marriage and the Family, 48,* 121–128.

Wolfgang, M., & Ferracuti, F. (1967). *The subculture of violence: Toward an integrated theory of criminology.* London: Tavistock.

PART II

THE PROBLEM

2

Transgenerational Triangles of Abuse: A Model of Family Violence

Philip G. Ney

Faculty of Medicine, University of British Columbia, Vancouver, BC, Canada

INTRODUCTION

In an attempt to explain why humanity's unhappy history, in particular family violence, repeats itself, I propose a model that requires the participation of perpetrator, victim, and observer. My research has shown that depending on the type and extent, family violence is transmitted from one generation to the next. Children blame themselves and become conflicted more often with verbal abuse than other types of abuse or neglect. Although the reenactment appears to be maladaptive, it is possible that humans are attempting to maintain an efficient homeostasis by trying to solve the conflicts that were engendered within them by the mistreatment. To avoid entropy, families will reenact violence similar to that of their forbears hoping to both see and understand how and why it happens. Hopefully the reenactment will provide them enough information so that their intrapsychic conflicts are resolved and the energy is not used inefficiently. To avoid a demise through entropy, humans strive to understand themselves, even if that means they must reenact the painful violence that inaugurated their confusion.

Why does humanity's unhappy history repeat itself? Why is the violence of every age so similar? Why do individuals so seldom learn from their own mistakes? Why do they often marry the same type of person they just divorced? Why do parents treat their children in the same abusive manner with which they were treated? Family violence is often handed from parent to parent, to the third and fourth generations. If collective and individual tragedy is reenacted, with the essential themes of history reappearing in successive generations, is the ultimate tragedy that mankind cannot learn from its mistakes? It seems so tragic and futile, but there may be some purpose. Is each replay only another opportunity to review the same scene, or is there some "drive" that impels mankind to reenact unresolved conflicts so that they may eventually learn from them? Maybe a study of family violence, particularly child abuse, will provide some insights into these ancient questions.

This chapter suggests a model to describe and to explain the transgenerational

Philip G. Ney, M.A., M.D., F.R.C.P. (C), F.R.A.N.Z.C.P is a clinical professor with the Department of Family Practice, Faculty of Medicine, University of British Columbia, Vancouver B.C., Canada. He is also the director of the Adolescent Unit, Jack Ledger House, Arbutus Society For Children, Victoria B.C.

child abuse. I found that some types of abuse are more likely than others to be transmitted from one generation to the next. Depending on the type and extent of abuse, children will blame themselves and become conflicted in their thinking and behavior. When they cannot be solved, these conflicts continue into their adult life. It seems that adults attempt to solve these conflicts by reenacting them. It is hypothesized that the reenactment results in a triangle of violence that requires the participation of the perpetrator, victim, and observer. Although the reenactment appears to be maladaptive, it may be an attempt to understand. It is possible that individuals must understand their conflicts because the human organism is attempting to function in the most efficient manner possible and maintain negative entropy. Human efficiency is diminished by intrapsychic and interpersonal conflict. An understanding and possible solution might be detectable in the reenactment of a major conflict.

TRANSGENERATIONAL ABUSE

Child abuse may become transgenerational because children seek revenge when they grow up. Miller and McCann (1979) found that children 1–6 years of age were likely to prescribe more punishment for intentional compared to accidental perpetrators of abuse. Children felt that punishment should be less if there had been some compensation for the victim and if the perpetrator had already been punished. They were more inclined to seek the punishment of a perpetrator than to compensate the victim, especially if the victims were known to them.

One possible reason for transgenerational child abuse is that the conflicts engendered by abuse and neglect become internalized. In a study of children hospitalized in a child psychiatric unit, we found (Ney, Moore, McPhee, & Trought, 1986) the child's tendency to blame himself depended on the type and extent of the abuse. From the child's point of view, it is safer to punish himself than hurt those on whom his existence depends. The child appeared to internalize conflict with his parents in preference to being alienated from them, possibly because that meant he might be neglected and not survive. He sought to be punished in order to end his parents' anger, which inclined them to reject or avoid him. The abused child was not only hurt by adults, he continued to hurt himself in ways similar to that in which he was hurt. As an adult he tended to become the punisher of those dependent on him, especially when his children made demands.

I (Ney, 1987a) found that verbal abuse is the most likely, and physical abuse the least likely, form of maltreatment to be transmitted from one generation to the next. I also found high correlations between how a mother was treated as a child and how she treated her child (Ney, 1988). There were also high correlations between how she treated her child and how she was treated by her husband. Moreover, we found the mother was treated by her husband in many ways similar to the treatment she received as a child. It appeared that some women select husbands that will treat them as they were treated by their parents. In a number of instances, the woman was treated by her second husband very much like she was by the first. Even when parents were determined to avoid perpetuating their experience of abuse, under conditions of stress many reverted to treating their children as they had been treated.

ROTATING TRIQUETRA

In the model I use to describe family violence, there is the necessary participation of the perpetrator, victim, and observer (PVO), forming a triangle or triquetra. The triquetra rotates according to time, place, and circumstance so that the roles of the PVO are somewhat interchangeable. A perpetrator can become the victim and the observer may become the perpetrator.

The child who is a victim of physical abuse becomes the abusing parent in the next generation. The sexual abuser of children changes from perpetrator to victim, assaulted by fellow inmates as soon as he is imprisoned.

The apparent perpetrator (P), victim (V), and observer (O) can change roles because within each of them there are facets of the other part. The sadistic perpetrator is also partly masochistic so that when a more sadistic individual overpowers him, he becomes surprisingly submissive. The bystander who takes covert delight in the gang rape of a woman, real or dramatized, given an opportunity may also become a perpetrator in the same activity. Although it is not recognized in law or in much of sociology, there is a certain arbitrariness to who is designated the victim, or the perpetrator, or the observer.

The direction in which the triquetra rotates will depend on the relative preponderance of the P, V, or O within each individual and on external circumstances, namely the rotation of other triangles with which the violent triquetra interacts. When a family expressing violence is taken to court, the mother who was the victim becomes the perpetrator, insisting that her husband who abused her and her children, be given the maximum sentence. In this particular court the judge has been criticized (victimized) by the media for his lenient handling of family violence. On this occasion he insists that the perpetrator (husband) receive a maximum sentence. The husband is imprisoned, thus becoming a victim, but he may soon beat up a fellow prisoner. Little cognizance is taken of the fact that the wife provoked him with verbal abuse or that his son, the apparent observer, set up a particular episode by providing the father with information that his wife had been seen kissing a stranger.

When it is possible to detect the relative preponderance of the other facets within the individual, it becomes possible to predict what will happen in the next episode. A child who so often stood by helplessly while his parents fought is likely to become mostly observer. If he identified more with his father, the apparent aggressor, than with his mother, the apparent victim, his next stronger tendency would be to become a physical abuser. He might select a mate with a tendency similar to that of his mother to provoke with belittling comments. If the perpetrator (father) is also to a great extent a victim, having been victimized by his own parents, he will not greatly protest the sentence of the court, feeling that he deserves anything that is handed to him. If the second most prominent feature in him is his tendency to be an observer, he will stand by while his fellow inmates abuse someone more passive.

In the triquetra PVPV (Fig. 2-1), the primary orientation (top of the triangle) is toward the perpetrator, whose next most common feature is his tendency to be a victim. This is also the orientation of a forensic psychiatrist, police officer, or judge. The newspaper reporter who is prominently a victim, will highlight the distress of the victim, portraying in detail that person's suffering and humiliation. If the victim's next most prominent feature is the tendency to be a perpetrator, it is possible to predict that in the next episode the triquetra will rotate in such a way that the victim assisted by the media seeks vengeance and may take justice into his own hands. Thus

ABUSE PARADIGM P.V.P.V.

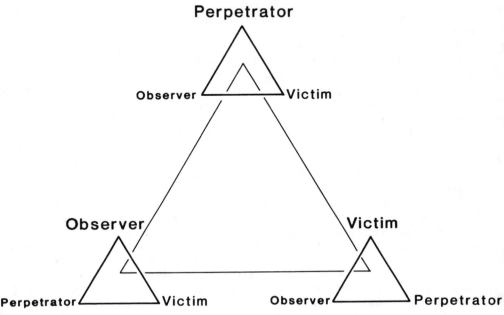

Figure 2-1

a shopkeeper will shoot a suspect robber and be applauded for what otherwise would be described as cold-blooded murder.

Quantum mechanics demonstrate how our experience of reality depends on the point of view we choose (Comfort, 1983). If we choose to see the episode of family violence from the victim's point of view, we will tend to succor the offended and punish the perpetrator. It may be just as objective to view reality from the perpetrator's point of view. It will help us understand why being badly abused as a child partly explains his aggressive behavior. Thus, whether our intervention is primarily punishing, sympathizing, or therapeutic is determined as much by our choice of perception as by our "objectivity" and clinical skill. Martin (1984) describes how a particular perspective has lead to neglect of male abusers. To become reasonably objective and sympathetically therapeutic may require that we consider everyone a victim, at least initially. This will allow us the opportunity to help the perpetrator, victim, and observer reconsider their positions. In this way we can introduce some flexibility into the triquetra.

The law puts a necessary emphasis on the responsibility of an individual to choose right from wrong. In doing so the legal system helps humanity to maintain a freedom of choice and insists that people take as much individual responsibility as they can. The therapeutic and legal points of view are irrevocably irreconcilable. This is probably how it should be. It highlights the importance of maintaining communication between the legal and helping professions, but avoiding collusion. Unfortunately as probation officers, policemen, and judges become increasingly aware of the complexity of people, it becomes harder for them to designate any one person as responsible for a violent act. Instead of attempting to be therapeutic, judges might determine who is guilty and what the sentence should be, but then provide an opportunity for that punishment to be proportionately distributed among all those who contributed to the violence.

The triquetra, which is nascent in the young adult, begins to first show itself when she or he chooses a mate. Most mating is not random, but assortative (Nielsen, 1964). Young people choose each other on the basis of subtle social and psychological characteristics. Unwittingly they find mates that represent another corner of their triquetra. The third corner may be an in-law, or later, a child. When a young husband and wife fight, the mother-in-law hears about it over the telephone, proportioning blame or sympathy to one or the other according to the characteristics within her that are prominently perpetrator, victim, or observer. I found (Ney, 1988) that many women were abused and neglected by their spouses in ways similar to their treatment by their parents, especially if they were abused verbally or neglected emotionally.

Unfortunately there is a persistent disinclination to regard children as victims who have some responsibility in initiating or maintaining their experience of abuse or neglect. This may be an expression of each person's tendency to distance himself or herself from death and his or her own destructive tendencies. Because it is hard to acknowledge our own tendencies to be perpetrator, victim, or observer in triquetra, we tend to assign the responsibility of violence only to the perpetrator. Robert Lifton (1986), who struggled with his awareness that Nazi doctors were also people, was afraid that providing a psychological understanding of the Nazi physicians would in some way excuse them.

THE ESSENTIAL ROLE OF THE OBSERVER

If, then, we are all partially responsible, we are all partially without excuse. There are very few even among the most concerned citizens who can state that they are doing as much as they could to prevent violence. If we try to distance ourselves from distress and evil, we will need to scapegoat someone. If we are able to admit our part in a triquetra, we will be better able to see the necessary participation of all and to provide sympathetic understanding. Our ability to treat depends on our awareness of the triquetra, our willingness to acknowledge our part, and our determination to help people stop repeating their inflexible repetitions.

As an observer it is virtually impossible to be so removed or so objective so as not to be involved. Often the key to violence is the part played by the observer, and therefore the observer is also responsible. The position held by the observer, literally his or her point of view, is determined by his or her own nature and nurture. This point of view determines the reality that one observes and reports, and to which one actively responds. Each observer has a greater vested interest in one kind of outcome. When it occurs it provides an existential payoff to confirm the person's world view. That payoff is only partly gratifying because it does not contribute to a solution of the inner conflict within the observer, although it does help sustain his or her familiar equilibrium.

Observers are vitally important to the perpetrator and the victim because they hold a potential solution to the personal dilemmas of each of the others. They can provide at least a partial resolution by a whole spectrum of responses from commenting to adjudicating. The observer can declare his or her observation, "I noticed when you did that, she did this." The observer may judge who is apparently right and who is apparently wrong, "It's your fault." Occasionally the observer may perceive, comment, judge, and intervene, "When I saw you do that, even though he may have started it, I decided it was mainly your fault and now you must leave."

Both the perpetrator and the victim will invite or attract an observer to each potential violent event and give him some authority and power. The observer will accept this role only on the condition that he remains relatively anonymous. The observer does not want to be implicated as party to the violence either with the victim or the perpetrator partly because the judicial system might hold him culpable, but also because a recognition of his role in a violent episode will escalate his inner conflicts beyond his self-control. When the observer does not perform as he is expected by the perpetrator and the victim, they both cry in disappointed rage, "You saw it happening, why didn't you do something?"

The observer is attracted to violence because (1) it provides him the opportunity to examine the conflicts in his own mind while he watches them enacted. (A clearer view might help him solve his inner tensions or learn a secret of his own dilemmas). (2) it provides stimulation and/or titillation, which prevents him from dealing with boredom; and (3) it will heighten his energies used in the attack of practical problems. He carefully chooses what to observe with these three factors unconsciously "in mind."

One cannot examine the role of the bystander without asking why society has been so long in recognizing the bystander's critical role in violence. It might be because people like to consider themselves objective observers able to solve their own or other people's problems without being implicated. It is possible that the observer's role has been neglected because of the present dominance of reductionistic science, which implies that it is possible to be an uninvolved observer. Observers may not wish to be implicated because the judicial system has been so punitive and they are afraid of being identified with the perpetrator.

Observing always suggests either the need to know more or to intervene. Observing violence always disturbs the personal and interpersonal equilibrium. To deny the observation to oneself or others usually results in an increased tendency to lie on all occasions and a diminished ability to perceive. The timeless question is not, "Did you know?," but "What did you do about what you did know?"

REPETITIONS OF ABUSE, TO PREVENT ENTROPY

The triquetra can describe how family violence occurs. For an explanation of why it occurs, and with apology to Carnot (1824) and others, I use the concept of entropy. For the purposes of this chapter entropy is the tendency for humans and human systems to dissipate energy in such a way that it is no longer useful for work, enjoyment or clear thinking. From conception humans are dying as well as growing. To survive they must renew their energy intake and conserve their energy utilization. To the extent that they use energy efficiently they can delay their inevitable demise. Most conflict consumes energy uselessly. Interpsychic turmoil makes it difficult to make adaptive choices. Individuals may spend all day attempting to make up their mind on an issue and feel exhausted without having accomplished any useful work. Not only does internal debate consume energy and take up thinking that could otherwise be devoted to useful or pleasurable thought, the conflict results in anxiety. Anxiety uses energy at a high rate because opposing systems cancel each other. The triceps and biceps both contract while the individual tries to decide whether he will strike someone or restrain himself. Organ function is made inefficient by tension.

To avoid consuming energy needlessly through conflict, the human organism persistently seeks to resolve both intrapersonal and interpersonal problems. Solutions may be achieved by thinking, by education, and possibly by discussions. When these fail, and they usually do with major conflicts, people create the opportunity to reexamine their part in conflicts by reenacting them. Having picked out the critical players from among workmates, friends, or family, they restage a minor tragedy. Hopefully, after the action is well established, an individual can withdraw, stand back from the action, and observe it objectively. Unfortunately having once been such an integral part of the action, it is impossible to withdraw without the reenactment collapsing. Thus very few people have an opportunity to objectively view their oft-repeated tragedies. Though this conflict reenactment appears to be only harmful and maladaptive, it is essentially purposeful. Unfortunately, without corrective feedback people usually cannot perceive or understand their contribution to conflict and they seldom learn from the repetition of their mistakes.

Any individual who needs to reenact conflicts from which he hopes to learn, will carefully select others to help him enact the unresolved drama. The selection is mostly unconscious but is justified on the grounds of compatibility. Finding the right job, establishing a warm friendship, or falling in love results in a warm, secure sensation: "I can't tell you why, but this seems very right to me." The close association with a preferred partner becomes a conflict usually when a crisis arises. The couple who have carefully selected each other so that their responses in critical situations are reasonably predictable and fit patterns of unresolved conflict from their past, will feel acute distress when the conflict arises. They feel predominantly anxious, but also confused because they have once again repeated a small tragedy without learning from it. In this way many relationships are conflicts looking for an occasion.

The occasion arises in a family when a child, or dependent, cries in discomfort. The cry evokes a memory in the parents of their own discomfort and awakens a dormant conflict. The conflict creates tension that results in the inefficient utilization of an individual's energy. After the conflict reenactment they feel tired and frustrated. It isn't long before they again feel an intense desire to solve the problems that keep reoccurring "to get out of this trap." They may respond to the child's cry first with nurture, but then with increasing aggression, because of their frustration.

The prelude to any particular crisis is a state of tension between husband and wife, with a third party (observer) often in the form of a mother- or father-in-law standing by. When the child's cry persists, the growing level of tension demands an expression and a solution. The energy consumption increases as the parents strive to control their impulsive anger. The rapidly depleting energy creates a sense of urgency. Most people try the easiest, most readily available solution, usually from a repertoire of familiar patterns. Yet both parents want to avoid abusing their child as they were abused, so they search for alternatives by consulting friends and counselors. If a new method is suggested, it may be tried, but is often too quickly discarded. The parents whose conflicts leave them with few energy reserves cannot attempt to quiet the child and also control their own impulsive response without feeling drained of energy they would prefer to spend enjoying themselves or each other. Therefore their anxiety is coupled with resentment: "This kid has no right to tire me out just when I'm looking forward to a good game of golf." They must find a quick solution. When the child once again cries the painful memories are intensified. The remembered pain, plus the frustration in not finding a more adaptive mechanism to handle the child, intensifies the conflict and the rapid depletion of energy. The parents' impulsive response surfaces from a reservoir of behaviors they learned as children: "Shut up or you'll really get it just like I used to."

The child's reaction to this threat is to cry with increased intensity, partly because his underlying need has not been met, and partly because his existence feels threatened. The mother's or father's self-control is overcome partly because they have less energy and partly because of the intensified internal struggle, "I am exhausted, I have no patience to argue with you." "Do what I say right now or you'll get a licking." Often the child is immobilized by anxiety and confusion. Because he doesn't respond correctly or not quickly enough, the parent strikes. The tendency to hit children is reinforced by a momentary cessation of conflict within the parent and by a pause in the child's irritating cry. The child soon begins again, this time both in fear and in anger stimulated by the pain. Because of that anger he may attempt to hit back at his parent. This provokes unrestrained aggression from the parent, "Don't you dare hit me." "Now you are really going to get it."

The intense child/parent conflict is aggravated by the parents' guilt, which arises from the realization that they have inflicted on their child the same kind of pain they experienced as children. In addition, because they identify with the abused child, they feel his distress. The abuse-restraint conflict might be further intensified by a rebuke from the observer in the triquetra, a parent or spouse who implies that kind of attack on a child is awful. "It's the worst thing you could have done." "Besides, anyone knows there are better ways of dealing with obstreperous children." The net effect is parents who are tired, frustrated, angry, overcome by guilt, conflicted, and so infuriated by the child's "rebellious behavior" that they lose control. The mother or father repeatedly hits the child until his or her rage is exhausted or until the pitiable state of the child evokes such remorse that he or she cannot continue.

Once the child has been beaten, there is a momentary lull in the conflict. As the parent and child disengage, the observer (spouse or grandparent) may berate them. The guilt induced by the observer, plus self-recrimination, intensifies the internal energy consuming conflict, thus priming the parent for another episode of the same behavior. The child's experience of having his appeals met by aggression instead of nurture induces a conflict within him. The frustration that his need was unmet and the pain from the abuse result in a desperation that surfaces whenever he becomes needy. Whenever he cries out of need, he also cries out of fear and anger. This puts a particular edge to his appeal. A piercing cry is more likely to evoke aggression rather than nurture from a parent. Thus, in a small but significant way, the victimized child is contributing to his own victimization.

The ensuing struggle within the child consumes his energy, making him despondent and easily frustrated. He is unable to tackle developmental tasks as efficiently. Consequently he fails in school and socializing. His parents and teachers urge him to try harder. While the child tries to comply because he wants to please his parents, which has survival value for him, he also has become somewhat distrustful. He may succeed at school by dint of urgent effort, but this leaves him with less energy to cope with the demands of a conflicted home life. In an effort to conserve his energy he withdraws, but then he is less able to interpret and respond adaptively to social situations at home. He is more prone to make social mistakes, and to irritate his parents when he should be quiet and compliant.

The child's fatigue makes him more demanding. He tries to borrow energy from his parents in order to keep developing, but they don't believe they have enough energy to deal with their own conflicts and life demands. They resent their child's appeal and will avoid him by finding other things to do, for example, get a job. Because of the increased deprivation, the child feels greater anger and becomes even more irritating in his attempts to appeal for nurture. He carries his conflicts into his peer world, but his demands are met by a similar type of avoidance from his peers who cannot sustain his need for nurture. In these ways the deprivation/aggression conflict becomes ingrained within the child. Because there is no one to help him answer the question, "Why do my parents hit me when I ask for help?," it is carried into his adult life. Because he did not solve the conflict as a child, he must solve it as an adult or use energy inefficiently. Unfortunately, he is no more rational than his parents were in selecting a mate. Unconsciously, he finds someone who will help recreate the experiences of his past. Although his guilt-ridden parents are set up to be the observers, he becomes the apparent perpetrator and his wife or child the victim, in another triquetra. Although he tries not to be aggressive with his own children, he finds himself perpetuating the peculiar propensity of his past. That realization so fills him with guilt he may leave the marriage. The family breakup now sets up a similar type of conflict in his children. They will become adults vainly searching for fulfillment in their spouses.

Abused and neglected children tend to blame themselves. Their tendency to take responsibility for family violence adds to the conflict that needs to be resolved. Unfortunately there are an insufficient number of trained individuals who either recognize or can treat the conflicts as they occur. Children might otherwise blame their parents, but they seem to understand that they need two parents in order to survive. They avoid increasing tensions within or between their parents to prevent a possible breakup when mother and father fight. Children will also intervene, attracting their parents' aggression, thereby making themselves scapegoats in order to resolve the conflict between parents. The abused child becomes both the punished and the punisher. The latter part of him only surfacing when he becomes an adult with demanding children of his own.

Although abuse has a damaging effect on children, neglect may have a more significant and more lasting deleterious result. Neglect leaves children with the sense of having been cheated of a reasonable childhood. That awareness stems less from comparing their own experience to that of others with nurturing, nonpunitive parents, and more from an intuitive awareness of what should have been the nature of parenting that would fill their needs. Children know their needs and strive for any experience to have them filled. They are also aware of what they might have become had they received the building blocks to their development at the appropriate times of their childhood.

Much of the rage in children that results in violence stems from a realization that they were cheated of an adequate childhood. The anger grows with their increasing consciousness that there is no one who can make up the deficiencies of their childhood. They can never become what they might have been. If people, adolescents in particular, cannot deal with that disappointment, if they cannot mourn the loss of a reasonable childhood and the person they could have been, there is a burning anger that erupts whenever a spouse, boss, or child disappoints them. Because adolescents cannot quite give up the possibility of finding the perfect parent, or surrender the eventuality of finding a perfect mate, they vainly search for someone, somewhere, to provide the patient guidance and persistent nurturing appropriate for children. They are bound to be disappointed. The resulting sense of deprivation and injustice fires many episodes of violence.

Adults are more likely to become involved in a "quid pro quo" relationship. Those who are looking for a completion of their childhood have an idealized view of another person, which is reinforced by the strong emotions associated with falling in love. It is only after they become committed to that person that they begin to realize how disappointing the relationship is going to be. The more the romance and the hype, the more the disappointment and it is usually mutual. When they cannot deal with the disappointment in each other, they look for their children to fill those needs. Disappointment in the children, especially those who are wanted children, is often the basis of future abuse and neglect.

TREATMENT

One intelligent, beautiful woman of 35 years I once treated had been the victim of childhood violence, perpetrated by her often drunk father and observed by her passive, tired mother. Having sworn not to marry a drinker or violent man, she carefully scrutinized a number of suitors. The man she married was gentle and considerate but she left him after three years: "He was a wimp." She then had a succession of three marital relationships with drunken, abusive men. Realizing the futility of trying to understand why "I was so stupid," she sought treatment. Within a short period she saw the pattern and worked through her intense ambivalence toward men. She then remarried the first gentleman and according to last report, was living happily ever after (well, at least most of the time).

If violence requires the participation of the perpetrator, victim, and observer, and if each episode is usually a reenactment of old problems that people are attempting to solve in order to maintain a positive energy state, then treatment will require a therapeutic reenactment with insight, retraining old behavior patterns, and sometimes additional sources of energy or rest. The insight may develop as an analysis of the reenactment in transference, or through recognizing the transactions in a family, or in the experience and comments generated during psychodrama. The necessary components of treatment will also require each individual to, as clearly as possible, indicate to themselves and their therapist what they feel they might have been, had the circumstances of their childhood been optimum for development. Having described what they should be, they are encouraged to take a snapshot or to draw a blueprint. With that picture or blueprint "pinned on the wall," they are better able to assess the difference between what they could have been and what they are. They will be now in a position to mourn their childhood and the person they might have been.

Therapy will be needed to bring the reenactment into focus by emphasizing critical features of the experience, heightening the emotions, and then pointing out the effects. A treatment program I have described elsewhere (Ney, 1987b) consists of seven stages through which people who have been abused or neglected are guided. Change will also require the retraining of old patterns of behavior. This may include role-plays, training in assertion, or cognitive restructuring. When the patient is debilitated or weak from conflict, nutrition, rest, exercise, and when necessary, antidepressants are also necessary.

CONCLUSION

Although our primitive sense of justice urges us to defend the injured and punish the aggressor, a closer scrutiny of violence indicates it doesn't often happen without the participation of perpetrator, victim, and observer. The triquetra of these three rotates according to time and circumstance so that any designation of who is one or the other is temporary and arbitrary.

The apparent futility of repetitious family violence might be purposeful. People reenact tragedies they have not learned to resolve, or understood why they must participate. They must understand or stay conflicted. Unresolved conflict consumes human energy with no benefit. To avoid a demise from entropy, every human strives to understand himself well enough to solve his intra- and inter-personal conflict, even if that means he must reenact the painful violence that inaugurated his confusion.

BIBLIOGRAPHY

Carnot, S. (1824). *Reflexion sur la puissance motrice du feu (Reflections on the motor power of fire)*. Paris, France: French Academy of Science.

Comfort, A. (1983). Existential psychiatry and quantum logic. *Psychiatry, 46*, 393–399.

Lifton, R. J. (1986). *The Nazi doctors: Medical killing and the psychology of genocide*. New York: Basic Books.

Martin, J. A. (1984). Neglected fathers: Limitations in diagnostic and treatment resources for violent men. *Child Abuse & Neglect, 8*, 387–392.

Miller, D. T., & McCann, C. D. (1979). Children's reactions to the perpetrators and victims of injustice. *Child Development, 50*, 861–868.

Ney, P. G., Moore, C., McPhee, J., & Trought, P. (1986). Child abuse: A study of the child's perspective. *Child Abuse & Neglect, 10*, 511–518.

Ney, P. G. (1987a). Does verbal abuse leave deeper scars: A study of children and parents. *Canadian Journal of Psychiatry, 32*, 371–378.

Ney, P. G. (1987b). The treatment of abused children: The sequence of events. *American Journal of Psychotherapy, 41*, 39–401.

Ney, P. G. (1988). Transgenerational child abuse. *Child Psychiatry & Human Development, 18*, 151–168.

Nielsen, J. (1964). Mental disorders in married couples (assortative mating). *British Journal of Psychiatry, 110*, 683–697.

3

The Assessment of Spousal Abuse: An Alternative to the Conflict Tactics Scale

Nancy R. Rhodes
Psychologist, Pasadena, California

INTRODUCTION

Research in domestic violence has been impeded by the lack of an instrument capable of measuring frequencies and intensities of violent behavior. The most notable scale devised for this purpose is the Conflict Tactics Scale (CTS). It is not very thorough, however, and inadequate to perform the functions needed for domestic violence research. The purpose of this study was to design a more effective instrument for measuring wife abuse. Thirty female victims of domestic violence participated in a pilot study of the questionnaire's criterion-related validity. Each subject completed the questionnaire and took part in a structured interview. Blind ratings of the frequency and severity of violence for each subject were made for both the interview and questionnaire. Sources of data were significantly correlated for frequency ($p < .05$) but not for severity ratings. The correlation between the severity ratings of the interviews and the questionnaires' severity scores was significant ($p < .05$).

BACKGROUND

Spousal abuse is an aspect of family life that was largely ignored by the public and generally avoided by behavioral scientists until the early 1970s. Since that time there has been an increasing body of literature exploring various dimensions of domestic violence. These studies may be characterized generally as historical, theoretical, and empirical.

The historical accounts of family violence, which documented the long tradition of wife battering and the way in which society has perpetuated such behavior, are extremely useful in terms of providing cultural perspective (Martin, 1976; Pleck, 1979; Schecter, 1982; Straus, 1976). However, they shed little light on the psycho dynamics

Nancy R. Rhodes, Ph.D., is a clinical psychologist currently in private practice.

This study was conducted as a doctoral dissertation at Fuller Theological Seminary, Graduate School of Psychology, Pasadena, California. The author gratefully acknowledges the guidance and assistance of her dissertation committee: Hendrika Vande Kemp, Ph.D. (Chair), Constance Doran, Ph.D., and Linda Mans Wagener, Ph.D. She also acknowledges Eva Baranoff, Ph.D., for her invaluable assistance in the data collection and preparation of this manuscript.

of family violence or on practical approaches to dealing with the problem. Theoretical explorations, which constitute the majority of the published studies, have been important in expanding our understanding of why certain individuals resort to violence within the family.

However, a comprehensive understanding of family violence requires that the results of empirical research be brought to bear on the issue. Researchers attempting to study family violence empirically have been confronted with methodological obstacles related both to availability of appropriate samples and reliable and valid instruments for operationally measuring the types and severity of spousal abuse. Consequently, most empirical studies to date have tended to utilize clinical populations that are readily accessible to researchers (Barnhill, Squires, & Gibson, 1982; Coleman, 1980; Flynn, 1977; Gelles, 1972; Hilberman & Munson, 1978; Pagelow, 1981; Rounsaville, 1978; Snyder & Fruchtman, 1981; Watson, Rosenberg, & Petrik, 1982). The study populations of these studies, which tend to be selected from shelters, medical facilities, or other convenient locations, limit the generalizability of the findings and lead to confusion between the victims' help-seeking behavior and factors related directly to family violence (Gelles, 1980, 1982).

MEASUREMENT OF SPOUSAL ABUSE
IN THE LITERATURE

Although most instruments designed to measure domestic violence have been relatively brief and somewhat oversimplified (Hudson & McIntosh, 1981; Makepeace, 1981; Stacy & Shupe, 1983), the Conflict Tactics Scale (CTS) developed by Straus (1974, 1979) is much more extensive. The CTS consists of a checklist describing actions that typically occur during family conflicts. Respondents are asked to indicate the frequency of each action by themselves and other family members both over the previous year and for the history of the family.

The CTS was used in a national study of 2,143 families (Straus, Gelles, & Steinmetz, 1980). The value of that study was somewhat mitigated by inherent weaknesses in the CTS. The CTS has been widely used in studies of family violence (Barling, O'Leary, Jouriles, Vivian, & Mac Ewen, 1987; Gelles, 1978; Browning & Dutton, 1986; Gully & Dengerink, 1983; Hornung, McCullough, & Sugimoto, 1981; Kratcoski, 1984; Schumm, Martin, Bollman, & Jurich, 1982; Yllo & Straus, 1981).

However, despite its widespread use, the CTS has certain flaws that should be addressed. First, the CTS makes the assumption that violence always occurs in the context of conflictual situations, and fails to recognize the possibility of violence in other contexts that have nothing to do with overtly conflictual situations (Martin, 1976). Second, the CTS has no method for assessing the *antecedents* of the violent actions, which leads to an analysis of behavior without taking into account the context in which the behavior occurred. This is likely to contribute to misunderstanding and possibly inaccurate conclusions.

A third weakness is that the CTS fails to address the meaning of the actions taken, or to deal with the fact that there are many different types of violent behaviors and ways of understanding and/or reacting to those behaviors (Denzin, 1984). That is, there are situations in which an individual's actions may differ significantly from his or her intentions, and this should be incorporated into analyses of conjugal violence. As Rosenbaum (1988) points out, there are many cases in which it would be valuable to know whether violent actions were initiative or retaliatory, instrumental or expressive, or intentional or accidental. The CTS does not provide this information.

Fourth, the items of the CTS lack uniformity, with some items being quite specific descriptions of violent acts and other items being phrased in such a general manner that they are prone to subjective interpretation. In addition, not all forms of violent behaviors are covered by the items. Fifth, the CTS makes no effort to assess the *consequences* of the violent actions. Violent encounters vary greatly in the types of actions, the intensity of those actions, and the nature of the short- and long-term consequences. The degree of physical danger and continuing psychological trauma is an important indicator of intensity, and this is not adequately captured on the CTS. Sixth, and finally, only one form of the CTS has been used to study widely differing forms of family violence: child abuse, sibling abuse, parent abuse, and spousal abuse. Each of these differs in terms of etiology, dynamics, and reporting aspects, and an overly broad instrument is likely to be insensitive to the differences in these types of abuse.

The current study was implemented in part to address these weaknesses and to develop a new instrument that addresses at least some of the weaknesses. Study objectives were (a) to develop a more effective and precise instrument for measuring spousal battering, and (b) to evaluate the usefulness of that instrument in a sample of women who had been abused. The longer-term goal was to provide a prototype for collection of data on larger and more representative samples in the future.

In contrast to the CTS, which provides only frequency counts of specific behaviors (many irrelevant to *spousal* battering per se), the instrument developed in the course of this study specifically measures both the nature and severity of the violence. All items on the instrument are related exclusively to spousal abuse; this was done in order to enhance the specificity and reliability of the response.

The instrument was also designed to be comprehensive, as reflected in the diverse dimensions for which data were collected:

- Identity of the perpetrator
- Identity of the victim
- Descriptive data (physical size and fitness, age) of both victim and perpetrator
- Antecedents of the violent episode
- Time of attack
- Nature of violent actions
- Frequency of each violent action
- Victim's actions in response to violence
- Weapons used
- Intensity and duration of attack
- Consequences of the attack

The decision to utilize a self-administered questionnaire was made based on the argument that anonymity would increase the willingness to respond openly and honestly (Oppenheim, 1966) and that this method is more efficient for gathering data from larger samples.

METHOD

Instrument Development

Stage 1: Development of Items

In order to develop a comprehensive pool of appropriate items, a detailed list of commonly occurring violent behaviors was compiled based on content analysis of 269 temporary restraining orders filed through the Stop Abusive Family Environments (S.A.F.E.) program in Pasadena, California. The use of restraining orders as the data source maximized reliability, in that the information describing domestic violence incidents contained was elicited under oath. This list of items was supplemented with descriptions of incidents from case reports described in accounts of spousal abuse (Martin, 1976; Walker, 1979).

The resultant list was then categorized into broad categories, with items being further classified by type and severity of violent action. Overlapping and similar items were identified and adjustments made in the category definitions.

Stage 2: Questionnaire Development

The items generated in Stage 1 formed the basis for the development of specific questions written at approximately eighth-grade level. Technical words, lengthy words, and words with multiple meanings were avoided, as were double negatives. All statements were kept short, clear, and to the point. Areas covered were dictated by issues raised in an in-depth review of the literature, as well as by the item development process.

Four-point response scales (ranging from "never" to "often") were developed for several of the questions. However, insufficient information was available to quantify all of the items regarding violent behaviors and resulting injuries. Consequently, respondents were asked to estimate the number of times that they experienced any of a number of types of violent behaviors.

Stage 3: Evaluation and Revision

The first draft of the questionnaire was reviewed by the members of a domestic violence research group made up of doctoral students with expertise in the field. These judges reviewed and critiqued the questions, and reached a consensus that the items in the pool adequately sampled the domain. Judges' comments and criticisms regarding design and wording of questions were utilized as a basis for revision of the instrument.

Stage 4: Preliminary Pilot Study

The questionnaire was then administered to five randomly selected battered women from the S.A.F.E. client population. After completing the questionnaire, each subject was interviewed regarding the questionnaire's content, clarity, readability, and sensitivity. A final set of revisions was made based on this feedback.

Subjects

Thirty women who had been in relationships involving three or more physically violent incidents participated in the study. These subjects were contacted through

S.A.F.E., local shelters, and a newspaper advertisement. Characteristics of the sample are shown in Table 3-1.

Procedure

Although this study was largely exploratory—thus making comprehensive assessment of validity and reliability unrealistic—it was considered essential to make at least an initial assessment of criterion-related validity of the instruments. This was done in order to provide a means of determining whether the questionnaire was eliciting the desired information, and to provide an empirical basis for subsequent instrument development. In addition, it provided a data base from which scales could be developed.

The criterion utilized for validation purposes consisted of a semi-structured interview exploring various aspects of the violent relationship. Given the inherent sensitivity of interviewing the victims of spousal violence, these interviews were conducted by two doctoral students who were knowledgeable about domestic violence and who had extensive interviewing experience. Interviews lasted approximately two hours and were audiotaped with the consent of the subjects.

All subjects were given both the instrument and the structured interview. Half of the subjects were interviewed first and half took the written questionnaire first.

Ratings and Scale Development

Scales were developed to rate the frequency and severity of the violence in each relationship. Thurstone equal-appearing interval scales were developed for all types of violence and injuries. Violent actions were coded based on intensity and the likeli-

Table 3-1 Profile of study sample

Age	20–63 years of age, Mean = 31.8 years
Education	10–16 years, Mean = 13.3 years
Employment	53.3% employed, 33.3% unemployed/homemaker, 13.3% student
Ethnicity	76.7% Caucasian, 13.3% Latino, 10.9% African-American
Relationship to perpetrator	46.7% separated, 10.0% divorced, 26.7% separated from former "live-in," 6.7% married, 10.0% other
Duration of relationship	3 months–31 years, Mean = 6.8 years
Length of time acquainted with perpetrator before first incident	1 month–11 years, Mean = 1.7 years
Total number of violent incidents	3–"hundreds," Mean = 46.8 incidents

hood of the action causing serious physical harm. Injuries were rated similarly. If the two scores differed in the intensity rating, the higher score was utilized.

Frequency and severity of violence were quantified based both on content analysis of the structured interviews and analysis of questionnaire responses. This was done independently by each of the two graduate students in order to assess inter-rater reliability.

RESULTS

Pearson product-moment correlation coefficients were utilized to assess inter-rater reliability. Ratings on both severity and frequency scales were highly correlated ($p <$ .01).

The ratings of questionnaires and structured interviews were also correlated as a means of assessing criterion-related validity. Questionnaire and interview ratings of frequency of violence were highly correlated, although the ratings of severity were not. In cases with discrepancies in the severity ratings, the questionnaire tended to yield the higher severity score.

Many subjects experienced difficulty in reporting the exact number of times that violent actions had occurred. However, they were able to indicate *whether* each action had ever occurred and to provide an estimate of the frequency of occurrence.

A profile of the most commonly occurring types of violent acts is shown in Figure 3-1. All of the subjects had experienced being thrown against a solid object, and most had experienced several different types of violent attacks.

Figure 3-2 shows a profile of the consequences of the violent acts.

DISCUSSION

In the past, spousal abuse has been treated as a fairly simple set of violent behaviors. The assumption was generally made that inquiring about a few representative violent actions would provide an adequate data base for analyzing levels of violence.

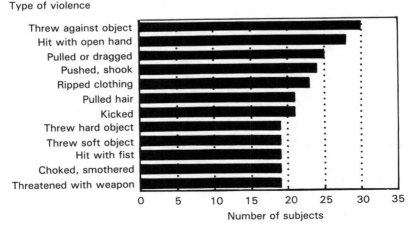

Figure 3-1 Frequency of occurrence of specific violent acts.

Type of injury

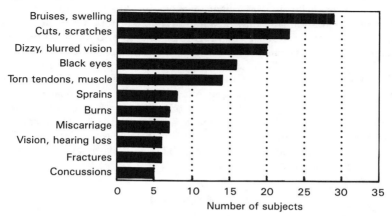

Figure 3-2 Frequency of specific types of injuries resulting from violence.

Results of the current study, however, suggest that the phenomenon of spousal abuse is more complex and that a more sophisticated approach is needed. The lack of a clear conceptual and operational definition has been a barrier to valid and reliable research on domestic violence in the past. The pool of items developed and refined in the current study is more comprehensive than that of the CTS, and hopefully addresses at least some of the weaknesses of that instrument.

It was hypothesized that the thorough procedures that were utilized in the instrument development phase would maximize the instrument's criterion-related validity. However, the correlations between the questionnaire and criterion (structured interview) severity ratings were not as high as had been expected, with the questionnaire yielding consistently higher severity ratings.

There are at least three possible explanations for this. First, it should be acknowledged that the two instruments take a different approach to assessing the severity of violence. While the structured interviews focused on the violence that occurred in three specific incidents, the questionnaire took a broader approach by referring to violence in the relationship in general. Second, the questionnaire asked quite explicit questions and allowed subjects to respond to a series of "menus" describing different types of violent actions. This is in contrast to the more open-ended interview format; many battered women may find it difficult to recall specific details of violent events or have trouble verbalizing in the interview situation. Thus, the subjects may have found it easier to describe the content of the violent encounters by checking off the types of violence. Third, the questionnaire may have encouraged a greater degree of openness than the face-to-face interview. The more distant and impersonal nature of completing a written questionnaire may have decreased the subjects' concerns that they give socially desirable responses. However, it is not possible to identify precisely the reasons for this finding until further research is carried out.

It is also important to acknowledge the limitations of self-report data in general. The concern in domestic violence research has traditionally been that the incidence of violence is likely to be underreported. The assumption of the current study was that the use of an extensive, semistructured interview would be the method least likely to underestimate violence. However, the findings showed that subjects reported lower levels of violence during the interview than on the self-report questionnaire. This suggests that the questionnaire may be a more reliable method for estimating severity of violence than the interview. In this regard, it should also be noted that the questionnaire methodology is more cost-effective in that there is no need to hire well-qualified interviewers and that it takes only 20–30 minutes to complete.

This preliminary study served to provide the basis for an objectively scorable instrument with reliable ratings for frequency and severity of spousal abuse. Future efforts will focus on improving the accuracy of the scoring system through continued expert review and pilot studies. Scoring methods will also be developed for other portions of the questionnaire, assessing such dimensions as psychological abuse and the distribution of violent incidents over time. This will lay the groundwork for more extensive validity and reliability studies.

BIBLIOGRAPHY

Barling, J., O'Leary, K., Jouriles, E. N., Vivian, D., & MacEwen, K. E. (1987). Factor similarity of the CTS across samples, spouses, and sites. *Journal of Family Violence, 2*(1), 37–54.

Barnhill, L. R., Squires, M. F., & Gibson, G. (1982). The epidemiology of violence in CMHC setting. In Hansen, J. C., & Barnhill, L. R. (Eds.), *Clinical approaches to family violence.* Rockville, MD: Aspen.

Browning, J., & Dutton, D. (1986). Assessment of wife assault with the Conflict Tactics Scale: Using couple data to quantify the differential reporting effect. *Journal of Marriage and the Family, 48*(2), 375–379.

Coleman, K. H. (1980). Conjugal violence: What 33 men report. *Journal of Marriage and Family Therapy, 42,* 623–668.

Denzin, N. K. (1984). Toward a phenomenology of domestic violence. *American Journal of Sociology, 90,* 483–513.

Flynn, J. P. (1977). Recent findings related to wife abuse. *Social Casework, 58,* 13–20.

Gelles, R. J. (1972). *The violent home.* Beverly Hills, CA: Sage.

Gelles, R. J. (1978). Violence toward children in the United States. *American Journal of Orthopsychiatry, 48,* 580–592.

Gelles, R. J. (1980). Violence in the family: A review of research in the seventies. *Journal of Marriage and the Family, 42,* 873–884.

Gelles, R. J. (1982). Applying research on family violence to clinical practice. *Journal of Marriage and the Family, 44,* 9–20.

Gully, K. J., & Dengerink, H. A. (1983). The dyadic interaction of persons with violent and nonviolent histories. *Aggressive Behavior, 9,* 13–20.

Hilberman, E., & Munson, K. (1978). Sixty battered women. *Victimology, 2,* 460–470.

Hornung, C. A., McCullough, B. C., & Sugimoto, T. (1981). Status relationships in marriage: Risk factors in spouse abuse. *Journal of Marriage and the Family, 43,* 675–692.

Hudson, W. W., & McIntosh, S. R. (1981). The assessment of spouse abuse: Two quantifiable dimensions. *Journal of Marriage and the Family, 43,* 873–888.

Kratcoski, P. C. (1984). Perspectives on intrafamily violence. *Human Relations, 37,* 443–454.

Makepeace, J. (1981). Courtship violence among college students. *Family Relations, 30,* 97–102.

Martin, D. (1976). *Battered wives.* San Francisco, CA: Glide.

Oppenheim, A. N. (1966). *Questionnaire design and attitude measurement.* New York: Basic Books.

Pagelow, M. D. (1981). *Woman battering; Victims and their experiences.* Beverly Hills, CA: Sage.

Pleck, E. (1979). Wife beating in nineteenth century America. *Victimology, 4,* 60–74.

Rosenbaum, A. (1988). Methodological issues in marital violence research. *Journal of Family Violence, 3,* 91–104.

Rounsaville, B. J. (1978). Theories in marital violence: Evidence from a study of battered women. *Victimology, 4,* 60–74.

Schecter, S. (1982). *Women and male violence.* Boston, MA: South End Press.

Schumm, M. A., Martin, M. J., Bollman, S. R., & Jurich, A. P. (1982). Classifying family violence. *Journal of Family Issues, 3,* 319–340.

Snyder, D. K., & Fruchtman, L. A. (1981). Differential patterns of wife abuse: A data-based typology. *Journal of Consulting and Clinical Psychology, 49,* 878–885.

Stacy, W. A., & Shupe, A. (1983). *The family secret.* Boston, MA: Beacon Press.

Straus, M. A. (1974). Leveling, civility, and violence in the family. *Journal of Marriage and the Family, 36,* 13–29.

Straus, M. A. (1976). Sexual inequality, cultural norms, and wife beating. *Victimology, 1,* 54–70.

Straus, M. A. (1979). Measuring intrafamily conflict and violence: The Conflict Tactics Scale. *Journal of Marriage and the Family, 41,* 75–88.

Straus, M., Gelles, R., & Steinmetz, S. (1980). *Behind closed doors: Violence in the American family.* New York: Anchor.

Walker, L. (1979). *The battered woman.* New York: Harper & Row.

Watson, C. G., Rosenberg, A. M., & Petrik, N. (1982). Incidence of wife-battering in male psychiatric patients: Are special treatment programs needed? *Psychological Reports, 51,* 563–566.

Yllo, K., & Straus, M. A. (1981). Interpersonal violence among married and cohabiting couples. *Family Relations, 30,* 339–347.

4

The Relationship Between Locus of Control and Level of Violence in Married Couples

Robert M. Theodore
Department of Psychology, Northwest Missouri State University, Maryville

INTRODUCTION

The present study investigated the relationship between locus of control and level of violence (abuse, victimization, nonabuse, and nonvictimization) in a marriage.

Sixty married couples chosen from churches and marital counseling groups responded to the Vocational Preference Inventory, Conflict Tactics Scale, and Adult Nowicki-Strickland Internal-External Locus of Control Scales.

Locus of control was predicted by time in counseling, history of family violence, income,and abuse. Abuse status was predicted by victim status, violence in the family of origin, marital status, income, and highest academic grade achieved. Victim status was predicted by abuse status, marital status, and time in counseling.

Analysis of variance found victims to have a significantly more external locus of control than nonvictims. Abusers were not significantly different from nonabusers on locus of control. Pearson product-moment correlations revealed significant relationships between abusive husbands and victimized wives and between nonabusive husbands and nonvictimized wives on measures of locus of control.

The hypothesis that locus of control and level of violence are related was supported.

Early literature on domestic violence focused on child abuse (Kemp, Silverman, Steele, Droegemueller, & Silver, 1962), examinations and descriptions of violence (Schultz, 1960; Snell, Rosenwald, & Robey, 1964), and women as victims of spouse abuse (Pizzey, 1977). Other publications were directed at the chaos in which some women were living (Martin, 1976; Pizzey, 1977), and vividly depicted the living conditions of some people in a way that stimulated interest and investigation.

Gelles (1980) called for more rigorous studies that would test proposed theories, increase the variety of measuring instruments, and use nonclinical samples to increase our understanding of abuse between spouses. As expected, the number of articles has

Robert M. Theodore, Ph.D., is currently in the Department of Psychology at Northwest Missouri State University.

The author thanks Wayne Lanning, Don Forrest, Arden White, Kathy Green, and Steve Heyman for their comments and support while working on the dissertation from which this chapter is derived.

increased. Even a television movie has portrayed an abusive relationship, a throwback to the early writings of Pizzey (1977) and Martin (1976). However, the general emphasis remains on discussions of personality (Wetzel & Ross, 1983), reasons for remaining in an abusive situation (Rounsaville, 1978), and treatment strategies (Gondolf, 1985). Furthermore, the primary research samples continue to be drawn from clinical populations.

Foundational research into spouse abuse was limited to wife battering in part because the women's movement provided motivation for further investigation, the accessibility of battered women in shelters, and the fact that traditional male roles did not encourage men to admit being victims or abusers. Even now, men as victims of abuse or mutual abuse between partners is rarely addressed (Steinmetz, 1978; Tkachuk, 1985). Literature continues to focus on what has become accepted as the "typical" situation in which the husband abuses the wife.

The actual problem to be explored (spouse abuse) in this chapter is more than a "typical" situation. It is more than a feminist issue or an issue for men. It is a humanitarian concern because domestic violence results in millions of men and women being injured physically, hospitalized, or in a few cases murdered.

Therefore, the purpose of the present study was to step beyond the stereotypic situation and investigate spouse abuse with regard to both the physically abusive husband or wife and a nonabusive population. To achieve a better understanding of the difference between an abusive and a nonabusive marriage, the study examined the relationship between levels of violence (abuse, victimization, nonabuse, and nonvictimization) and locus of control.

Locus of control, a construct couched within social learning theory, is said to be a personality variable that can be expressed as an internal orientation or an external orientation depending on the style learned as a child (Rotter, 1966). An example of external locus of control (or belief in external causality) was exemplified when women checking into a shelter were measured for locus of control (Lewis, 1982). It was found that these women blamed their husbands for their life circumstances. In other words, they expressed an external orientation. On the other hand, Walker (1984) reported that abused women tended to score high in internal control (i.e., believing they could control their life circumstances). In counseling, it has been observed that men externalize responsibility. One study found that correlated locus of control to abusive behavior in men (Rouse, 1984).

Therefore, it appears that the dynamic of external locus of control may be operating in the hostile marriage. However, there is no conclusive evidence as to the effect of locus of control in abusive marriages or harmonious marriages. Numerous and sometimes conflicting reports exist in the literature regarding symptoms and correlates of abuse (Gondolf, 1985; Lewis, 1982; Rouse, 1984; Walker, 1984; Wetzel & Ross, 1983). A small number of the theories or symptoms have been researched. Although some data exist on locus of control in abused wives, the literature is relatively limited regarding husbands (neither abusers nor victims) on locus of control and no records of a nonabusive group being used for comparison were found.

Straus, Gelles, and Steinmetz (1980) report that people in an abusive marriage perform the same abusive behaviors as their parents. The connection between the marital violence and social learning in this study is established by asking respondents if their parents ever hit each other during an argument and relating violence in the family of origin to the respondents' present behavior. A limitation, however, is that it cannot be determined by this study if locus of control is learned from the originative family. Although it may be inferred by a high positive correlation between abuse and external locus of control that locus of control orientation is learned, it is not possible to determine whether the abusive behavior or the locus of control orientation came first.

Nevertheless, the present study seems to be a first investigation into locus of control and levels of violence (abusers, victims, nonabusers, and nonvictims). By studying the relationship between level of violence and locus of control, it may be possible to identify the role of locus of control in a violent marriage.

Also, income (Rounsaville, 1978), level of education (Hornung, McCullough, & Sugimoto, 1981), gender (Steinmetz, 1978; Straus et al., 1980), and church attendance (Star, 1978) have been identified as variables that may account for locus of control orientation and incidence of domestic violence. Therefore they are appropriately considered in the analysis of the data.

Two other variables considered in the present study, self-esteem and traditional sex role (Walker, 1979), have been suggested as characteristics of abusive husbands. Achievement (Phares, 1976) was found to be related to locus of control and may be related to marital violence. For instance, people who tend to be less achievement oriented tend to be more external, in other words, they tend to believe that powerful others control their lives as may be the case with abusers. Finally, a subject's time spent in counseling could have some effect on level of violence and locus of control, thus it was also considered.

Although the purpose of the present study was to investigate the relationship between locus of control and violence, and other variables, it was designed to answer specifically the following questions.

1. What is the relationship between an abusive husband's locus of control and a victimized wife's locus of control?

2. Do victims of physical abuse and nonvictims have the same locus of control?

3. Do abusers and nonabusers have the same locus of control?

4. What is the relationship between a nonabusive husband's locus of control and a nonvictimized wife's locus of control?

5. Do achievement, age, highest academic grade level achieved, self-esteem, traditional sex role, violence in family of origin, church attendance, income, gender, abuse, victim, and time spent in counseling predict locus of control in men and women?

6. Do achievement, age, highest academic grade level achieved, self-esteem, traditional sex role, violence in family of origin, church attendance, income, gender, victim, locus of control, and time spent in counseling predict abusive behavior in men and women?

7. Do achievement, age, highest academic grade level achieved, self-esteem, traditional sex role, violence in family of origin, church attendance, income, abuse, gender, locus of control, and time spent in counseling predict victimization (i.e., being a victim of physical abuse) in men and women?

8. What are the differences between identified counseling group participants' demographics and church population demographics?

METHOD

Subjects

For the reported study, 528 potential respondents were contacted, (264 married couples). Forty five percent of those individuals contacted returned questionnaires. A total of 120 selected respondents (60 married couples) was used in the present study. Six couples were separated and one couple completed a divorce during the time of data collection. Because the one couple had just completed divorce proceedings during the data collection period, it was decided to include their scores for analysis. The respondents selected for the study were between the ages of 23 and 56.

The majority of subjects (married couples) were selected from four churches. However, seven of the couples volunteered from a sexual assault and family education project and counseling groups for victims and abusers. Although the sample was sufficient to identify relationships and assess differences, it was not intended to be representative of the area populations.

The respondents were chosen via stratified random sampling from each of the church groups, but included all the reported abusers and victims from all groups. A stratified sample from the churches was used because using the whole group of returned questionnaires would have produced a disproportionately large sample of nonabusers and nonvictims. For statistical purposes, a more balanced number of cases was desired.

Eligible couples were selected in each church from mailing lists provided by pastors. Participating couples (selected from the mailing lists) were assigned separate code numbers by the church's secretary. The instrument packet that each couple received and the instruments that were to be completed by the husband and the wife had a code number that corresponded to the number on the church's list written on it. The return envelope included in each instrument packet also had the couple's code number stamped on it. A list of the numbers that corresponded to the numbers assigned to the parishioners was kept by the secretary for future reference.

The researcher also kept a record of the code numbers assigned by each church. Each church also had a unique set of code numbers so that it could be identified. By means of the list of numbers, it was possible to keep a record of the instruments returned from each church. As couples returned their questionnaires, their code numbers were scratched off the list. The code numbers enabled follow-up procedures.

Follow-up was conducted ten days to two weeks after the instruments were mailed by the church secretary. To remind respondents to return the questionnaires, postcards were sent to couples (those code numbers remaining on the primary researcher's list) via the mailing list retained by the church secretary.

For the project and counseling groups, the instrument packets were distributed by project administrators and counselors and collected by them. Approval for data collection was obtained from project administrators and group leaders. The instrument packets were coded by number and the numbers assigned to those who were participating in the study. The completed questionnaires were mailed back to the primary researcher.

Instruments

The Conflict Tactics Scale (CTS) was chosen to measure levels of violence in a marriage. Factor analysis of the CTS suggested three factors, reasoning, verbal aggression, and assault (violence) (Straus, 1979).

Reliability was established by mean item-total correlations. For husbands, correlations for reasoning, verbal aggression, and violence were .74, .73, and .87 respectively. Similar correlations were reported for wives (Straus, 1979). Concurrent validity, construct validity, and face validity are discussed in Straus et al. (1979, 1980).

The Nowicki-Strickland Internal-External Control Scale for adults (ANS-IE) was designed to assess the construct of locus of control and was chosen for this study for that purpose. Furthermore, the ANS-IE has been found to be a valid, reliable instrument for measuring locus of control in non-college populations (Nowicki & Duke, 1974; S. Nowicki, Jr., & M. P. Duke, personal communication, May 1986).

The Vocational Preference Inventory (VPI) was chosen because it has repeatedly been found to be a valid and reliable measure of achievement, traditional sex role, and self-esteem, the independent variables in this study. Validity and reliability data have been published (Andrulis, 1977; Holland, 1985).

PROCEDURE

Identified subjects were mailed a coded packet of materials including the Conflict Tactics Scale, the locus of control scales, and the Vocational Preference Inventory. Included in each packet was a letter explaining the purpose of the study, the date by which the instruments were to be returned, and an explanation that follow-up contacts would be made if the tests were not returned on time. Participants were informed in the letter that all information would be kept confidential and that names would be used only for distribution and collection.

Subjects were categorized as either victims, abusers, nonvictims, or nonabusers by their responses to the violence questions on the Conflict Tactics Scale (CTS). An abuser, by definition, was an individual who reported (on the CTS violence scale) using physical violence toward his spouse more than two times. An individual who reported being the victim of physical violence more than two times was categorized as a victim.

On the other hand, a husband reporting, for example, hitting his wife and being hit in return, was classified as a combination of victim/abuser. (Wives were classified in a similar manner). Thus certain individuals were classified as both victim and abuser. Similarly, those who reported less than two occurrences of abuse and victimization were categorized as nonabuser/nonvictim. Combined cases of this nature were legitimate for this study because the focus was on the relationship between the locus of control of victims and the locus of control of abusers, not necessarily the difference between husbands and wives. However, for specific hypotheses, the distinction (between abusive husbands and victimized wives) was made for the analysis. Furthermore, none of the research hypotheses compare abusers and victims on any particular variable. Therefore, using the scores of people who fit both abuser and victim categories did not confound the analysis.

Abuser status and victim status were independent variables in the study. Incidence of physical abuse was assessed in terms of rate reported for the 12 months prior to receiving the packet of instruments.

Each subject received two CTS instruments. The first scale asked for the respondent's use of conflict tactics during the past year and determined if the respondent was abusive. The second scale determined if the respondent was a victim by asking for the subject's perception of his or her spouse's use of tactics. The CTS determined the incidence of violence tactics on a six-point Likert scale.

The dependent variable in the study was locus of control. The Locus of Control Scales (Nowicki & Duke, 1974) use a forced choice response format—the respondent must choose either a "yes" or a "no" response for each item. A high score indicates an external locus of control and a low score an internal locus. Each subject was asked to complete a Locus of Control Scale.

In addition to the data collected via the Locus of Control Scale and CTS, the following demographic information was gathered for each subject: gender; highest academic grade level achieved; income; time spent in counseling; violence in the family of origin; and rate of church attendance. The demographic variables were considered independent variables.

The demographic variables were also used to determine if significant differences exist between the church populations and the identified abuse/victim populations from the project and counseling groups. The church populations and counseling groups were compared on relevant demographics, income, highest grade level achieved, and church attendance. These demographics were chosen for comparison because it was believed that counseling group subjects might be in a lower socioeconomic group, lower achievers in academics, or might not attend church as often as those respondents from the church population.

If the two groups differed significantly, then the final analysis would be considered with this limitation in mind. It is important to retain the data particularly from the identified abuse and victim groups because they are the subjects of particular concern and what differentiates them from the church groups may, in the final analysis, be of considerable importance. Of equal interest would be the finding of no difference between the two groups.

Other independent variables such as achievement, self-esteem, and traditional sex role were measured with the (Vocational Preference Inventory) VPI. These variables were included because they have been found to be related to abusive behavior (Straus et al., 1980) and therefore may account for a portion of the variance in the research. The VPI is a self-administered paper and pencil inventory. The subject responds by indicating "yes" or "no" regarding like or dislike for the particular occupations. Vocational interests are determined by an individual's responses to test items. A high score in a particular vocational category (e.g., status) indicates a preference for occupations in that area and suggests certain personality characteristics in the respondent.

RESULTS

Stepwise multiple correlations were used to determine the variables that would predict either of the criterion variables (abuse, victim, or locus of control). Analysis of variance was used to assess the differences between either victims and nonvictims or abusers and nonabusers. To discover the relationship between the locus of control of abusive husbands and victimized wives, Pearson product-moment correlations were used. Likewise, the correlations between the locus of control of nonabusers and nonvictims was assessed with Pearson r. The differences between church respondents and counseling group participants were determined by t-tests.

Comparison of Groups

Although question eight was the last, it was vital to the study because it determined if the backgrounds of the sample of abusers and victims from counseling groups and the church sample were different. A finding of significant difference would require separate analysis for each group (as if they were two different samples). It was not the main question of the study, but would affect the analysis of the other questions depending on its outcome. Therefore, it is considered first.

Question eight was addressed in two ways. First, subjects seen in counseling (*n* = 14, seven couples) were compared with all church subjects (*n* = 101) for different background information. Then, only those couples who were identified as victims or abusers from each group were compared for different background information.

Table 4-1 summarizes results comparing specified demographics for identified abusers and victims attending counseling for violence, and church attenders. No significant difference was found for income or church attendance. However, there was a significant difference in the number of years of school completed (*p* = .007). Those subjects seen in counseling reported fewer years of school completed (*M* = 13.28, *SD* = 2.75) compared to subjects reporting no abuse and no counseling (*M* = 15.31, *SD* = 2.54).

Thus, the background information between the two groups seemed similar and it was reasonable to include the identified abusive population as a part of the sample.

In order to ascertain any difference between couples chosen from counseling groups and chosen church couples who reported marital violence (both in counseling and not), further analysis was performed. No significant difference was found for income (*p* = .10) or church attendance (*p* = .23). The two groups were found to be significantly different on the number of academic grades (school years) completed (*p* = .008; mean church group = 14.8, *SD* = 2.61; mean counseling group = 12.3, *SD* = 2.41). Again, the groups seemed sufficiently similar to treat both groups in one pool for analyses of primary questions.

Abusive Husbands/Victimized Wives

A significant positive relationship (*r* = .673, *p* = .017) was found between abusive husbands' and victimized wives' locus of control. Approximately 45% of the variance was accounted for by locus of control scores of abusive husbands and victimized wives.

The correlation between nonabusive husbands' locus of control and nonvictimized wives' locus of control was also significant (*r* = .423, *p* = .007). Therefore, the locus of control for nonabusive husbands and nonvictimized wives is significantly positively related. The correlation for the nonvictimized wives and nonabusive hus-

Table 4-1 Differences between identified counseling group participants and the church population

	Church subjects			Subjects in counseling				
	N	Mean	SD	N	Mean	SD	t	P
Income	101	3.17	1.07	14	2.57	1.22	1.91	.059
Grade level	101	15.31	2.54	14	13.28	2.75		.007
Church attendance	101	.97	.17	14	.92	.27	.79	.429

bands (r = .423) was found to be significantly different, chi-square (N = 2,1 df) = 9.06, p = .01, from the correlation of abusive husbands and victimized wives (r = .672). This indicates that violent couple's locus of control differs from nonviolent couples' and that violent couples tend to be relatively homogeneous in their locus of control orientation.

Victims Versus Nonvictims and Abusers Versus Nonabusers

Findings related to questions two and three are depicted in Tables 4-2 and 4-3, respectively. A significant difference was found between the locus of control of victims and nonvictims (p = .021). Victims' (M = 9.50, SD = 3.72, n = 10) locus of control was more external than nonvictims' (M = 7.20, SD = 4.59, n = 10), in other words, significantly better than chance. However, no significant difference was found between abusers and nonabusers on locus of control (p = .742).

The results shown in Table 4-3 also indicate no significant difference between abusers' and nonabusers' locus of control, although a significant difference was found between the locus of control of victims and nonvictims. Unweighted means analysis was used to adjust for discrepancies in cell size in the analysis of variance. Unequal cell size appears to have had no effect.

Locus of Control

Table 4-4 contains a summary of the analysis performed to determine if locus of control was significantly predicted by the independent variables stated in question five. Predictors that were found to be significant included time spent in counseling (r = .395), father's abusive behavior, in other words, violence in family of origin (r = .375), income (r = −.298), and abuse (r = .175).

Significantly related to locus of control were time spent in counseling, violence in the family of origin, income, and abuse. These four predictors accounted for 31% of the variance in the prediction of locus of control.

Abusive Behaviors

Significant predictors of abusive behavior included victim (r = .468), father's behavior, in other words, violence in the family of origin (r = .410), marital status (r = .477), income (r = −.398), and highest academic grade achieved (r = −.184). These five predictors accounted for 48% of the variance in predicting abuse. Although not significant, locus of control (r = .179) represented 3% of the variance and was entered next in the equation. Significant predictors of abuse are shown in Table 4-5.

Table 4-2 ANOVA for the comparison of the locus of control for abusers vs. nonabusers and victims vs. nonvictims

Source	SS	DF	Mean square	F	Significance
Main effects	169.897	2	84.949	4.315	.016
Victim	108.193	1	108.193	5.496	.021
Abuser	2.152	1	2.152	.109	.742
Abuser × victim	.998	1	.998	.051	.882

Table 4-3 Unweighted means analysis comparison of abusers vs. nonabusers and victims vs. nonvictims

Source	SS	DF	MS	F	p
Abuse	1.01	1	1.01	<1	ns
Victimization	6.89	1	6.89	4.92	.05
A × B interaction	.47	1	.47	<1	ns
Residual	—	144	1.40	—	—

Victimization

The relationship between the dependent variable victim and the predictor variables is shown in Table 4-6. Significant predictors of victim status included abuse ($r = .469$) and marital status ($r = .415$). Time spent in counseling ($r = .372$) was not considered significant, although it could be considered marginal.

Time spent in counseling, abuse, and marital status significantly predicted victimization and accounted for 30% of the variance in prediction of victimization.

DISCUSSION

The present study was undertaken because of the physical pain and mental anguish resulting from domestic violence and to assess the role of locus of control in domestic violence.

The results of this study support the observations that external locus of control is related to level of violence and are consistent with previous research (Lewis, 1982; Rouse, 1984). For example, locus of control scores for victims were significantly more external than nonvictims, and abuse was significantly related to locus of control.

Clearly, locus of control orientation plays a significant role in the dynamics of a marriage. For nonvictims and nonabusers, it may be that a more internal orientation contributes to a more reasoning (less violent) method of resolving conflict. Theoretically, individuals with an internal locus of control (hereafter referred to as internals) take responsibility for the outcome of events or activities in their lives (Rotter, 1966). They feel more in control of themselves and their situation. When problems arise, such as marital conflict, the internal spouse will be more introspective. In other words, internals look at their parts in the interaction and modify their own behaviors to resolve the situation (Phares, 1976). The important factor is that internals may take more responsibility for their success and failure in a marriage when compared to externals.

Table 4-4 Stepwise multiple regression for the dependent variable locus of control

Step	Predictor variable	F value to enter	Signif.	Multiple R	R squared	Simple R
1	Counseling	19.5	.000	.395	.156	.395
2	His. family violence	14.2	.000	.508	.258	.375
3	Income	4.5	.039	.536	.288	− .298
4	Abuse	4.0	.048	.561	.314	.175
5	Grade level	3.5	.064	.581	.338	− .305

Table 4-5 Stepwise multiple regression table for the dependent variable abuse

Step	Variable	F to enter	Signif.	Multiple R	R squared	Simple R
1	Victim	29.459	.000	.468	.219	.468
2	His. family violence	24.041	.000	.605	.365	.410
3	Marital status	9.093	.003	.646	.417	.477
4	Income	7.640	.007	.677	.458	−.398
5	Grade level	3.976	.049	.691	.478	−.184
6	Locus of control	2.524	.115	.701	.504	.179

People with an external locus of control (hereafter referred to as externals) perceive others as controlling the events in their lives, even their emotional well-being (Nowicki & Duke, 1974; Rotter, 1966). Externals tend to describe marital conflict as a matter of bad luck. The main characteristic of externals is that they do not feel in control of their lives (i.e., outcomes of events). Counselors have identified the externals' belief in powerful others in statements such as, "she makes me angry" or "my life would be better if only he or she would change." That is, externals see their spouses as being the sources and controllers of their misery (Gondolf, 1985; Walker, 1979; Wetzel & Ross, 1983).

More evidence is provided that externality and violence are related. Sadowski and Wenzel (1982) determined that high externals reported more hostility than internals, a finding that was supported in the present research. A significant positive relationship was found between abuse and locus of control. This positive correlation (the prediction of locus of control by abuse) suggests that external locus of control and spouse abuse are related.

In the present study, locus of control (external) was predicted by time spent in counseling. This may suggest that subjects experiencing physical abuse at the hands of their spouses are suffering emotionally and are seeking help. It may also mean that external subjects of the study were seeking a powerful other (a counselor) to solve their problems, as the literature suggests (Phares, 1976).

Time spent in counseling also predicted victimization, although it did not predict abuse. This finding probably results from the fact that more counseling resources are available for victims than abusers. An alternative explanation is that abusers may not seek counseling as frequently as victims. As expressed by an abuser, "I thought I could handle it without help" (Gondolf, 1985, p. 53).

Another predictor of locus of control was violence in the family of origin. This outcome supports the theoretical premise of the present study, that abuse is learned. Furthermore, it seems that the father's behavior is more influential than the mother's

Table 4-6 Stepwise multiple regression for the dependent variable victim

Step	Variable	F to enter	Signif.	Multiple R	R squared	Simple R
1	Abuse	30.160	.000	.469	.220	.469
2	Marital status	7.807	.006	.523	.273	.415
3	Time in counseling	3.820	.053	.547	.298	.372
4	His. family violence	3.996	.086	.564	.319	.064

behavior in predicting abuse and locus of control. The mother's behavior did not predict locus of control or abuse.

Research literature provides supportive evidence that violence in the family of origin and father's behavior are important factors in the transmission of marital violence. Rounsaville (1978) reports that between 39 and 74% of men surveyed were physically abused or observed physical violence between their parents. However, Straus et al. (1980) and Kalmus (1984) suggest that although the father's behavior may have slightly more influence in the transmission of violence than the mother's behavior, it is not necessarily true that males will become abusers or females victims.

The present study supports previous research that found that income is a factor in marital violence (Rounsaville, 1978; Straus et al., 1980). Spouse abuse was greater in lower income families.

Other predictors of marital violence included marital status, abuse, and victimization. Marital status became a predictor because several of the violent couples were separated at the time of data collection, whereas all nonviolent couples were married and living together at the time of the study.

An apparent trend is seen throughout this study that is consistent with previous research. It is that in a violent marital relationship, external locus of control is a predominant factor for the victim and also for the abuser. From this study, locus of control could not be identified as the cause of spouse abuse. However, it may be said that the belief in a powerful spouse controlling one's life becomes a catalyst to violence. This catalyst works best in an environment that is ready for ignition. This environment includes low income, low academic achievement, and a history of family violence.

With respect to these findings, the implication for treatment is that, through counseling, clients' learned locus of control orientation and concomitant behavior may be modified. Phares (1976) indicates that locus of control orientation may be modified. Furthermore, counselors working with abusers have observed that external orientation may be modified through cognitive and/or behavioral intervention (Lewis, 1982; Waldo, 1987).

Clearly, more research in this area is needed to determine if counseling (either group or individual) creates a change of orientation from external to internal and as a consequence, a decrease in abuse. Also, future studies and the counseling profession would benefit from theory based research conducted on broader research samples. Research samples continue to be drawn primarily from treatment centers and groups. These sample restrictions preclude generalization of results to other populations and thus limit our understanding of domestic violence and nonviolent relationships. To maximize our effectiveness with clients, it is equally important to understand what makes a relationship healthy as it is to know what makes it violent.

BIBLIOGRAPHY

Andrulis, R. (1977). Adult assessment: A source book of tests and measurements of human behavior. Springfield, IL: Charles C Thomas.

Gelles, R. J. (1980). Violence in the family: A review of research in the seventies. *Journal of Marriage and the Family, 42*(4), 873–885.

Gondolf, E. W. (1985). Fighting for control; A clinical assessment of men who batter. *Social Casework: The Journal of Contemporary Social Work, 66*(1), 48–54.

Holland, J. L. (1985). *Vocational preference inventory (VPI)*. Odessa, FL: Psychological Associates.

Hornung, C. A., McCullough, C. B., & Sugimoto, T. (1981). Status relationships in marriage: Risk factors in spouse abuse. *Journal of Marriage and the Family, 43*(3), 675–692.

Kalmus, D. (1984). The intergenerational transmission of marital aggression. *Journal of Marriage and the Family, 46*(1), 11–19.

Kemp, H., Silverman, F., Steele, B., Droegemueller, W., & Silver, H. (1962). The battered child syndrome. *Journal of the American Medical Association, 181*(1), 17–24.

Lewis, L. A. (1982). Internal-external locus of control in battered women. (Doctoral Dissertation, Fielding Institute, Santa Barbara, California). Dissertation Abstracts International 43:2711B.

Martin, D. (1976). *Battered wives.* San Francisco, CA: Glide Publications.

Nowicki, S., & Duke, M. P. (1974). A locus of control scale for college as well as non-college adults. *Journal of Personality Assessment, 38,* 136–137.

Phares, E. J. (1976). *Locus of control in personality.* Hillsdale, NJ: General Learning Press.

Pizzey, E. (1977). *Scream quietly or the neighbors will hear.* Hillsdale, NJ: Ridley Enslow.

Ponzetti, J. J., Cate, R. M., & Koval, J. (1982). Violence between couples: Profiling the male abuser. *The Personnel and Guidance Journal, 61*(4), 222–224.

Rotter, J. B. (1966). Generalized expectancies for internal versus external control of reinforcement. *Psychological Monographs: General and Applied, 80*(1, Whole No. 609).

Rounsaville, B. J. (1978). Theories in marital violence: Evidence from a study of battered women. *Victimology: An International Journal, 3*(1–2), 11–31.

Rouse, L. (1984). Models, self-esteem, and locus of control as factors contributing to spouse abuse. *Victimology: An International Journal, 9,* 130–141.

Sadowski, C., & Wenzel, D. (1982). The relationship of locus of control dimensions to reported hostility and aggression. *The Journal of Psychology, 112,* 227–230.

Schultz, L. (1960). The wife assaulter. *Journal of Social Therapy, 6*(2), 103–112.

Snell, J., Rosenwald, R., & Robey, A. (1964). The wife beater's wife: A study of family interaction. *Archives of General Psychiatry, 11,* 107–113.

Star, B. (1978). Comparing battered and nonbattered women. *Victimology: An International Journal, 3*(1–2), 32–44.

Steinmetz, S. K. (1978). The battered husband syndrome. *Victimology: An International Journal, 2,* 499–509.

Straus, M. A. (1979). Measuring intrafamily conflict and violence: The conflict tactics scale. *Journal of Marriage and the Family, 41*(1), 75–88.

Straus, M. A., Gelles, R., & Steinmetz, S. (1980). *Behind closed doors.* New York: Doubleday.

Tkachuk, M. (1985). Battered and nonbattered womens' attitudes towards violence between women and men. (Doctoral Dissertation, University of Wyoming). Dissertation Abstracts International 46:2081B.

Waldo, M. (1987). Also victims: Understanding and treating men arrested for spouse abuse. *Journal of Counseling and Development 65*(7), 385–388.

Walker, L. E. (1979). *The battered woman.* New York: Harper & Row.

Walker, L. E. (1984). *The battered woman syndrome.* New York: Springer.

Wetzel, L., & Ross, M. (1983). Psychological and social ramifications of battering: Observations leading to a counseling methodology for victims of domestic violence. *The Personnel and Guidance Journal, 62*(1), 423–428.

5

Social Isolation and Wife Abuse: A Research Report

Joyce McCarl Nielsen
Russell K. Endo
Barbara L. Ellington
Institute of Behavioral Science, University of Colorado, Boulder

INTRODUCTION

The purpose of this chapter is to present quantitative data on the relation between social isolation and wife abuse from two separate studies and then to examine the nature of this association more precisely.[1] It is important to investigate this relation because, although many researchers and writers (e.g., Petersen, 1980; Pfouts, 1978; Rounsaville, 1978; Schuyler, 1976; Stark, Flitcraft, & Frazier, 1979) have assumed that there is an association between isolation and wife abuse, no one has actually tested this assumption using quantitative data. Indeed, much of the support for such an association is based on extrapolations from child abuse research (see Gelles, 1980). Further, data that do exist on the specific relation between social isolation and wife abuse (in contrast to child abuse) are found primarily in descriptive studies. Gelles (1974) and Dobash and Dobash (1979), for example, inductively come to the conclusion that isolation is related to abuse, but neither actually tests this hypothesis. Moreover, Dobash and Dobash (1979) treat isolation as a constant condition and offer largely conceptual evidence for the relation between isolation and wife abuse. There are two additional limitations of previous work. First, the available data do not pro-

Joyce McCarl Nielsen is associate professor of sociology at the University of Colorado-Boulder, and was principal investigator of the two studies (conducted under the auspices of the Institute of Behavioral Science, University of Colorado-Boulder) upon which this chapter is based. Her teaching and research interests include the sociology of sex and gender, social psychology, and women studies. Her recent publications include *Sex and Gender in Society; Perspectives on Stratification,* Waveland Press, 1990, and *Feminist Research Methods: Exemplary Readings in the Social Sciences,* Westview Press, 1990.

Russell K. Endo is an urban sociologist and was associate director of the two research projects at the Institute of Behavioral Science, University of Colorado-Boulder, upon which this chapter is based. He teaches ethnic studies courses at the University of Colorado.

Barbara L. Ellington is senior acquisitions editor at Westview Press, Boulder, Colorado. She was a research anthropologist on the two research projects at the Institute of Behavioral Science, University of Colorado-Boulder upon which this chapter is based.

[1]The authors thank Richard Gelles for his critical comments and suggestions on an earlier version of this chapter and the Aurora (Colorado) Community Mental Health Center for its support in the data collection phase of this research. This research was funded in part by a grant from the Colorado Commission on Higher Education. The results of a preliminary analysis of some of the data have been reported in: Russell Endo, Barbara L. Ellington, and Joyce McCarl Nielsen, Wife abuse in western energy boomtowns, *International Journal of Sociology of the Family, 14* (Autumn 1984), 269–281.

vide information about how isolation and wife abuse are related in time: does isolation precede or is it a consequence of battering? Second, the available data and even theoretical discussions do not address the issue of who is isolated—the victim, the offender, or the family as a whole. Many studies assume, for instance, that women who are victims of abuse become socially isolated as a result. Others (e.g., Cantoni, 1981) argue that less socially integrated men are more inclined to be violent. Still others (e.g., Gelles, 1974; Ball, 1977) use the family as the unit of analysis. Thus the social isolation of abused women, their spouses, and their families as a whole needs to be measured separately.

There has, of course, been some speculation with regard to the temporal ordering of social isolation and wife abuse. Gelles (1974) and Dobash and Dobash (1979) view the woman's isolation as both a cause and a consequence of abuse. On the one hand, the presence of physical violence in the home could lead to isolation, either because the victim does not want others to find out or because others, knowing or suspecting violence, avoid the couple. On the other hand, Gelles prefers the argument that isolation precedes family violence and is as much a cause as a consequence of it. In this respect he notes that many of his subjects explained their lack of friends without direct reference to the problem of violence.

In this chapter we use quantitative data from two separate studies to examine (1) whether there is a relation between isolation and wife abuse; (2) if so, whether social isolation characterizes the women, their spouses, or their families as a whole; and (3) the temporal ordering of isolation and wife abuse.

METHOD

Study 1 Samples

Two separate samples were generated for Study 1. First, we interviewed 25 battered and 26 never-battered women who resided in a relatively small ranching and farming community in western Colorado. They were recruited through advertising, referrals from social service agencies, a telephone survey, and ethnographic fieldwork.[2] The advertising consisted of notices that briefly described the purpose of the study, guaranteed anonymity to respondents, and offered monetary compensation for transportation and childcare costs. Notices were published in the local newspaper, posted in public places throughout the community, and read on the air by the local radio station. Cooperating social service agencies included the town's mental health center and alcohol and drug abuse programs; the police and sheriff's departments also made referrals. The telephone survey involved calling every 20th name in the local phone directory, which contained approximately 3,500 residential listings, and conducting a brief interview that asked about general community problems, including

---

[2]We used these different recruitment methods with the intention of comparing the resulting subsamples on key variables. However, because of the small sizes of the subsamples, we were unable to make any comparisons.

wife abuse.[3] At the end of the telephone interview, respondents were asked whether violence had been a problem in their family. Regardless of the answer, they were told about the study and invited to participate in a two- to three-hour face-to-face interview session; again, confidentiality and anonymity were assured and monetary compensation for childcare and transportation was offered. Ethnographic fieldwork was used to recruit battered women for two reasons. First, in this small community, it proved to be a more effective way to identify and contact battered women for our study than the more visible methods described above.[4] Second, because of our focus on social isolation, we were particularly interested in locating and interviewing abuse victims who had not previously been in communication with public agencies.[5]

To complement this sample of battered and never-battered women, we generated a second Study 1 sample consisting of the 181 ninth-grade students at the local high school. These students completed a questionnaire on family and community life that included questions about physical abuse among family members.

Study 2 Sample

In a second study, we interviewed 50 battered women and 23 natural helpers who resided in a large suburb of a Colorado metropolitan area. Natural helpers were neighbors or friends who functioned as resource persons for others in need—in this case, battered women.[6] Subjects were again recruited through advertising, referrals from social service agencies, and ethnographic fieldwork. The natural helpers were interviewed as a comparison group because almost all had nonabusive partners[7] and because they were recruited in the same way as the battered women.[8]

Table 5-1 shows some of the background characteristics of the battered and nonbattered women in Studies 1 and 2 and their spouses. In general, these two sets of women/spouses were fairly similar. One noteworthy difference is that the spouses of the nonbattered women had higher mean incomes than the spouses of the battered women.

The Study 1 sample of high school students consisted of about an equal number of

---

[3]Because of disconnected phones and households that could not be reached—each number was tried at least three times at different times of the day—the number of households contacted was 143 rather then the approximately 175 estimated. Of these, 120 (84%) completed the survey. Although random digit dialing is frequently used in telephone surveys to ensure that unlisted numbers are included, we did not use this procedure because the proportion of unlisted numbers in this rural area was small and because the local telephone company requested that we not use random digit dialing.

[4]The authors acknowledge the contribution of Dr. Carla Littlefield, who conducted the ethnographic fieldwork.

[5]Because it is almost impossible to generate a random sample of battered women, especially in a relatively small rural community, these 25 battered and 26 never-battered women were not necessarily representative of the battered and never-battered women of this community. However, comparisons with existing data from the local area showed that our two sample groups were fairly representative in terms of background and socioeconomic characteristics of the total population of women and families.

[6]The activities of the natural helpers included providing information about daycare options and other services, taking care of children on an emergency basis, and being generally available to give aid, especially in times of crisis.

[7]Two of the natural helpers were living with batterers but their inclusion in the natural helper subsample did not affect the results reported in this article.

[8]The subsamples of battered women and natural helpers were relatively independent. In only seven cases did a battered woman and a natural helper report having a mutual relationship.

Table 5-1   Background data on battered and nonbattered women and their spouses: Studies 1 and 2

Variable	Study 1		Study 2	
	Battered women[a]	Non-battered women[b]	Battered women[c]	Non-battered women[d]
Woman's race				
White	100%	100%	88%	87%
Other	0	0	12	13
	100%	100%	100%	100%
Woman's mean age	34	30	33	39
Spouse's mean age	37	32	37	41
Couple's years residence in comm.				
Less than 5 years	88%	69%	Mean = 6.8 yrs.	Mean = 7.4 yrs.
5 years or more	12	31		
	100%	100%		
Woman's occupation				
Prof./Tech.	20%	31%	54%	55%
Cler./Sales	28	31	29	22
Craftsman	12	0	0	0
Operative	36	35	18	24
Service	4	4	0	0
Laborer	0	0	0	0
Farm/Ranch	0	0	0	0
	100%	100%	100%	100%
Spouse's occupation				
Prof./Tech.	20%	31%	44%	47%
Cler./Sales	4	4	9	4
Craftsman	64	62	31	35
Operative	4	0	7	0
Service	8	4	9	4
Laborer	0	0	0	0
Farm/Ranch	0	0	0	0
	100%	100%	100%	100%
Woman's mean years education	12.9	13.2	13.1	13.6
Spouse's mean years education	11.6	13.4	13.1	13.0
Woman's mean income[e]	3.7	3.0	5.5	5.3
Spouse's mean income	7.0	8.3	7.0	8.7

[a]$N = 25$
[b]$N = 26$
[c]$N = 50$
[d]$N = 23$
[e]Income categories: 1. No earned income; 2. Less than $2,500; 3. $2,500–4,999; 4. $5,000–6,999; 5. $7,000–9,999; 6. $10,000–12,999; 7. $13,000–15,999; 8. $16,000–19,999; 9. $20,000–24,999; 10. $25,000–29,999; 11. 30,000–34,999; 12. $35,000–39,999.

females (52%) and males (48%). The students' mean age was 15.1 years, and they averaged 5.1 years residence in the community. Twenty-five percent of the students' fathers were in professional/technical occupations; 7% were in clerical/sales positions; 20% were craftsmen; 30% were operatives; and 12% were service workers, laborers, or worked on farms/ranches.

Measurement

To measure wife abuse in the Study 1 high school sample, we used an index of violence based on questions that asked whether the father pushed/shoved, hit, or physically fought with the mother when he became angry at her.[9,10] Social isolation in the Study 1 high school sample was measured by indices of the parents' frequency of interaction with friends/neighbors and frequency of interaction with relatives (how often they visited, wrote, and phoned); an index of parents' participation in voluntary organizations; and an index of family participation in various public activities such as attending church, sporting events, movies, school events, and going shopping and camping. Similar items (frequency of interaction with friends/neighbors and relatives; participation in voluntary organizations; family's participation in public activities) were used to measure isolation with the sample of battered and nonbattered women in Study 1. In addition, we developed an index based on the woman's ability to rely on friends, neighbors, and relatives in times of illness, financial troubles, or other crises.

In Study 2 we more precisely measured the isolation of the woman, her spouse, and the family as a whole. The isolation of the women was measured, as in Study 1, by indices of their frequency of interaction with friends/neighbors and relatives and an index of their participation in voluntary organizations. An additional measure was adapted from Barrera (1981) and included the total number of different individuals with whom a woman had interacted in various contexts such as talking about personal matters; getting and giving advice, loans, help with various activities, and support for ideas; and getting together for fun or relaxation. To measure the isolation of a woman's spouse, we used indices of his frequency of interaction with friends/neighbors and relatives and an index of his participation in voluntary organizations; these are similar to the measures used in Study 1. The isolation of the family as a whole was measured by an index of family participation in various public activities (as in Study 1).[11]

For the subsample of battered women in Study 2, the isolation of the women, their spouses, and their families was measured for four different periods: in the few months prior to the first battering incident (Time 1); in the few months prior to the worst battering incident; in the few months prior to the end of the spousal relationship (if applicable); and at the time of the interview. For the subsample of natural helpers in Study 2, the isolation of the women, their spouses, and their families was measured

---

[9]We asked about violence on the part of both parents, but there were very few reported cases of husband abuse. In any case, our theoretical interest is in wife abuse.

[10]Because of space limitations, we do not list the questions that comprise the indices used in our research, nor do we present data on responses to these individual questions or on the range of values, means, standard deviations, and reliability of each index. This information is available from the authors on request. It should be noted that all of the indices used in our research were found to be reliable using Cronbach's alpha.

[11]All of the measures described in this paragraph were based on questions asked of the women.

for two time periods: in the first few months of marriage (Time 1); and at the time of the interview. Mean values for these isolation measures are shown in Table 5-2.

In the literature on wife abuse, there is frequent reference to jealousy on the part of the spouse, and it is reasonable to expect that such jealousy may be an important factor in producing social isolation, at least for women in abusive relationships. Therefore we asked the battered women in Study 2 to indicate the extent to which their spouses acted jealous when they (the women) went out with friends and how often the spouses restricted their activities as a result. An index of jealousy was created from these questions. Not surprisingly, the responses to these questions markedly distinguished the battered women from the natural helpers. For example, 66% of the battered women reported that their spouses acted jealous a lot when they went out with friends, compared with only 14% of the natural helpers. Also, 68% of the battered women said that their spouses restricted their activities a lot compared with 23% of the natural helpers.

In Study 2, we adapted Straus's (1979) Conflict Tactics Scale to measure the frequency of battering by asking the battered women about their spouses' use of various conflict tactics. Table 5-3 compares some of our overall results with those from Straus's national study. Not surprisingly, the men in our research were much more violent. The proportion of men in our study who had ever used various conflict tactics with their wives ranged from 18 to 96%, compared with a range in Straus's

Table 5-2 Social isolation over time of battered women (BW) and natural helpers (NH), their spouses, and their families: Study 2[a]

Variable	Time 1		Around time worst battering	Around time end relatshp.	At time interview	
	BW[b]	NH[c]	BW (only)	BW (only)	BW	NH
Woman						
Mean score different interpers. contacts	83.1	88.3*	82.7	78.7	90.8	102.0*
Mean score freq. interact. w/friends, relatives, neighbrs.	25.4	31.7*	23.2	22.4	24.4	32.2*
Mean score particip. volunt. org.	1.4	1.7*	1.4	1.5	1.4	3.3*
Spouse						
Mean score freq. interact. w/friends, relatives, neighbrs.	26.6	32.0*	27.0	27.5	27.5	32.3*
Mean score particip. volunt. org.	1.4	1.6*	1.4	1.5	1.5	1.7*
Family as a whole						
Mean score particip. public activities	15.4	17.2*	14.3	14.0	14.3	16.7*

[a]Higher scores indicate more social activity (i.e., less isolation)
[b]$N = 50$; Time 1 = the few months prior to the first battering incident
[c]$N = 23$; Time 1 = the first few months of marriage
*Difference between battered women and natural helper groups statistically significant ($p < .05$, ANOVA)

study of 4 to 23%. However, in both studies, the percentages decreased dramatically as the severity of the violent act increased. In our study, the mean number of battering incidents for the entire husband-wife relationship was 51. In 30% of the families, husbands used violence from several times a month to every day. An index of battering frequency was created from the questions about the spouses' use of conflict tactics.

Finally, for the subsample of battered women in Study 2, we constructed an index of battering *severity* that included the number of battering incidents and interviewers' ratings of the overall degree of psychological and physical abuse in the relationship.[12]

RESULTS

Isolation-Wife Abuse Relation: Study 1

To examine the relation between social isolation and wife abuse using the Study 1 high school data, we regressed the violence index on the four social isolation indices and the following eight variables: socioeconomic status (father's occupation); presence of alcohol problems in the family; presence of drug problems in the family; length of residence in the community; dwelling type (mobile home vs. other types); parent's marital situation (mother-stepfather vs. other types); family size; and gender of the student respondent. We included the first three variables (socioeconomic status, alcohol problems, and drug problems) because of their potential relation with family violence. The next three variables (length of residence, dwelling type, marital situation) were selected because the sociological literature on rapid growth in western communities[13] suggests their association with family violence; for example, newcomers, mobile home dwellers (who were likely to be physically as well as socially isolated), and mother-stepfather marital situations were expected to have higher levels of family conflict. Family size and gender of the student respondent were primarily

[12]Measures for the battered and nonbattered women (including natural helpers) who were interviewed in these studies were pretested with volunteers from a different community from the ones in which our research took place.
[13]Rapid population growth characterized both communities in which our research took place.

Table 5-3 Use of conflict tactics involving physical force: Study 2 (battered women only) and Straus's national sample (1979)

Percent of husbands who ever did following to their wives[a]	Study 2 sample[b]	Straus's national sample
Threw something	84	17
Pushed, shoved, grabbed	96	23
Slapped	84	18
Kicked, bit, hit with fist	84	9
Hit or tried to hit with something	64	10
Threatened with knife or gun	76	6
Used knife or gun	18	4

[a]As reported by the wives
[b]$N = 50$

included as control variables.[14] For the regression analysis, we adopted the causal assumption preferred by Gelles—that isolation precedes abuse. (This particular temporal ordering was examined more closely in Study 2 and will be discussed later.)

Table 5-4 shows the results of the regression analysis. The family activities measure had the highest coefficient, and the coefficients for parents' frequency of interaction with friends/neighbors and frequency of interaction with relatives were also statistically significant ($p < .05$). The only isolation measure that did not affect wife abuse was parents' participation in voluntary organizations. This may have reflected the relative lack of variation on this variable (few parents belonged to such organizations), or it may have been due to the student respondents' lack of knowledge about the extent of their parents' activities. On the other hand, it is also possible that participation in voluntary organizations, unlike other types of social interaction, was simply not related to battering. Table 5-4 also shows that the presence of drug problems and alcohol problems in the family and the parent's marital situation affected wife abuse.

Comparisons between the social isolation of the battered and never-battered women interviewed in Study 1 also confirm the isolation-wife abuse connection. There were statistically significant differences ($p < .05$, chi square; data not shown) between the two groups, with the battered women being more isolated in terms of frequency of interaction with friends/neighbors, frequency of interaction with relatives, and family participation in public activities. In addition, battered women were less likely than nonbattered women to report that they could rely on relatives, neighbors, and friends in times of illness, financial troubles, or other crises. No statistically significant differences were found with regard to participation in voluntary

[14]Possible problems due to multicollinearity were investigated and found not to exist.

Table 5-4 Standardized regression coefficients from regression of violence index on eleven explanatory variables: Study 1, high school sample[a]

Independent variables	Index of violence[b]
Parents' freq. of interaction with friends/neighbors	− .11*
Parents' freq. of interaction with relatives	− .12*
Family participation in public activities	− .28*
Parents' participation in voluntary orgs.	− .01
Socioeconomic status	− .08
Alcohol problems in family	.16*
Drug problems in family	.12*
Length of residence in community	− .07
Dwelling type[c]	− .05
Parents' marital situation[d]	− .18*
Family size	− .07
Gender of student respondent[e]	− .16*
R^2	.21

[a]$N = 181$
[b]Higher values indicate greater violence
[c]Mobile home = 1; other = 2
[d]Mother and stepfather = 1; other = 2
[e]Female = 1; male = 2
*$p < .05$

organizations; this is similar to the finding about voluntary organizations from the high school data.

Isolation-Wife Abuse Relation: Study 2

To examine the relation between social isolation and wife abuse in Study 2, we compared the battered women and the natural helpers. The results, as seen in Table 5-2, again show a relation between isolation and abuse. At Time 1, as well as at the time of the interview, battered women had fewer different interpersonal contacts than the natural helpers, and both the battered women and their spouses had less interaction with friends/neighbors and relatives and participated less in voluntary organizations. Also, the families of the battered women participated less in public activities than the families of the natural helpers. All of these differences were statistically significant ($p < .05$, ANOVA).

Isolation-Wife Abuse Temporal Order: Study 2

With regard to the temporal ordering of the isolation-battering relation, the results from Study 2 (Table 5-2) suggest that isolation precedes battering because, at Time 1, the battered women, their spouses, and their families were more isolated than the natural helpers, their spouses, and their families respectively. At the same time, there is evidence that social isolation is a consequence of battering. The isolation of the battered women increased after Time 1 (the first battering incident) until the time of the interview as did the isolation of their families as a whole, although the differences between time periods were not statistically significant ($p > .05$, ANOVA). In contrast, the isolation of the natural helpers and their spouses decreased after Time 1 (the first few months of marriage), though the isolation of their families did increase.

Who Is Isolated? Study 2

With respect to the issue of who is isolated in a family characterized by wife abuse, a case can be made using the Study 2 data discussed above that the battered women, their spouses, and their families as a whole are all isolated when compared to their natural helper counterparts. To further address this issue, we used the Study 2 data collected from the battered women and regressed the index of battering frequency and the index of battering severity on three indices that measured the overall isolation of the battered women, their spouses, and their families as a whole. The results, seen in Table 5-5, show that the isolation of the women and their families but not their spouses affected battering frequency and severity.

Jealousy: Study 2

As mentioned earlier, the spouses of the battered women in Study 2 exhibited more jealousy than those of the natural helpers. In a further analysis of these data, we found that, for the battered women, the index of jealousy was correlated with the index of the woman's overall isolation ($r = .28$, $p < .05$) and also with the index of battering severity ($r = .52$, $p < .05$). We therefore examined these relations for various time periods. We found that jealousy was not correlated with the woman's isolation around the time of the first battering incident, around the time of the end of her spousal

Table 5-5 Standardized regression coefficients from regression of index of battering frequency and index of battering severity on indices of woman's, spouse's, and family's isolation: Study 2 (battered women only)[a]

Independent variables[b]	Index of battering frequency[c]	Index of battering severity[d]
Index of woman's isolation	.44*	.34*
Index of spouse's isolation	.08	.01
Index of family's isolation	.48*	.41*
R^2	.24	.18

[a]$N = 50$
[b]Higher values indicate greater isolation
[c]Higher values indicate a greater frequency of battering
[b]Higher values indicate greater battering severity
*$p < .05$

relationship (if applicable), or at the time of the interview, but it was correlated with isolation around the time of the worst battering incident ($r = .20, p < .05$). Further, jealousy was found to be correlated with battering severity around the time of the worst battering incident ($r = .23, p < .05$).

DISCUSSION

The relation between social isolation and wife abuse might be explained in at least two ways. The first is a monitoring/feedback interpretation, the idea that isolated individuals and families may be cut off from important social controls insofar as other people function as monitors of behavior (Gelles, 1974). That is, battering may occur because some behaviors don't get monitored and individuals consequently don't receive messages from others that violence is an inappropriate method for resolving conflicts. Garbarino (1977) and Suedfeld (1974) also discuss the importance of getting realistic feedback about one's behavior, especially during times of crisis and/or role transition (marriage, parenthood, etc.). Although not tested directly, this explanation is consistent with our findings.

A second explanation of why isolation and wife abuse are related emphasizes social control. As discussed earlier, our results from Study 2 support Gelles's preference for the isolation-precedes-battering temporal order. However, the social isolation of the battered women also increased after the first battering incident. All of this is consistent with the argument that battering is one way of controlling a woman's social activity. Dobash and Dobash (1979) provide the most comprehensive discussion of this line of reasoning. They argue that, in their social position as wives, women's activities are restricted to the home, that this isolation in the home begins early in a marriage, and that it increases as husbands develop power and control over their wives' activities and as the women's household and childcare duties increasingly restrict their outside activities. They stress the social isolation of all women, and argue that it increases with marriage and that it is exacerbated by being abused physically.

In summary, the purpose of this chapter is to contribute to theoretically guided research on wife abuse by helping to clarify the nature of its association with social isolation. We have shown that isolation is related to wife abuse; that it is important to examine the isolation of the woman, her spouse, and her family as a whole; that isolation seems to both precede and result from battering; and that jealousy is at times related to social isolation and battering severity. We have considered both the monitoring/feedback and control interpretations as possible explanations of the relation between social isolation and wife abuse.

BIBLIOGRAPHY

Ball, M. (1977). Issues of violence in family casework. *Social Casework, 58*(1), 3–12.
Barrera, M. (1981). Social support in the adjustment of pregnant adolescents: Assessment issues. In B. Gottlieb, (Ed.), *Social networks and social support* (pp. 69–95). Beverly Hills, CA: Sage.
Cantoni, L. (1981). Clinical issues in domestic violence. *Social Casework, 62*(1), 3–12.
Dobash, R. E., & Dobash, R. P. (1979). *Violence against wives.* New York: The Free Press.
Garbarino, J. (1977). The price of privacy on the social dynamics of child abuse. *Child Welfare, 56*(9), 565–575.
Gelles, R. J. (1974). *The violent home.* Beverly Hills, CA: Sage.
Gelles, R. J. (1980). Violence in the family: A review of research in the seventies. *Journal of Marriage and the Family, 42*(4), 143–155.
Petersen, R. (1980). Social class, social learning, and wife abuse. *Social Science Review, 54*(3), 390–406.
Pfouts, J. H. (1978). Violent families: Coping responses of abused wives. *Child Welfare, 57*(2), 101–111.
Rounsaville, B. (1978). Theories in marital violence: Evidence from a study of battered women. *Victimology, 3*(1–2), 11–13.
Schuyler, M. (1976, November). Battered wives: An emerging social problem. *Social Work, 21,* 488–491.
Stark, E., Flitcraft, A., & Frazier, W. (1979). Medicine and patriarchal violence: The social construction of a "private" event. *International Journal of Health Services, 9*(3), 461–493.
Straus, M. (1979). Measuring intrafamily conflict and violence: The conflict tactics (CT) Scale. *Journal of Marriage and the Family, 41,* 75–88.
Suedfeld, P. (1974). Social isolation: A case for interdisciplinary research. *The Canadian Psychologist, 15*(1), 1–15.

6

An Analysis of Crisis Calls by Battered Women in the City of Atlanta

Komanduri S. Murty
Julian B. Roebuck
Department of Criminal Justice, Clark Atlanta University, Atlanta

INTRODUCTION

This is a quantitative analysis of 9,919 battered women's crisis calls to the Atlanta Council of Battered Women from January 1, 1983, to December 31, 1984. Study focus is on incidence and volume, victims' sociodemographic characteristics, the battery situation, and services rendered by the council. The findings suggest that crisis call information may be utilized as a supplement to survey data on battered women. Moreover, this analysis demonstrates that qualitative data on the battery situation may be quantified.

PREVIOUS RESEARCH

The literature on battered women, that is, women who are deliberately physically injured by males with whom they are married or cohabiting, has increased dramatically in the United States since 1975 as a major component of family violence (Martin, 1977; Moore, 1979; Straus, Gelles, & Steinmetz, 1980; Walker, 1979). The proliferating scholarly books and articles published, the conferences and workshops held, the legal deliberations made, and the press coverage on this subject indicate its emergence as a social problem. Further, this phenomenon has become the province of several concerned groups: victims' and women's rights advocates, journalists, legislators, law enforcers, therapists, and researchers. Social workers, the police, courts,

Komanduri S. Murty, who holds a Ph.D. in sociology (demography and quantitative methodology), is an associate professor and chairman of the Department of Criminal Justice Administration at Clark Atlanta University. He was formerly the Research Director of the Population Research Center, Waltair, India. He has published journal articles in the areas of demography, economics, and criminology. He is currently the Project Director of Fulton County's Pre-Trial Intervention Program and Project Director of the Fulton County's Job Opportunities in Security Service Program.
Julian B. Roebuck, who holds a Ph.D. in sociology from the University of Maryland, is a research professor in the Department of Criminal Justice Administration at Clark Atlanta University. He has published articles and books in the areas of deviant behavior, criminology, and race relations and is currently researching with Dr. Murty in the area of violent crime in Atlanta.

psychologists, psychiatrists, and sociologists are the major professionals concerned with the etiology, treatment, prevention, and research related to this problem.

Although the literature on battered women is of a wide and overlapping range and somewhat amorphous, it may be tentatively ordered into eight categories: (1). General and historical; e.g., Goode, 1971; Steinmetz, 1974; Dobash and Dobash, 1979; Masumura, 1979; Walker, 1979; Roy, 1982; Davis, 1987; (2). Theoretical and etiological; e.g., Gelles, 1974; Steinmetz, 1977; Kumasai, 1979; Straus and Hotaling, 1980; Long, Witte, & Karr, 1983; Caplan, 1984; (3). Victims' reactions; e.g., Aguirre, 1985; Turner & Shapiro, 1986; Browne, 1987; Morrison, Van Hasselt, & Bellack, 1987; (4). Process; e.g., Goldstein, Davis, & Herman, 1975; Dutton & Painter, 1981; Erchak, 1984; (5). Personality profile; e.g., Roy, 1977; Hartik, 1978; Sugarman & Cohn, 1980; Gradal, 1982; Gellen, Hoffman, Jones, & Stone, 1984; (6). Treatment; e.g., Fleming, 1979; Goldstein & Page, 1981; Bowen, 1982; McCarthy, 1982; Descher, 1984; Gordon & Gordon, 1984; (7). Frequency and severity of injury; e.g., Straus, 1978; Snyder & Fruchtman, 1981; Okun, 1983; Barnett & Lopez-Real, 1985; (8). Legal recourse; e.g., Truninger, 1971; Eisenberg & Micklow, 1977; Kleclner, 1978; Bowker, 1983; Moore, 1985; Staff, 1986.

The literature discloses a dearth of specific quantitative data on the frequency and severity of women battery, the victims' reactions to battery, the battery process, and the analysis of crisis calls and services rendered by counseling agencies. This deficiency may be attributed to several factors: (a) Family violence did not become a public issue until the late 1960s and early 1970s; (b) Official reporting systems for recording incidence of family violence have been slow to develop. Many still consider what happens within the family to be a private matter; (c) Though several states recently have enacted family violence acts and provided funds for sheltering victims (Search Group Inc., 1984), the traditional tabulation of wife battery under the legal assault category still persists; (d) The response by police, district attorneys, and judges to violence in the family including wife battery has been traditionally slow, mild, and noncriminal; (e) Officials in the past have usually referred wife battery cases to social agencies; and (f) Many women fail to follow through in pressing charges against assaultive husbands (Gelles, 1974; Davis, 1987).

METHOD

Source of Data

For the purpose of this research we collected, tabulated, and analyzed cross-sectional data on wife battery from the Atlanta Council for Battered Women (CBW), the city's major domestic violence intervention agency. Apart from receiving direct hot-line calls from victims, this agency generally receives wife beating referrals from the police and other agencies.

Council for Battered Women—Overview

The CBW was established in July 1975 by the Atlanta YWCA task force. The major objective of the council is to provide the following services to battered women callers: (a) 24-hour telephone crisis hot line; (b) phone counseling and referrals; (c) client emergency shelter; (d) children's recreational and educational programs; (e) follow-up programs; (f) client vocational educational programs; (g) staff in-service training; (h) volunteer service programs.

Gelles and Straus (1979, p. 15) estimated that more than two million wives are beaten by their husbands each year. The Atlanta police received approximately 5,000 battered women's calls per month in 1983. By conservative estimates, studies show that only one in ten incidents of women battering is reported to the police (Davis, 1987). The metro Atlanta CBW is one of more than 300 shelters throughout the United States that services battered women. Throughout its existence, it has been an active, efficient agency in providing alternative services for battered women, and therefore receives strong community support. The CBW maintains a 24-hour crisis line that currently receives more than 700 calls a month (500 calls per month during the research period). Twenty-two professional counselors and 70–100 volunteers (with at least college degrees) cover the crisis line. The CBW is staffed by 24 full-time professional staff members, including one crisis-line coordinator with a master's degree in social work.

The CBW has a children's program, which among other things, attempts to break the cycle of child abuse. In addition to counseling services, its members promote the agency through media appearances, public speeches, advertising, and coordinated professional and civic workshops. In a large measure the council determines public policy relating to domestic violence in Atlanta. The council was granted United Way Agency status in January 1983 and is supported financially by the city of Atlanta, Fulton and Dekalb counties, federal agencies, and several metro churches, civic groups, and foundations.

Unit of Analysis

With the consent and cooperation of the CBW we analyzed the woman battery crisis calls for a period of two years (January 1, 1983, to December 31, 1984). All calls were received by female social-worker counselors who logged in case history information on a specific case-history format. This format was utilized by all phone counselors as well as counselors who provided later casework services. Although many callers subsequently visited the CBW office for further services, we were concerned only with the initial crisis call data as recorded in case histories. Each telephone call was considered to be an independent event (that is, we assumed no relationship between calls, nor did we attempt a cohort analysis).

Operational Definitions

We utilized content analysis in this study to assess woman battery as determined from telephone calls to the CBW in terms of: incidence and volume; victims' sociodemographic characteristics; the battery situation; and services rendered to victims. For a discussion of content analysis, see Berelson (1952), Holsti (1969), and Krippendorff (1980). The content analysis suggested the following subcategories and corresponding definitions:

Incidence and Volume

This category designates the total number of telephone calls by caller type: (a) new caller is a first-time caller to the CBW; (b) old caller is one who has previously called the CBW; and (c) third-party callers are those caller reporters who live outside of the battered women's domicile: family members of client; friends/neighbors; police/ domestic intervention unit; social service agency; hospital/doctor; lawyer; employer; personal counselor; minister; others.

Sociodemographic Characteristics

1. Source of council knowledge—Family, friend/neighbor, police/domestic crisis intervention unit, social service agency, hospital/doctor, lawyer, employer, advertisement and/or media, counselor, minister, other.
2. Client's residence—Client's residence at time of call by county (Fulton, De-kalb, Cobb, Clayton, Gwinnett, Rockdale, Douglas) in Georgia and residence outside the state.
3. Client's race—White, black, Asian, Hispanic, other.
4. Client's age—Under 18 years, 18–29 years, 30–39 years, 40–49 years, 50–59 years, and 60 years and over.
5. Marital status—Single, married, separated/divorced, and widowed.
6. Number of children—Total number of children (0–14 years old) living in the household.

The Battery Situation

1. Prior verbal interaction between perpetrator and victim—(a) flow: from perpetrator to victim; victim to perpetrator; and, between victim and perpetrator; (b) content.
2 Verbal interaction between perpetrator and victim during the battery (same as above).
3. Immediate post battery verbal interaction between perpetrator and victim (same as above).
4. Type of physical force (pushes, shoves, slaps, punches, stabs, knocks, kicks, butts, bites, scratches, blows with objects, stomps, other).
5. Extent of physical injury: (a) minor—black eyes, superficial bruises, sprains and scratches; (b) moderate—fractured noses and/or limbs, loss of teeth, severe bruises and strains; and (c) severe—concussions, multiple contusions, multiple fractures, hemorrhage, loss of consciousness, and life-threatening conditions.
6. Victim's response during and immediately following the battery—(a) self-defense and counterattack; (b) screams for help; (c) temporary flight (running away); (d) leaving the perpetrator and the household; (e) living with or without perpetrator at the time of instant call; (f) visit to doctor; (g) report to police; (h) other.
7. Use of drugs and/or alcohol immediately prior to the battery: (a) by victim; (b) by perpetrator; (c) by both; (d) by none.
8. Involvement of children during the battery: (a) presence of children; (b) participation of children.
9. Battery history: (a) the frequency of past battery; (b) victim's response to past batteries.

Services Rendered

1. Direct phone service—(a) Phone counseling by counselor who utilizes a problem-solving approach that provides the client with information necessary for the protection of herself and her children (i.e., on the basis of the client's explanation of her problem and situation). (b) Information on options: The counselor on the basis of client's explanation of her problem furnishes her with a large base of knowledge

about several agencies that might render her services including information about legal recourses.

2. Direct advocacy—The counselor directs the client to specific agency sources for immediate help: law enforcement, social agency, church, legal (attorney/district attorney), hospital/doctor, emergency mental health, emergency housing, permanent housing, and other. The callers under study were considered acute cases that needed some kind of help.

Data Analysis

Incidence and Volume

The CBW received 4,502 crisis calls from women varying in age from under 18 years of age to over 60 years of age in 1983, and provided emergency shelter for 171 women and 243 children during this period. In 1984 the CBW received 5,417 calls and provided emergency shelter for 741 women and 850 children. Women who had not contacted the council before accounted for approximately 65% of the total calls in 1983 and in 1984. Repeat callers, women who had called the council previously, made 20% of the calls. The remaining 15% were third-party callers (other than victim or perpetrator). One-third of these third-party callers had called the CBW before about a prior battery incident involving the same couple. The majority of the third-party calls were from family members (29.5%), and friends/neighbors (29.35%). The remainder were as follows: social service agencies (20.65%); hospitals/doctors (7.46%); police/domestic crisis intervention unit (7.23%); lawyers (2.8%); employers (.44%); personal counselors (.29%); ministers (.74%); and others (.88%).

Clients' Sources of Knowledge

The clients' sources of knowledge about the CBW were as follows: police/domestic crisis intervention unit (22.78%); social service agency (21.0%); friends and neighbors (15.3%); family members (11.57%); hospital/doctor (11.57%); advertisement and media (4.27%); lawyer (3.7%); counselors (1.6%); ministers (.53%); and employers (.18%). Seven percent of the victims did not give the source of knowledge.

Victim's Sociodemographic Characteristics

The largest proportion (44.25%) of total calls were received from Fulton County residents as expected, because the majority of metro Atlanta's population lives in this county, which is CBW's home base. Dekalb, Clayton, Gwinnett, Cobb, Rockdale, and Douglas counties contributed to 21, 5, 5, 3.8, 1.2 and .8% of the calls respectively. A sizable number of calls (4.65%) were from Georgia females who resided outside the metro Atlanta area. Out of state calls accounted for only 1.58% of total calls. Most in this category were from women visiting the metro Atlanta area with their mates. Twelve percent of the callers did not designate residence.

White women made 44.33% of the total calls; black women, 36.93%; Hispanic, .85%, and Asian, .62%. According to the 1980 census the Atlanta Standard Metropolitan Statistical Area (S.M.S.A.) consisted of 597,000 white females aged 16 years and over (73% of females of all races) and 191,000 black females (24%). Black females made 37% of CBW calls, thus indicating a higher frequency of battery victims than was the case for white females. The sex ratios for whites was 92 men per 100 women and for blacks 81 men per 100 women. This differential shows that the supply of men to women was lower for blacks than whites, and may mean that black males felt freer to push women around than did white males. Furthermore, traditionally, black women have been less likely to report physical abuse by their mates to public agencies than have white women. Therefore the differential rate between black and white females may have been even greater than the CBW call statistics indicate. Women who did not report their race made 7.26% of the total calls.

The largest number of calls were received from women aged 18–29 (32.95%) followed by the age groups 30–39 (24.93%); 40–49 (7.19%); 50–59 (2.8%); and 60 years or over (.98%). Women under 18 years made only .10%.

Women in the age categories 18–29 and 30–39 were probably more actively involved in male/female relationships that triggered violence than those in the older age categories. Ninety-two percent of all callers said they were legally married; the remaining 8% reported living with boyfriends.

Women in these two age categories had also been more exposed to the equal rights movement (that fosters the denouncement and the public airing of wife battery) than older women. Older women may have been more culturally inhibited and therefore, may have refrained from calling the CBW as readily. Further, these women may have already escaped from previously experienced abusive situations, via terminated relationships (separation, divorce, or widowhood). Additionally, older women (i.e., above 40 years) were probably less likely to have had male mates around than younger women.

Moreover, older women were probably less frequently physically abused by mates than were younger women because they probably experienced fewer adjustment problems related to finance, sexual jealousy, children, and other marital difficulties. Newman (1979, pp. 145–146) found these latter adjustment problems, among others, to be correlates of family violence, especially wife abuse. Ninety six percent of all callers to the CBW had up to three children aged from 0–12 years (a median of 4.7). We may therefore infer a nexus of young married women with children and wife battery.

We know from criminal statistics that young males (18–35) are more criminally violent than older age groups, and that the age group 18–24 is the most violent. The proclivity of young males to violence may account for the more frequent CBW calls from younger women than from older women. This may be imputed from the likelihood that younger males more frequently form sexual unions with counterparts, younger females, than with older females.

The Battery Situation

Verbal interaction immediately prior to and during the battery. In almost all cases (97%) the woman batterer directed a tirade of verbal abuse (including profane and obscene language) toward the victim that expressed his temporary overall dissatisfaction with the conjugal relationship. More often than not he blurted out during the battery a series of generalized, irrational, and trivial verbalizations that made no sense to the victim. Typical remarks of one batterer follow: "You're no damn good and you need a good beating. I'm tired of the whole mess. I'm gonna kick your ass, you bitch." The victim usually (in 65% of the cases) sustained the attack in silence. The remainder argued back and frequently denied any basis for the battery. As one victim stated to her husband during a physical attack, "You're wrong. I'm a good woman; you have no right to beat up on me like this. Why are you doing this to me?"

Use of physical force and extent of injury. Physical injuries varied from minor (superficial bruises, whelps, sprains, and scratches) to moderate injuries (black eyes, broken noses, fractured limbs, and deep bruises) to severe injuries (multiple fractures and contusions, broken jaws, missing teeth, loss of blood, loss of consciousness, and concussions). These injuries resulted from pushes, shoves, slaps, blows, kicks and butts; knocks with the hands, fists, feet, head, and at times hard inanimate objects (sticks, rods, canes, ropes, belts, chains, guns, knives). Fifty percent of the callers reported mild injuries. That is, they suffered from one or more of the following: superficial bruises and sprains, scratches, nosebleeds, and black eyes resulting from pushes, shoves, slaps, and fist blows. Thirty-five percent reported moderate injuries. That is, they suffered from one or more of the following: deep bruises, incapacitating sprains, broken noses, bleeding cuts, fractured body limbs and bones, resulting from fist blows, kicks, and the use of belts and hard objects. Fifteen percent reported serious injuries. That is, they suffered from concussions, multiple fractures, multiple contusions, missing teeth, loss of blood, loss of consciousness, and other life-threatening damages, resulting from fist blows, kicks, stabs, knocks, stomps, use of sticks and other hard objects. Most suffered in silence because of fear and the wish to keep their attack secret from neighbors. As one victim reported: "I was afraid if I hollered out he would beat me more. And I did not want my neighbors to know." Those who cried out loudly, screamed or shouted with pain said that, "It did no good." One victim stated on the phone: "He threatened to beat me harder if I hollered out. I did, and he beat me harder."

Victims responses to the instant battery. Only in 5% of the cases did the victims attempt a counterattack or a means of self-defense (i.e., fought back with their hands or physical objects). All of these were unsuccessful and resulted in additional physical injury. Another 9% attempted unsuccessfully to escape (i.e., to run away). Some (about one-third) left the home temporarily (from one hour to an overnight stay) immediately after the beating.

Visit to an M.D. (following the instant battery call). Nearly 20% of callers reported that they had visited a doctor as a consequence of the instant battery.

Use of drugs and alcohol in the battery situations. All victims denied the use of alcohol and/or drugs at the time of the instant battery. The victims reported that only 30% of the perpetrators were intoxicated (with alcohol) at the time of the battery. None were very drunk. Less than 25% claimed that alcohol contributed to the battery situation.

Threats during and after the battery. Sixty-seven percent of the victims reported that the perpetrators threatened them either during or shortly after the battery; in other words, with further physical injury should they leave them, tell others, or seek assistance from outside agents (police, sheriff, CBW, family, neighbors, friends, preachers, doctors).

Involvement of the children in the battery. In only 16% of the cases were the victim's children present. In 80% of these cases the children were also (mildly or moderately) battered. Frequently the victims had anticipated the potential battery situation and had consequently placed their children outside the home (with neighbors, family, friends, in-laws, etc.) prior to the battery. Most victims reported that they sensed when a battery was imminent.

First time or multiple victimization calls. Eighty percent of the first time callers reported that they had been battered at least once before the instant call. More than half reported two or more prior beatings.

Services Rendered

Staff counselors who received the battery calls provided one or more of the following services: direct phone counseling to 74.73%; specific information about other helping agencies, including legal recourses, to 24.2%; made referrals to law enforcement agencies to 26.51%; made referrals to other social agencies to 20.02%; provided emergency housing facilities (shelters) to 12.42%; provided permanent housing facilities to 11.4%; suggested legal recourse measures to 14.08%; referred 2.13% to emergency mental health services; and directed 2.13% to medical service agencies. The staff counselors who received the calls advised most of the callers (85%) to seek further counseling beyond CBW telephone counseling services; in other words, individual counseling at the CBW itself and/or at other agencies.

CONCLUSION AND DISCUSSION

To our knowledge, this is the first quantitative study on battered women that analyzes crisis telephone call data collected in a large metropolitan area. Although limited in scope, this study not only deals with victims' sociodemographic characteristics, but also with the quantitative aspects of the battery situation and agency services. Although the findings for the most part agree with those found elsewhere in survey data, they provide additional insight into the dynamics of the battery situation; for example, verbal interaction, the use of physical force, the victim's response, threats, battery frequency, and so forth.

We found the majority of the battered women calls to the CBW were from white, young (18–29 years), married, Fulton County residents, with children up to 12 years. The battered women were verbally and physically abused without a verbalized rational basis. Most received mild to moderate injuries and did not retaliate or leave their mates. Most were threatened with further physical harm during and after the battery; were physically and mentally cowed; and were terrorized. Twenty percent visited a doctor as a consequence of the instant battery. Children were involved infrequently. In only 30% of the cases did the victim report that the perpetrator was intoxicated, and most did not feel that alcohol contributed to the battery situation. Eighty percent of the first time callers reported multiple victimization. The CBW offered a wide range of services from telephone counseling to legal advocacy counsel and directions.

Unfortunately we have no sociodemographic data on the batterers or their definitions of the battery situations. From the crisis call analysis it appears that the batterers were more responsible for the battery episodes than their mates; and that they were less rational and more physically aggressive than their victims. The intense and insidious fear of the battered women as expressed in the crisis calls is one of the most important findings. No calls were received from single or married women who were engaged in only casual sexual relationships.

Going beyond the data it could be conjectured that these deep south women may have reacted to battery in a more docile manner than would have their counterparts from less traditional environments. Although Atlanta is a large metropolitan area, it appears more provincial and "small townish" than many other metropolitan areas.

Many young people from 18 to 39 are immigrants from small southern towns and rural areas. Certainly we need regional comparisons of batterers and those battered.

BIBLIOGRAPHY

Aguirre, B. E. (1985). Why do they return? Abused wives in shelters. *Social Work, 30,* 350–354.

Barnett, O. W., & Lopez-Real, D. I. (Nov. 1985). *Women's reactions to battering and why they stay.* Paper presented at the American Society of Criminology. San Diego, CA.

Berelson, B. (1952). Content analysis in communication research. Glencoe, IL: The Free Press.

Bowker, L. H. (1983). Battered wives, lawyers, and district attorneys: An examination of law in action. *Journal of Criminal Justice, 2,* 403–412.

Browne, A. (1987). *When battered women kill.* New York: Free Press.

Bowen, N. H. (1982). Guidelines for career counseling with abused women. *Vocational Guidance Quarterly, 31,* 123–127.

Caplan, P. J. (1984). The myth of women's masochism. *American Psychologist, 39*(2), 130–139.

Davis, L. (1987). Battered women: The transformation of a social problem. *Social Work, 32,* 306–311.

Descher, J. P. (1984). *The hitting habit: Anger control for battering couples.* New York: The Free Press.

Dobash, R. E., & Dobash, R. (1979). *Violence against wives: A case against patriarchy.* New York: The Free Press.

Dutton, D., & Painter, S. L. (1981). Traumatic bonding: The development of emotional attachments in battered women and other relationships of intermittent abuse. *Victimology: An International Journal, 6*(1–4), 139–155.

Eisenberg, S., & Micklow, P. (1977). The assaulted wife: Catch 22 revisited. *Women's Rights Law Reporter, 1,* 3–4.

Erchak, G. M. (1984). The escalation and maintenance of spouse abuse: A cybernetic model. *Victimology: An International Journal, 9*(2), 247–253.

Fleming, J. B. (1979). *Stopping wife abuse.* Garden City, NJ: Anchor Doubleday.

Gelles, R. J. (1974). *The violent home: Study of physical aggression between husbands and wives.* Beverly Hills, CA: Sage.

Gelles, R. J., & Straus, M. A. (1979). Violence in the American family. *Journal of Social Issues, 35,* 15–39.

Gellen, M. I., Hoffman, R. A., Jones, M., & Stone, M. (1984). Abused and nonabused women: MMPI profile differences. *Personnel and Guidance Journal, 62,* 601–604.

Goldstein, J. H., Davis, R. W., & Herman, D. (1975). Escalation of aggression: Experimental studies. *Journal of Personality and Social Psychology, 31,* 162–170.

Goldstein, R. K., & Page, A. W. (1981). Battered wife syndrome: Overview of dynamics and treatment. *American Journal of Psychiatry, 138,* 1036–1044.

Goode, W. J. (1971). Force and violence in the family. *Journal of Marriage and the Family, 33,* 624–636.

Gordon, S., & Gordon, J. (1984). *A "better safe than sorry" book: A family guide for sexual assault prevention.* New York: Ed-U Press.

Gradal, B. W. (1982). A study of locus of control and sex-role typology in two groups of battered women. *Dissertation Abstracts International.* (University Microfilms 82-15:143).

Hartik, L. M. (1978). Identification of personality characteristics and self-concept factors of battered wives. *Dissertation Abstracts International.* (University Microfilms 78-18:190).

Hosti, F. (1969). *Presentation of crime in newspapers.* Minneapolis, MN: Minneapolis Sociological Press.

Kumasai, F. (1979). Social class, power and husband–wife violence in Japan. *Journal of Comparative Family Studies, 10*(1), 91–105.

Kleckner, J. H. (1978). Wife beaters and beaten wives: Co-conspirators in crimes of violence. *Psychology, 15*(1), 54–56.

Krippendorff, K. (1980). *Content analysis: An introduction to its methodology.* Beverly Hills, CA: Sage.

Long, S. K., Witte, A. D., & Karr, P. (1983). *Family violence: A microeconomic approach. Social Science Research, 12*(4), 363–392.

Martin, D. (1977). *Battered wives.* New York: Pocket Books/Simon and Schuster.

Masumura, W. T. (1979). Wife abuse and other forms of aggression. *Victimology: An International Journal, 4*(1), 46–59.

Moore, D. A. (1979). *Battered women.* Beverly Hills, CA: Sage.

Moore, J. M. (1985). Landmark court decision for battered women. *Response, 8*(4), 5–8.

Morrison, R. L., Van Hasselt, V. B., & Bellack, A. S. (1987). Assessment of assertion and problem-solving skills in wife abusers and their spouses. *Journal of Family Violence, 2*(3), 227–237.

Newman, G. (1979). *Understanding violence.* New York: Lippincott.

Okun, L. E. (1983). A study of women abuse: 300 battered women taking shelter, 199 women-batterers in counseling. *Dissertation Abstracts International.* (University Microfilms 83-18:576).

Roy, M. (Ed.) (1977). *Battered women: A psychological study of domestic violence.* New York: Van Nostrand Reinhold.

Roy, M. (1982). *The abusive partner: An analysis of domestic battering.* New York: Van Nostrand Reinhold.

Search Group Inc. (1984). Information policy and crime control strategies. Washington, DC: U.S. Department of Justice.

Snyder, D. K., & Fruchtman, L. A. (1981). Differential patterns of wife abuse: A data based typology. *Journal of Consulting and Clinical Psychology, 49,* 878–885.

Staff, M. (1986). Police found to be making more arrests for domestic violence. *Criminal Justice Newsletter, 3.*

Steinmetz, S. (1974). *Violence in the family.* New York: Dodd and Mead.

Steinmetz, S. (1977). *The cycle of violence: Assertive, aggressive, and abusive family interaction.* New York: Prager.

Straus, M. A. (1978). Wife beating: How common and why? *Victimology: An International Journal, 2,* 443–458.

Straus, M. A., Gelles, R. J., & Steinmetz, S. K. (1980). *Behind closed doors: Violence in the American family.* New York: Doubleday/Anchor Press.

Straus, M., & Hotaling, G. T. (Eds.) (1980). *The social causes of husband–wife violence.* Minneapolis, MN: University of Minnesota Press.

Sugarman, D. B., & Cohn, E. S. (1980). Wife abuse versus child abuse: Do people differ in their attributions of responsibility to the victim and offender? Paper presented at the Annual Meeting of the Eastern Psychological Association, Washington, DC.

Turner, S., & Shapiro, C. (1986). Mourning the death of a relationship. *Social Work, 31,* 372–376.

Truninger, E. (1971). Marital violence: The legal solutions. *Hastings Law Review, 13,* 159–176.

Walker, L. E. (1979). *The battered women.* New York: Harper and Row.

PART III

WOMEN WHO KILL

7

Female Murderers and Their Motives: A Tale of Two Cities

Coramae Richey Mann
Department of Criminal Justice, Indiana University, Bloomington

Field research data from police department homicide files in Chicago and Houston for 1979 and 1983 tend to support earlier studies that found that women who kill give self-defense and emotional reasons (anger, revenge) as motives for murder. The 114 female murderers in these random samples acted alone and did not preplan the murders, which were intersexual, intraracial, and intrafamilial. Neither social characteristics such as race and employment status, prior arrest history, or previous violent arrest history influenced motive. Although most of the offenders appeared to come from the lower economic strata, there were few instances of an economic motive. Where available, final court dispositions are reported. The preliminary results of the present study involving two cities and a portion of a continuing study that will include Atlanta, Los Angeles, New York City, and Baltimore, indicate the primary homicide cause when women are the offenders is the result of an argument or fight. Several research questions developed from the study will be applied to the larger data set in forthcoming analyses.

Researchers have only recently directed empirical attention to female offenders, who, with the exception of those subjects described in prostitution studies, comprise a group largely ignored until the last decade or so. Even with an increasing number of studies of female offenders of various types, little effort has been directed to women who commit criminal homicide and the motives or rationales behind such murders.[1] The major purpose of the exploratory descriptive study reported here is to add to the

Dr. Coramae Richey Mann has advanced degrees in clinical psychology and sociology from Roosevelt University and the University of Illinois at Chicago. Her professional career has been devoted to research, teaching, and activism related to "victims" of the juvenile and criminal justice systems: youths, racial minorities, and women. She has published a number of articles on these topics and a textbook, *Female Crime and Delinquency*. As a Ford Foundation Research Fellow, she tracked female felons from arrest through sentencing in an observational study. A proposed book, *Deadliest of the Species*, will be based on her current research on arrested female murderers throughout the country. Professor Mann is currently on the faculty of the Department of Criminal Justice at Indiana University as a full professor.

The author deeply thanks former Chicago Superintendent of Police Fred Rice and former Houston Chief of Police Lee P. Brown, for permitting access to their police records and homicide data; Captain Tim Reddick and Dr. Edmond True for their computer assistance; and two anonymous reviewers for their helpful comments.

The research was made possible by a faculty grant from the Florida State University.

[1]The terms "homicide" and "murder" are used interchangeably here because "murder" is the term used by both the Chicago and Houston homicide departments and the *Uniform Crime Reports*. Homicide is the killing of a human being, while murder is a criminal homicide.

small but growing body of research and literature on this female offender group and discover if women who kill today do so for the same or different reasons than those reported in 1958 in Wolfgang's pioneer study and by researchers in the intervening years.

REVIEW OF RELATED PREVIOUS RESEARCH

Whereas Wolfgang reported self defense/justifiable (50.6%) as the most frequently given motive in 1958, since that time, although there is considerable scatter across the various reasons proffered for the homicide, the most often cited motive seems to be psychological and emotional causes. Gibbs, Sullivan, and Vega (1977) report the most frequent, or 34.6% of the motives, in this category, as do Wilbanks (1983) with 59.6%, and Weisheit (1984) who found that 30% of the female homicide offenders had revenge as a motive. Although not listing proportions, Totman (1978) also reported revenge and self-preservation as the primary motives for women who kill.

Similar to Wolfgang's findings, Ward, Jackson, and Ward (1969) also list self defense (24%) as the most frequent rationale given by the incarcerated Florida female murderers studied. This coincides with the second most frequent reason for killing another person found by most of the studies addressing homicide motive—self-defense, "self-preservation," or other forms of justifiable action. Claiming innocence may be another way of declaring the homicide justifiable, but such an inference is difficult to make from the data reported in three studies listing this motive (Ward et al., 1969; Suval & Brisson, 1974; Gibbs et al., 1977). A related problem of interpretation from previous studies concerns those female murderers who stated the homicide was "someone else's fault," a rationale that might suggest a claim of innocence (Ward et al., 1969; Weisheit, 1984).

A final definitional perplexity is noted in studies citing economic reasons as the murder motive (Wolfgang, 1958; Wilbanks, 1983; Weisheit, 1984). It is not possible to ascertain from these reports whether the rationale in these instances relates to the commission of an economic crime that resulted in a homicide, for example, armed robbery, or if there was a direct economic motive for the killing, such as murder for insurance money.

The present analysis attempts to more clearly define motive by defining *psychological* motives as those peculiar to mentally ill offenders; and *emotional* motives as anger, rage, jealousy, and the like, or those that stem from immediate reactive emotional states; and further dichotomizes *economic* motives into indirect (in the commission of another crime) and direct (for personal financial gain).

METHODS

The Sample

The study group reported in this chapter consists of 114 randomly selected cleared homicide cases from Chicago and Houston for the years 1979 and 1983 in which the offenders were women. These women ranged in age from 12 to 61 years (mean = 32 years) and were predominantly black (79.8%) with the remaining offenders almost equally divided between white (10.5%) and Hispanic (9.6%). Cases were sampled for the years 1979 and 1983 in order to observe any possible changes that may have occurred over this time period.

The basis for the selection of the cities in the study was the national homicide rates for the years examined: 9.7 per 100,000 in 1979, and 8.3 per 100,000 in 1983. Fifteen states were identified as meeting these criteria and within those states Chicago and Houston were found to be higher than the respective rates for both years and therefore selected.[2] One-third (33.3%) random samples of female murderers arrested in 1979 and 1983 in Chicago and Houston were selected using Tables of Random Numbers (Blalock, 1972, pp. 554–557), resulting in a total of 60 cases from Chicago (1979 = 33/99; 1983 = 27/81) and 54 cases in the Houston sample (1979 = 30/89; 1983 = 24/72).[3]

Procedure

The complete homicide files of the sampled cases for 1979 and 1983, some of which included autopsy reports, and any other police record sources such as arrest folders, fingerprint files, and F.B.I. reports were minutely examined. Information obtained from these documents was recorded on individual research schedules after each case had been assigned a code number to insure confidentiality. The seven-page schedule included *demographic and social characteristics* of the offender (age, race, marital status, education, employment status, maternal status) and victim (age, race, occupation); *offense data* (offense day/date/time/location, motive, weapon or method used in the murder, premeditation, whether committed alone or with others, alcohol/ drug involvement, arrest date, amount of bond, final disposition); *criminal justice data* (previous arrest/conviction records of offender and victim, violent histories of offender and victim); and the victim-offender relationship.

Approximately one week was spent in each city abstracting information from the files. Several follow-up contacts to obtain missing and additional data, such as court dispositions, were also made after leaving the field sites.

FINDINGS

Profile

A profile of the female murderer and her crime reveals an offense that is primarily intersexual, intraracial, and intrafamilial; committed by an offender who tends to be about 32 years of age, black (79.8%), unemployed (62.6%), a mother (85.5%), and ever married or common-law married (67.7%). She acts alone in the commission of the murder (90.4%), kills someone close to her (75.4%) with a gun (57.9%), usually a pistol (87.1%), in a residence, on a weekend night. These female offenders committed the murders alone (90.4%) and the majority (71.1%) did not preplan or premeditate the homicide. In the 76 cases in which information was available, 36.8% of the

---

[2]Other cities included in the study are Atlanta, Los Angeles, New York City, and Baltimore. At this writing all of the data from the other cities have not been analyzed for inclusion in this chapter. The 1979 homicide rate for Houston was 40.4 and in 1983, 32.4. For Chicago these rates were 27.9 and 24.1, respectively. Another important factor considered in the selection of cities in such research is access to the police files.

[3]Time and budget considerations prohibited inclusion of all of the cases for Chicago (N = 180) and Houston (N = 161) for the two years.

women were under the influence of alcohol at the time of the offense, and only 9.9% were affected by narcotics; but in no instance was being under the influence of a substance given as a motive by the offender. The victims, on the other hand, had been drinking in 60% of the cases where data were available (N = 85). Autopsies revealed that 20.2% of the victims were drunk. Similar to their murderers, few victims were under the influence of narcotics (5.4%).

Motive

A statistical analysis of the *motive* variable, show in Table 7-1, reveals that the probability is .005 that this variable is a result of simple random sampling. It is clear that self-defense (44.2%) and emotional reasons (23%) are the most frequent motives given by the female murder suspects in Chicago and Houston since they account for two thirds of the reasons given in the combined data. However, a closer inspection of the individual cities (Table 7-2) reveals that the Houston sample is the major contributor to the self defense motive witnessed in the finding that in 1979, 60% of the Houston women gave such a rationale for the murder, as did 54.2% in 1983. Chicago, on the other hand, had substantially lower self defense motives given than Houston (34.4% in 1979; 32.2% in 1983) in both years yet over twice the proportion of emotional reasons than Houston, or 28.1% compared to Houston's 10% in 1979 and 37% compared to Houston's 16.7% in 1983.

Motive was examined by condition of the victim to determine whether the victim

Table 7-1 Percentage distribution of motive variables, Chicago and Houston, by year

Motive	Percent by year[a]		
	1979 (N = 63)	1983 (N = 51)	Total (N = 114)
Not responsible			
Innocent	3.2	3.9	3.5
Self-defense	46.8	41.2	44.2
Defense of others	—	7.8	3.5
Accident	9.7	2.0	6.2
Under influence	—	—	—
Others' fault	1.6	—	.9
Physiological	—	—	—
Psychological	8.1	3.9	6.2
Justifiable		1.6	3.9
Responsible			
Multiple	3.2	—	1.8
Emotional	19.4	27.5	23.0
Economic	3.2	3.9	3.5
Argument/Fight	4.8	7.8	6.2
Senseless	—	2.0	.9
Unknown	—	—	—
Totals[b]	100.0	100.0	100.0

[a]Adjusted frequencies.
[b]Because of rounding, percentages may not add to totals.

Table 7-2 Percentage distribution of motive variables, Chicago and Houston, by year

| | Percent by year[a] | | | | | |
| | Chicago | | | Houston | | |
Motive	1979 (N = 33)	1983 (N = 27)	Total (N = 60)	1979 (N = 33)	1983 (N = 27)	Total (N = 60)
Not responsible						
Innocent	—	3.7	1.7	6.7	4.2	5.6
Self-defense	34.4	29.6	32.2	60.0	54.2	57.4
Defense of others	—	7.4	3.4	—	8.3	3.7
Accident	12.5	—	6.8	6.7	4.2	5.6
Others' fault	3.1	—	1.7	—	—	—
Psychological	9.4	3.7	6.8	6.7	4.2	5.6
Responsible						
Multiple	3.1	—	1.7	3.3	—	1.9
Emotional	28.1	37.0	32.2	10.0	16.7	13.0
Economic	3.1	3.7	3.4	3.3	4.2	3.7
Argument/Fight	6.3	11.1	8.5	3.3	4.2	3.7
Senseless	—	3.7	1.7	—	—	—
Totals[b]	100.0	100.0	100.0	100.0	100.0	100.0

[a]Adjusted frequencies.
[b]Because of rounding, percentages may not add to totals.

was incapacitated (e.g., asleep, ill, drunk, helpless, infirm) or not. The presumption was that such a condition might contribute to the motive, for example in a woman's reluctance to continue caring for an invalid; the opportunity to "equalize" a situation when the victim was asleep; or a possible precipitating factor in the homicide resulting from a drunken encounter between the victim and offender. This was not found to be a significant factor, but there were individual cases such as one in which a drunken male victim challenged the female homicide offender through such inflammatory statements as, "Come on, bitch, kill me," while baring his chest. She met the challenge.

Responsibility Versus Non-Responsibility

The motive variable was recoded into *not responsible* (innocent, self defense, accident, other's fault, defense of others, under the influence, physiological, psychological, and justifiable) and *responsible* (emotional, economic, argument/fight, senseless, and multiple reasons). An examination of possible explanatory variables was then introduced in crosstabulations of these classifications. Although no significant difference was indicated when race was dichotomized into minority and nonminority, there was a tendency for the nonminority group to claim they were not responsible for the murder (75%) more so than the minority group (56.4%). Similarly, in terms of age and motive, although those over age 25 were slightly more likely to deny responsibility for the murder (60%) than the women under 25 years of age (50%), this was not a statistically significant difference.

It was not surprising to find a significant difference between the responsible and not responsible groups when premeditation of the murder was introduced. Those women who were responsible premeditated the crime (76.9%), although those claiming they were not responsible for the murder were not as likely to have preplanned it (69.1%).[4]

The method chosen to perpetrate the murder was recoded as gun/no gun, because a firearm, usually a pistol, was the preferred weapon in 57.9% of the total cases. A significant difference was found between Chicago and Houston in the choice of weapons with Chicago women choosing a knife more frequently (46.7%) than Houston female murderers (20.4%).[5] The reverse was true in Houston, where women preferred guns (75.9%), in many cases long guns, compared with female murderers in Chicago (41.7%). A majority of the women who denied responsibility for the murder used a gun (65.3%), whereas 60.5% of those who claimed responsibility did *not* use a gun in the homicide. This significant difference[6] suggests that the women who clearly had murder in mind (assumed responsibility for it) used whatever was most available at the time. Such an interpretation tends to support the earlier contention that women who kill use a household weapon, most often a knife (Wolfgang, 1958). It is also possible that those women using a gun and disclaiming responsibility for the murder did so in self-defense.

Victim-offender relationship was re-categorized into family and nonfamily. Nonfamily includes friends, acquaintances, and strangers as victims. Family is defined here as both blood ties and intimate, interpersonal relationships such as common-law married or lovers, as well as interpersonal associations with legal ramifications, in other words, married, separated, and divorced. The relationship between the offender and her victim was not significantly related to motive, although there was a slight tendency for a female offender to deny responsibility for the murder when a family member was concerned (60.5%), compared with a homicide involving a nonfamily victim (53.1%).

Other Motives

Women arrested for murder in both Chicago (6.8%) and Houston (5.6%) were inclined to define the murder as an "accident"; however, statements such as "He walked into the knife," or "I just meant to scare him with the gun," lacked credibility, particularly when examined in conjunction with other circumstances involved in the incident.

Although robbery constituted 10.5% of the motives in murders listed by the F.B.I. in 1979 (U.S. Department of Justice, 1980, p. 12), and 10.6% in 1983 (U.S. Department of Justice, 1984, p. 12), only one 1979 case of prostitution robbery in Chicago and a 1983 tavern robbery in Houston were identified as felony murders by the women studied. In fact, economic reasons as a motivation for murder comprised only 3.5% of the cases for both cities and years. The other two cases involved an infanticide, because "we couldn't afford it" (another baby in the family), and a murder resulting from an argument over a narcotics sale.

---

[4]Significant at the .0002 level with chi square equal to 17.2 with two degrees of freedom.
[5]Significant at the .0005 level with chi square equal to 12.31 with two degrees of freedom.
[6]Significant at the .01 level with chi square equal to 5.85 with one degree of freedom.

Criminal Justice Data

In order to determine if the female murderers had a prior history of crime and thus explore a criminal subculture perspective, offenders' previous arrest records and convictions were examined. No significant differences in motive were found between those women with criminal histories and those without. An analysis of the available arrest records or verified information that the female offender had no arrest record ($N = 91$) revealed that less than one-third (30.8%) of the women who killed had previous violent arrest histories. Separate analyses of the violent history variable by city produced a different picture. Female murderers in Chicago comprised 81.5% of those subjects in the study with prior violent arrest histories, which was significantly different from the Houston offenders (18.5%).[7] Another interesting finding concerning violent arrest histories of these offenders is that violent criminal histories increased from 1979 to 1983 for both Houston and Chicago. In Chicago 31.3% of the female murderers in 1979 had violent arrest histories; by 1983, 54.2% did. The comparable percentages for Houston were 8.7% in 1979 and 25% in 1983.

The final court disposition, located in 108 of the 114 cases, revealed that 56.1% of the female criminal homicide offenders received prison sentences, with a mean of 16 years to serve (median = 9.6 years).[8] Although nonminorities were more likely to avoid a prison sentence (83.3%) than minorities (70.8%), this finding was not statistically significant. Not surprisingly, female criminal homicide offenders who premeditated the murder were more likely to go to prison (48%) than those who did not preplan the crime (20.8%), but nonetheless more than half of the women who planned the murder (52%) did not get a prison sentence.[9] A woman who killed a nonfamily person was significantly more likely to be sent to prison than if she killed someone close to her.[10] Only 20.8% of women who killed "family" went to prison, compared with 45.2% of those who had nonfamily victims.

Not unexpectedly, 85.5% of the women who denied responsibility for the homicide were not sentenced to prison, whereas 46.7% of those who were responsible received prison sentences.[11] Interestingly, we again find that a higher proportion of those responsible for the murder (53.3%) were not sent to prison.

A final significant difference relates to prison time and motive. Prison sentence was broken down into none, low (under 10 years), and high (10 years or more). As predicted, those women who stated they were not responsible for the murder, and presumably the court agreed, received lesser sentences (none or low) than those who admitted their homicide responsibility.[12] But even the group giving motives indicating responsibility for the murder did not fare badly because 50% did not receive prison time, 22.7% were in the low sentencing category, and only 27.3% were given 10 years or more to serve.

---

[7]Significant at the .03 level with chi square equal to 8.36 with three degrees of freedom.

[8]Only aggregate numbers are reported because analysis by city and year yields numbers too small to be meaningful.

[9]Significant at the .04 level with chi square equal to 7.07 with two degrees of freedom.

[10]Significant at the .02 level with chi square equal to 5.39 with one degree of freedom.

[11]Significant at the .0006 level with chi square equal to 11.18 with one degree of freedom.

[12]Significant at the .0003 level with chi square equal to 16.28 with two degrees of freedom.

SUMMARY AND DISCUSSION

The findings of the motive data on a random sample of 114 female criminal homicide offenders in Chicago and Houston for the years 1979 and 1983 tend to support previous studies of female murderers who report emotional reasons or self-defense as the primary motives given for the homicide. Some variation by city and year was found in the present study. In Houston, self-defense was the most frequently given rationale, with emotional reasons next. On the other hand, Chicago female suspects indicated self-defense over emotional reasons in 1979, but the reverse in 1983. When the years are combined, both reasons were equally given (32.2% each) in Chicago.

Other characteristics of this offending group indicate that women do not preplan their murders, and usually act alone in the commission of the offense. There were no significant differences between minority and nonminority women in terms of motive, although nonminority female murderers tended to claim nonresponsibility for the event more so than the minority women. Whether the victim was family or not had no bearing on the motive, nor did the condition of helplessness of the victim. Only four cases involving an economic motive were identified in the study, which suggests money or material gain are not primary reasons for women to kill. Although their high unemployment status indicated that female homicide offenders in Chicago and Houston possibly come from a lower income stratum, there was no evidence of a criminal or violent subcultural phenomenon in terms of prior criminal record or violent criminal history. Nonetheless, increases in violent offense arrest histories were noted in both cities from 1979 to 1983.

The final court disposition in the murder cases indicates that more than one-half of the women who committed criminal homicide in these two cities received prison sentences, especially those who premeditated the murder. But a woman who killed a family member or someone with whom she was involved in an intimate relationship was less likely to go to prison than if her victim was not a family member. Of those women who had motives indicating a responsibility for the murder, only slightly more than one-fourth received prison sentences of 10 years or more.

Although Chicago and Houston are cities with two of the highest murder rates in the country, these findings on the motives of women who kill provide only a partial picture of this offender and her rationale for taking another's life. Ongoing data collection in Atlanta, Los Angeles, New York City, and Baltimore will hopefully complete the portrait begun in this tale of two cities, because the homicide files of these six cities collectively represent the majority of such cases in the United States. These preliminary findings suggest a number of questions to be addressed with the final data set: (1) What, if any, differences exist between black and nonblack female murderers in choice of victim, motive, weapon choice, and other circumstances of the homicide? (2) Are there any significant differences between the races relative to sex or age of the victim? (3) Is there any validity to the "subculture of violence" theory as applied to women? (4) Does an economic theory of crime pertain to female murderers? (5) Is the profile of female killers today any different than that of Philadelphia in 1958? (6) Are there racial differences in the sentencing of women who kill? (7) Does limited access to proper medical care affect trauma-induced mortality? (8) Are victim-precipitation and/or the "battered woman syndrome" valid indicators of female homicide offenses? (9) Is a black life devalued by the courts? and most importantly, (10) Are black women committing black genocide?

The few studies of criminal homicide that explore gender and race report black women with the second highest offender (and victim) rates, preceded by black men and followed by white men and white women respectively (e.g., Sutherland & Cressey, 1978; Riedel & Lockhart-Riedel, 1984; Mann, 1986). Clearly the involvement of black women in criminal homicide is significantly higher than that of white, Hispanic, Asian, or Native American women in the United States. Because homicide is predominantly an intraracial event, the usual victim of a black female murderer is another black, most often a man. Black men are also the primary targets of black male criminal homicide offenders. Thus, murder has become "epidemic" within the black community with black men having the highest victim rates of homicide in the country (58.5 per 100,000), followed by black women with a rate of 13.2 per 100,000 (Riedel, 1984, p. 53). The ongoing research described in this chapter is an attempt to explore the reasons behind this form of black-on-black genocide through an examination of the circumstances and motives involved in cleared homicide cases.

BIBLIOGRAPHY

Blalock, H. M. (1972). *Social statistics.* New York: McGraw Hill.

Gibbs, D. L., Sullivan, I. J., & Vega, M. (Nov., 1977). Homicides committed by females in the state of Florida. Unpublished paper presented at the annual meeting of the American Society of Criminology, Atlanta, GA.

Mann, C. R. (1986). The black criminal homicide offender in the United States. *Report of the Secretary's Task Force on Black and Minority Health, Volume V: Homicide, suicide, and unintentional injuries.* Washington, DC: U.S. Government Printing Office.

Riedel, M. (Nov., 1984). Issues in the study of black homicide. Unpublished paper presented at the annual meeting of the American Society of Criminology, Cincinnati, OH.

Riedel, M., & Lockhart-Riedel, L. (1984). Issues in the study of black homicide. Unpublished paper presented at the annual meeting of the American Society of Criminology.

Sutherland, E. H., & Cressey, D. R. (1978). *Criminology.* Philadelphia: Lippincott.

Suval, E. M., & Brisson, R. C. (1974). Neither beauty nor beast: Female criminal homicide offenders. *International Journal of Criminology and Penology, 2,* 23–34.

Ward, D. A., Jackson, M., & Ward, R. (1969). Crimes of violence by women. In D. Mulvihill & M. Tomin, (Eds.), *Crimes of violence* (pp. 843–910). Washington, DC: U.S. Government Printing Office.

Weisheit, R. A. (1984). Female homicide offenders: Trends over time in an institutionalized population. *Justice Quarterly, 1,* 471–489.

Wilbanks, W. (1983). Female homicide offenders in the United States. *International Journal of Women's Studies, 6,* 302–310.

Wolfgang, M. E. (1958). *Patterns in criminal homicide.* Philadelphia: University of Pennsylvania Press.

Totman, J. (1978). *The murderers: A psychosocial study of criminal homicide.* San Francisco: R and E Research Associates.

U.S. Department of Justice. (1980). *Uniform crime reports for the United States.* Washington, DC: U.S. Government Printing Office.

U.S. Department of Justice. (1984). *Uniform crime reports for the United States.* Washington, DC: U.S. Government Printing Office.

8

Women, Murder, and Male Domination: Police Reports of Domestic Violence in Chicago and Philadelphia

Noel A. Cazenave
Department of Sociology, University of Connecticut, Storrs

Margaret A. Zahn
Department of Sociology, University of North Carolina, Charlotte

INTRODUCTION

When presented without context specific detail, results from existing survey studies of homicide and domestic violence may be very misleading. A recent National Institute of Justice study of homicide in the United States found that in 57% of the cases of family homicide (nearly all of which involved adults in intimate relationships), the victim was male and in 43% she was female (Riedel, Zahn, & Mock, 1985, p. 25). Earlier studies, (e.g., the prototypical study of homicide in Philadelphia by Marvin Wolfgang, 1958) also reported near parity of homicide victimization between husbands and wives. For example, Wolfgang (1958) noted that although 53 of the 100 marital homicide[1] cases he studied had wives as victims and 47 of the victims were husbands, when all types of homicides were considered, males were much more likely to be involved as both offenders and victims than were females. In addition, females were more likely to be homicide offenders and victims in marital relationships than was the case for males. Although 41% of all women killed were murdered by their husbands, only 11% of the men who were killed were assaulted by their

Noel A. Cazenave is associate professor of sociology at the University of Connecticut. His teaching and research interests include poverty and inequality, racism and public policy, social movements, and political sociology. He is currently conducting a study of Social Science Experts and Community Participation in Precursors to the U.S. "War on Poverty." He is also in the planning stages of projects on racism and U.S. welfare policy, and African Americans and movements for economic justice.

Margaret A. Zahn is professor of sociology and chair of the Department of Sociology, Anthropology, and Social Work at the University of North Carolina at Charlotte. She was director of a nationwide study on homicide funded by the National Institute of Justice and has published extensively in the area of violence, including a recent coedited book on *Violence: Patterns, Causes and Public Policy.* She is currently vice-president of the American Society of Criminology.

[1]Wolfgang's figures include both victims who were legally married and those involved in common-law marriage relationships. In referring to Wolfgang's findings the terms "married," "husbands," and "wives" include references to common-law marriages.

wives. However, when a man was killed by a woman it was most likely to be by his wife. Finally, husbands tended to kill more violently than did wives.

In their pioneering research on family violence, Murray Straus and his associates also encountered statistics that, without further explanation, could be misleading. They found comparably high rates of violence for husbands and wives[2] (Straus, Gelles, & Steinmetz, 1980). Unfortunately, these statistics reveal nothing about who initiated the violence and its relative consequences for the males and females involved (Gelles, 1979). For example, in a reanalysis of data presented by Steinmetz that showed that men and women are equally inclined to kill one another, Pleck, Pleck, Grossman, & Bart (1977) found that wives were seven times as likely as husbands to murder in self-defense. Straus (1976) is also cautious about the possible misinterpretation of homicide statistics. He states that, in many incidences, whether a homicide is committed is determined by the presence of knives or guns. Straus further suggests that wives are more likely to resort to the use of such weapons because of their relative lack of physical strength as compared to their husbands. As indirect support for this view Straus again referred to the Wolfgang study (1985), which found that in those husband-wife murders where it could be shown that the victim precipitated the assault, 85% of the cases involved the husband as the aggressor. Finally, Straus notes that although because of their general superiority in physical strength and adeptness in the use of physical violence, it might be expected that men would be less violent in their homicidal attacks, Wolfgang found instead that husbands were much more likely to engage in homicides involving multiple stabbing, cutting, or shooting, or a severe beating, than were wives. Straus concluded that the existing literature on family violence and domestic homicide do not explain why indeed, " . . . wives are much more often the victims of violence by their husbands than the reverse" (Straus, 1976, p. 54). Straus asserts that an understanding of this difference entails an analysis of the social structure that promotes both sexual inequality and cultural norms supportive of violence against women.

The controversies over the appropriate analysis of violence against women are not limited to the interpretation of official statistics, however. In fact, Straus himself has been criticized; not because of his explanation of statistics, but as a result of his choice of analytical concepts. For example, Dobash and Dobash (1979) are critical of the use of the concept of marital violence and of the modern systems approach to the study of family violence because they feel that both obscure the fact that violence in the home is not simply a battle between equals but is most likely to be aimed at female victims to ensure their continued subjugation. That is, to be understood, violence against wives cannot simply be treated as an aspect of marital or family violence but must be placed within its sociohistoric context and explained through concepts and theories specific to its own needs.

In a paper appropriately titled "Mutual Combat and Other Family Violence Myths," Berk, Berk, Loseke, and Rauma (1981) identified two approaches to the study of spousal violence. The first of these uses what they refer to as a "rubric of family violence" to treat spousal violence as a form of "mutual combat" where, "The problem then is not violent men, but violent people" (1981, p. 1). Their alternative approach entails placing spousal violence within the broader context of male domination and the subjugation of women. This latter strategy is most consistent

[2]As was the case with the Wolfgang study, here "husbands" and "wives" refer to people involved in either legal or common-law marriages.

with feminist theory on the victimization of women; most particularly, the concept of patriarchal domination.

WOMEN, VIOLENCE, AND PATRIARCHAL DOMINATION

The issues of rape and assault emerged in the 1970s as key agendas of the women's movement. These concerns are stressed by those committed to the advancement of women because of their belief that as long as men are allowed to dominate women physically through their generally superior physical strength and aggressive skills, women could be "kept in their place" physically, regardless of their individual or collective abilities.

Susan Brownmiller's (1975) *Against Our Will: Men, Women, and Rape* helped make this connection explicit and played a major role in the reconceptualization of rape from a sexual act to an act of aggression through which men, both individually and collectively, have historically coerced and controlled women. The concept of patriarchal domination (what we will refer to as male domination in the remainder of this chapter) was also espoused as an explanation of violence against women by Del Martin (1977) in *Battered Wives*. Martin stated that the ultimate cause of wife beating is sexual inequality. Consequently, wife beating will persist as long as there are unequal power relationships between men and women and violence can be used to further tip the scale in favor of male supremacy.

One of the first attempts to apply the concept of male domination to social science research on violence against women was Dobash and Dobash's (1979) *Violence Against Wives*. The Dobash's research provided this perspective with both a method and credibility. Their method is referred to as the context specific approach. This research strategy is based on the philosophy that violence against wives cannot adequately be explained through the computerized reconstruction of reality based on the analysis of abstract variables collected through survey research. As they put it (1979, p. 30), "The essence of the context specific approach is that the social world can be understood only by exploring human behavior in the setting in which it occurs." These scholars contend that such an analysis makes it clear that culturally, historically, and socially, wife abuse is different from any other form of family violence and can best be conceptualized as a mechanism of coercive control to maintain ancient but continuing patterns of male domination.

A strength of the context specific approach, as the Dobashs use it, is that it entails the presentation of numerous data-rich case illustrations that reveal the context of meaning of violent episodes in a way that survey research cannot. Through them a common pattern emerges in which violence against wives is used by men to exercise their perceived authority as "heads" of households. Whether she is beaten because "the dinner is late," "she answers him back," or "there is not enough starch in his shirt," the real issue is clear—she is not conforming to the demands of the patriarchal system.

Such case study data are essential to both the application of the context specific approach and the verification of the male domination perspective. This perspective has not been tested more because of the heavy emphasis of family violence studies on survey research methods. However, some work is now being done to demonstrate that positivistic research strategies and a male domination conceptual perspective are not inimical (Berk et al., 1981; Yllo, 1981).

Although Zahn's (1975, p. 401) research on female homicide victims found support for what she referred to as the sex role hypothesis and the view that " . . . among females, the female role and the attached family role continue to be the dominant influences in shaping the life, and death, of females," the substantive importance of homicide—the ultimate violence against women—to the women's movement, its potential theoretical significance in testing the key feminist perspective of male domination, and the abundance of homicide case material make this void in the homicide literature conspicuous. The impact of male domination on female homicide victims and offenders is the primary focus of the present study. Official homicide case study data are used to address the following two questions: (1) Are the structure and dynamics of domestic homicides involving male victims and female victims the same, or are there gender specific differences? and, (2) If noteworthy gender specific differences exist, do they reveal patterns that can best be explained through the use of gender stratification concepts and theory?

METHOD

This analysis is based on 83 homicide incidents involving men and women in intimate relationships in Philadelphia and Chicago taken from a study of American homicide by Riedel, Zahn, and Mock (1985).

The larger study from which these case narratives[3] are derived consists of two major components: (1) an analysis of United States homicide patterns and trends from 1968 to 1978 through the use of the FBI *Uniform Crime Reports* and, (2) an analysis of homicide patterns in eight United States cities for the year 1978 through the use of police and medical examiner office records. It is from this second component that the cases discussed in the following analysis are drawn.

The Subsample

Time and space considerations do not permit an examination of all cases of murder involving women in intimate heterosexual relationships as offenders or victims for each of the eight cities studied. Therefore, only the cases from Chicago and Philadelphia are included in the analysis. These cities were chosen because they are the largest cities included in the study, those for which there is the greatest amount of comparative data collected in other studies, and because they are representative of their geographic regions. Chicago and Philadelphia are also similar in their age and race composition. Finally, the regions they represent, the North Central and Northeast, respectively, fit the 1968 through 1978 national homicide trend pattern best and are most similar of the eight cities to national statistics in the sex of victims.[4]

In this analysis, the term "domestic homicide" is used in a specific way to refer to homicides involving men and women in current or past intimate relationships who may or may not share the same domicile. This includes men and women who are presently, or were formerly, legally married, living in a common-law relationship, or involved in a relationship described by the police or medical examiner's office as

[3]These "narratives" were constructed by the authors from police and medical examiner's reports.
[4]Other cities included in the larger study, but not in the present analysis, are St. Louis in the North Central region, Newark in the Northeastern region, Dallas and Memphis in the Southern region, and a city under the pseudonym "Ashton" in the Western region.

"boyfriend/girlfriend." As the last category implies, not all of these cases fit the family homicide victim/offender characterization used in the larger study. For example, not all family homicide relationships discussed in the general survey report involved intimate heterosexual relationships. Homicides involving parent and children or siblings were also included in those family homicide statistics.

Thirty-nine of the 83 cases are taken from the police department and medical examiner's records of Philadelphia and 44 cases come from the police department records of Chicago. Altogether, there are 42 female victims and 41 male victims comprising the subsample.

Data Analysis

Data to be reported in the following analysis include gender-related homicide patterns involving: victim/offender relationship; murder methods and weapons; gender dynamic differences in homicide aggressor and the most violent homicide offenders; and a typology of homicide cases for the two cities based on police reported offender motivation and precipitating events.

Because the overwhelming majority of the victims (79%) and the offenders (86%) for which data on race are available are black or Hispanic, no analyses are done by race for this small subsample of cases. Finally, homicide case narratives will be reported to illustrate major homicide types discussed in the analysis.

Advantages and Disadvantages of Police and Medical Examiner's Records

As we mentioned previously, the advantage of case material over survey research is that the nature of a particular phenomenon can better be uncovered by observing common patterns and sequences that emerge in given contexts. That is, one is able to gain a gestalt view of what is being studied rather than having to rely on the reconstruction of the relationships between rather abstract variables. Such data are also generally richer in what they reveal about the meanings and motivation of certain acts for key actors. Finally, in comparing the relative advantages of police and medical examiner's records, Zahn (1980) notes that generally the police are better able to reconstruct the events of a crime scene because they have first contact with the crime situation on which the statistics are based. On the other hand, medical examiner's records provide better evidence as to the cause of death and the presence of alcohol or other drugs in the victims.

The use of such records also entail major disadvantages. There are technical problems of validity and reliability. For example, neither the police nor medical examiners know exactly what happened, and they have varying degrees of success in reconstructing the events that occurred. As Zahn observed (1980), information like victim-offender relationship and motive are often difficult to detect and such data may vary in subsequent reports and records based on who is collecting the data and what additional information may be available. Finally, the quality of homicide reports differs from official to official, office to office, and city to city, based on the competence and commitment of various individuals and institutions in collecting accurate and complete information.

There have also been debates as to the appropriateness of social science research based on official statistics. Douglas (1971) thinks that by relying on official statistics, social scientists abdicate their search for the truth and place themselves in the compromising position of accepting the facts, figures, and ultimately the worldview of official institutions of social control.

For those interested in phenomenological research there are other pitfalls. For example, although Kitsuse and Cicourel (1963) are not as pessimistic about the use of official statistics as Douglas, they caution that, to the extent that these statistics are useful, it is in the understanding of the meanings, motivations, interpretations, and actions of official record keepers, not those on whom such records are actually kept. That is, strictly speaking, the reader's understanding of homicide acts is limited to the secondhand and sometimes distorted perceptions of the police and medical examiners who attempt to reconstruct these events and of the researchers who construct narratives from them.

Finally, Gulotta and Vayaggini (1976) note that the demands of language structure often impose a logic on phenomenological reality that is not actually present. They observe, for example, that the need of language for " . . . a subject to perform an act and an object to suffer its impact . . ." (p. 57) may result in simplistic, mechanical, and deterministic descriptions that do not adequately report reciprocal influences or system-governed events. For example, in ex post facto research based on police reports where both the police and researchers are literally trying to piece events together without any real knowledge of causal events, a fallacy of false logical sequences may appear. That is, what may seem to be a logical order of events may be, although logical, an erroneous attempt at the reconstruction of events not known.

Although, as Douglas (1971) suggests, participant observation studies may be needed to fully comprehend the meaning and context of human events, official case data may be of some value in uncovering sequences and contexts that take us beyond the limitations of traditional survey research. Even with their limitations and biases they do offer some beginning insights for those interested in the contextual nexus of women and American homicide.

FINDINGS AND DISCUSSION

Socioeconomic Status and Relationship Involvements of the Homicide Victims

As Table 8-1 shows, occupationally the victims are generally of low socioeconomic status (SES). In addition to the fact already discussed that most of the victims and offenders are racial minorities, nearly one-third of the male and a fourth of the female victims are unemployed. Finally, when the female housewives are added to those who are unemployed, almost half of the female victims are in an economically precarious predicament that might limit their options in escaping from abusive or threatening relationships.

As is expected for low SES people, the common-law marriage relationships for this subsample are relatively common (see Table 8-2). In fact, both male and female homicide victims are slightly more likely to have common-law marriage relationships than to be legally married. It should also be noted that female homicide victims are much more likely to be involved in a boyfriend/girlfriend relationship than male victims. In contrast with male victims, those women who do not actually share a domicile with men are equally as likely to be victims as women who co-

Table 8-1 Occupation and sex of victim

Occupational category	Sex of victim	
	Male	Female
Professional, managerial, entrepreneur	1	1
White collar nonprofessional	1	3
Skilled or semiskilled blue collar	8	5
Operative	5	2
Unskilled laborer	5	4
Housewife	0	10
Unemployed	13	10
N/A	8	7
Totals	41	42

reside with husbands. This can be further seen in the greater number of female as compared to male victims who are in estranged marital relationships or who were formerly in a boyfriend/girlfriend situation. Thus, when women kill they kill men with whom they are living. Men also kill their female cohabitants, but in addition, kill their estranged spouses and their girlfriends. For the female victims some other factors seem to be at work that go beyond simply the increased time at risk associated with living together.

Gender-Related Homicide Patterns

Table 8-3 documents that, consistent with previous homicide studies (e.g., Wolfgang, 1958), there are gender differences in the use of murder methods and weapons. Male offenders are much more likely to use guns, while females tend to use knives. Finally, only male offenders commit beating or strangulation homicides. That is, male offenders are more likely to use a weapon specifically designed to kill, injure, or physically overpower their victims, while female offenders are more likely to use kitchen utensils, which Wolfgang (1958) has suggested may be utilized to compensate for their relative lack of physical strength. As shall be seen in the next section, these findings are but one source of evidence that male offenders may be more likely to be aggressors than female offenders, who more commonly engage in self-defense related violence.

Table 8-2 Victim/Offender relationship and sex of victim

Victim/Offender relationship	Sex of victim	
	Male	Female
Coreside in legal marriage	14	9
Coreside in common-law marriage	15	11
Estranged from former marriage	4	7
Boyfriend/Girlfriend	8	15
Totals	41	42

Table 8-3 Murder method and weapon and sex of offender

Murder method/weapon	Sex of offender	
	Male	Female
Shooting/gun	26	16
Stabbing/knife	7	22
Beating/fists or objects	5	0
Strangulation/hands	2	0
Other	1	2
N/A	1	1
Totals	42	41

Gender and Homicide Aggressor

Consistent with the findings just discussed, very clear gender related tendencies are revealed regarding the gender of homicide aggressors and of victim initiated incidents. The data show that in 53 of the 58 cases (or 91%) for which information is available the initiator of physical violence is male. Put another way, no matter whether the man or the woman ultimately becomes the victim, in more than 90% of the cases, it was the man who initiated the violence.

In brief, in support of the male domination perspective and opposed to the view that homicide is equally as likely to involve female as male aggressors, in the overwhelming majority of these domestic homicide incidents in Chicago and Philadelphia a man was the aggressor. This is true even in those cases where the offender is female.

Gender and Severity of Violence

Not only are men more likely to be the aggressors in homicide cases involving women as either offender or victim, they also tend to be more violent in their homicides. Using Wolfgang's (1958) definition of a violent homicide as " . . . one involving two or more acts of stabbing, cutting, or shooting, or a severe beating," (Straus, 1976, p. 55) it was found that, when such information is available (Table 8-4), male offenders engaged in 18 homicide incidents involving multiple blows compared to only 5 for female offenders. That is, despite their generally superior strength and greater access to guns, which imply that the homicides they are involved in against women require relatively less effort, the male offenders tend to, in fact, be more violent in their actions and to inflict damage much beyond that which would produce death. Women, on the other hand, are more likely to stab or shoot their victim once.

Table 8-4 Severity of physical attack by sex

Number of physical blows	Male offender	Female offender
One	21	36
Two or more	18	5
No information	3	0
Totals	42	41

Gender, Motivation, and Precipitating Events

In order to develop a typology of homicide cases, each domestic homicide incident was read and categorized according to the precipitating event reported or the offender's apparent motive. Eight distinct categories were identified. Five of these categories provide information that is helpful in understanding the possible motives involved. The accident, other, and motivation and precipitating events unknown categories are much less useful in the descriptive types they provide.

Most of the five descriptive homicide categories in Table 8-5 reveal gender specific homicide patterns. The largest categories of homicide cases for both men and women are gender related. The major class of cases involving female offenders and male victims is self-defense, and the largest category of cases involving male offenders and female victims is precipitated by the offender's response to the victim's attempt to leave the relationship.

Further support for the view that the largest single category of cases is gender related are the facts that: (1) all of the self-defense homicide cases involve female offenders and male victims, and (2) 12 of these 18 cases include beatings to the woman prior to the homicide.

A good example of such a case is the following narrative based on a case involving a male victim employed as a cook, where neither the age nor race of the victim or offender is specified:

> The offender was verbally abused and smacked several times during the night and early morning. When they arrived at friends' the victim continued to verbally humiliate the offender. After they left they walked. The victim punched the offender and knocked her to the ground. The offender pulled out a .22 caliber pistol from her purse and shot the victim in the chest. The offender admitted shooting the victim, "because he had been beating on her."

In 7 of the 18 self-defense cases there is evidence of alcohol use by either the victim or the offender. The following is an example of such a case, involving a 60-year-old unemployed black male janitor as the victim and his 48-year-old black wife as the offender.

> The victim came home drunk and hit his wife in the nose. She bled. The victim picked up a knife. The offender picked up a bottle. The victim and offender argued and fought. The offender hit the victim in his face with a bottle and then stabbed him several times.

Many of these cases occurred early in the morning, suggesting a pattern of arguments that began after the husband returned home from a night of drinking.

The second largest category of homicides and the largest class involving female victims and male offenders consisted of cases in which the victim (nearly always female) unsuccessfully attempted to leave the relationship. Although both categories are gender specific, in contrast with the self-defense narratives, none of these cases involved beatings at the time of the immediate homicide incident and none of these reports mentioned drunkenness or heavy drinking on the part of either the offender or the victim. Compared to the self-defense narratives, these incidents seem to be much less spontaneous and much more instrumental in nature. This can be seen vividly in the cases that fit an execution style slaying pattern, during which there was little argument or discussion. The following narrative involves a 36-year-old black female victim, employed as a postal clerk, and her 48-year-old black ex-boyfriend.

Table 8-5 Precipitating event in domestic homicide by sex of offender

Event	Male	Female
Self-defense	0	18
Attempting to end relationship	12	2
Jealousy	5	1
Argument over money	3	3
Domestic quarrel:		
Various causes	5	6
Accident	4	0
Other	2	2
Motivation and precipitating		
events unknown	11	9
Totals	42	41

The offender knocked on the door of the victim's residence. When the door was opened by the victim's son the offender entered the home and ordered the son upstairs. The offender then walked to the bedroom of the victim. Upon seeing the offender the victim closed and locked the door. The offender forced the door open and fired several shots at the victim; two of which struck her in the head. The offender then left the house using the rear door from which he had entered. Letters were found that indicated that the offender had attempted to patch up the relationship that the victim wanted to discontinue. The offender had been previously arrested and convicted on three occasions for noncompliance with a court order, resisting arrest, and breach of peace.

In another case, involving a 22-year-old black female, who was employed as a United States Customs worker, and her ex-husband: "The offender came up behind the victim and shot her in the head while she was on an El (elevated subway train) platform."

Other cases involved arguments precipitated by the offenders who wanted to continue or renew a relationship, or jealousy about the victims seeing or intending to see other men. In all these "victim attempted to leave the relationship" type homicides, the killings appear to entail the enforcement of norms held by the offender that death is the penalty for the failure of the victim to continue the relationship.

Both of the major categories of homicide discussed thus far seem to support the theory of male domination as an explanation for certain forms of violence involving women. The beatings prevalent in the self-defense homicide, and the prohibition of women leaving relationships evident in the second category of cases, suggest not only a strong element of male domination but actual ownership norms. Apparently, many of these men operate under the assumption that they are entitled to exercise physical dominion over women and that women may not leave relationships as they choose. Again, both of these norms imply ownership.

It might also be expected that jealousy precipitated homicides would reflect this "ownership" pattern, where the victim is treated essentially as nontransferable chattel. But to what extent are such homicides gender specific? That is, are men and women equally as likely to engage in jealousy precipitated assaults, or do they, again, reveal patterns of male domination? Although the numbers of jealousy related homicides are too small to allow for definitive conclusions, they do reveal a pattern consistent with the other "ownership" related findings already discussed. As Table 8-5 shows, in cases of jealousy precipitated homicides, five out of six of these cases involve men as offenders. In most of these jealousy precipitated homicides, women were killed by jealous men to whom they were married currently or had been married previously, or men with whom they were cohabitating or intimately involved. The following narrative of a 44-year-old Puerto Rican female victim, who was self-employed as a tailor, and her 44-year-old Puerto Rican husband is an illustration.

> When the police arrived they were met by the victim's and offender's daughter who told them that the mother was in back of the family store and had been shot by her father. The offender entered the store and said, "I am the man, I shot my wife." The offender told the police that he and his wife had been having domestic problems because she was seeing another man.

It also appears that "ownership" rights are not considered to be reciprocal when it comes to gender and jealousy related homicides. There are no cases in which a woman killed a man because of her jealousy of his actions. In one of the jealousy precipitated cases, a woman killed a man who initiated an argument over allegations of her seeing another man. Both produced weapons during the struggle. In two other jealousy precipitated homicide incidents, it was the women who were murdered after they confronted their partners about seeing other women. This category is illustrated by the following narrative of a 42-year-old female victim and her husband for whom the race of the participants and the age of the offender are not known.

> The victim saw her husband in a car with another woman. An eyewitness to the incident indicated that the victim came after her husband with a claw hammer and broke the car window. During the ensuing argument the offender pulled a gun, shot the victim in an arm, chased her to the bedroom where her son was sleeping, and shot her in the back. The offender then called the police and admitted to the shooting.

In brief, consistent with the male domination perspective, women are not only murdered by jealous husbands, they are also killed when they express their jealousy to men they accuse of being "unfaithful." The penalty for women who are either unfaithful or who complain about the infidelity of the men with whom they are involved is the same—death.

Although the three homicide categories already discussed provide the best illustrations of male domination related homicides involving women, there are other relevant cases that fit the remaining, less gender specific categories. For example, four of the cases categorized as domestic quarrel/various causes involve beatings. For these beating cases there is one male victim and three female victims. The male victim domestic quarrel case that involved a beating was precipitated by a victim who attempted to physically coerce his girlfriend into dancing nude in a nightclub he owned. The cases with female victims involved beatings associated with arguments about cleaning up an apartment, the victim's cooking, and the victim's use of narcotics. Domestic argument related homicides in which the precipitating events are known and there is no indication of a beating at the time of the homicide incident include the following, for male victims: a quarrel over an earlier beating that the victim had administered to the offender's sister, which resulted in the sister running away; a disagreement over appropriate sexual conduct; the victim's use of narcotics; the offender spending time with friends; and the victim's not coming home to take the offender's daughter to the hospital. For female victims these nonbeating related arguments focused on the victim's court petition to support three children, and the offender's desire for custody over a son born outside of her marriage. Even some of these cases appear to involve patterns of male domination.

When arguments over money are involved, men and women are equally likely to be offenders. This is also true in "other" arguments (i.e., arguments about events other than leaving the relationship and jealousy). The following narrative case of an unemployed female and common-law husband, where their races and ages are unknown, provides an example of a money argument homicide that also involved a beating.

> The victim and offender argued over the offender's "spending the welfare money and not paying the bills." The offender struck her with fists and a number of blunt instruments. She fell backward and struck her head on a radiator. The husband carried her to the bedroom, tried unsuccessfully to awaken her, changed her clothes, and carried her to the bedroom where he placed her on a chair. The offender called the police.

Another interesting finding, although there are far too few cases for it to be definitive, is the four incidents described as "accidents" in police reports. All four of these involved female victims. Three of these incidents had no witnesses, and two of the accidents are "suspicious." One offender claimed that the victim tripped and fell on a knife. The following is another example of a suspicious accident involving a Puerto Rican housewife and her husband.

> The son visited his mother and father and brought a handgun and showed it to the father. The son checked the trigger. The father checked the trigger and pointed the gun at the wife and pulled the trigger and shot her in the head. The husband and son told the police that the victim was shot by unknown persons while she was looking out the back door. The husband later gave a statement to the police where he admitted shooting her while playing with the gun. The police report indicated that the police suspected that there was a marital quarrel involved.

In brief, this analysis of gender and the offender motivation and precipitating events associated with homicide in Chicago and Philadelphia is consistent with previous findings that reveal clear gender related patterns. It suggests that a male domination perspective is not only useful, but necessary for a full understanding of their structure and dynamics.

SUMMARY AND CONCLUSION

The existing research on gender and family violence and gender and homicide has provided statistics and conceptualizations that are often confusing and misleading. An issue of particular relevance to homicide and family violence researchers alike is the extent to which violence against women is simply a form of domestic violence or should be treated as a gender specific phenomenon characterized by identifiable patterns of male domination.

Eighty-three homicide cases involving men and women in intimate relationships in Chicago and Philadelphia were analyzed to determine if there were gender-related patterns of homicide. It was found that many of these murders were gender specific. Both gender differences in the use of murder weapons, and the descriptions of the homicide incidents, suggest a tendency toward more male aggression and more female defensive behavior in these cases. Males tended to be the initial aggressors in homicide incidents even when the ultimate offenders were female; and when males were the offenders, their actions tended to be more violent. Female offenders were most likely to kill in self-defense, while men were more likely to kill when the victim attempted to leave the relationship. In general, findings support a male domination view of women and homicide. They suggest that domestic homicides with women as victims tend to be motivated primarily by male offenders' desire for the maintenance of the gender-based status quo and the enforcement of "ownership" norms, while those homicides with male victims are more likely to be precipitated by the attempts of women to change or escape what is seen as a threatening or intolerable situation. The small size of the sample and the limitations associated with data derived from police and medical reports make these findings tentative. They do suggest, however, the need for additional research on women, murder, and male domination.

This study's findings on gender and homicide patterns support the view that many murders involving women are gender specific. For example, men and women differ in the murder methods and weapons used and in the nature of intimate victim/offender relationships involved. Although female homicide offenders are more likely to use knives (typically available from kitchens), men are more likely to utilize guns, beatings, and strangulation. These differences suggest a tendency toward more male aggression and more female defensive behavior in homicides. Although men are at greater risk when they reside with women with whom they are intimately involved, women are likely to be victims, even if they are simply involved in boyfriend/girlfriend relationships. They also have a greater chance than men of being victimized by offenders from estranged or previous relationships.

The findings on gender, homicide aggressors, victim precipitated homicide, and severity of violence also support the view of gender specific violence supportive of male domination. Men are more likely to be the aggressors in homicide incidents even when the ultimate offenders are women. Similarly, when homicides are victim precipitated, the victim is typically a man. Finally, men are generally more violent (i.e., use multiple blows in the homicides they commit) than are women.

Gender specific patterns are also suggested by most of the descriptive motivation/precipitating event homicide categories identified. Such patterns are particularly true of Chicago. The largest class of male victims involved female self-defense homicide cases, and for female victims they are concerned with the almost exclusively female victims attempted to leave relationship category. These various categories of homicides differ not only in the offenders' motivation but in the extent to which the aggression is relatively spontaneous, as in self-defense cases, or instrumental and apparently norm-enforcement related, as in those categories in which men seem to operate under "ownership" norms that men may harm women physically if they attempt to leave relationships or if they express an interest in other men. These findings support a male domination view of homicide that assumes that although domestic homicides with women as victims tend to be motivated primarily by a desire by male offenders for the maintenance of the gender based status quo, homicides involving male victims are more likely to be precipitated by the attempts of women to change or escape what is seen as a threatening or intolerable situation or system.

Although these findings provide tentative support that the variable of gender and the perspective of male domination are important in understanding women and murder in the United States, limitations in the subsample and data mandate that these conclusions be treated with caution. Their greatest value is in what they suggest is needed in the way of future research.

Implications for Further Research

Research is needed using race, ethnicity, and class as variables to determine how these factors affect the structure and dynamics of gender related homicide, and how they impact the way that the "actions" of victims and offenders are conceptualized, reported, and adjudicated. Additional research is needed on women, self-defense, murder, and the similarities and differences between those cases and others involving women as homicide victims. Finally, interactionist research strategies that are specifically designed to test gender related concepts and theories could make an important contribution in uncovering the sequential processes and patterns necessary to understand the gender specific context of American homicides involving women. Such research should use multiple data sources (e.g., police and medical examiner's records, court records, and in-depth interviews with offenders and witnesses) and methods (e.g., the analysis of official statistics and records and participant observation studies of police investigations and the local communities in which such homicides occur).

Additional research on women and homicide can make significant contributions to both our substantive and theoretical understanding of violence against women. Such knowledge may ultimately facilitate the development of effective public policy to challenge one of the still remaining physical obstacles impeding the full liberation and actualization of women.

BIBLIOGRAPHY

Berk, R. A., Berk, S. F., Loseke, D. R., & Rauma, D. (1981, July). Mutual combat and other family violence myths. Paper presented at the National Conference for Family Violence Researchers, University of New Hampshire, Durham.
Brownmiller, S. (1975). *Against our will: Men, women, and rape.* New York: Bantam.
Dobash, R. E., & Dobash, R. (1979). *Violence against wives: A case against the patriarchy.* New York: Free Press.
Douglas, J. D. (1971). *American social order: Social rules in a pluralistic society.* New York: The Free Press.
Gelles, R. J. (1979). The truth about husband abuse. In R. Gelles (Ed.), *Family violence* (pp. 137–144). Beverly Hills, CA: Sage.
Gulotta, G., & Vayaggini, M. (1976). The offender-victim system. In E. C. Viano (Ed.), *Victims and society* (pp. 50–59). Washington, DC: Visage Press.
Kitsuse, J. I., & Cicourel, A. V. (1963). A note on the uses of official statistics. *Social Problems, 11,* 131–139.
Martin, D. (1977). *Battered wives.* New York: Pocket Books.
Pleck, E., Pleck, J., Grossman, M., & Bart, P. (1977). The battered data syndrome: A comment on Steinmetz's article. *Victimology, 2*(3/4), 680–683.
Riedel, M., Zahn, M. A., & Mock, L. F. (1985). The nature and patterns of American homicide. Washington, DC: U.S. Department of Justice.
Straus, M. A. (1976). Sexual inequality, cultural norms, and wife beating. *Victimology, 1,* 54–76.
Straus, M. A., Gelles, R. J., & Steinmetz, S. K. (1980). *Behind closed doors: Violence in the American family.* Garden City, NY: Anchor.
Swigert, V. L., & Farrell, R. A. (1976). *Murder, inequality, and the law.* Lexington, MA: Lexington Books.
Wolfgang, M. E. (1958). *Patterns in criminal homicide.* Philadelphia: University of Pennsylvania Press.
Yllo, K. (1981, July). Using a feminist approach in quantitative research: A case study. Paper presented

at the National Conference for Family Violence Researchers, University of New Hampshire, Durham.

Zahn, M. A. (1975). The female homicide victim. *Criminology, 13,* 400–415.

Zahn, M. A. (1980). Homicide in the twentieth century United States. In J. A. Inciardi and C. E. Faupel (Eds.), *History and crime: Implications for criminal justice policy* (pp. 111–132). Beverly Hills, CA: Sage.

PART IV

VIOLENCE IN DATING RELATIONSHIPS

9

Sexual Abuse in Dating Relationships

Maureen A. Pirog-Good
School of Public and Environmental Affairs, Indiana University,
Bloomington

INTRODUCTION

This chapter examines factors that influence women inflicting and sustaining sexual abuse in dating relationships. We analyze the influence of women's past experiences, specifically whether they have witnessed or experienced violence in childhood; their self-esteem; and characteristics of their dating history including their total number of dates over the past year, their number of dating partners, and whether they were deeply involved in a relationship. Utilizing the 171 white, heterosexual females, we find that women who inflict and sustain sexual abuse have low self-esteem and date frequently. Additionally, the number of dating partners has a positive and significant effect on the number of sexually abusive incidents sustained by women.

In the dating population, sexual abuse occurs more frequently than physical abuse (Stets & Pirog-Good, 1987b; compare Makepeace, 1987, and Korman & Leslie, 1982). Moreover, the lesser intimate forms of sexual abuse are the most common (Kanin, 1957; Korman & Leslie, 1982; Stets & Pirog-Good, 1987b). Nonetheless, most of the dating violence literature has focused exclusively on physical, nonsexual abuse (Makepeace, 1981; Laner & Thompson, 1982; Cate, Henton, Koval, Christopher, & Lloyd, 1982; Henton, Cate, Koval, Lloyd, & Christopher, 1983; Bogal-Allbritten & Allbritten, 1985; Roscoe & Benaske, 1985; Stets & Pirog-Good, 1987a), or date rape (Russell, 1982; Kilpatrick, Veronen, & Best, 1984; Koss, Leonard, Beezley, & Oros, 1985). This research examines factors associated with a wide variety of sexually abusive acts. Using retrospective, self-report survey data, we estimate models designed to predict women inflicting and sustaining sexual abuse.

Maureen A. Pirog-Good is an associate professor of public policy analysis in the School of Public and Environmental Affairs (SPEA) at Indiana University. She has a B.A. and an M.A. in economics from Boston College as well as a Ph.D. in policy analysis from the University of Pennsylvania. Upon completing her Ph.D. in 1981, Dr. Pirog-Good taught in the Finance Department of the Wharton School at the University of Pennsylvania. Her current areas of research and expertise include teenage parenting, child support enforcement, programs for abusive men, and physical and sexual abuse in dating relationships. She coedited *Violence in Dating Relationships: Emerging Social Issues*, published by Praegar in 1989. Her articles have appeared in a wide variety of journals including *Social Psychology Quarterly, Social Science Quarterly, Journal of Social and Personal Relationships, Public Budgeting and Finance, Contemporary Policy Issues*, and *Sociological Methods and Research*. In addition, Dr. Pirog-Good has conducted research for numerous organizations including the Brookings Institution, the U.S. Department of Transportation, the Ford Foundation, the Rockefeller Foundation, and the Woodrow Wilson School at Princeton University. On the subject of programs for abusive men, she has served as an expert witness for the U.S. Department of Justice.

THEORY AND HYPOTHESES

We adopt the perspective that the causes of sexual abuse are multiple. That is, the probabilities of inflicting and sustaining sexual abuse are conditioned on a variety of influences such as individuals' past experiences, feelings about themselves, and the nature of their current relationships. Those factors that we examine include witnessing abuse between parents as a child, experiencing child abuse, self-esteem, and characteristics of one's dating history including the total number of dates over the past year, the number of dating partners, and whether or not the respondent was deeply involved in a relationship.

Witnessing and Experiencing Abuse

Learning theorists indicate that aggression is learned through early life experiences (Bandura, Ross, & Ross, 1961). In adulthood, violence emerges between intimates as a result of repeating behaviors that one has observed or experienced when young. Thus, we hypothesize that witnessing and experiencing abuse in childhood will positively influence inflicting and sustaining abuse while dating.

Within the dating violence literature, some support for the generational transmission of violence is evidenced (Laner & Thompson, 1982; Bernard & Bernard, 1983; Roscoe & Benaske, 1985), while others have found that it is only relevant in explaining men's involvement in abusive relationships (Stets & Pirog-Good, 1987a; Gwartney-Gibbs, Stockard, & Bohmer, 1987). Although the results have been somewhat inconsistent on the generational thesis of violence, it still continues to be an important theory predicting abuse (Hotaling & Sugarman, 1986) and thus is included in our analysis.

Self-Esteem

Marital and dating violence research reveals that low self-esteem influences abuse (Walker, 1979; Goldstein & Rosenbaum, 1985; Hotaling & Sugarman, 1986; Deal & Wampler, 1986). The social psychological literature suggests that low self-esteem may bring about deviant behavior (Kaplan, 1980, 1982a, 1982b). Consequently, we hypothesize that low self-esteem will positively influence inflicting and sustaining sexual abuse in courtship.

Dating Characteristics

Several characteristics of the individual's dating history are included in this analysis. First, the number of dating partners over the past year and the total number of dates are included as measures of the opportunity for sexual abuse to occur. Exposure to more personalities and more frequent dating may increase the probabilities of inflicting and sustaining sexual abuse by increasing one's exposure to situations in which such abuse might occur.

Second, we examine the degree of behavioral involvement in dating relationships. Most research in courtship violence reveals that the more serious the relationship, the greater the likelihood that abuse will occur (Cate et al., 1982; Laner & Thompson, 1982; Laner, 1983; Henton et al., 1983; Sigelman, Berry, & Wiles, 1984; Roscoe & Benaske, 1985; Stets & Pirog-Good, 1987a; Arias, Samios, & O'Leary, 1987). Dating relationships in which there is high behavioral involvement may be characteristic of a deeper level of commitment, individuals knowing each other for a longer time, and possessing intimate knowledge about each other. If commitment to the relationship is breached (perhaps by dating another) or sensitive information about oneself is disclosed to others, it may be the basis for inflicting or sustaining abuse. Thus, we expect behavioral involvement, a characteristic of serious relationships, to positively influence inflicting and sustaining courtship violence.

METHODS

Sample and Data

During the spring of 1986, a random sample of 56, upper-level classes at a large Midwestern university was obtained. Letters were sent to each professor in the sampled classes explaining our research and asking them if they would agree to have their students participate in our study. Of the 56 professors solicited, 25 agreed to participate in this study. Refusals, as well as those willing to participate, were evenly distributed across disciplines and class sizes. The reasons for refusing to participate included "the class was cancelled," "insufficient class time," and "the student and professor met on a one-on-one basis and confidentiality of the questionnaire could not be insured."

The pen and paper survey instruments were administered to students in attendance by their professors. The classes were instructed as to the seriousness of the project, insured that their responses were anonymous, and were allowed 40 minutes to complete the questionnaire. No students refused to participate. Individuals excluded from the study were nonwhite or had not dated within the past 12 months. Inferences concerning racial differences in abusive relationships could not be made reliably given that fewer than 10 nonwhite responses were obtained. The final sample included 171 usable responses from white females who had dated within the past 12 months. Because of the relatively small sample size and potential selectivity biases introduced by the sampling methods, the representativeness of this sample cannot be guaranteed.

The survey instrument covered four broad areas including demographic information, witnessing and experiencing violence in childhood, self-esteem, and dating information. With regard to the dating information, each respondent provided information on as many as four dating partners. Individuals dating more than four partners were asked to provide information on the four dating partners whom they regarded as the most important. The format of the questionnaire was primarily multiple choice, though several open-ended questions were included.

Measures

To measure whether respondents inflicted sexual abuse (INFLICT) within the past year, they were asked if they had *used* each of the following sexual activities *against their partner's will* with up to four dating partners: (1) necking, (2) chest fondling, (3) genital fondling, (4) oral sex, and (5) intercourse. These items formed a scale with an omega reliability (Heise & Bohrnstedt, 1979) of .98. Respondents were also asked if they *sustained* these sexual activities *against their own will* with up to four dating partners (SUSTAIN). These items formed a scale with an omega reliability of .82. The incidence of sexual abuse was measured by summing the number of sexually abusive incidents across all partners for each respondent.

To measure whether respondents witnessed parental violence (PARENTV) and/or experienced violence as a child (CHILDV), we used the "violence" tactics items from the Conflict Tactics Scale (CTS) (Straus, 1979). The eight "violence" tactics include physically coercive acts ranging in severity from "pushing, grabbing, or shoving" to "using a knife or gun." Respondents indicated the frequency with which their parents used each "violence" tactic with one another and with the respondent during the worst year of their childhood. Each act of violence was weighted for seriousness (Straus, 1982), then cumulated.

The measure of self-esteem (SELFEST) was the Rosenberg Self-Esteem Scale (Rosenberg, 1979). The scale has high reliability, and concurrent and construct validity.

Three dating history variables were constructed to capture both the opportunity for abuse to occur as well as the depth of involvement with one's dating partners. The measures that proxy the opportunity for abuse to occur include the number of dating partners (NUMPART) and the total number of dates (TDATES) within the past year. The degree to which a woman was deeply involved in a relationship (INVOLVED) is a dummy variable that equals one if the respondent had dated one or more partners at least once a week for at least six months.

RESULTS

The average respondent was 21 years of age. The typical woman had an average of two dating partners and 76 dates during the past year. Seventy percent of the women were deeply involved in a relationship. Twenty-eight percent of the respondents had witnessed acts of violence between their parents and 80% reported being the target of at least one act of physical aggression by their parents.

Sixteen percent of the women reported inflicting sexually abusive behavior. The most frequent forms of sexual behavior forced on their partners were necking (13%), followed by genital fondling (6%), oral sex (4%), intercourse (3%), and chest fondling (2%). More women reported sustaining sexual abuse. Twenty-six percent of the respondents reported a sexual victimization by one or more dating partners within the prior 12 months. In order of decreasing frequency, respondents most frequently experienced necking (15%), chest fondling (12%), genital fondling (11%), oral sex (11%), and intercourse (9%) against their will.

When sexual abuse occurs, it appears to become an established pattern of behavior. For those women who inflicted sexual abuse, there was an average of 56 abusive sexual acts in the past year. For women who sustained sexual abuse, there was an average of 37 sexually abusive acts that they sustained. Thus, many individuals may view mild forms of sexual abuse as normal.

To explore, in a multivariate context, the determinants of sexual abuse, we estimated tobit models. Tobit models are appropriate when the dependent variable has a lower limiting value of zero for most observations but takes many values for the remaining observations (Amemiya, 1974). Most respondents neither inflicted nor sustained sexual abuse, but among those who had, there was diversity in the frequency of these acts. Results of our tobit models appear in Table 9-1. Maximum likelihood ratio tests indicate that both models are significant at the .001 level.

Table 9-1   Means and standard deviations of the variables and tobit estimates for inflicting and sustaining sexual abuse for women

Variables	Mean	SD	Tobit estimates	
			INFLICT ABUSE	SUSTAIN ABUSE
CONSTANT			184.18	29.15
PARENTV	6.53	25.40	− .54	− .02
CHILDV	14.10	29.16	− .13	.29
SELFEST	31.96	3.96	− 11.81**	− 4.43**
NUMPART	2.01	1.15	− 39.64	14.25**
TDATES	75.71	43.89	2.45***	.49**
INVOLVED	.70	.46	− 110.5*	− 13.54
INFLICT	8.79	54.76		
SUSTAIN	9.68	31.15		

$*p < .10; **p < .05; ***p < .001$.
$N = 171$ for both equations.
The maximum likelihood ratio tests for both equations are significant at the .001 level.

As indicated in Table 9-1, low self-esteem and frequent dating predict inflicting sexual abuse. A deep involvement in a relationship exerts a large, negative, and modestly significant effect on the propensity to be sexually abusive. Low self-esteem, the number of dating partners, and the frequency of dating predict victimization.[1] These findings are discussed below.

Self-Esteem

The results indicate that low self-esteem is positively related to the number of sexually abusive acts inflicted. However, small decreases in self-esteem among women with high or average levels of self-esteem will not result in behavioral changes. Because we are interested in behavioral change, we calculated the threshold values of self-esteem below which further decreases in self-esteem would result in increases in the frequency of sexually abusive acts. To do this, we used the regression coefficients in Table 9-1, set the values of PARENTV, CHILDV, and TDATES to their means, and systematically varied the remaining independent variables as indicated in Table 9-2.

As shown in Table 9-2, when the number of dating partners increases, the threshold values of self-esteem decline. That is, as the number of dating partners increases, self-esteem must fall to progressively lower levels before increases in inflicting sexual abuse occur. Additionally, the threshold values of self-esteem below which behavioral changes are observed are considerably higher for women who are not deeply involved in a dating relationship.

Self-esteem also predicts sustaining sexual abuse. In Table 9-1, we see that a one-point decrease in self-esteem increases the number of sexual victimizations by 4.43

[1]The correlation between the variables TDATES and INVOLVED was .70 indicating some degree of collinearity. When the variable INVOLVED was excluded from the models, TDATES remained significant for using and receiving sexual abuse. When the variable TDATES was excluded from the models, INVOLVED remained nonsignificant. These results indicate that collinearity did not affect the estimates in our models.

over one year. However, the threshold values in Table 9-2 suggest that small decreases in self-esteem for women with average or above average values of self-esteem will not affect sexual victimization. Decreases in self-esteem will increase victimizations only if the decreases in self-esteem are very large, causing self-esteem to fall below its threshold or if a woman begins with a very low value of self-esteem. Also, we find that self-esteem must fall below progressively lower levels as the number of dating partners increases before increases in sexual victimizations will occur.

Because of the limitations of the data, the fact that low self-esteem predicts inflicting and sustaining sexual abuse among women should be viewed cautiously. Although diminished self-esteem may increase the probabilities of inflicting and sustaining sexual abuse, it is also possible that abused or abusive women have lower self-esteem as a consequence of sexual aggression. Future research should employ panel data to help determine causality.

Dating Frequency

The second variable that exerts a strong significant effect on inflicting and sustaining sexual abuse is the total number of dates in the preceding year. Turning first to inflicting sexual abuse, Table 9-1 reveals that each additional date increases the predicted number of sexually abusive acts by 2.45. Threshold values of dating frequency above which further increases in dating would result in increases in the frequency of sexually abusive acts were calculated. Results are given in Table 9-3.

Table 9-3 reveals that for women who are deeply involved in a relationship, and who have one, two, three or four partners, their dating frequency must exceed 142, 159, 175, and 191 dates per year, respectively, before an increase in sexual abuse will occur. For women who are not deeply involved, the threshold values of the frequency of dating are lower. Regardless of whether or not they were deeply involved in a dating relationship, only three respondents or 2% of our sample actually exceeded these threshold values. Thus, while the effect of increasing one's dating frequency on the number of sexually abusive acts committed is quite large, it is only discernible for

Table 9-2 Threshold values of self-esteem below which behavioral changes are observed for inflicting and sustaining sexual abuse under conditions of an involved and not involved relationship for up to four partners

Number of partners	INFLICT ABUSE		SUSTAIN ABUSE	
	INVOLVED = 0	INVOLVED = 1	INVOLVED = 0	INVOLVED = 1
1	27	18	19	16
2	24	15	22	19
3	21	11	25	22
4	17	8*	29	26

*This value falls below the minimum score on the self-esteem scale. Therefore, self-esteem has no effect on inflicting sexual abuse.

The values of PARENTV, CHILDV, and TDATES were set at their sample means of 6.53, 14.1, and 75.71, respectively. Because INVOLVED is a dichotomous variable, the sample mean, .70, is not meaningful. Therefore, results are presented for women who are or are not deeply involved in a relationship (INVOLVED = 1, INVOLVED = 0, respectively.).

Table 9-3   Threshold values of the number of dates above which behavioral changes are observed for inflicting and sustaining sexual abuse under conditions of an involved and not involved relationship with up to four partners

	INFLICT ABUSE		SUSTAIN ABUSE	
Number of partners	INVOLVED = 0	INVOLVED = 1	INVOLVED = 0	INVOLVED = 1
1	97	142	192	220
2	114	159	163	191
3	130	175	134	162
4	146	191	105	133

The values of PARENTV, CHILDV, and SELFEST were set at their sample means of 6.52, 14.1, and 31.96, respectively. Because INVOLVED is a dichotomous variable, the sample mean, .70, is not meaningful. Therefore, results are presented for women who are or are not deeply involved in a relationship (INVOLVED = 1, INVOLVED = 0, respectively).

those women who date *very* frequently and fall into the upper extremes of the dating frequency distribution.

Dating frequency also significantly and positively predicts sustaining sexual abuse. However, the women who actually experience sexual victimization as a result of increased dating again fall into the extreme right tail of the dating frequency distribution. Women who are not deeply involved must have an average yearly dating frequency in excess of 192, 163, 134, and 105 if they date one through four individuals, respectively. Women who are deeply involved must date even more frequently to increase the probability of sustaining sexual abuse. Only 3% of all respondents exceeded these threshold values.

Other Variables

Other variables that predict inflicting and sustaining sexual abuse include the number of dating partners and a deeply involved relationship. For women with a deep involvement, every partner above five increases sustaining sexual abuse by 14 sexual acts a year or slightly more than one per month (see Table 9-1). Women without a deep involvement will not experience increased sexual victimization unless they increase their number of dating partners above six. For each partner in excess of six, an increase in sexual victimization of slightly more than one per month is predicted.

Whether a woman is deeply involved in a dating relationship exerts a very large and modestly significant effect on the number of sexually abusive acts perpetrated. We view this variable as a measure of one's depth of involvement in a relationship and had anticipated a positive effect. Contrary to our expectations, the effect is negative, indicating that women who are deeply involved are less likely to be sexually abusive, although, for women with average characteristics, this effect is not observable. The effect of a deep involvement only becomes discernible as self-esteem decreases, the number of dating partners declines, and/or dating frequency increases.

DISCUSSION

We thought that women who witnessed physical abuse between parents *and* experienced violence as a child would be more likely to inflict and sustain sexual abuse because they had learned that aggression was acceptable. However, the results provide no support for this hypothesis. One reason why childhood experiences may not predict sexual abuse is because of the poor recollection of students in retrospective studies like ours. Alternatively, witnessing and experiencing physical, *nonsexual* abuse in childhood may not affect *sexual* abuse in adulthood. Rather, it may be that sexually abused children are more likely to be sexually abusive or victimized in adulthood. Future research should explore this possibility.

We found that perpetrators and victims of sexual abuse while dating have low self-esteem. It must be remembered, however, that a small decrease in a woman's self-esteem will not increase the frequency of inflicting or sustaining sexual abuse unless the woman already has a very low self-esteem. Moreover, in instances where a woman is deeply involved in a relationship, her self-esteem must be at an extremely low level before further decreases in self-esteem will influence inflicting or sustaining sexual abuse. Therefore, if we slightly lower the self-esteem of women who are average or above average on self-esteem, an increase in the probabilities of sexual abuse will not occur.

Women with low self-esteem may be more likely to inflict sexual abuse because they may feel that through sexuality, they are wanted, desired, loved, and thus important. This, in turn, would act to raise their self-esteem (Kaplan, 1980). Women with low self-esteem may be more likely to sustain sexual abuse because they may feel that they deserve it. Although there is theoretical support for the relationship between self-esteem and sexual abuse found in this study, as discussed above, the limitations of cross-sectional data require us to acknowledge the distinct possibility that inflicting or sustaining sexual abuse may diminish self-esteem.

Turning to the characteristics of the relationship, we viewed dating frequency as a measure of the opportunity for abuse to occur. Our results do indicate that the more frequently a woman dates, the greater her risk of being sexually abusive or sexually victimized. Also as the number of dating partners increases, sexual victimization is more likely to occur. By exposing herself to a larger number of dating partners, the potential for conflict over sexual issues increases.[2] On the other hand, behavioral involvement does not predict sexual victimization and has a large but weakly significant effect on inflicting sexually abusive behavior.

In general, the findings in this research indicate that, for women, a low self-esteem and the opportunity for sexual abuse to occur influence inflicting and sustaining sexual abuse while dating. Clearly, this is not all there is to sexual abuse. This chapter does not examine situational factors that may influence sexual abuse. For example, a woman may be more likely to use sexual abuse at a particular place, for example, her home, where she feels more in control of her mate and the situation, and where she feels freer to initiate sexual activity. Additionally, sexual activity may occur against one's own or the other's will because there is a lack of communication of one's sexual

---

[2]The number of partners a woman is dating could operationalize the depth of involvement in a relationship. That is, the fewer the number of partners a woman is dating, the greater the possibility that she is involved with one person. However, the variable INVOLVED provides a more direct measure of the depth of involvement in a relationship.

desires. Future research needs to explore situational factors such as these that may influence sexual abuse.

BIBLIOGRAPHY

Amemiya, T. (1974). Multivariate regression and simultaneous equation models when the dependent variables are truncated normal. *Econometrica, 42,* 999–1011.

Arias, I., Samios, M., & O'Leary, K. D. (1987). Prevalence and correlates of physical aggression during courtship. *Journal of Interpersonal Violence, 2,* 82–90.

Bandura, A., Ross, D., & Ross, S. A. (1961). Transmission of aggression through imitation of aggressive models. *Journal of Abnormal and Social Psychology, 63,* 575–582.

Bernard, M. L., & Bernard, J. L. (1983). Violent intimacy: The family as a model for love relationships. *Family Relations, 32,* 283–286.

Bogal-Allbritten, R. B., & Allbritten, W. L. (1985). The hidden victims: Courtship violence among college students. *Journal of College Student Personnel, 26(3),* 201–204.

Cate, R., Henton, J., Koval, J., Christopher, F. S., & Lloyd. S. (1982). Premarital abuse: A social psychological perspective. *Journal of Family Issues, 3,* 79–80.

Deal, J. E., & Wampler, K. S. (1986). Dating violence: The primacy of previous experience. *Journal of Social and Personal Relationships, 3,* 457–471.

Goldstein, D., & Rosenbaum, A. (1985). An evaluation of the self-esteem of maritally violent men. *Family Relations, 34,* 425–428.

Gwartney-Gibbs, P. A., Stockard, J., & Bohmer, S. (1987). Learning courtship aggression: The influence of parents, peers, and personal experiences. *Family Relations, 36,* 276–282.

Heise, D. R., & Bohrnstedt, G. W. (1979). Validity, invalidity, and reliability. In E. F. Borgatta & G. W. Bohrnstedt (Eds.), *Sociological methodology* (pp. 104–129). San Francisco: Jossey-Bass.

Henton, J., Cate, R., Koval, J., Lloyd, S., & Christopher, F. (1983). Romance and violence in dating relationships. *Journal of Family Issues, 4,* 467–482.

Hotaling, G. T., & Sugarman, D. B. (1986). An analysis of risk markers in husband to wife violence: The current state of knowledge. *Violence and Victims, 1,* 101–124.

Kanin, E. J. (1957). Male aggression in dating-courtship relations. *American Journal of Sociology, 63,* 197–204.

Kaplan, H. H. (1980). *Deviant behavior in defense of self.* New York: Academic Press.

Kaplan, H. (1982a). Self-attitudes and deviant response. In M. Rosenberg & H. H. Kaplan (Eds.), *Social psychology of the self-concept* (pp. 452–465). Arlington Heights, IL: Harlan Davidson.

Kaplan, H. (1982b). Deviant behavior and self-enhancement in adolescence. In M. Rosenberg & H. H. Kaplan (Eds.), *Social psychology of the self-concept* (pp. 466–482). Arlington Heights, IL: Harlan Davidson.

Kilpatrick, D. G., Veronen, L. J., & Best, C. L. (1984). Factors predicting psychological distress among rape victims. In C. R. Figley (Ed.), *Trauma and its wake: The study of treatment of post-traumatic stress disorder* (pp. 113–141). New York: Brunner/Mazel.

Korman, S. A., & Leslie, G. R. (1982). The relationship of feminist ideology and date expense sharing to perceptions of sexual aggression in dating. *The Journal of Sex Research, 18,* 114–129.

Koss, M. P., Leonard, K. E., Beezley, D. A., & Oros, C. J. (1985). Non-stranger sexual aggression: A discriminant analysis of the psychological characteristics of undetected offenders. *Sex Roles, 12,* 981–992.

Laner, M. R. (1983). Courtship abuse and aggression: Contextual aspects. *Sociological Spectrum, 3,* 69–83.

Laner, M. R., & Thompson, J. (1982). Abuse and aggression in courting couples. *Deviant Behavior: An Interdisciplinary Journal, 3,* 229–244.

Makepeace, J. M. (1981). Courtship violence among college students. *Family Relations, 30,* 97–102.

Makepeace, J. M. (1986). Social factor and victim-offender differences in courtship violence. *Family Relations, 38,* 87–91.

Roscoe, B., & Benaske, N. (1985). Courtship violence experienced by abused wives: Similarities in patterns of abuse. *Family Relations, 34,* 419–424.

Rosenberg, M. (1979). *Conceiving the self.* New York: Basic Books.

Russell, D. E. (1982). *Rape in marriage.* New York: Macmillan.

Sigelman, C. K., Berry, C. J., & Wiles, K. A. (1984). Violence in college students' dating relationships. *Journal of Applied Social Psychology, 14(6),* 530–548.

Stets, J. E., & Pirog-Good, M. A. (1987a). Violence in dating relationships. *Social Psychology Quarterly,*
    52, 225–233.
Stets, J. E., & Pirog-Good, M. A. (1989). Patterns of physical and sexual abuse for men and women in
    dating relationships: A descriptive analysis. *Journal of Family Violence, 4*(1), 63–76.
Straus, M. A. (1979). Measuring intrafamily conflict and violence: The conflict tactics scale. *Journal of*
    Marriage and the Family, 41, 75–88.
Straus, M. A. (1982). A reevaluation of the conflict tactics scale violence measures and some new mea-
    sures. Durham, NH: Family Violence Research Program.
Walker, L. E. (1979). *The battered woman.* New York: Harper and Row.

10

Male Versus Female Initiation of Aggression: The Case of Courtship Violence

Alfred DeMaris
Bowling Green State University, Ohio

INTRODUCTION

This chapter examines the commonly held assumption that female violence in relationships is primarily a response—either defensive or retaliatory—to prior aggression on the part of the man. A biracial sample of 865 students attending four universities in the Southeast yielded a subsample of 218 respondents who reported violence in a current or previous relationship and who further identified the usual initiator of violence in the relationship. Regardless of race, reports of male and female respondents were in agreement that when one partner could be said to be the usual initiator of violence, that partner was typically the woman. The data suggest that, at least for courting relationships, a substantial amount of interpersonal violence is initiated by women. A productive direction for future research would be to focus on violence as a process that involves inputs from both partners.

The theoretical position that violence is best understood in terms of factors that lead one sex to assault the other characterizes much of the sociology of family violence. In particular, the family violence problem is usually conceptualized by researchers as the problem of men assaulting women, in the interest of maintaining a culturally prescribed position of dominance within the family (Allen & Straus, 1980; Dibble & Straus, 1980; Pagelow, 1985; Straus, 1977; Straus, 1980; Wardell, Gillespie, & Leffler, 1983; Yllo, 1983). The fact that men resort to using violence to attain this end is attributed to the influence of many factors, including the intergenerational transmission of proviolent attitudes and behavior (Kalmuss, 1984), the imbalance of resources between partners in a relationship (Allen & Straus, 1980; Hornung, McCullough, & Sugimoto, 1981), life events stress (Farrington, 1980; Makepeace, 1983), and the perception of a "license to hit" that accrues to marital or quasimarital relationships (Cate, Henton, Koval, Christopher, & Lloyd, 1982; Straus, 1980).

This position tends to encourage the view that female violence in relationships is predominantly responsive, rather than offensive. Although most survey data show

Alfred DeMaris is an associate professor in the Department of Sociology at Bowling Green State University, in Ohio. His areas of specialization are the family and quantitative methods. Research interests include both basic and applied research on family violence and other indicia of family distress. Articles generated by his research on family violence have appeared in *Journal of Family Issues, Social Service Review,* and *Social Casework.*

that women report being physically aggressive with their partners at rates approaching those for men (Straus & Gelles, 1986), most are of the opinion that such "aggression" is primarily defensive, or perhaps, retaliatory. The situation in which it is the woman who actually initiates most of the violence is considered atypical (Straus & Gelles, 1986; Makepeace, 1986; Pleck, Pleck, Grossman, & Bart, 1978; Saunders, 1986; Stets & Pirog-Good, 1987).

The issue is not easily resolved from current data because most studies to date have not allowed a clear identification to be made of who actually initiated most or all of the violent encounters, except when only the man or the woman is reported to be the violent partner. Even in the latter case, however, it is not firmly established that the woman is the aggressor. For example, if the respondent is the husband or boyfriend, he may only be underreporting his own violence (Edelson & Brygger, 1986). If the respondent is a woman, there is still the possibility that her actions constituted a "preemptive strike," designed to prevent what she perceived to be an impending attack by her partner (Saunders, 1986).

Very few studies have asked respondents to identify which partner was the primary initiator of violence. Some exceptions are the studies by Saunders (1986) and Makepeace (1983). Saunders's study of 52 battered women seeking help through shelters and counseling found that most of these respondents described their own violence as self defense or fighting back; only five women indicated that much of their violence was initiated by them (Saunders, 1986). Makepeace asked respondents in courting relationships to identify who first used violence in their relationship, and what their own motives for using violence were. He found a tendency for respondents to perceive the other person as initiator regardless of sex, although 27.7% of men and 22.9% of women claimed to be the first to use violence. Regarding motives for violence, he found that slightly more than one-third of the females, 35.6%, claimed self defense. However, despite the fact that 64.4% had other motives, Makepeace concluded that "female use of violence, even when for the conscious purpose of causing harm, is predominantly self-defensive" (Makepeace, 1986, p. 385).

This study further explores the initiation of violence in premarital relationships with a sample of both white and black college students. Although violence during courtship is not expected to mirror the dynamics of marital violence, many argue that the patterns are similar, and that courtship violence provides a "training ground" for later marital aggression (Laner & Thompson, 1982; Makepeace, 1981; Roscoe & Benaske, 1985). It is therefore fruitful to examine male-female differences in initiation of violence during courtship in an attempt to shed additional light on the role that female-initiated violence plays in heterosexual relationships.

HYPOTHESES

Prior conceptualization and research led to the formation of several research hypotheses. The first follows directly from the assumption that men are the primary initiators of aggression. *Hypothesis 1: Men will be more likely than women to be reported by both sexes to initiate violence in relationships.*

Another sex difference reported for married couples in the literature is that husbands tend to see relationships as mutually violent, while wives tend to see them as husband-violent (Browning & Dutton, 1986). Assuming that this difference applies to relationships in general leads to the next hypothesis. *Hypothesis 2: Men will be more likely to report that violence was mutually initiated and that violence was female-initiated, compared to women.*

All acts of violence are not of the same intensity. Often a distinction is made between minor and severe violence (Straus & Gelles, 1986; Kalmuss & Straus, 1982). Although men would be expected to initiate both more often than women, it is plausible that women might be more likely to initiate minor than severe violence. One would therefore expect level of violence to interact with sex differences in initiation as follows: *Hypothesis 3: The sex difference in initiation hypothesized above (Hypothesis 1) will be greater for severe violence than for minor violence.*

It is of further interest to explore whether potential sex differences in initiation of violence vary by race. With a few exceptions, research in this area is largely confined to white populations; much less is known about the dynamics of relationship violence among blacks. There are almost no data on courtship violence for this ethnic group.

Compared to whites, blacks have been found to be both more likely to approve of, and to have actually used, interspousal violence, although most of these differences disappear when socioeconomic status is controlled (Cazenave & Straus, 1979; Lockhart, 1987). In the current study, then, blacks might be more likely than whites to take responsibility for being the aggressor, by virtue of their greater endorsement of interpersonal violence in relationships. *Hypothesis 4: Blacks will be more likely than whites to report that violence was initiated by the respondent.*

Finally, there is no evidence to suggest that black women are any more likely than white women to initiate violence. Therefore, it is expected that there will be no interaction of race with the relationship between sex and initiation. *Hypothesis 5: Male-female differences in initiation of violence will be the same regardless of race.*

For statistical purposes, all hypotheses will be subjected to two-tailed tests to allow for the possibility of accepting an alternative hypothesis that is contrary in either direction from the null.

METHODS

The data for this paper come from a larger study of courtship violence, based on a sample of black and white college students attending four different universities in the Southeast. The enrollment at two schools was primarily black, another was racially mixed, and the fourth was primarily white. Selection of universities in this fashion was purposefully done in order to ensure roughly equivalent numbers of blacks and whites in the final sample. Respondents were solicited through introductory sociology classes at each school, and data were gathered via questionnaires completed during class.

Respondents who either had never had a heterosexual involvement, or who were currently married were eliminated from the sample. There remained a total of 865 individuals who reported being either currently involved or having had a heterosexual involvement at some time. The final sample constitutes a subset of this group.

The Sample

The race and sex distribution for the 865 respondents in the larger study was as follows: 27.1% were black women, 14.9% were black men, 33.3% were white women, and 24.7% were white men. Median age for the group as a whole was 20. The majority were either freshmen or sophomores (74.2%), while 18.5% were juniors, 6.9% were seniors, and .3% reported "other" as their classification. There were no graduate students in this group.

An examination of declared majors indicated that virtually all fields were represented, although social sciences and history may be somewhat overrepresented, with 14% in this category. Other fields claimed by substantial proportions of the sample were business (24.4%), health professions (14%), education (7.1%), and engineering (6.5%). About 5% were undecided. Sixty-eight percent were currently involved in a relationship, while 32% were not.

The sample for this chapter consists of a subset of 218 of these respondents who stated that either they or their partners had been violent in their current or most recent relationship, and who further provided usable information regarding which partner usually initiated the violence. In the total sample, 37.4% reported inflicting violence, while 31% reported sustaining violence.

Measures

The variables for this study were sex, race, level of violence, and usual initiator of violence. The occurrence of violence was measured by the Conflict Tactics Scale (Straus, 1979). In particular, those individuals who reported inflicting or sustaining any of the acts from "threw something at the other" through and including "used a knife or gun" were considered to have experienced violence. Following previous usage (Straus & Gelles, 1986; Kalmuss & Straus, 1982), the items "threw something at the other," "pushed, grabbed, or shoved the other," and "slapped the other" were considered minor; all other acts were considered severe violence. Respondents who indicated engaging in only minor violence were coded "minor" on this variable. All others were coded "severe."

The usual initiator of violence was assessed with the following item: "If you and your partner have *both* been violent in your current or most recent relationship, which of the following statements best describes who usually threatened to hit *first, started* pushing or shoving, or threw the *first* slap or punch?" The answer categories were "my partner always initiated the violence," "my partner usually initiated the violence," "my partner and I were equally responsible for initiating the violence," "I usually initiated the violence," "I always initiated the violence." The first two responses were coded "partner initiated," the third, "both equal," and the last two, "respondent initiated."

Most of those who answered this item were people who reported both themselves and their partners to have been violent. However, a number of respondents answering this item had reported only one person to have been violent, and that that person was also the usual initiator. These were also included as usable responses. Hence, to be included in the analysis, respondents had to have answered the item regarding initiation. This requirement was imposed in order to avoid the problem, discussed above, of inferring that a particular partner was the usual initiator based solely on being the only one identified as having been violent.

Analysis

Loglinear analysis was employed to select the most parsimonious model that provided an adequate fit to the data. In so doing, the research hypotheses were tested by examining whether or not a specified two- or three-way relationship had to be included in the final model. Model selection began with an examination of the fit of all models of uniform order, up to order four. Subsequently, starting with the lowest-order model that still provided an adequate fit, backward elimination was employed to arrive at the most parsimonious model. During backward elimination, a term was eliminated as long as (a) the remaining terms provided a good fit to the data, as assessed by G^2 and its associated probability, and (b) the partial test for the elimination of that term was nonsignificant (Agresti, 1984; Bishop, Feinberg, & Holland, 1975; Feinberg, 1980).

FINDINGS

The test of the models of uniform order revealed that the model containing all second-order, but no third-order, terms provided an adequate fit to the data (G^2 = 16.5, p > .05). Or, alternatively, the test indicates that the hypothesis that all three-way and higher-order interactions are zero cannot be rejected. Therefore, Hypothesis 5 is supported, but Hypothesis 3 is not.

Table 10-1 presents the results of the backward elimination procedure staring with the full second-order model. Shown are: the "best model" at the end of each cycle in which a term is considered for elimination, the fit of the model that excludes that term (df, G^2, Prob), and the partial test for the difference in fit of the model with and without that term (df,* G^2,* Prob*). Three terms in the model can be eliminated

Table 10-1 Results of model selection using backward elimination from full 2nd order model: [LR] [LI] [LS] [RI] [RS] [IS][a]

Best model	Term deleted	df	G^2	Prob	df*	G^2*	Prob*
Full 2nd order		9	16.50	.057			
	[IS]	11	32.89	.001	2	16.39	.001
	[RS]	10	20.29	.027	1	3.79	.052
	[LS]	10	16.74	.080	1	.24	.625
	[RI]	11	18.21	.077	2	1.71	.425
	[LI]	11	23.08	.017	2	6.58	.037
	[LR]	10	17.62	.062	1	1.12	.289
[IS] [RS] [RI] [LI] [LR]		10	16.74	.080			
	[IS]	12	33.95	.001	2	17.21	.001
	[RS]	11	20.70	.037	1	3.96	.047
	[RI]	12	18.43	.103	2	1.70	.428
	[LI]	12	24.14	.020	2	7.40	.025
	[LR]	11	18.03	.081	1	1.30	.255
[IS] [RS] [LI] [LR]		12	18.43	.103			
	[IS]	14	36.99	.001	2	18.56	.001
	[RS]	13	23.74	.034	1	5.31	.021
	[LI]	14	25.82	.027	2	7.39	.025
	[LR]	13	19.72	.103	1	1.28	.257
[IS] [RS] [LI][b]		13	19.72	.103			
	[IS]	15	38.50	.001	2	18.78	.001
	[RS]	14	25.25	.032	1	5.53	.019
	[LI]	15	27.33	.026	2	7.61	.022

[a]L = Level of violence; I = Usual initiator; R = Race; S = Sex.
[b]Final model.

without causing a significant change in fit. These are the terms for the relationships between sex and level of violence (LS), race and usual initiator (RI), and race and level of violence (LR). Because the RI term was not significant, Hypothesis 4 was not supported.

The last three lines in the table indicate that the relationships between sex and usual initiator of violence (IS), sex and race (RS), and level of violence and usual initiator (LI) are all significant and therefore cannot be dropped. The final model contains these three second-order relationships and provides a reasonably good fit to the data ($G^2 = 19.72, p > .1$).

Table 10-2 shows the loglinear parameter estimates and ratios of these estimates to their asymptotic standard errors for the three terms IS, RS, and LI. Under the null hypothesis that a particular parameter is zero, these ratios are approximately distributed as standard normal random variables, and can be compared to a Z-table to assess whether or not a particular effect is significant. Under the two-tailed alternative hypothesis, estimated effects that are approximately twice their standard errors would be significant. A significant effect, in this case, implies that the observed cell frequency represents a significant departure from what would be expected if that particular parameter were zero (Agresti, 1984).

The parameter estimates for the relationship between sex and race indicate that the sex distribution in the sample is not the same for blacks and whites. Among blacks there are more women, and among whites, more men, than one would expect if race and sex were independent.

An interesting relationship emerges between level of violence and who is reported to be the usual initiator. Compared to the severe violence group, those reporting only

Table 10-2 Parameter estimates and ratios of estimates to their asymptotic standard errors for 2nd order terms in the final model

Term	Parameter estimate (estimate/asymptotic SE)	
	Male	Female
Initiate		
Both equal	.171	−.171
	(1.68)	(−1.68)
Partner	.273	−.273
	(2.66)	(−2.66)
Respondent	−.443	.443
	(−4.06)	(4.06)
Race		
Black	−.169	.169
	(−2.35)	(2.35)
White	.169	−.169
	(2.35)	(−2.35)
	Minor level	Severe level
Initiate		
Both equal	.269	−.269
	(2.42)	(−2.42)
Partner	.004	−.004
	(.03)	(−.03)
Respondent	−.273	.273
	(−2.23)	(2.23)

minor violence tend more often to see the violence as mutually initiated. On the other hand, those reporting severe violence tend to see themselves as the initiators. Perhaps minor violence is less memorable, and respondents are therefore less able to recall accurately who first became physically aggressive. Severe violence, being more noteworthy, lends itself more readily to accurate recall of the specific circumstances surrounding the episode, including who initiated the violence.

The parameter estimates for the relationship between sex and usual initiator show that Hypothesis 1 was not supported. Men tend to report that violence was either mutually initiated or initiated by the partner, while women congruently report that violence was usually initiated by themselves. This can be seen more clearly by examining Table 10-3, which shows the collapsed crosstabulation of sex with usual initiator for the sample as a whole. The data suggest a fairly strong level of agreement, among both sexes, that when one partner was the usual initiator, that partner was more likely to be the woman (reported by 41% of men and 49% of women, respectively).

Although men were somewhat more likely to report that violence was mutually initiated, compared to women (39% compared to 28%), the ratios of parameter estimates to standard errors in Table 10-2 indicate that these cell frequencies do not represent significant departures from what would be expected under the hypothesis of no effects for these cells. The other four cell frequencies, however, do represent significant departures from independence. However, Table 10-3 further shows that, in fact, men in the sample are slightly *less* likely to report the woman as initiator, compared to women. Therefore, Hypothesis 2 was not supported in this study.

DISCUSSION

This chapter has examined the commonly held assumption that when women are violent in relationships, such violence is typically a response to prior male violence, rather than being initiated by women of their own accord. The data presented herein suggest that, at least for courting relationships, such is not the case. In this study, both men's and women's reports indicated that when one partner could be said to be the usual initiator of violence, that partner was most often the woman. This finding was the same for both black and white respondents.

Some cautions need to be introduced in interpreting these results. First, the data are from a limited and nonrandom sample. The respondents were all college students

Table 10-3 Unconditional distribution of usual initiator by sex, for the entire sample. Table shows percent (N) in each category

	Sex	
Initiate	Male	Female
Both equal	39 (31)	27 (38)
Partner	41 (33)	24 (33)
Respondent	20 (16)	49 (67)
Total	100 (80)	100 (138)

taking introductory sociology classes at universities in the Southeast. They were reporting on violence in nonmarital relationships only. Therefore, the results have limited generalizability beyond a population of this complexion.

However, even if they were to apply generally to the case of courtship, it is not clear that the patterns observed here would apply to marriage. Although many researchers suggest that the dynamics of courtship and marital violence are quite similar (Laner & Thompson, 1982; Makepeace, 1981; Roscoe & Benaske, 1985), others have taken issue with this position, suggesting that models of spouse abuse are not strong predictors of aggression during courtship (DeMaris, 1987). It is entirely possible that women are more physically aggressive during courtship because they are much freer to leave relationships at will. In consequence, they may be at more liberty to strike out at their partners, knowing that they are not constrained to live day-by-day with potential adversaries who are typically larger and stronger than they are.

Returning to the case of courtship, on the other hand, the data do suggest that a substantial proportion of female violence in these relationships is neither defensive nor retaliatory. Both types of "responsive" violence presume that the other partner has initiated the first attack. However, 41% of the men and 49% of the women in this study indicated that the woman was the usual initiator of violence in the relationship.

Although more research needs to be conducted to determine whether or not the present findings are an anomaly, the implication of this study is that the emphasis on the man as aggressor in relationship violence may be somewhat counterproductive to a complete understanding of this phenomenon. Undeniably, male-initiated assaults on women constitute the most serious and most frequent scenarios in relationship violence, as others have shown (Pagelow, 1985; Saunders, 1986). Yet these cases in themselves do not describe the full range of scenarios encountered. Another substantial part of relationship violence consists of mutually assaultive couples and couples in which the woman is the primary initiator of aggression.

Nevertheless, the point should be made very clear that regardless of who initiates violence, the adversaries are not evenly matched. When, as in this study, women report initiating "violence," this is not to be construed to be identical to male-initiated violence in terms of consequences to the recipient. Because heterosexual pairing is characterized by differential size, strength, and fighting ability that favors the man, aggression initiated by him usually has far more serious implications.

The importance of female-initiated aggression lies not so much in its consequences—although these can frequently be severe—as in its importance to the understanding of the "construction" of a violent relationship as a *process* involving input from both partners. Violence is an interpersonal rather than purely intrapersonal phenomenon: it takes at least two partners to have a violent relationship. The sequence of events that culminates in a violent episode is fueled by a variety of situational, psychological, social, and interactional factors. As research has verified, the other partner's violence is a major input in this sequence (Dibble & Straus, 1980). An important consequence of female initiation of violence is that it may well provide a man, not initially inclined to hit a woman, with a sense that such a response is justified as either "self-defense" or "retaliation." Such an exchange may then eventuate in serious injury to her.

A productive direction for future research might be to further explore the *initiation* of aggression, in an effort to understand the processes by which relationships *become* violent. Of particular interest are the factors that enable women to initiate attacks in the face of adversaries who, in most cases, outclass them in fighting ability. Perhaps it is a shared, yet unstated, recognition of the unfairness inherent in such an imbalance that allows women to take such a bold step. As others have noted, female violence is often not taken seriously by men, who feel that their partners are unable to do any serious damage (Pagelow, 1985). Norms among men generally dictate that it is unfair to fight with a significantly smaller or weaker opponent, and, further, that it is cowardly or beneath one's dignity to hit a woman. It may be that these attitudes and norms facilitate a level of female aggressiveness within intimate relationships that does not exist in society at large. It remains for future studies to examine these processes in greater detail.

BIBLIOGRAPHY

Agresti, A. (1984). *Analysis of ordinal categorical data.* New York: Wiley.
Allen, C. M., & Straus, M. A. (1980). Resources, power, and husband-wife violence. In Murray A. Straus & Gerald T. Hotaling (Eds.), *The social causes of husband-wife violence* (pp. 188–208). Minneapolis, MN: University of Minnesota Press.
Bishop, Y. M. M., Fienberg, S. E., & Holland, P. W. (1975). *Discrete multivariate analysis: Theory and practice.* Cambridge, MA: MIT Press.
Browning, J., & Dutton, D. (1986). Assessment of wife assault with the conflict tactics scale: Using couple data to quantify the differential reporting effect. *Journal of Marriage and the Family, 48,* 375–379.
Cate, R. M., Henton, J. M., Koval, J., Scott, F. C., & Lloyd, S. (1982). Premarital abuse: A social psychological perspective. *Journal of Family Issues, 3,* 79–90.
Cazenave, N. A., & Straus, M. A. (1979). Race, class, network embeddedness and family violence: A search for potent support systems. *Journal of Comparative Family Studies, 10,* 281–300.
DeMaris, A. (1987). The efficacy of a spouse abuse model in accounting for courtship violence. *Journal of Family Issues, 8,* 291–305.
Dibble, U., & Straus, M. A. (1980). Some social structure determinants of inconsistency between attitudes and behavior: The case of family violence. *Journal of Marriage and the Family, 42,* 71–80.
Edleson, J. L., & Brygger, M. P. (1986). Gender differences in reporting of battering incidences. *Family Relations, 35,* 377–382.
Farrington, K. M. (1980). Stress and family violence. In Murray A. Straus & Gerald T. Hotaling (Eds.), *The social causes of husband-wife violence* (pp. 94–114). Minneapolis, MN: University of Minnesota Press.
Fienberg, S. E. (1980). *The analysis of cross-classified categorical data.* Cambridge, MA: MIT Press.
Hornung, C. A., McCullough, B. C., & Sugimoto, T. (1981). Status relationships in marriage: Risk factors in spouse abuse. *Journal of Marriage and the Family, 43,* 675–692.
Kalmuss, D. (1984). The intergenerational transmission of marital aggression. *Journal of Marriage and the Family, 46,* 11–19.
Kalmuss, D., & Straus, M. A. (1982). Wife's marital dependency and wife abuse. *Journal of Marriage and the Family, 44,* 277–286.
Laner, M. R., & Thompson, J. (1982). Abuse and aggression in courting couples. *Deviant Behavior, 3,* 229–244.
Lockhart, L. L. (1987). A reexamination of the effects of race and social class on the incidence of marital violence: A search for reliable differences. *Journal of Marriage and the Family, 49,* 603–610.
Makepeace, J. M. (1981). Courtship violence among college students. *Family Relations, 30,* 97–102.
Makepeace, J. M. (1983). Life events stress and courtship violence. *Family Relations, 32,* 101–109.
Makepeace, J. M. (1986). Gender differences in courtship violence victimization. *Family Relations, 35,* 383–388.
Pagelow, M. D. (1985). The "battered husband syndrome": Social problem or much ado about little? In N. Johnson (Ed.), *Marital violence* (pp. 172–195). London: Routledge and Kegan Paul.
Pleck, E., Pleck, J. H., Grossman, M., & Bart, P. B. (1978). The battered data syndrome: A comment on Steinmetz' article. *Victimology, 2,* 680–683.
Roscoe, B., & Benaske, N. (1985). Courtship violence experienced by abused wives: Similarities in patterns of abuse. *Family Relations, 34,* 419–424.
Saunders, D. G. (1986). When battered women use violence: Husband-abuse or self-defense? *Victims and Violence, 1,* 47–60.

Stets, J. E., & Pirog-Good, M. A. (1987). Violence in dating relationships. *Social Psychology Quarterly, 50,* 237–246.

Straus, M. A. (1977). A sociological perspective on the prevention and treatment of wifebeating. In Maria Roy (Ed.), *Battered women: A psychosociological study of domestic violence* (pp. 194–239). New York: Van Nostrand Rheinhold.

Straus, M. A. (1979). Measuring intrafamily conflict and aggression: The conflict tactic (CT) scale. *Journal of Marriage and the Family, 41,* 75–88.

Straus, M. A. (1980). The marriage license as a hitting license: Evidence from popular culture, law, and social science. In Murray A. Straus & Gerald T. Hotaling (Eds.), *The social causes of husband-wife violence* (pp. 39–50). Minneapolis, MN: University of Minnesota Press.

Straus, M. A., & Gelles, R. J. (1986). Societal change and change in family violence from 1975 to 1985 as revealed by two national surveys. *Journal of Marriage and the Family, 48,* 465–479.

Wardell, L., Gillespie, D. L., & Leffler, A. (1983). Science and violence against wives. In David Finkelhor, Richard J. Gelles, Gerald T. Hotaling, & Murray A. Straus (Eds.), *The dark side of families* (pp. 69–84). Beverly Hills, CA: Sage.

Yllo, K. (1983). Sexual equality and violence against wives in American states. *Journal of Comparative Family Studies, 14,* 67–86.

11

Factors Related to Physical Violence in Dating Relationships

Diane R. Follingstad
Larry L. Rutledge
Kay McNeill-Harkins
Darlene S. Polek
Department of Psychology, University of South Carolina, Columbia

INTRODUCTION

Understanding violence in dating relationships is still in the infancy stage. To date, research has not fully explained this phenomenon and its associated factors. In this study, 210 college women returned a questionnaire that operationalized many of the hypothesized ideas regarding dating violence. The actual occurrence of controlling behaviors by the man along with a propensity by the woman to allow even a slight degree of control by the man were found to be the strongest predictors of whether females had been physically abused. Other significant predictors were romanticism, a belief that physical dominance by the man is fun, a family history of adults modeling physical force, and a tendency to reveal information that may have the potential to be

Diane R. Follingstad is a professor in clinical psychology at the University of South Carolina. She received her Ph.D. in clinical psychology from the University of Colorado in 1974. She is also a Diplomate in Forensic Psychology as certified by the American Board of Professional Psychology. Her primary research interests have been in the areas of physical violence in adult relationships and forensic psychology. She has published in such journals as *clinical psychology Review, Journal of Family Violence, Law and Human Behavior,* and *Journal of clinical psychology.*

Larry L. Rutledge received his Ph.D. in clinical-community psychology from the University of South Carolina in 1987. Prior to that he obtained a Master's Degree from California State University in 1981. His current interests are primarily in neuro-psychological assessment and his present position is at the North Fulton Regional Hospital in the Atlanta area. He has published in such journals as *Journal of Family Violence* and *Journal of Interpersonal Violence.*

Kay McNeill-Harkins has her Ph.D. in clinical-community psychology from the University of South Carolina, which she received in 1989. She previously had a master's degree in public health, which was awarded in 1973 from the University of North Carolina. Her current position is at the Berkeley County Mental Health center in South Carolina where she specializes in sexual abuse issues and heads the sexual abuse program. She also has a part-time private practice. She has been a co-author of an article published in the *Journal of Family Violence.*

Darlene S. Polek is a clinical psychologist at the Veterans Administration Medical Center in Augusta, Georgia. She completed her Ph.D. at the University of South Carolina in Columbia, where she developed an interest in women's issues and domestic violence. Her internship at the Medical College of Georgia led to an interest in family systems and anxiety disorders. She is currently involved in research on secondary traumatization of female spouses and children of patients suffering from combat-related posttraumatic stress disorder. She has co-authored articles in such journals as *Law and Human Behavior, Journal of Family Violence,* and the *Journal of Interpersonal Violence.*

used against oneself. Factors that did not distinguish between women who had or had not experienced physical violence in a dating relationship were traditional sex role attitudes, attitudes toward love, self-esteem levels, and belief in justifications for the use of physical force in relationships. A parsimonious scale of items that reliably distinguished between abused and nonabused women in dating relationships was developed based on the significant factors.

Prior investigations of physical violence in dating relationships on college campuses have focused on establishing prevalence data, looking at demographics and on developing theories as to the causes of the violence (Bogal-Allbritten & Allbritten, 1985; Cate, Henton, Koval, Christopher, & Lloyd, 1982; Laner & Thompson, 1982; Makepeace, 1981, 1983; Roscoe & Callahan, 1985; Sigelman, Berry, & Wiles, 1984). Estimates of physical violence on various campuses by these researchers appear to be fairly consistent with the rates of dating physical violence at approximately 20-25% of questionnaire respondents. Although these pioneering studies in the area of college dating violence have done much to answer questions of incidence and prevalence, the germinal theories that these researchers have developed from their questionnaire data need to be verified empirically. In addition, more investigation needs to occur in the area of attitudes and personality variables to add to the current knowledge of demographic relationships and beginning suggestions of causal relationships.

General models and *post hoc* evaluations about abusive relationships have not fully explained abuse in *dating* relationships. That is, although theories to explain the general area of abuse in adult relationships have developed rapidly, many of the "explanations" that are chiefly applicable to marital violence do not seem to fit dating relationships. For example, explanations given by abused married women such as staying in the relationship for the children's sake, depending financially on the man, or believing that divorce is wrong are not explanations typically given by women as reasons for staying in a violent dating relationship.

Causes for violence in dating relationships have often been speculated upon *after* collecting data on college subjects rather than from initial hypotheses that were then empirically investigated. However, several of the prior studies are important jumping-off points for further investigation of dating violence.

After Makepeace (1981) concluded a study on college dating, he theorized that violent incidents in college dating relationships occurred due to a lack of rules or limits in these relationships ("Premarital Violence," 1981). Cate et al. (1982) theorized that in some cases, college students may equate physical force with love. They found this attitude in one-third of the couples who had remained together after one or more violent episodes. Laner and Thompson (1982) hypothesized that abusive and aggressive behaviors were more likely to occur in "more involved" relationships. They speculated that a greater intensity of involvement may give rise to physical incidents because of an implied right to influence the other person. Involved relationships were also thought to be characterized by a knowledge of which of the partner's vulnerabilities and fears might be used to hurt or threaten the partner. Although these factors *may* be found in long-term relationships, it is also possible that these factors might instead be related to the personalities of the individuals involved in the relationship (e.g., some people may divulge few vulnerabilities even in a long-term relationship). Thus, the Laner and Thompson (1982) hypothesis may be premature in establishing "involvement" as a causal factor in the occurrence of physical force in dating relationships. Based on their survey data, Lander and Thompson (1982) also hypothesized three other factors that might be involved in abusive dating relationships: (a) abuse as a child of one or both members of the dating couple; (b) traditional sex roles in the relationship; and (c) a belief by the partners that violence connotes deeper feeling (i.e., love) ("Premarital Violence," 1981). The attitudinal and personality variables investigated by Sigelman et al. (1984) revealed traditional sex role attitudes in men who abused and low social desirability in women who abused and were abused.

The present study attempted to clarify preexisting studies by separating data collection for the two sexes (i.e., only women were utilized) and by investigating a wider range of attitudinal and personality variables in the same study. Included in this study are a large number of theorized factors from both the dating and the marital abuse literature. Seven variables in the present study were based on hypotheses and results of the studies on dating violence discussed above. This investigation attempted to operationalize ideas of previous researchers, for example, Makepeace's (1981) idea that violence occurs due to a lack of rules or limits in these relationships. Operationalizing the hypotheses, however, often resulted in the necessity of developing scales and items to meet specific purposes. For example, one group of items was developed to measure various controlling behaviors women were likely to allow men to engage in toward them. These items were based on the hypothesis that physical violence is an extension of milder forms of controlling behavior used to influence women. A second group of items measured the controlling behaviors actually engaged in by men in all of the women's dating relationships. Third, a previously developed measure of attitudes toward feminism and women's roles was included to test for endorsement of traditional sex roles. The fourth and fifth groups of items (which were developed to assess hypothesized variables) tested the degree to which the belief that physical force is a demonstration of love and beliefs about romantic love were related to the presence of physical force. Also developed for this study were a sixth group of items measuring the woman's childhood experience of physical or verbal abuse and a seventh variable assessing the type and amount of personal information a woman would be likely to reveal in a dating relationship.

The investigators also added several other variables that have been identified as psychological factors in spouse abuse that appeared germane to dating relationships as well as some other conceptually relevant ones from clinical experience and literature on abused women. (a) As physical dominance by a man may be valued by some women, and because physical force could be perceived as an extension of this idea, several items assessing attitudes toward physical dominance of the man over the woman were included. (b) Low self-esteem has been found in women abused by their spouses (e.g., Follingstad, 1980). It is uncertain though whether these women began the relationships with low self-esteem or developed it as a result of a lack of mastery they experienced in not being able to reduce the violence toward them. To further explore the relationship of this variable to violence, a scale of self-esteem was included. (c) Researchers (e.g., Gelles & Cornell, 1985; Martin, 1976; Truninger, 1971; Walker, 1979, 1984) have suggested that beliefs of abused women often contribute to their acceptance of the use of physical force against them. Therefore, prior researchers' hypotheses of justifications advanced by abused women as to why their partner used force against them were included. (d) Various studies (e.g., Gelles, 1972, 1976; Giles-Sims, 1983; Owens & Straus, 1975) have suggested that seeing physical abuse modeled as a problem-solving style in childhood is a significant factor in the use of violence or tolerance of violence as an adult. Therefore, an assessment of the presence of physical and/or verbal abuse occurring between adults in the home and abuse of the subject as a child was assessed. (e) Several writers in the area of domestic violence have underscored the isolation of the battered women (e.g., Bowker, 1984; Walker, 1979, 1984). They theorized that a lack of both corrective feedback and resources contribute to the woman's lack of power in the relationship. Therefore social supports were assessed as well as whether the woman maintained her social supports after entering into a significant relationship with a man.

METHOD

Subjects

Subjects were 210 single women who were either undergraduate or graduate students at the University of South Carolina. Ages ranged from 17 to 45 with a mean age of 20.8 and a standard deviation of 2.92. The scoring for year in school was 1 = freshman, 2 = sophomore, 3 = junior, 4 = senior, and 5 = graduate student. The mean school year was 2.80 with a standard deviation of 1.30. Black women constituted 7.5% of the sample of women. The women returning the questionnaires closely paralleled the available university statistics of undergraduate versus graduate women and white versus black women, thus being a representative sample. ANOVAs were run on demographic variables to determine whether significant differences existed between the levels of the variables. As no differences were located, demographics were not used as covariates and all subjects were run in the same analyses.

Subjects were solicited from the library and the student union, two locations on campus where it was assumed *all* students had a likelihood of being present rather than specific classes or interest groups. Approximately 550 questionnaires were handed out by female research assistants who asked passing women if they were single. The women were asked to complete the questionnaires and return them in addressed and sealed envelopes through campus mail to insure anonymity and confidentiality. Approximately 40 of the returned questionnaires were not included in the data analysis due to incompleteness.

One specific instruction was included regarding qualification for participation. As the questionnaire dealt with violence within a courtship, one item asked the woman whether she had ever been in at least one serious dating relationship. This was defined as a relationship that lasted at least several months with the couple spending considerable time together. In addition, the couple should have also considered the relationship significant and somewhat more than a casual, intermittent dating arrangement. Thus, it is believed that many questionnaires were not returned due to women deciding they did not meet the criteria for inclusion in the study.

Measures

As a number of measures had to be developed to specifically test a variety of the hypotheses, the types of items, rationales, and scoring information are included in this section under individual scale titles. However, only significant items of the developed scales are actually reported in the Results section for the sake of brevity.

Control Scale (CS)

Forty-seven items were developed to test the relationship of a lack of limits with violence in dating relationships from the literature on spouse abuse dealing with emotional abuse and from clinical experience. They were devised to tap controlling behaviors that could be engaged in by the man, and which the woman might allow. The items were written in statement form typically beginning with the words "I would allow. . . ." Subjects first checked whether these attempts at controlling their behavior had *ever happened,* and second indicated on a four-point Likert scale the degree to which they would be likely to *allow* the behavior to happen in a relationship (i.e., very likely, quite likely, somewhat likely, not likely at all). "Allow" was defined for the subjects as meaning they would let it happen and not actively try to stop it, even though they might not like it. The controlling behaviors ranged from milder forms of control (e.g., allowing the male to drive if he insisted; serving him, such as bringing him a beer, if he thought it was her duty; allowing him to decide the evening's activities most of the time) to moderate forms (e.g., giving in to unreasonable demands if he threatened to leave her or date someone else; letting him call her names and ridicule her in front of others; letting him decide whether she could have friends of either sex) to severe forms of control (e.g., forcing sexual activity; hitting her for doing something "wrong"; allowing him to physically threaten someone else he thought was interfering with their relationship).

Separate pretesting of these items indicated that 93 college men and women viewed individual items similarly as to the degree of control, in other words, there were no significant differences by sex on a ten-point rating scale of degree of control (from not controlling at all to extremely controlling) for individual items. Women, however, tended to consistently perceive the behaviors as slightly more controlling than the men did. Means of the degree of control for the items ranged from 3.02 to 8.56. Items that proved to be significant are listed in the Results section.

Self-Esteem Scale (SE)

This scale measures the self-acceptance aspect of self-esteem and was devised by Rosenberg (1965). The scale consists of ten items answered on a four-point Likert scale from strongly disagree to strongly agree. It is considered to be a unidimensional scale and was originally given to a sample of more than 5,000 advanced high school students from ten random New York schools. Since then, a wide variety of samples has been used and similar results occurred with adults. A test-retest correlation was found to be .85 and a reproducibility coefficient of .92 was determined, thereby establishing reasonable reliability of the measure. This scale also has reasonable convergent and discriminant validity.

Love Scale (LS)

Rubin (1970) started with the assumption that love is an interpersonal attitude and developed a scale to assess the construct of romantic love. Three components make up the scale: (a) affiliative and dependent need; (b) a predisposition to help; and (c) an orientation of exclusiveness and absorption. Although he did not assess the reliability of his scale, he was able to determine a good degree of discriminant validity for his scale (small correlations with a liking scale) and convergent validity as demonstrated by a laboratory study in which couples who were more in love according to the scale spent more time gazing into one another's eyes. A Likert scale of four points ranging from strongly disagree to strongly agree was the possibility for response options.

Justification Scale (JS)

Twenty-two reasons why a boyfriend might use physical force against a girlfriend were listed, including loss of temper, mental illness, discipline, the boyfriend's unhappiness about other aspects of his life, intoxication, and so forth. Subjects were instructed to decide on a four-point scale from strongly agree to strongly disagree whether the use of physical force directed by their boyfriend toward themselves would be *justifiable* if it were due to each of the 22 reasons.

FEM Scale

This ten-item scale is an abbreviated version of the original scale developed by Smith, Ferree, and Miller (1975). The FEM Scale assesses acceptance or rejection of central beliefs of feminism. Subjects respond on a four-point Likert scale ranging from strongly disagree to strongly agree. Reliability was reported to be .91. A validity test was conducted by determining the relationship between the FEM Scale and involvement in and subjective identification with the women's movement with resulting correlations at the .01 probability level.

Dominance

Individual items were developed by the investigators to assess additional factors that were hypothesized to be related to violence in courtship. Three dominance items tapped attitudes of the female subjects toward a man demonstrating physical power over them. This was asked first regarding playful physical overpowering that felt like fun and was not hurtful and second, where the physical dominance has hurtful consequences. The third dominance item tapped the theorized equation of hitting with love. Again, four Likert response options ranged from strongly agree to strongly disagree.

Romanticism

Romanticism items developed the themes of extreme loyalty for someone should you be in a serious or sexual relationship; the idea that "hate means love"; and the concept that jealousy is good for a relationship because it indicates the partners care for each other. Five questions were developed of which the significant ones are discussed in the Results section. Strongly disagree, disagree, agree, and strongly agree were the possible answers that subjects could give.

History of Abuse

Four history of abuse questions tapped the presence and frequency of physical and/or verbal abuse toward the subject as a child, as well as the presence and frequency of both types of abuse between adults in the subject's home. Verbal abuse was stated to be "ridicule, name-calling, and harassment." Physical abuse as a child was defined as "more than simple discipline for misbehavior and/or resulting in injuries." To assess the effects of modeled abuse between adults, subjects were asked whether they had ever seen adult members in the home use physical force toward each other. Subjects answered these questions on a five-point frequency basis of never, rarely, several times a year, monthly, weekly, or more.

Social Supports

Social support items asked each subject whether she had at least one same sex friend or at least one family member in whom she could confide "almost everything" to which she answered either yes or no. Another item asked whether the female continued to confide in these persons while in a significant relationship with a male.

Personal Information

To develop the theorized idea of increased personal vulnerability (which has no known measure to date) being related to physical violence, four of the questions asked about the likelihood that a subject would reveal personal information and fears in a dating relationship as well as in friendships. One question assessed the degree to which the revealed information in the dating relationship has the potential to be used against the subject by the other person to make her feel unhappy at a later time (i.e., vulnerability).

Physical Abuse

One final question determined whether the subjects had ever been in a relationship in which physical force was used toward them. The definition of physical force indicated any use of physical means that could be considered aggressive or potentially hurtful. Examples of this included being slapped, grabbed, or shaken as well as more serious physical force such as being choked, kicked, threatened with a weapon, or having an object thrown at them.

RESULTS

Because of the possibility of chance significance with the large number of variables being assessed, a conservative statistical approach was chosen. Initially a random subsample of 25% of the subject population was selected on which to conduct the analyses. The random subsample of 25% of the total sample of subjects yielded 12 subjects who reported physical force and 36 subjects with no physical force. (Of the original 210 subjects, 48 women revealed the occurrence of physical force in a dating relationship.) When significant ANOVA, chi square, or Cramer's V analyses occurred for the subsample between women who had experienced physical force in a relationship (PF) versus women experiencing no physical force (NPF), the analyses were then conducted on the whole sample of subjects for the significant items. This was done to reduce the possibility of chance significance, increase the reliability of the findings, and therefore also increase the validity of the results. Where significance was obtained for both the subsample and the sample, these items were then viewed as reliably distinguishing between women who had been physically abused and those who had not.

PF subjects appeared to closely parallel the demographic statistics of the 210 subjects in general. The age mean of PF women was 20.8, with a standard deviation of 2.43, year in school mean was 2.80 with a standard deviation of 1.25, and 7.5% of the women were black.

Factors Related to Physical Violence in Dating Relationships

Control

An ANOVA for the subsample compared PF women with NPF women on the entire scale of controlling behaviors. A significant difference was found ($F = 4.59$, $p < .03$) (see Table 11-1). This significant relationship was also demonstrated for the entire sample ($F = 3.63, p < .05$). Women who had experienced physical force were more likely to allow controlling behaviors on the part of men in a relationship and were less likely to try to stop these behaviors. Because it was believed that only some of the items contributed to the significance and because the goal for this study was to produce a more parsimonious set of discriminating factors, ANOVAs were conducted on the 47 individual items. Eight items that were either significant or very near significance for the sample were combined into a subscale (eight-item control questionnaire) that proved to be highly significant for both the subsample ($F = 20.81$, $p < .00001$) and the sample ($F = 11.75, p < .0007$). The 95% confidence intervals for this subscale strongly suggest that subjects experiencing physical force in a dating relationship allowed only slightly more of the controlling behaviors. In differentiating between the two groups though, this small difference is very important (see Table 11-1). The most severely controlling items did *not* discriminate between PF women and NPF women. This suggests that women experiencing physical violence were only allowing control by the men at mild or moderate levels. The individual significant items from the control questionnaire are as follows:

CQ19—I would allow him to frequently mention my faults in front of other people.

CQ22—I would allow him to tell me things that he thought I'd done wrong in my life.

CQ27—If he threatened to leave me or date someone else, I would give in to his demands, even if they were unreasonable.

CQ28—I would allow him to check on me to see if I actually went where I said I was going.

CQ33—I would allow him to get his way more often than mine to keep peace.

CQ43—I would allow him to have the final decision of what to watch on television when we were together.

CQ44—I would allow him to decide whether I could have male friends.

CQ45—I would allow him to accuse me of infidelity or seeing other men behind his back.

Romanticism

The five romanticism items were significant as a scale when a comparison of PF and NPF women was conducted for the subsample of the subjects ($F = 4.71, p < .03$). However, the relationship did not hold true for the entire sample ($F = .48, p > .05$) (see Table 11-1). Thus, in accordance with our conservative statistical approach, the significance of the total score for the subsample was viewed as possibly due to chance. Therefore, it is not expected that the total romanticism scale will reliably distinguish between the two groups. However, two of the individual scale items were significant both for the subsample and the sample. Women who had experienced physical force responded with a higher level of agreement to the following two items: Rom4—It is flattering to have a man who is jealous of you, because it indicates how

Table 11-1 One-way ANOVAs of dependent variables by women with and without physical violence in a dating relationship

Dependent variables	Subsample (N = 48)			Sample (N = 210)		
	F	p	95% Confidence level	F	p	95% Confidence level
Control scale	4.59	.03	PF[a] 78.4 to 95.3 NPF 75.0 to 82.4	3.63	.05	PF[a] 77.6 to 88.2 NPF 76.5 to 80.4
Control 19, 22 28, 33, 43, 44, 45 (Control subscale)	20.81	.00001	PF 12.1 to 16.8 NPF 9.9 to 11.3	11.75	.0007	PF 11.3 to 13.6 NPF 10.3 to 11.2
Control subscale Romance 18 & 19 Dominance 11	27.32	.00001	PF 23.1 to 29.0 NPF 19.1 to 21.1	21.97	.00001	PF 21.8 to 24.7 NPF 19.8 to 20.9
Romance 18	4.94	.03	PF 2.1 to 3.3 NPF 1.9 to 2.4	4.04	.04	PF 2.2 to 2.7 NPF 2.0 to 2.3
Romance 19	3.77	.05	PF 1.9 to 2.5 NPF 1.6 to 2.0	8.18	.004	PF 2.0 to 2.4 NPF 1.7 to 2.0
Feminism scale	.00	.96				
Love scale	.83	.36				
Self-esteem scale	.115	.73				
Justification scale	.009	.92				

[a]PF = Subject experiencing physical force directed toward her in a dating relationship. NPF = No physical force experienced.

much he cares; and Rom5—In serious relationships, almost all one's loyalty and energy should be devoted to one's boyfriend rather than friends. Table 11-1 lists the significance levels for both the sample and population comparisons for these two items.

Dominance

Dominance items did not significantly differentiate between the two groups of women as a scale, either for the subsample or for the sample (see Table 11-1). However, one of the items proved significant for the subsample and sample. PF women agreed more frequently and to a greater degree with the following item than NPF women, $(F = 4.02, p < .05)$: Dom1—It is exciting to have a man demonstrate his physical power over you in a way that is fun and not hurtful.

Combining the two romanticism items and the one dominance item with the shortened scale of controlling behaviors yielded an extremely significant subscale for discriminating between the two groups of women. For the subsample, the F was 27.32 $(p < .00001)$ and for the sample, the F value was 21.97 $(p < .00001)$.

Table 11-1 lists the 95% confidence intervals for the significant scales and items. These confidence intervals indicate the scores within which 95% of the subjects' scores in each group fell.

Happen Scale

Controlling behaviors that subjects marked as actually having happened to them were analyzed using chi square analyses. The items were combined as a Happen scale and women with and without abuse from the subsample were compared to determine whether the number of controlling behaviors they had experienced differed across groups. The significance level for the entire Happen scale approached significance for the subsample, $(X^2 = 3.45, p < .06)$, so the chi square analysis was also conducted for the entire population of subjects (see Table 11-2). The comparison for the sample of college women indicated a significant difference for the happen scale $(X^2 = 15.91, p < .0001)$.

The assumption that only some of the 47 items would actually contribute to the significance of the entire Happen Scale led to chi square analyses of individual items. Where significant or nearly significant probability values occurred for the subsample of 48 subjects, chi square analyses were then conducted for the entire sample. Table 11-2 delineates probability and chi square values for the 13 items found to discriminate between the PF and NPF females. The content of the individual items is as follows:

Happen1—I told him everyone who telephoned me if he asked.

Happen7—He frequently mentioned my faults when we were alone.

Happen14—He wanted me not to look at men, even a passing glance, when we were out together.

Happen21—He decided whether I could have female friends.

Happen23—He called me names and ridiculed me when we were alone.

Happen24—He would hit me if I'd done something wrong.

Happen25—He insisted I do things because I was a woman (e.g., wash dishes).

Happen28—He checked on me to see if I actually went where I said I was going.

Happen31—He wanted to know with whom I had past sexual experiences and I told him.

Table 11-2 Chi-Squares and Cramer's Versus of dependent variables by PF and NPF women[a]

Dependent variables	Subsample ($N = 48$)		Sample ($N = 210$)	
	X^2	p	X^2	p
Happen scale	3.45	.06	15.91	.0001
Happen 1	3.56	.05	5.53	.01
Happen 7	2.74	.09	13.83	.0002
Happen 14	3.02	.08	11.12	.0009
Happen 21	3.01	.08	19.87	.00001
Happen 23	4.39	.03	16.54	.00001
Happen 24	13.28	.0003	28.23	.00001
Happen 25	5.71	.01	16.73	.00001
Happen 28	8.28	.004	40.73	.00001
Happen 31	3.22	.07	3.37	.06
Happen 37	4.02	.04	13.09	.0003
Happen 45	3.89	.04	36.86	.00001
Happen 46	6.55	.01	38.88	.00001
Happen 50	4.02	.04	20.66	.00001
Physical abuse 4	9.42	.002	6.07	.01
Personal info 3	3.92	.04	5.01	.02

[a]All significant findings were in the direction of PF females more likely to report the behavior than NPF females.

Happen37—He wanted me not to speak back to any men who tried to talk to me even when I was out by myself.

Happen45—He accused me of infidelity and seeing other men behind his back.

Happen46—He threatened to physically hurt another person he thought was interfering with our relationship.

Happen50—He wanted me not to speak back to any man who tried to talk to me when we were out together.

All of the significant findings for these Happen items were in the direction that if women had been in a physically violent relationship, they were more likely to report the controlling behavior having occurred. The item content seems very much in line with the jealousy, possessiveness, power issues, and traditional sex-role attitudes suggested in research and clinical studies of men who abuse.

Physical or Verbal Abuse as a Child

Of the items assessing physical and verbal abuse in the home of each subject, only one item differentially discriminated between PF and NPF subjects: Physical abuse4—Did you ever see adult members in your home use physical force? PF females were more likely to have witnessed violence *between adults* in the family of origin. A Cramer's V analysis was significant for the subsample of subjects ($V = 9.42$, $p < .002$) as well as for the sample ($V = 6.07$, $p < .01$), (see Table 11-2). Contrary to prior findings, physical abuse directed toward the subject herself as a child was not a significant factor in differentiating between PF and NPF women. In addition, verbal abuse in the home, whether directed toward the subject herself or between adults in the home, did not discriminate between the two groups of women.

Personal Information

One item tapping the type and amount of information revealed by a woman in a dating relationship showed significant differences for Cramer's V analyses done on both the subsample and sample: Personal info3—To what degree does the information you reveal in a significant relationship have the *potential* to be used against you by the other person to make you feel unhappy at a later time? PF women were more likely to reveal "quite a bit" or "a lot" of the type of information which could be potentially used against them at a later period of time (subsample, $V = 3.92, p < .04$; sample, $V = 5.01, p < .02$). The other aspects of this factor (i.e., having someone to confide in, maintaining a confidential relationship even when in a dating relationship, and revealing general fears and personal information while in a serious dating relationship) did not discriminate between PF and NPF women. The qualitative aspect of the information revealed (i.e., the type that has the potential to be used against you) appears to be the important factor for discriminating between the two groups.

Reliability Estimates

The split-half reliability of the attitudinal items consisting of the significant control, romanticism, and dominance items was computed using the Spearman correlation coefficient. From this, the reliability of the whole test was estimated to be .71. Similarly, the estimate of reliability was computed for all of the significant behavioral (i.e., happen) items, yielding a reliability estimate of .75.

Factor Analysis

To determine whether the conceptualized items in the significant subscales actually constituted one or more factors, the control scale items, the Romanticism items, and the dominance item were subjected to a factor analysis. After rotation with Kaiser normalization, two major factors emerged. All of the eight control scale items loaded .33 to .58 on the first factor of the factor matrix and all of these items loaded more strongly on the first than the second factor. In contrast, neither of the romanticism items nor the dominance item loaded well on the first factor, but rather the three items ranged from .42 to .66 on the second factor. This gives empirical support for placing these significant items in two separate subscales for further analyses and suggests content similarity of the two factors.

The significant happen items were also subjected to a factor analysis. These 13 items appeared to form a cohesive conceptual factor as all 13 loaded most strongly on the first factor except for one item. Loadings ranged from .32 to .75, with all but two items loading .42 and stronger. The Eigenvalue for the first factor was 3.95.

Multiple Correlations and Variance

In order to determine the amount of variance accounted for in assigning women to abused versus nonabused categories, a multiple correlation was computed using all of the significant items (happen, control, romanticism, dominance, history of abuse, and personal information). The multiple R was .64 and the R^2 was .41. With just these subscales of items, 41% of the variance of a very complex multidimensional problem was identified.

Significant correlations between attitudinal items and behavioral items were apparent. The Control subscale was significantly correlated with the Romanticism items

$(r(208) = .24, p < .01$ and $r (208) = .38, p < .01)$, the Dominance item $(r (208) = .19, p < .05)$ and the Happen subscale $(r (208) = .22, p < .01)$.

Nonsignificant Scales and Items

It is important to note that several of the attitudinal measures did not yield significant differences between the PF and NPF subjects. A subject's score on the FEM Scale, measuring acceptance of core beliefs of feminism, showed virtually no relationship with violence experienced during courtship (see Table 11-1). The love scale, reflecting attitudes toward someone you are in a significant relationship with, as well as the self-esteem scale, assessing acceptance toward one's self, were both nonsignificant factors when comparing the two groups of women. No justifications for physical incidents in a relationship, neither the total scale score nor individual items, discriminated between PF and NPF women.

DISCUSSION

The results of this study appear to be useful for several reasons. First, the inclusion of many variables based on the results of prior research, as well as others included as conceptually relevant from spouse abuse literature and clinical experience, permitted a more comprehensive study of factors and their interrelationships linked to dating violence. Second, the attitudinal items appear to be highly significant for differentiating between women who had experienced physical violence in a dating relationship and those who had not. These items, therefore, constitute parsimonious scales for further research.

The variables that discriminated between women who have or have not experienced violence in a dating relationship demonstrated that many of the explanations offered for this phenomenon do not hold true. For example, holding traditional attitudes toward sex roles does not appear to make a woman more likely to have been a victim of physical force while in a dating relationship. Although these results conflict with the ideas of Laner and Thompson (1982), they are not surprising, as feminism versus traditionalism appears to be a broad concept that may not be relationship specific. Similarly, holding stronger attitudes of exclusivity, helpfulness, and loyalty (i.e., love) toward one's dating partner did not seem to be a factor. Neither self-esteem nor justifications as to why a man might use physical force had a bearing on whether a woman would more likely be a victim of physical force in a dating relationship. It is important to consider that these data may contrast with spouse abuse literature due to the possibility that less physical force over shorter periods of time may occur in dating relationships. Therefore, the dating violence may not have the impact on self-esteem that ongoing physical force in a marriage might have. However, the results suggest that possessing lower self-esteem to begin with does not seem to predispose one to receiving physical force in a dating relationship.

The strongest actual predictors of dating violence were the occurrence of controlling behaviors by a man in the relationship and a propensity of a woman to allow a man to exert slightly more control over her than other women allow. In addition, women who have been the victim of force tend to romanticize jealousy and possessiveness, to believe that physical domination can be fun, and have a family history in which adults modeled physical force.

The types of controlling behaviors in relationships reported most frequently by the women experiencing physical force indicated that their male partners appeared jealous, possessive, traditional in sex-role orientation, and concerned with power. One can speculate from this picture that men with propensities for engaging in controlling and physically forceful behavior may be drawn to women who are likely to allow even *small* amounts of control over their behavior and may be likely to seek them out in relationships. Another possibility is that these men may consistently engage in controlling type behaviors in any dating relationship they may encounter, but only some women may tolerate the behaviors due to past history or attitudinal factors. One could also speculate that physical incidents on the part of the man may be an extension of behaviors used to control the woman and may appear when other forms of control are not successful.

The extent to which a woman might allow a man to have control over her may in turn be determined by the "romantic" attitudes she possesses and how much she believes physical domination by the man and emotional vulnerability belong in a male-female relationship. Witnessing physical violence between adults in her family may also increase her tolerance for physical force in her own relationship. This is not to suggest that the woman wishes for or condones physical force toward her, but rather that she may feel she has no alternative but to allow it to occur. What is important to note is that it seems the woman needs to permit the man to exercise only a small amount of control to possibly create a climate in which more control may be exerted. Women who had experienced physical force directed toward them were *not* more likely to believe they would allow severe forms of control.

The subscales and items that significantly distinguished between women who had experienced physical force and those who had not should be very useful in further research. Some predictive validity appears evident for the factors investigated in this study, as comparisons were made between college women who had experienced physical incidents and those who had not. The items were also deemed to be reliable for basic research purposes according to Nunnally's (1978) standards. As suggested by the percentage of variance accounted for, the significant items have indeed been shown to make a valuable contribution to understanding the differences between the two groups of women. By demonstrating the usefulness of these self-report attitudinal and behavioral items, these scales and items can be used to test other possible factors.

As these data relate only to college dating, comparison studies need to determine the similarity or difference of these results to other dating relationships. This sample also has limitations due to regional and age variables and therefore generalizations must be made with caution. Extended samples for comparison are certainly warranted. As more is understood regarding factors relating to dating and marital violence, further relationships among variables will need to be explored.

Future research into the phenomenon of dating violence should also determine if significant differences exist between subjects who experienced just one incident of violence and those who experienced repeated incidents—this distinction could account for two very different patterns of behavior and attitudes. The identification of differences among the women who have experienced physical force may shed even greater light on physical violence in dating relationships.

BIBLIOGRAPHY

Bogal-Allbritten, R. B., & Allbritten, W. L. (1985). The hidden victims: Courtship violence among college students. *Journal of College Student Personnel, 26,* 201-204.

Bowker, L. H. (1984). Coping with wife abuse: Personal and social networks. In A. R. Roberts (Ed.), *Battered women and their families.* New York: Springer.

Cate, R. M., Henton, J. M., Koval, J., Christopher, F. S., & Lloyd, S. (1982). Premarital abuse: A social psychological perspective. *Journal of Family Issues, 3,* 79-90.

Follingstad, D. R. (1980). A reconceptualization of issues in the treatment of abused women: A case study. *Psychotherapy: Theory, Research and Practice, 17,* 294-303.

Gelles, R. J. (1972). *The violent home.* Beverly Hills, CA: Sage.

Gelles, R. J. (1976). Abused wives: Why do they stay? *Journal of Marriage and the Family, 38,* 659-668.

Gelles, R. J., & Cornell, C. P. (1985). *Intimate violence in families.* Family Studies Text Series 2. Beverly Hills, CA: Sage.

Giles-Sims, J. (1983). *Wife battering: A systems theory approach.* New York: The Guilford Press.

Laner, M. R., & Thompson, J. (1982). Abuse and aggression in courting couples. *Deviant Behavior; An Interdisciplinary Journal, 3,* 229-244.

Makepeace, J. M. (1981). Courtship violence among college students. *Family Relations, 30,* 97-102.

Makepeace, J. M. (1983). Life events stress and courtship violence. *Family Relations, 32,* 101-109.

Martin, D. (1976). *Battered wives.* San Francisco, CA: Glide.

Nunnally, J. C. (1978). *Psychometric theory.* New York: McGraw-Hill.

Owens, D. J., & Straus, M. A. (1975). The social structure of violence in childhood and approval of violence as an adult. *Aggressive Behavior, 1,* 193-211.

Premarital violence: Battering on college campuses. (1981). *Response to Violence in the Family Newsletter, 4,* 1.

Roscoe, B., & Callahan, J. (1985). Adolescents' self-report of violence in families and dating relationships. *Adolescence, 20,* 545-553.

Rosenberg, M. (1965). *Society and the adolescent self-image.* Princeton, NJ: Princeton University Press.

Rubin, Z. (1970). Measurement of romantic love. *Journal of Personality and Social Psychology, 16,* 265-273.

Sigelman, C. K., Berry, C. J., & Wiles, K. A. (1984). Violence in college students' dating relationships. *Journal of Applied Social Psychology, 5,* 530-548.

Smith, E. R., Ferree, M. M., & Miller, F. D. (1975). A short scale of attitudes toward feminism. *Representative Research in Social Psychology, 6,* 51-56.

Truninger, E. (1971). Marital violence: The legal solutions. *Hastings Law Review, 23,* 259-276.

Walker, L. E. (1979). *The battered woman.* New York: Harper & Row.

Walker, L. E. (1984). *The battered woman syndrome.* New York: Springer.

PART V

THE MALE BATTERER

12

Male Batterers: Evidence for Psychopathology

Renata Vaselle-Augenstein
William Lyon University

Annette Ehrlich
California State University, Los Angeles

INTRODUCTION

Clinical and empirical data on the personality characteristics of male batterers are reviewed. That evidence suggests that, as a group, batterers have an identifiable set of personality characteristics: dependence, depression, anxiety, low self-esteem, paranoia, dissociation from their own feelings, poor impulse control, antisocial tendencies, and hostility toward women. The evidence also suggests that, although psychopathology may not be present in all cases, there is psychopathology in many men who batter. There appear to be different personality types among batterers. A multifactor description of battering is offered, in which both personality and nonpersonality factors are taken into account. Implications of the personality data for treatment of batterers are considered.

The behavior of batterers, men who inflict open, deliberate, and systematic physical injury on their wives or girlfriends, has been the subject of considerable discussion (for earlier reviews of the literature, see Davidovich, 1990; Edleson, Eisikovits, & Guttmann, 1985; Gelles, 1980; Goodstein & Page, 1981; Hamberger & Hastings, 1988a; Hotaling & Sugarman, 1986; Stahly, 1977/1978; Tolman & Bennett, 1990). In the past, much emphasis has been placed on the causative role played by nonpersonality factors, such as alcohol and drug abuse (Gayford, 1983), unemployment and other sources of environmental stress (Straus, Gelles, & Steinmetz, 1980), social approval of violence (Straus, 1977/1978), and sex-role stereotyping (Sonkin, Martin, & Walker, 1985).

Until recently, the personality dynamics of the batterer were not seen as important.

Dr. Renata Vaselle-Augenstein is a clinical psychologist in private practice in Los Angeles. She specializes in working with batterers who are referred by the courts or who ask for help voluntarily. She continues to do research and is working on a book on the psychodynamics and treatment of the abusive syndrome.

Dr. Annette Ehrlich is a physiological psychologist who is a Professor in the Psychology Department at California State University in Los Angeles. She has an extensive list of previous publications, most of which deal with animals. Her present interest is in the application of traditional experimental methodology to clinical problems, and her most recent papers deal with pain control, personality of gang members, and adolescent drug use.

Although a small number of authors argued otherwise (Bernard & Bernard, 1984; Gayford, 1975; Gillman, 1980; Rounsaville, 1978), the majority view, until the mid 1980s, seemed to be that psychopathology is present in only a small percentage of batterers, somewhere between 10% and 20% (Bach, 1980; Bograd, 1984; Dutton, 1984; Dutton, Fehr, & McEwen, 1982; Gelles & Cornell, 1983; Gondolf, 1985; Purdy & Nickle, 1981; Smith, 1984; Sonkin et al., 1985; Straus, 1977/1978; Straus et al., 1980; Walker, 1981; Watts & Courtois, 1981). Indeed, batterers sometimes were described as "normal, healthy males" (Smith, 1984) who had the same psychological problems as other men but who lacked adequate coping skills (Walker, 1981; Weitzman & Dreen, 1982).

Since the mid 1980s, evidence for the existence of psychopathology in more than a small minority of batterers has accumulated (Allen, Calsyn, Fehrenbach, & Benton, 1989; Cadsky & Crawford, 1988; Gondolf, 1988; Hamberger & Hastings, 1986; Hastings & Hamberger, 1988; Shupe, Stacey, & Hazlewood, 1987). As a result, there has been increasing recognition of the fact that more attention needs to be paid to the personality dynamics of batterers (Hotaling & Sugarman, 1986; Tolman & Bennett, 1990). However, there is still resistance to that shift in focus (Dutton, 1988; Edleson et al., 1985; Margolin, 1987; Neidig, Friedman, & Collins, 1986; Pattison, 1985). The major purpose of the present review is to summarize the evidence for personality problems and psychopathology in male batterers. The issue is important because it has implications for treatment of batterers.

One point needs to be made clear at the outset. Much of the material reviewed is clinical. Further, although appropriate comparison groups of nonbatterers were included in most of the empirical studies that will be discussed here, some studies (e.g., Hamberger & Hastings, 1986; Schuerger & Reigle, 1988) lacked such groups. However, these limitations are less serious than they might be, for the empirical studies confirm and extend the much larger body of clinical data. It is possible now to begin to put together an account of personality dynamics and psychopathology in batterers.

PERSONALITY DYNAMICS OF BATTERERS

Dependence

An observation commonly made by practitioners who work with batterers is that they are extremely dependent on their wives (Bernard & Bernard, 1984; Bowlby, 1984; Coleman, 1980; Dutton et al., 1982; Elbow, 1977; Kelly & Loesch, 1983; Purdy & Nickle, 1981; Rounsaville, 1978; Shupe et al., 1987; Symonds, 1978; Watts & Courtois, 1981; Wetzel & Ross, 1983). Supportive evidence comes from a controlled study (Doherty, 1983) in which a significantly higher level of dependence, as assessed by scores on the Rotter Incomplete Sentences Blank, was found in batterers than in nonbatterers. Batterers also have been described as being dissociated from their own feelings (Kelly & Loesch, 1983; Weitzman & Dreen, 1982). Purdy and Nickle (1981) argue that it is dissociation that leads the batterer to become unusually dependent on his wife; she is perceived as the individual whose function it is to deal with feelings.

Because the thought of being left by their wives induces panic (Coleman, 1980) and "abandonment anxiety" (Weitzman & Dreen, 1982), batterers use coercive means, such as battering and the threat of suicide, to keep their wives with them

(Bowlby, 1984). Rounsaville (1978) found that 71% of his sample of battered wives reported that their husbands had threatened to commit suicide if they left. When coercive measures fail and the woman leaves, the batterer often is unable to accept the fact that the relationship is over. Even five years after the divorce or separation, the batterer still may be following and harassing his victim (Rounsaville, 1978; Walker & Browne, 1985).

Although they are dependent, batterers evidently are ambivalent about that dependence. According to some clinicians, the first abuse occurred on an occasion when dependency of one or the other partner became an issue, for example, on the honeymoon, when the wife announced her pregnancy, or the birth of the first child (Dutton, 1984; Rounsaville, 1978; Wetzel & Ross, 1983).

Intimacy

The ambivalence about dependency that was just described accords with another observation made by clinicians, which is that batterers have problems with respect to intimacy and boundaries (Dutton, 1984; Dutton et al., 1982; Gondolf, 1985; Hallschmid, Black, & Checkley, 1985; Symonds, 1978, 1984; Walker & Browne, 1985; Weitzman & Dreen, 1982). They want and need to have a relationship that is close, but then they fear the intensity of the relationship and the possibility of losing control. The outcome is that batterers feel both emotionally isolated and also exaggeratedly dependent on their wives or girlfriends.

Two empirical studies provide support for the observations of clinicians. Allen et al. (1989) tested a large sample of batterers on the FIRO-B, a test that assesses need to associate with people, have control over others, and experience affectionate or emotional involvement with others. There was no control group, but the data were compared with normative population data reported by other investigators. The resulting test profiles suggested that batterers have difficulty expressing affection, are uncomfortable around others, are cautious about initiating and developing close relationships, and are highly selective about who gets close.

In the other empirical study (Hastings & Hamberger, 1988), there was a control group of nonbatterers. All subjects took a battery of tests that included the Millon Clinical Multiaxial Inventory, the Beck Depression Inventory, and the Novaco Anger Scale. Significant differences between batterers and nonbatterers were found on most of the personality test scales, and the differences, in general, indicated greater pathology in the batterers. The conclusion about lack of comfort in intimate relationships was based not on a single finding but rather on the pattern of findings.

Jealousy

Along with dependence, batterers exhibit considerable suspicion. Vaselle-Horner and Ehrlich (in press) found that batterers obtained significantly higher scores than nonbatterers on the paranoia scale of the Minnesota Multiphasic Personality inventory. Maiuro, Cahn, Vitaliano, Wagner, and Zegree (1988) found that batterers scored higher than nonbatterers on a measure of suspicion extracted from the same test, as did men who were generally assaultive.

Clinical reports are in agreement. The degree of jealousy and possessiveness about their wives and girlfriends exhibited by batterers seems to be pathological (Bowlby, 1984; Coleman, 1980; Gayford, 1983; Kelly & Loesch, 1983; Rounsaville, 1978;

Saunders, 1984; Shupe et al., 1987; Walker, 1981; Wetzel & Ross, 1983). When battered women are interviewed, they report that their husbands isolate them—even from friends and family (Bowlby, 1984; Coleman, 1980; Kelly & Loesch, 1983; Rounsaville, 1978; Saunders, 1984; Walker, 1981; Wetzel & Ross, 1983). Conversations with other men are viewed with great suspicion (Rounsaville, 1978; Walker, 1981). In Gayford's (1983) study, respondents reported that beatings to extract confessions of supposed infidelities were common. According to Gayford (1983) and Rounsaville (1978), the battering victim cannot win because friendships with other women, like relationships with other men, are discouraged and can lead to accusations of lesbianism.

Assertion and Need for Control

A few observers have described batterers as unassertive, even passive, men who are paired with very assertive women (Davidson, 1978; Gelles, 1974; Saunders, 1984; Snell, Rosenwald, & Robey, 1964). However, the more usual description of batterers is that they are men who have an excessive need to be in control. They do not allow their wives to make any independent decisions, and they want to know everything that their wives do. Further, they like to be in charge of all aspects of the family's life, such as finances and recreation (Coleman, 1980; Dutton, 1984; Gondolf, 1985; Myers & Gilbert, 1983; Rounsaville, 1978; Symonds, 1978; Walker, 1981). According to Dutton et al. (1982) and Dobash and Dobash (1977/1978), batterers regard their wives and girlfriends as chattel and are threatened by even the most moderate assertions of independence. On the basis of data provided by wives, Dobash and Dobash (1984) analyzed events that preceded an attack. They found that violence occurred at the point at which the woman could be perceived as having challenged the man's authority.

It may be that power needs are best understood in relation to other aspects of the batterer's personality. Thus, Allen et al. (1989) have argued that, if batterers attempt to control others, they do so not out of a need to dominate but rather because they feel inadequate in close relationships. Dutton and Strachan (1987) argue that the high need for power in batterers is relevant only when it occurs in conjunction with poor verbal ability. In their study, responses to the Thematic Apperception Test showed that batterers were not significantly different in need for power from unhappily married men, but they were significantly less verbally assertive than both maritally happy and maritally unhappy nonbatterers. The conclusion reached by Dutton and Strachan (1987), that batterers perceive some danger in intimate relationships with women, is not in disagreement with the views presented by Allen et al. (1989).

Maiuro, Cahn, and Vitaliano (1986) carried the analysis of a verbal assertion deficit still farther. They administered the Assertiveness and Aggression Inventory, a test that employs separate scales to assess ability to refuse requests, as distinct from ability to initiate requests. The findings showed that batterers and nonbatterers did not differ significantly on the measure of refusal assertiveness, but batterers were significantly lower on the measure of request assertiveness. Because batterers also were more hostile than nonbatterers, the conclusion drawn was that batterers can defend their rights, but they have difficulty with the positive expression of needs. The authors concluded that their data agreed with the interpretation offered by clinicians, that the excessive need for control exhibited by batterers is related to a difficulty in intimate relationships.

Unhappiness and Dissatisfaction

There is evidence that batterers experience a high level of unhappiness and dissatisfaction with their lives, both at home and at work (Hotaling & Sugarman, 1986). Clinical observers report a low level of self-esteem, coupled with a sense of powerlessness in terms of controlling their own lives (Currie, 1983; Elbow, 1977; Gondolf, 1985; Myers & Gilbert, 1983; Rae-Grant, 1983; Saunders, 1984; Shupe et al., 1987; Symonds, 1984; Taylor, 1984; Walker, 1981; Weitzman & Dreen, 1982). High levels of hostility, depression, and anxiety also have been reported (Elbow, 1977; Symonds, 1978). Empirical data support these observations.

Doherty (1983) and Harris (1988) found that, by comparison with nonbatterers, batterers had a significantly lower level of self-esteem, as assessed by scores on the Tennessee Self-Concept Scale. Goldstein and Rosenbaum (1985) reported a similar difference between batterers and nonbatterers when self-esteem was assessed by means of the Rosenberg Self-Esteem Scale. In the latter study, participants took an additional test in which they were presented with hypothetical situations involving wives who acted in ways that opposed their husbands. Batterers perceived more situations as damaging to their self-esteem than nonbatterers.

Along similar lines, Vaselle-Horner and Ehrlich (in press) reported that batterers had significantly lower scores than nonbatterers on the ego strength scale of the Minnesota Multiphasic Personality Inventory, a scale that assesses feelings of personal adequacy. Schuerger and Reigle (1988) and Harris (1988) also found evidence for low ego strength in batterers. Schuerger and Reigle's (1988) data came from scores on the Psychological Inventory and the Sixteen Personality Factors Questionnaire. In their case, the comparison was between their test results for 250 batterers and published norms on the same tests. Harris's (1988) data came from a study in which a direct comparison was made between batterers and nonbatterers on the Sixteen Personality Factors Questionnaire.

In two uncontrolled studies, clinically high levels of anxiety were reported in batterers. Sonkin et al. (1985) administered the Minnesota Multiphasic Personality Inventory, and Schuerger and Reigle (1988) used the Psychological Screening Inventory and the Sixteen Personality Factors Questionnaire. Two controlled studies also revealed a high level of anxiety in batterers. Doherty (1983) reported that batterers obtained significantly higher scores than nonbatterers on the Taylor Manifest Anxiety Scale, and Hastings and Hamberger (1988) obtained similar results when batterers and nonbatterers were compared on the Millon Clinical Multiaxial Inventory. The latter authors also found a significantly higher level of somatic complaints in batterers than in nonbatterers.

For hostility and depression, as well, supportive data for clinical observations come from both controlled and uncontrolled studies. Clinically high levels of hostility and depression in a group of batterers were reported by Sonkin et al. (1985), on the basis of scores on the Hostility Toward Women Scale and the depression scale of the Minnesota Multiphasic Personality Inventory, respectively. Hastings and Hamberger (1988), who compared batterers and nonbatterers on the Beck Depression Inventory, found that batterers were significantly more depressed than nonbatterers. Maiuro et al. (1988) found that batterers scored higher than nonbatterers on hostility, assessed by means of the Buss-Durkee Hostility Inventory, but in this regard they were like men who are generally assaultive outside the family as well as within it. Where batterers differed from all other men who were tested was in the fact that the hostility, as well as the suspicion mentioned in an earlier section, was accompanied by a high level of depression.

Anger, Aggression, and Impulse Control

Interviews with battered women indicate that episodes often are set off by seeming trifles, such as an unironed shirt or a late meal (Martin, 1978; Pagelow, 1981; Shupe et al., 1987). There is evidence, too, that batterers often have a history of aggression. Somewhere between 44% and 67% of batterers who are seen in treatment programs are found to have had previous violent relationships with women (Carlson, 1977; Coleman, 1980; Gayford, 1983; Sonkin et al., 1985; Walker & Browne, 1985) or to have been arrested previously for other crimes of violence, including assaulting other men (Carlson, 1977; Gayford, 1975; Rounsaville, 1978; Shields & Hanneke, 1983; Stewart & deBlois, 1981). Taken together, the two lines of evidence have suggested to some clinicians that batterers are individuals who are lacking in impulse control (Bowlby, 1984; Coleman, 1980; Currie, 1983; Rounsaville, 1978; Shupe et al., 1987; Walker, 1981; Wetzel & Ross, 1983).

Empirical studies provide support. Bernard and Bernard (1984) and Sonkin et al. (1985), on the basis of scores on the Minnesota Multiphasic Personality Inventory, reported poor impulse control in the batterers they tested. Schuerger and Reigle (1988), similarly, found evidence for impulsivity in the single group of batterers they tested on the basis of combined data from the Sixteen Personality Factors Questionnaire and the Psychological Screening Inventory. Vaselle-Horner and Ehrlich (in press) found that batterers had significantly higher scores than nonbatterers on the hypomania scale of the Minnesota Multiphasic Personality Inventory, a scale that assesses unstable mood.

Not everyone agrees, however, that batterers lack impulse control. Opposing clinical evidence is as follows: Batterers direct most of their aggression toward wives and girlfriends rather than coworkers (Bograd, 1988); they sometimes wake their victims from sleep in order to beat them up (Follingstad, 1980; Pagelow, 1981; Shainess, 1979); when they hit, batterers aim where the blows will not show; and they usually stop before they kill their victims (Sonkin et al., 1985). All of these findings suggest that batterers are capable of at least some degree of control, that in fact they store up aggression and wait until it can be discharged safely against weaker individuals. According to Guerney, Waldo, and Firestone (1987), it is because they seek outlets for aggression that batterers interpret harmless events angrily; they may also deliberately engineer events so that they can express aggression.

Whether batterers are seen as lacking in impulse control or, in opposite terms, as being rigid, compulsive, and over-controlled (Bach, 1980; Elbow, 1977; Gondolf, 1985), may not be the critical issue. What the evidence just reviewed suggests is that, as Guerney et al. (1987) and Maiuro et al. (1988) have argued, batterers have longstanding and serious problems with the expression of anger and aggression. Consequently, attempts to blame the victim for "inciting" the violence by nagging (Kleckner, 1978; Mushanga, 1983; Szinovacz, 1982) are inappropriate. Fortunately, there seems to be general agreement now that victim characteristics and behavior are unrelated to battering (Hotaling & Sugarman, 1986). However, attempts to explain battering by calling it a "relationship" problem persist (Bach, 1980; Bagarozzi & Giddings, 1983; Deschner, 1984; Margolin, 1987; Neidig, 1984; Weitzman & Dreen, 1982).

Some clinical observers say that there is an association, in the batterer's mind, between sexual arousal and violence. Evidence for that association comes from reports (Bowker, 1983; Sonkin et al., 1985) showing that marital rape is common in batterers. Dutton (1984), Sonkin et al. (1985), and Dutton et al. (1982) all describe the batterer as someone who not only learned, in childhood, to respond to anger with violence, but who also experiences all arousal as anger.

For the batterer, violence seems to be an addictive behavior, one that escalates with time, both in frequency and in severity. Because the victim evidences pain and submits to her aggressor, the man is reinforced for his behavior. Also, escalation may occur because the batterer tries to maintain a constant level of effect as the victim habituates (Sonkin et al., 1985; Walker & Browne, 1985). Here, it is worth noting that batterers often have problems with other forms of addiction, as well. High levels of alcohol and drug use have been reported in batterers (Bernard & Bernard, 1984; Carlson, 1977; Fitch & Papantonio, 1983; Gayford, 1983; Gondolf, 1985; Hastings & Hamberger, 1988; Rounsaville, 1978; Schuerger & Reigle, 1988; Sonkin et al., 1985; Steward & deBlois, 1981; Tolman & Bennett, 1990).

Use of Defense Mechanisms

Whether batterers feel remorse—or even are capable of doing so—is doubtful. Earlier, Walker (1978) had argued that, after a violent episode, there was a "honeymoon" period, during which the man was contrite and loving. Indeed, it was these recurrent periods of kindness that were thought by Walker to contribute to the ambivalence displayed by abused women when opportunities arose to leave the relationship. Subsequently, however, data began to accumulate to show that remorse is a rare event.

Dobash and Dobash (1984), in a study of Scottish men, found that only a minority of batterers expressed regret, even after an unusually severe attack. According to Dobash and Dobash, contrition, if it is expressed at all, occurs only after the first attack, when the man is afraid that the woman will leave, but not subsequently. Similarly, Kelly and Loesch (1983) found, in a study of American women, that victims were divided more or less evenly in their views when asked whether their husbands were sorry after the attacks.

Further evidence comes from the reports of psychotherapists who treat batterers. Although Dutton et al. (1982) and Symonds (1978) commented on the presence of anxiety and guilt about their violent behavior in batterers, by far the more common observation (Coleman, 1980; Elbow, 1977; Gondolf, 1985; Shupe et al., 1987; Walker, 1981; Watts & Courtois, 1981; Weitzman & Dreen, 1982) has been that the batterer feels little guilt or concern, other than the concern caused by the possibility of his own arrest and trial or the permanent loss of his spouse. The findings of Hastings and Hamberger (1988) confirm these clinical reports. On the basis of the difference in test profiles between batterers and nonbatterers on the Millon Clinical Multiaxial Inventory, these authors concluded that batterers are lacking in empathy for others. They simply do not understand that other individuals, especially those regarded as weaker, have rights.

Related to the apparent lack of remorse is an extremely high level of denial. Wetzel and Ross (1983) describe batterers who only notice the sometimes severe injuries of their victims the next day and then enquire innocently, "What happened to you?" Dobash and Dobash (1984) recount how, after a severe battering, the man may calmly ask for some ordinary service like having the woman make him a cup of tea and completely ignore the issue of whether her injuries allow her to carry out routine domestic chores.

In treatment programs, the level of denial is even more apparent (Bernard & Bernard, 1984; Ptacek, 1988). When pressed about their behavior, batterers omit important details and lie (Purdy & Nickle, 1981), minimize the extent of the woman's injuries ("I just pushed her a little," Wetzel & Ross, 1983), and deny responsibility for their actions ("I lost control" or "I had a difficult day at work," Purdy & Nickle, 1981). "She fell wrong" is a common remark (Walker, 1981, p. 84). Other, associated defense mechanisms noted by psychotherapists are projection of the blame onto the victim ("She asked for it," Gondolf, 1985) and rationalization ("I had to hit her to quiet her down," Coleman, 1980). Even men whose arrest records indicate that they administered severe beatings that stopped just short of killing their victims deny, minimize, and rationale their behavior when they begin treatment (Shupe et al., 1987).

Some support for these clinical observations comes from an apparently anomalous finding of Hastings and Hamberger (1988). These investigators found that, contrary to their expectation, batterers scored significantly lower than nonbatterers on the Novaco Anger Scale. The finding is reasonable if, as the authors argue, batterers tend to minimize and to deny their own aggression.

Jekyll-Hyde Personality

In light of the negative descriptions offered up to this point, it may seem contradictory to note that batterers sometimes are described as nice, humorous, charming, and sensitive. Actually, some clinicians see the batterer as having a Jekyll-Hyde type of personality. Although restrictive toward his wife and family, he can be personable in situations in which intimacy is not involved (Bernard & Bernard, 1984; Purdy & Nickle, 1981; Sonkin et al., 1985; Wetzel & Ross, 1983). According to Hastings and Hamberger (1988), batterers may present an agreeable impression in superficial interactions "that do not challenge or threaten the batterer's tenuous rigid adjustment. . . . It is only when the relationship has become important, and when the batterer's sense of control is threatened, that the negative features such as violence and intimidation emerge" (p. 43). The batterer reacts to situations that would seem trivial to others with extreme threat and anger.

An empirical study by Dutton (1988) provides evidence for the interpretation just offered. Batterers were compared with two groups of nonbatterers, happily married and maritally dysfunctional, and also with a group of generally assaultive men. The test situation was one in which videotapes of scenes involving power interactions between husband and wife were viewed. Where the female was shown initiating independent action, batterers perceived more abandonment than the other three groups. They also reported more anger and said that, if they were presented with a similar situation in their own lives, they would use physical aggression to regain control.

Alienation and Psychopathic Tendencies

Schuerger and Reigle (1988) found that their large sample of batterers scored above the population norm on those scales of the Psychological Screening Inventory that assessed alienation and nonconformity. In fact, the test results for a substantial proportion of participants were found to resemble those of incarcerated criminals. The conclusion reached by Schuerger and Reigle was that batterers are pathologically deviant.

Hastings and Hamberger (1988) reported similar findings. In their study, batterers scored significantly higher than nonbatterers on scales of the Millon Clinical Multiaxial Inventory that assess alienation and nonconformity. Additional evidences comes from a study by Vaselle-Horner and Ehrlich (in press). They found that batterers obtained significantly higher scores than nonbatterers on two scales of the Minnesota Multiphasic Personality Inventory, schizophrenia and psychopathic deviancy, that assess alienation and tendencies toward antisocial behavior. On the psychopathic deviancy scale, the mean score for batterers was in the range considered to be pathological.

ARE BATTERERS DIFFERENT FROM OTHER MEN?

Marital Unhappiness and Assaultiveness

Rosenbaum and O'Leary (1981) and also Telch and Lindquist (1984) have argued that some personality characteristics presently ascribed to batterers really are not specific to them but rather are shared by all men who are experiencing marital difficulties. However, in a number of the studies described earlier (Dutton, 1988; Dutton & Strachan, 1987; Goldstein & Rosenbaum, 1985; Hastings & Hamberger, 1988; Vaselle-Horner & Ehrlich, in press), this factor was controlled. Batterers were found to differ significantly on some, if not all, measures from nonbatterers who were maritally unhappy. Moreover, the differences were always in the expected direction, with batterers exhibiting more psychopathology than nonbatterers. Marital unhappiness, then, is not what distinguishes batterers.

A similar point arises with respect to the question of whether a meaningful distinction can be made between batterers and men who are generally assaultive. Both clinical and empirical data suggest that there is some overlap between the groups, but batterers, nevertheless, have some unique characteristics (Cadsky & Crawford, 1988; Dutton, 1988; Maiuro et al., 1988; Shields, McCall, & Hanneke, 1988).

Psychopathology and Types of Batterers

The evidence reviewed up to this point, both clinical and empirical, suggests that, as a group, batterers have an identifiable set of personality characteristics: dependence, depression, anxiety, low self-esteem, paranoia, dissociation from their own feelings, poor impulse control, antisocial tendencies, and hostility toward women. The evidence also suggests that there is psychopathology in many, if not all, batterers. There is no reason to assume, however, that all batterers are alike. What a number of investigators have suggested is the existence of various types (Allen et al., 1989; Cadsky & Crawford, 1988; Maiuro et al., 1988; Shields et al., 1988; Sonkin, 1988). Empirical attempts to distinguish such types have been made by Hamberger and Hastings (1986) and by Gondolf (1988).

Hamberger and Hastings (1986) administered the Millon Clinical Multiaxial Inventory to a sample of batterers and factor-analyzed the scores. Three main factors that were indicative of personality disorder were identified: borderline or schizoid, narcissistic or antisocial, and passive-dependent/compulsive. Based on the extent to which they had various combinations of high and low scores on each factor, batterers were divided into eight subgroups, seven of which could be characterized as pathological.

Group 1 was volatile and overreactive with poor impulse control. Men in this group had the Jekyll-Hyde personality and conformed to the DSM-III diagnostic category of borderline personality. Group 2 was rigid about rules and regulations; for them, punishment was administered unemotionally. They conformed to the DSM-III category of narcissistic or antisocial personality. Group 3 was rebellious, hostile, dependent, and low in self-esteem. They conformed to the DSM-III category of dependent or compulsive personality. Group 4 was the classic psychopathic personality—angry, aggressive, and antisocial. Group 5 had pronounced mood swings and a borderline personality. Group 6 was superficially charming but sensitive to rejection and apt to respond aggressively when dependency needs were not met. Group 7 was characterized by marked dependency needs, anxiety, and depression. Group 8 was low on all factors, and it was the only group that showed no clear pathology.

In a follow-up study, in which there was a control group of nonbatterers and the Millon Clinical Multiaxial Inventory was administered again, Hastings and Hamberger (1988) were able to demonstrate significant differences between batterers and nonbatterers on two of the three factors identified earlier: borderline and passive-aggressive.

Gondolf (1988) reported a cluster analysis on measures of batterer characteristics that were derived from interviews with a very large sample (more than 500) of battered women. Three batterer types were distinguished. The first, labeled "sociopathic," was likely to have been sexually abusive as well as physically abusive and was likely, too, to have been arrested for violent and drug-related crimes. This type was estimated to account for only 7% of batterers. The second type, labeled "antisocial," was also physically and verbally abusive but was less likely to have been generally violent and less likely to have been arrested. This type was estimated to account for 41% of batterers. The third type, the "typical batterer," engaged in less severe verbal and physical abuse, was less likely to have been arrested, was more likely to be apologetic after the battering, and conformed most closely to the prevalent clinical picture of the batterer. Victims were most likely to return to this third type, which was estimated to account for 52% of batterers. As Gondolf (1988) noted, some of the findings agreed with the description given by Hamberger and Hastings (1986) of the sociopathic/narcissistic batterer.

DISCUSSION

The suggestion that batterers are not normal men has met with considerable resistance. One objection is that calling the batterer pathological seems to ignore the larger social context in which battering occurs, the violence in society (Straus, 1977/1978), and the social approval of violence against women (Bograd, 1984). A second objection is that putting a psychiatric label on the batterer seems to absolve him of responsibility (Brennan, 1985; Edleson et al., 1985; Gondolf, 1988; Watts & Courtois, 1981). If he is sick, he is to be pitied and is not to be held accountable for his actions. A third objection is that calling the batterer pathological suggests that battering ought to be rare (Bograd, 1988; Zoomer, 1983); yet, the evidence shows that battering is not rare (Gelles, 1980). A fourth and final objection is that focusing on what are seen as underlying problems that "cause" battering means that attention is diverted from the main issue, which is the need to end the man's violence (Adams, 1988).

The objections just cited are by no means trivial. However, recognition of the role played by individual pathology in battering does not necessarily mean that social-cultural factors, developmental history, environmental factors, and other important contributing causes need to be ignored or discounted. Neither is it necessary to adopt the extreme position that nothing is important other than individual pathology. Nor does acceptance of the existence of individual pathology in batterers mean that they should not be held responsible for their actions. " . . . a focus on psychological characteristics of batterers in no way condones, excuses, or deflects responsibility for the violence of men toward women" (Hamberger & Hastings, 1988a, p. 764).

Perhaps the most reasonable approach is to view battering as having many determinants. Consider, for example, the role played by sexism. There is no evidence that batterers are more sexist than other men (Dutton, 1988; Hotaling & Sugarman, 1986; Rosenbaum, 1986a). Yet, sexism undoubtedly plays a role in battering. As other authors have pointed out, sexism is endemic to the male socialization process (Hotaling & Sugarman, 1986; Sonkin, 1988). There is social approval of violence (Straus et al., 1980), especially when it is directed at women (Bograd, 1984; Walker, 1981). Training begun in the family is reinforced outside by the media (Sonkin et al., 1985) and by social institutions like the legal system and religion (Adams & McCormick, 1982). Thus, the role of sexism is to provide a *context* within which battering can occur.

As another example of other factors, consider the role played by developmental history. A high proportion of batterers experienced or witnessed violence in the home (Hotaling & Sugarman, 1986; Tolman & Bennett, 1990). For the man who had such experiences, the lesson is that violence is an acceptable mode of interpersonal interaction, even in an intimate relationship (Bernard & Bernard, 1983; Carlson, 1977; Stahly, 1977/1978). The specific behaviors involved in battering are modeled, and there is, correspondingly, a lack of modeling of more appropriate ways in which to express anger and to resolve differences (Guerney et al., 1987). Thus, the importance of developmental factors is not that the man is doomed to repeat whatever happened in his own childhood, but rather that his childhood learning experiences provide him with a set of expectations about family interactions and also with a specific set of behaviors to be used in interactions with others.

As yet another example of the role played by other factors, consider the relationship between battering and use of alcohol and other drugs. As noted earlier, there is evidence for a high level of substance abuse in batterers (Hamberger & Hastings, 1986; Hotaling & Sugarman, 1986; Schuerger & Reigle, 1988; Sonkin et al., 1985). Some authorities describe substance abuse as an environmental factor that can trigger battering. Alcohol, in particular, has been described as a disinhibitor of aggression (Guerney et al., 1987; Shupe et al., 1987). However, alcohol and other substances are perhaps best seen not as triggers but as excuses. Men drink when they want to hit (Gondolf, 1988), and the use of alcohol and other chemicals allows the man to avoid personal responsibility for his behavior (Ponzetti, Cate, & Koval, 1982).

The significance of the examples just given is that no attempt is being made here to deny the fact that a full explanation of battering must take into account other issues besides personality and psychopathology. However, factors like sexism, developmental history, and substance abuse are important only to the extent that they act on an individual with a particular constellation of personality traits (e.g., poor impulse control, dissociation, low ego strength). In the final analysis, it is the individual man who acts. Even in a violent and sexist society, not all men become batterers (Rounsaville, 1978; Sonkin, 1988). As Breines and Gordon (1983) point out: " . . . no act of violence is merely the expression of a social problem (or culture) such as poverty or unemployment or male domination; each is also the personal act of a unique individual" (p. 530). If more attention is directed toward psychodynamic issues, that change should in no way affect attempts by feminists to change the larger social system within which battering occurs and is condoned. The need to increase sanctions against violent behavior and to change sexist attitudes remains.

IMPLICATIONS FOR TREATMENT

Most treatment programs rely heavily on cognitive training; batterers are taught appropriate communication and problem-solving skills, as well as ways to control anger (Chen, Bersani, Myers, & Denton, 1989; Deschner, 1984; Edleson, 1984; Waldo, 1987). Some therapists add training in assertion and relaxation (Deschner, 1984; Edleson, 1984; Hamberger & Hastings, 1986b) and either specifically challenge the man's sexist expectations about the need to be in control (Adams, 1988) or at least attempt to model nonsexist interactions (Bern & Bern, 1984; Bernard & Bernard, 1984).

However, regardless of these variations and, whether men are seen in groups (Chen et al., 1989; Currie, 1983; Dutton, 1984; Edleson, 1984; Gondolf, 1985; Waldo, 1987) or the batterer and his victim are seen as a couple (Harris, 1986; Margolin, 1979; Taylor, 1984), what characterizes virtually all programs is that treatment is brief, is oriented around the acquisition of new skills, and is more educative than therapeutic. What seems to be lacking is any systematic attempt to deal with psychodynamic issues in depth. Although it is not always stated explicitly, the rationale for most current treatment programs seems to be that: (1) the batterer is an essentially normal male whose difficulties lie primarily in two areas: anger control and communication; and (2) the man will stop battering if he is shown a more effective way in which to deal with his anger and to communicate his needs.

Whether these brief, educative training programs actually work is not clear. Although some clinicians admit that their success rate is low (Deschner, 1984; Schuerger & Reigle, 1988; Walker, 1981), many others claim that their programs are successful (Bern & Bern, 1984; Deschner & McNeil, 1986; Dutton, 1986; Hamberger & Hastings, 1988b; Poynter, 1989; Rosenbaum, 1986b). However, there is a problem about how success is defined. According to Walker and Browne (1985), of the small number of men who complete training programs, at least half continue their violent behavior with new partners after they leave treatment. Where the relationship remains intact, success may mean only that the violence is reduced but not eliminated entirely (Baum, Brand, Colley, & Cooke, 1987) or that the man is not seen again in court (Roberts, 1987). Also, beatings may stop but verbal and emotional harassment may continue (Brennan, 1985; Edleson & Syers, 1990; Gondolf, 1987). Even if a standard definition of success were adopted, the assessment problem would remain. Only a small number of evaluative studies come close to being methodologically adequate in that there was an untreated and randomly assigned control group (Harris, Savage, Jones, & Brooke, 1988), the problem posed by the high attrition rate in treatment programs was taken into account (Chen et al., 1989), and appropriate statistical analyses were done (Chen et al., 1989).

The evidence reviewed here suggests strongly that there is a need to rethink current treatment modes. Although several authors have recognized that need, the major suggestion seems to be that treatment programs be longer (Bernard & Bernard, 1984; Brennan, 1985; Gondolf, 1987; Hamberger & Hastings, 1988b; Shupe et al., 1987; Sonkin, 1988), so that attention can be paid to drug and alcohol problems (Sonkin, 1988), marital difficulties (Shupe et al., 1987), and ethical development (Gondolf, 1987). Because we believe that many batterers exhibit serious psychopathology, we would argue that treatment not merely be longer but that a specific attempt be made to deal with deeper psychodynamic issues. By giving the women who live with them a false sense of security (Gondolf, 1988; Tolman & Bennett, 1990), clinicians who treat batterers with serious psychopathology by means of short-term and essentially non-depth interventions may do more harm than they realize.

BIBLIOGRAPHY

Adams, D. (1988). Treatment models of men who batter: A profeminist analysis. In Kersti Yllo & Michele Bograd (Eds.), *Feminist perspective on wife abuse* (pp. 176–199). Beverly Hills, CA: Sage.

Adams, D. C., & McCormick, A. J. (1982). Men unlearning violence: A group approach based on the collective model. In M. Roy (Ed.), *The abusive partner: The analysis of domestic battering* (pp. 170–197). New York: Von Nostrand Reinhold.

Allen, K., Calsyn, D. A., Fehrenbach, P. A., & Benton, G. (1989). A study of the interpersonal behaviors of male batterers. *Journal of Interpersonal Violence, 4*, 79–89.

Bach, G. R. (1980). Spouse killing: The final abuse. *Journal of Contemporary Psychotherapy, 11*, 91–103.

Bagarozzi, D. A., & Giddings, C. W. (1983). Conjugal violence: A critical view of current research and clinical practices. *The American Journal of Family Therapy, 11*, 3–15.

Baum, F., Brand, R., Colley, D., & Cooke, R. (1987). Preventing family violence: The evaluation of a group for men who are violent towards their partners. *Australian Journal of Sex, Marriage and Family, 8*, 173–183.

Bern, E. H., & Bern, L. L. (1984). A group program for men who commit violence towards their wives. *Social Work with Groups, 7*, 63–77.

Bernard, M. L., & Bernard, J. L. (1983). Violent intimacy: The family as a model for love relationships. *Family Relations, 32*, 283–286.

Bernard, J. L., & Bernard, M. L. (1984). The abusive male seeking treatment: Jeckyll and Hyde. *Family Relations, 33*, 543–547.

Bograd, M. (1984). Family systems approaches to wife battering: A feministic critique. *American Journal of Orthopsychiatry, 54*, 558–568.

Bograd, M. (1988). Feminist perspectives on wife abuse: An introduction. In Kersti Yllo & Michele Bograd (Eds.), *Feminist perspectives on wife abuse* (pp. 11–27). Beverly Hills, CA: Sage.

Bowker, L. H. (1983). Marital rape: A distinct syndrome? *Social Casework, 64*, 347–352.

Bowlby, J. (1984). Violence in the family as a disorder of the attachment and caregiving systems. *The American Journal of Psychoanalysis, 44*, 9–27.

Breines, W., & Gordon, L. (1983). The new scholarship on family violence. *Signs, 8*, 490–531.

Brennan, A. F. (1985). Political and psychosocial issues in psychotherapy for spouse abusers: Implications for treatment. *Psychotherapy, 22*, 643–654.

Cadsky, O., & Crawford, M. (1988). Establishing batterer typologies in a clinical sample of men who assault their female partners. *Canadian Journal of Community Mental Health, 7*, 119–127.

Carlson, B. E. (1977). Battered women and their assailants. *Social Casework, 22*, 455–460.

Chen, H. T., Bersani, C., Myers, S. C., & Denton, R. (1989). Evaluating the effectiveness of a court-sponsored treatment program. *Journal of Family Violence, 4*, 309–322.

Coleman, K. H. (1980). Conjugal violence: What 33 men report. *Journal of Marital and Family Therapy, 6*, 207–213.

Currie, D. W. (1983). A Toronto model. *Social Work with Groups, 6*, 179–188.

Davidovich, J. R. (1990). Men who abuse their spouses: Social and psychological supports. *Journal of Offender Counseling, Services and Rehabilitation, 15*, 27–44.

Davidson, T. (1978). *Conjugal crime*. New York: Hawthorn Books.

Deschner, J. P. (1984). *The hitting habit: Anger control for battering couples*. New York: Freedom Press.

Deschner, J. P., & McNeil, J. S. (1986). Results of anger control training for battering couples. *Journal of Family Violence, 1*, 111–120.

Dobash, R. E., & Dobash, R. P. (1977/1978). Wives: The "appropriate" victims of marital violence. *Victimology, 2*, 426–442.

Dobash, R. E. & Dobash, R. P. (1984). The nature and antecedents of violent events. *British Journal of Criminology, 24*, 269–288.

Doherty, J. F. (1983). Self-esteem, anxiety and dependency in men who batter women. Dissertation Abstracts International 44A: 1384.

Dutton, D. G. (1984). Interventions into the problem of wife assault: Therapeutic, policy and research implications. *Canadian Journal of Behavioral Science, 16*, 281–297.

Dutton, D. G. (1986). The outcome of court-mandated treatment for wife assault: A quasi-experimental evaluation. *Violence and Victims, 1*, 163–175.

Dutton, D. G. (1988). *The domestic assault of women: Psychological and criminal justice perspectives*. Newton, MA: Allyn & Bacon.

Dutton, D. G., Fehr, B., & McEwen, H. (1982). Severe wife battering as deindividuated violence. *Victimology, 7*, 13–23.

Dutton, D. G., & Strachan, C. G. (1987). Motivational needs for power and spouse-specific assertiveness in assaultive and non-assaultive men. *Violence and Victims, 2*, 145–156.

Edleson, J. L. (1984). Working with men who batter. *Social Work, 29*, 237–242.

Edleson, J. L., & Syers, M. (1990). Relative effectiveness of group treatments for men who batter. *Social Work Research and Abstracts, 26*, 10–17.

Edleson, J. L., Eisikovits, Z., & Guttman, E. (1985). Men who batter women: A critical review. *Journal of Family Violence, 6*, 229–247.

Elbow, M. (1977). Theoretical considerations of violent marriages. *Social Casework, 58*, 515–526.

Fitch, F. J., & Papantonio, A. (1983). Men who batter: Some pertinent characteristics. *The Journal of Nervous and Mental Disease, 171*, 190–192.

Follingstad, D. R. (1980). A reconceptualization of issues in the treatment of abused women: A case study. *Psychotherapy: Theory, Research and Practice, 17*, 294–303.

Gayford, J. J. (1975). Wife-battering; A preliminary survey of 100 cases. *British Medical Journal, 1*, 194–197.

Gayford, J. J. (1983). Battered wives. In Richard J. Gelles & C. P. Cornell (Eds.), *International perspective on family violence* (pp. 123–128). Lexington, MA: Heath.

Gelles, R. J. (1974). *The violent home*. Beverly Hills, CA: Sage.

Gelles, R. J. (1980). Violence in the family: A review of research in the seventies. *Journal of Marriage and the Family, 42*, 873–885.

Gelles, R. J., & Cornell, C. P. (1983). Introduction: An international perspective on family violence. In Richard J. Gelles & C. P. Cornell (Eds.), *International perspectives on family violence*. Lexington, MA: Heath.

Gillman, I. S. (1980). An object-relations approach to the phenomenon and treatment of battered women. *Psychiatry, 43*, 346–358.

Goldstein, D., & Rosenbaum, A. (1985). An evaluation of the self-esteem of marital, violent men. *Family Relations, 34*, 425–428.

Goodstein, R. K., & Page, A. W. (1981). Battered wife syndrome: Overview of dynamics and treatment. *American Journal of Psychiatry, 138*, 1036–1043.

Gondolf, E. W. (1985). Fighting for control: A clinical assessment of men who batter. *Social Casework, 66*, 48–54.

Gondolf, E. W. (1987). Changing men who batter: A developmental model for integrated interventions. *Journal of Family Violence, 2*, 335–349.

Gondolf, E. G. (1988). Who are those guys? Toward a behavioral typology of batterers. *Violence and Victims, 3*, 187–203.

Guerney, B., Jr., Waldo, W., & Firestone, L. (1987). Wife-battering: A theoretical construct and case report. *The American Journal of Family Therapy, 15*, 34–43.

Hallschmid, C. A., Black, E. L., & Checkley, K. L. (1985). The core boundary: A conceptual analysis of interspousal violence from a construct-system perspective. *International Journal of Offender Therapy and Comparative Criminology, 29*, 15–34.

Hamberger, L. K., & Hastings, J. E. (1986). Personality correlates of men who abuse their partners: A cross validation study. *Journal of Family Violence, 1*, 323–341.

Hamberger, L. K., & Hastings, J. E. (1988a). Characteristics of spouse abusers consistent with personality disorders. *Hospital and Community Psychiatry, 39,* 763–770.

Hamberger, L. K., & Hastings, J. E. (1988b). Skills training for treatment of spouse abusers: An outcome study. *Journal of Family Violence, 3,* 121–130.

Harris, J. (1986). Counseling violent couples using Walker's model. *Psychotherapy, 23,* 613–621.

Harris, R., Savage, S., Jones, T., & Brooke, W. (1988). A comparison of treatments for abusive men and their partners within a family-service agency. *Canadian Journal of Community Mental Health, 7,* 147–155.

Hastings, J. E., & Hamberger, L. K. (1988). Personality characteristics of spouse abusers: A controlled comparison. *Violence and Victims, 3,* 31–48.

Hotaling, G. T., & Sugarman, D. B. (1986). An analysis of risk markers in husband to wife violence: The current state of knowledge. *Violence and Victims, 1,* 101–123.

Keith, H. S. (1988). A comparison of consort batterers and non-batterers on measures of impulsivity, dependency, locus-of-control orientation, and self-esteem. *Dissertation Abstracts International, 49/08-B:*3441.

Kelly, E. M., & Loesch, L. C. (1983). Abused wives: Perceptions during crisis counseling. *American Mental Health Counselors Association Journal, 5,* 132–140.

Kleckner, J. H. (1978). Wife beaters and beaten wives: Co-conspirators in crimes of violence. *Psychology, 15,* 45–54.

Maiuro, R. C., Cahn, T. S., & Vitaliano, P. P. (1986). Assertiveness deficits and hostility in domestically violent men. *Violence and Victims, 1,* 279–289.

Maiuro, R. D., Cahn, T. S., Vitaliano, P. P., Wagner, B. C., & Zegree, J. B. (1988). Anger, hostility, and depression in domestically violent versus generally assaultive men and nonviolent control subjects. *Journal of Consulting and Clinical Psychology, 56,* 17–23.

Margolin, G. (1979). Conjoint marital therapy to enhance anger management and reduce spouse abuse. *The American Journal of Family Therapy, 7,* 13–23.

Margolin, G. (1987). The multiple forms of aggressiveness between marital partners. How do we identify them? *Journal of Marital and Family Therapy, 13,* 77–84.

Martin, D. (1978). Battered women: Society's problem. In J. R. Chapman & M. Gates (Eds.), *The victimization of women* (pp. 111–142). Beverly Hills, CA: Sage.

Mushanga, T. M. (1983). Wife victimization in East and Central Africa. In J. Gelles & C. P. Cornell (Eds.), *International perspectives on family violence* (pp. 139–146). Lexington, MA: D. C. Heath.

Myers, T., & Gilbert, S. (1983). Wifebeaters' group through a women's center: Why and how. *Victimology, 8,* 238–248.

Neidig, P. H. (1984). Women's shelters, men's collectives, and other issues in the field of spouse abuse. *Victimology, 9,* 464–476.

Neidig, P. H., Friedman, D. H., & Collins, B. S. (1986). Attitudinal characteristics of males who have engaged in spouse abuse. *Journal of Family Violence, 1,* 223–233.

Pagelow, M. D. (1981). *Women-battering: Victims and their experiences.* Beverly Hills, CA: Sage.

Pattison, E. M. (1985). Violent marriages. *Medical Aspects of Human Sexuality, 19,* 57–74.

Ponzetti, J. J., Jr., Cate, R. M., & Koval, J. E. (1982). Violence between couples: Profiling the male abuser. *Personnel and Guidance Journal, 61,* 222–224.

Poynter, T. L. (1989). An evaluation of a group program for male perpetrators of domestic violence. *Australian Journal of Sex, Marriage, and Family, 10,* 133–142.

Ptacek, J. (1988). Why do men batter their wives? In K. Yllo & M. Bograd (Eds.), *Feminist perspectives on wife abuse* (pp. 133–157). Beverly Hills, CA: Sage.

Purdy, F., & Nickle, N. (1981). Practice principles for working with groups of men who batter. *Social Work with Groups, 4,* 111–122.

Rae-Grant, Q. (1983). Family violence—myths, measures, and mandates. *Canadian Journal of Psychiatry, 28,* 505–512.

Roberts, A. R. (1987). Psychosocial characteristics of batterers: A study of 234 men charged with domestic violence offenses. *Journal of Family Violence, 2,* 81–93.

Rosenbaum, A. (1986a). Of men, macho, and marital violence. *Journal of Family Violence, 1,* 121–129.

Rosenbaum, A. (1986b). Group treatment for abusive men: Process and outcome. *Psychotherapy, 23,* 607–612.

Rosenbaum, A., & O'Leary, K. D. (1981). Marital violence: Characteristics of abusive couples. *Journal of Counseling and Clinical Psychology, 49,* 63–71.

Rounsaville, B. J. (1978). Theories of marital violence: Evidence from a study of battered women. *Victimology: An International Journal, 3,* 11–31.

Saunders, D. G. (1984). Helping husbands who batter. *Social Casework, 65,* 347–353.

Schuerger, J. M., & Reigle, N. (1988). Personality and biographic data that characterize men who abuse their wives. *Journal of Clinical Psychology, 44,* 75–81.

Shainess, N. (1979). Vulnerability to violence: Evidence from a study of battered women. *Victimology, 3,* 11–31.

Shields, N. M., & Hanneke, C. R. (1983). Attribution process in violent relationships: Perceptions of violent husbands and their wives. *Journal of Applied Social Psychology, 13,* 515–527.

Shields, N. M., McCall, G. J., & Hanneke, C. R. (1988). Patterns of family and nonfamily violence: Violent husbands and violent men. *Violence and Victims, 3,* 83–97.

Shupe, A., Stacy, W., & Hazlewood, L. (1987). *Violent men, violent couples: The dynamics of domestic violence.* Lexington, MA: D. C. Heath.

Smith, S. (1984). The battered woman: A consequence of female development. *Women and Therapy, 3,* 3–9.

Snell, J. E., Rosenwald, J., & Robey, A. (1964). The wife-beater's wife. *Archives of Psychiatry, 2,* 107–109.

Sonkin, D. J. (1988). The male batterer: Clinical and research issues. *Violence and Victims, 3,* 65–79.

Sonkin, D. J., Martin, D., & Walker, L. E. A. (1985). *The male batterer: A treatment approach.* New York: Springer.

Stahly, G. B. (1977/1978). A review of select literature of spousal violence. *Victimology, 2,* 591–607.

Stewart, M. A., & deBlois, C. S. (1981). Wife abuse among families attending a child psychiatry clinic. *Journal of the American Academy of Child Psychiatry, 20,* 845–862.

Straus, M. A. (1977/1978). Wifebeating: How common and why? *Victimology: An International Journal, 3–4,* 443–458.

Straus, M. A., Gelles, R., & Steinmetz, S. (1980). *Behind closed doors: Violence in the American family.* Garden City, NY: Anchor.

Symonds, M. (1978). The psychodynamics of violence prone marriages. *The American Journal of Psychoanalysis, 38,* 213–222.

Symonds, M. (1984). Discussion of "violence in the family as a disorder of the attachment and caregiving system." *The American Journal of Psychoanalysis, 44,* 29–31.

Szinovacz, M. E. (1982). Economic resources, wife's skepticism, and marital violence. *International Journal of Family Psychiatry, 3,* 419–437.

Taylor, J. W. (1984). Structured conjoint therapy for spouse abuse cases. *Social Casework, 65,* 11–18.

Telch, C. F., & Lindquist, C. U. (1984). Violent versus nonviolent couples: A comparison of patterns. *Psychotherapy, 21,* 242–248.

Tolman, R. M., & Bennett, L. W. (1990). A review of quantitative research on men who batter. *Journal of Interpersonal Violence, 5,* 87–118.

Vaselle-Horner, R., & Ehrlich, A. (in press). Psychopathology of men who batter. *Victimology.*

Waldo, M. (1987). Also victims: Understanding and treating men arrested for spouse abuse. *Journal of Counseling and Development, 65,* 385–388.

Walker, L. E. (1978). Treatment alternatives for battered women. In J. R. Chapman and M. Gates (Eds.), *The victimization of women* (pp. 111–142). Beverly Hills, CA: Sage.

Walker, L. E. (1981). Battered women: Sex roles and clinical issues. *Professional Psychology, 12,* 81–91.

Walker, L. E., & Browne, A. (1985). Gender and victimization by intimates. *Journal of Personality, 53,* 179–195.

Watts, D. L., & Courtois, C. A. (1981). Trends in the treatment of men who commit violence against women. *Personnel and Guidance Journal, 60,* 245–249.

Weitzman, J., & Dreen, K. (1982). Wife beating: A view of the marital dyad. *Social Casework, 63,* 259–265.

Wetzel, L., & Ross, M. A. (1983). Psychological and social ramifications of battering: Observations leading to a counseling methodology for victims of domestic violence. *Personnel and Guidance Journal, 61,* 423–428.

Zoomer, O. J. (1983). On the social causes and function of violence against women. *International Journal of Offender Therapy and Comparative Criminology, 27,* 173–183.

PART VI

APPROACHES AND INTERVENTIONS

13

Translating Theory into Practice: A Conceptual Framework for Clinical Assessment, Differential Diagnosis, and Multi-Modal Treatment of Maritally Violent Individuals, Couples, and Families

Susan E. Hanks
California School of Professional Psychology, Berkeley/Alameda

INTRODUCTION

Staunch adherence to either political philosophies or rigid clinical paradigms does disservice to the men, women, and children who suffer the emotional and physical pain of domestic violence. Psychological, sociological, sociocultural, and feminist theories, as well as the existent empirical research, regarding the causes and consequences of marital violence must be bridged in integrating psychotherapeutic interventions with other modes of interventions. A conceptual framework is presented upon which multi-modal clinical services for maritally violent families can be based. A typology of maritally violent families is identified with implications for differential diagnosis, assessment, and clinical intervention. A therapist's countertransferential reactions, which can be expected, are described with recommendations for staffing patterns that mitigate professional burnout and prevent agency demoralization.

The prevalence of violence within the family histories of clinical populations (Herman, 1986; Hilberman, 1986; Jacobson, Koehler & Jones-Brown, 1987), as well as within the general population (Hotaling & Sugarman, 1987; Rosenbaum & O'Leary, 1981; Straus, 1978) has been well documented. In spite of increased specialization,

This chapter was awarded the Alumni Special Recognition Award by the Simmons College School of Social Work, Alumni Association, 1990 Annual Awards Program, Boston, Massachusetts.

Susan E. Hanks, S.M., L.C.S.W., is a Board Certified Diplomat in Clinical Social Work. She is the Founding Director of The Family & Violence Institute at the California School of Professional Psychology in Berkeley/Alameda. The Family & Violence Institute is a clinical treatment, training, and research project whose purposes are to intervene in the psychological causes and consequences of violence within the family, to train mental health practitioners and researchers to work effectively with this population, and to contribute to the body of knowledge within the field of family violence.

Ms. Hanks maintains a private clinical and consulting practice in Berkeley, CA. She is a member of the adjunct clinical, teaching, and research faculty at the California School of Professional Psychology. She is a Doctoral Candidate at the California Institute for Clinical Social Work.

however, most services for maritally violent families have been, and will continue to be, provided in traditional mental health and social service settings by clinicians whose education ill-prepares them to intervene appropriately. Sophisticated clinical theory and technique must be adapted and interwoven with social system interventions in treating the psychological causes and consequences of marital violence. Interventions that can be replicated in traditional mental health settings and integrated into the graduate level training programs of mental health practitioners need to be developed.

This chapter presents a conceptual framework upon which clinical services for maritally violent families can be based. A multi-modal treatment approach grounded in the psychodynamic theories of object relations (Fairbairn, 1952; Guntrip, 1969; Kernberg, 1984) and family systems (Scharff & Scharff, 1987; Slipp, 1984) and integrated with sociocultural and feminist perspectives (Bograd, 1982; Breines & Gordon, 1983; Griswold, 1986; Hanks, 1984; Stark & Flitcraft, 1988) is proposed. A typology of maritally violent families is identified with implications for differential diagnosis, assessment, and clinical intervention. Expectable countertransference reactions are presented. Staffing patterns are recommended that mitigate professional burnout and agency demoralization.

RECONCILING PARADIGMS

The literature is flooded with a host of presumed causes, predictors, and theories explaining marital violence (Gelles, 1979; Hotaling & Sugarman, 1987) and challenging the appropriateness of psychotherapeutic interventions. Clinicians should be informed and appreciative of the collective heuristic value of this debate.

The feminist perspective argues that family violence is produced by a patriarchal culture in which male power dominates. Societal norms and values are viewed as historically condoning marital violence (Bograd, 1984; Dobash & Dobash, 1979; Griswold, 1986; Hanks, 1984). Accordingly, one of the concrete issues that confronts the battered woman's movement is resisting the mental health profession's tendency to disavow a feminist analysis.

The sociological perspective argues that violence is not a reflection of individual pathology but is a fundamental aspect of human association. Violence is viewed as a nearly universal and normal, in other words, statistically frequent and culturally approved, aspect of family life (Gelles, 1979). Social system and environmental interventions are thus deemed appropriate.

The psychological perspective that defines physical violence as an abnormal manifestation of individual pathology has been widely critiqued for viewing human behavior independent of its social-political or interpersonal context. This perspective has the dubious, although well deserved, distinction of being historically most responsible for promulgating "victim blaming" notions that make a battered woman's actions the cause of her partner's violence (Bograd, 1982; Breines & Gordon, 1983; Hilberman, 1980). Psychodynamic and family systems theories (Cook & Frantz-Cook, 1984; Gilman, 1980; Hanks & Rosenbaum, 1977) are viewed with particular suspicion (Bograd, 1984). In an effort not to replicate victim blaming notions, the behavioral and social learning theories of learned helplessness (Walker, 1979), traumatic bonding (Dutton & Painter, 1981), and posttraumatic stress (Walker, 1989) have been applied to explain the debilitating behavioral reinforcements experienced by women in violent relationships.

It is difficult to transfer to actual clinical practice either empirical research findings or feminist theories on the causes and consequences of marital violence (Gelles, 1982). As Gelles (1979) states, it is extremely unlikely that family violence will be amenable to simplistic, single variable explanations. Simple empirical results, or statements repeated by early authors in the field until they gained the status of "law" (Gelles, 1979), do not necessarily inform sound clinical practice. In addition, the lumping together of types, levels, and populations has limited both knowledge building and utility because it obfuscates distinguishing subtleties (Hobbs, 1987). All maritally violent families are not the same. Families differ in the intrapsychic functioning of the individual members, in the man's and woman's functioning as a marital pair, in the family's functioning as a unit, and in the social-political context in which they live. The type, frequency, severity, and meaning of the violent behavior itself differs from couple to couple. The response of the battering man, battered woman, and the child/witness to marital violence is different (Pagelow, 1981; Snyder & Fruchtman, 1981; Stullman, Schoenenberger, & Hanks, 1987). Each of the emergent feminist, sociological, and psychological perspectives are necessary but insufficient unto themselves to explain adequately and to treat this prevalent family, clinical, and social problem.

TRANSLATING THEORY INTO PRACTICE

Defining Violence

Marital violence occurs between two adults in a mutually defined significant, intimate "marital" relationship, which may or may not be legally sanctioned. Marital violence refers to physical battering, in other words, the use of physical force or restraint carried out with the intent of causing physical pain or injury to another person. The physical battering may be accompanied by psychological, sexual, and/or property violence. Marital violence may also occur concurrently with other forms of violence within the family, such as child physical abuse or child sexual abuse. Marital violence, therefore, is a behavior, or set of behaviors, and does not constitute a psychological syndrome unto itself (Ceasar, 1985; Greenberg, 1987). It is multiply determined, the result of many different sets of intrapsychic, interpersonal, environmental and sociocultural dynamics.

Marital violence jeopardizes the physical safety of each individual in the family, whether abuser, victim, or child/witness. It has a psychologically debilitating effect on each individual family member as well as on the functioning of the family as a unit. Marital violence results in short- and long-term psychological sequelae and latent violence prone propensities within the family system even after the physical battering ceases (Bowlby, 1984; Kaufman & Ziegler, 1987).

Client Characteristics

An adequate clinical conceptual framework and clinical intervention strategy must encompass a view not only of the individuals involved but also of the family as a unit. Although much has been reported about the dynamics of maritally violent couples (Geller & Wasserstrom, 1985; Parnell, 1983; Rosenbaum & O'Leary, 1981; Rosenbaum & O'Leary, 1986), the literature is surprisingly sparse in regard to the impact of marital violence over time on the functioning of the family as a unit.

Early research in marital violence focused extensively on the battered woman because she was the most accessible family member (Hanks & Rosenbaum, 1977; Hilberman & Munson, 1978; Walker, 1979). In a recent review of victim characteristics (family histories, personality characteristics, and behaviors), only a woman's witnessing violence in her family of origin was consistently associated with being battered (Hotaling & Sugarman, 1987). There is no direct evidence that battered women have a clinically diagnosable character disorder to a greater extent than non-battered women. Personality and symptomalogical differences among battered women are viewed as consequences, not causes, of battering (Walker, 1984).

In the research on men who batter, no one psychological syndrome has been identified that is consistently associated with wife battering. Their characteristics are variously described in the literature as those of borderline, narcissistic, paranoid, or antisocial personality disorders, although these labels are rarely ascribed (Brennan, 1985; Ceasar, 1985; Coleman, 1980; Fitch, 1983; Greenberg, 1987; Herman, 1986; Hotaling & Sugarman, 1987; Rosenbaum & O'Leary, 1981). Witnessing violence and being battered as a child are reported frequently in childhood histories of adult male batterers (Brennan, 1985; Ceasar, 1985; Greenberg, 1987; Hotaling & Sugarman, 1987; Sonkin & Durphy, 1982; Sonkin, Martin, & Walker, 1985).

Research on children who witness marital violence clearly notes the psychological trauma they experience (Carlson, 1977; Emory, 1989; Hughes & Barad, 1983; Jaffe, Wolfe, Wilson, & Zak, 1986a; 1986b; Rosenbaum & O'Leary, 1981; Stullman, Schoenenberger, & Hanks, 1987; Wolfe, Jaffe, Wilson, & Zak, 1985; Wolfe, Zak, & Wilson, 1986), regardless of whether they have witnessed the violence between their parents or have themselves been the targets of violence. The effects of such a life experience will vary according to the age, sex, and developmental level of the child witness; the frequency, severity, and type of violence witnessed; the role within the family that the child witness assumes vis-a-vis the abused mother, the abusive father, and his or her siblings; and the ability of the primary caretaker, usually the mother, to buffer the repeated stress of the violence. Concepts of cumulative stress and posttraumatic stress disorder have been applied to child witnesses of maternal abuse (Eth & Pynoos, 1985). Children who witness family violence risk repeating this behavior in their own peer and adult relationships (Kaufman & Zigler, 1987).

Clinical Interventions

Research on treatment outcomes in marital violence is in its early stages (Gondolf & Russell, 1986; Rosenbaum & O'Leary, 1986). A "one size fits all' treatment approach is inappropriate as it may expect the psychologically impossible of many clients. Multi-modal treatment (combining individual, couple, family, group therapy for men, group therapy for women, and play therapy for children) seems to have the greatest impact. Different modes of therapy can be adapted to the needs of the client(s), can be offered both concurrently and consecutively, and can change over time as the needs of the client(s) change.

Treatment Stages

Telephone triage, while not to be considered psychotherapy over the phone, serves the multiple functions of brief crisis intervention, general education, screening for appropriateness for psychotherapy, and information and referral. Decisions and interventions made by the triage person require sophisticated assessment skills, knowledge of the dynamics of marital violence, and familiarity with community resources.

Clinical assessment may consist of up to four clinical interview sessions, psycho-diagnostic testing (especially the MMPI), and acquiring reports from allied agencies or practitioners. The purposes of assessment are: (1) to understand the family emotional climate before, during and after episodes of violence; (2) to determine the level of danger; (3) to differentially diagnose and screen for major impulse control disorders, sociopathy, affective disorders, chronic or acute underlying psychotic processes, significant drug and/or alcohol dependence, posttraumatic stress disorder, and/or the battered woman's syndrome; (4) to ascertain motivation and capacity for behavioral and psychotherapeutic change; and (5) to individualize a treatment approach.

If the client is an individual man in a relationship with a woman he has battered, at least one collateral contact is made with the battered woman by a clinician other than the man's therapist to corroborate the history of violence, accurately assess her safety, and inform her of her partner's participation in the treatment program. If a couple is seen conjointly during the assessment phase, at least one individual interview with each partner is conducted in order to assess the level of fear and intimidation.

Treatment Goals

The overall goals of treatment are to assist the client(s) in making the transition from a violent to a nonviolent relationship style and to ameliorate the debilitating psychological effect the violence has had on the individuals within the family and on the family's functioning as a unit. Because psychotherapy is not the only, nor necessarily the most effective, mode of intervention for stopping violence, clinical interventions are best structured in conjunction with other modes of intervention, for example, shelter services, police intervention, medical care, housing and financial assistance, or legal consultation. Short-term treatment focused on behavior change and ego mastery is appropriate when violence results from developmental and/or environmental crises (Type I, below). Longer-term treatment is appropriate when the goal is working through the cumulative psychological trauma of abuse (Type II, below). In some cases, psychotherapy with a primary focus on marital violence is ineffective (Type III, below) or contraindicated (Type IV, below).

Therapeutic Stance

Traditional clinical neutrality is not appropriate in situations of marital violence. The therapist must genuinely believe and state clearly to the client(s) that violence is an unacceptable behavior because of the risk for physical and psychological injury. The person who is violent is responsible for controlling his or her behavior.

The potential for violence can never be ignored. The therapist must continually reassess the potential for danger in the relationship and not collude with either the man's, woman's, or couple's denial and minimization of this potential. Research has shown that while a battered woman may over-report her violence, a man who batters tends to under-report his (Walker, 1989). In some relationships, both partners will report violent behavior; however, the therapist must understand that the man and the woman often have differing motivations for the use of violence within a relationship. The woman's use of violence may be motivated by self-protection, beginning in the

Contraindicated: to indicate the inadvisability of

relationship after she has been battered on a number of occasions, whereas the man may have been the first to use violence in the relationship, employing it for the purposes of control and intimidation (Parnell, 1983). The woman is usually at greater risk for physical injury than the man.

The fundamental stance regarding the continuation or dissolution of the marriage should be neutral. It is not the therapist's marriage to be saved or terminated but rather the client's to work on, should he or she so choose. Terminating the relationship should not be a prerequisite for initial or continuing participation in treatment. Indeed, requiring a client to terminate a relationship may be a manifestation of an over-anxious countertransference reaction on the part of the therapist. However, if a client(s) chooses to separate either temporarily or permanently, his or her attempts to separate are respected and supported.

Caveats Regarding Techniques

Utilizing behavioral techniques in therapy can be initially useful in some cases. The therapist, however, should guard against simplification and the premature use of directives as they can be techniques that are utilized based on the naive notion that telling people what to do will result in their doing it (Scharff & Scharff, 1987). The use of such directive techniques can often result in false compliance with the treatment process, in which little long-term behavioral change or insight is achieved. Retreat to these techniques by a therapist can often be a manifestation of countertransference anxiety regarding the potential for violence. Use of the "time-out" technique is contraindicated, for example, with a borderline character disordered man because abrupt separation at a time of heightened affective arousal can be experienced as abandonment and may heighten, rather than minimize, the potential for violence. A sociopathic man may utilize behavioral interventions punitively and passive-aggressively with his partner; for example, his taking a "time out" in order to avoid responsibility for his actions.

In the early stages of treatment, the use of direct verbal confrontation of a man's denial and minimization of his current violence must be coupled with an empathic therapeutic stance. A man's denial and minimization of his own violence, and often his denial and minimization of his own childhood abuse, may defend against repressed homicidal childhood rage felt toward his abusive parent(s). Direct verbal confrontation prior to the building of a solid therapeutic alliance may exacerbate feelings of rage and self-hatred and can lead to violent acting-out toward his partner or toward himself in the form of suicidal depression. Similarly, extracting a "confession" as a prerequisite for entry into treatment from a man with a narcissistic disorder may be experienced as a humiliation, whereas a sociopathic man who is skilled at false compliance can superficially "confess" in the absence of genuine insight or guilt.

Influence of Violence in Childhood

A battering man with a childhood history of family violence who as a child utilized the defense of identification with the aggressor will be initially unable to empathically recognize the frightening impact his behavior has had on his partner and/or children (Miller, 1983). This initial identification, however, can be modified as the man comes to recognize (through the therapist's empathic mirroring) his own terror during these

episc   ience as a
victi   ) does not
repo   g parental
disci   perceives
as de

A   , is often
initia   decontex-
tualiz   onse to it
(Reik   episodes
of abι   ' account
for he   violence
and tc   ory may
also eː   ponse to
their ρ

TYPOLOGY OF MARITALLY VIOLENT FAMILIES

A typology of maritally violent families has evolved out of the author's clinical practice and community consultation over the past 15 years with hundreds of adults and children in domestically violent families. The typology is a compilation of previously uncorrelated clinical observations that have been integrated with empirical research in the field of family violence and with an object relations and family systems theoretical perspective. Although no person, couple, or family will fit a type perfectly, it is hoped that the typology will have heuristic value in illuminating distinguishing subtleties among this population and in informing clinical practice.

Type I: Violence as an Acute Affective Storm Within a Primary Relationship Manifesting a Failure to Master a Family Developmental Stage and/or Cope with an Overwhelming Life Crisis

History and Type of Violence

These episodes of violence are acute, that is, not ingrained within the fabric of the relationship. Violence may have occurred more than once but it is usually within the recent past prior to the initiation of therapy. Physical violence is not accompanied by other types of psychological, sexual, or property violence. However, it may still have resulted in significant injuries to the woman. Violence is mutually dystonic to both partners who describe it as "out of character" for the current relationship and other past relationships. Both the man and the woman are alarmed at its occurrence and clearly, mutually state that it must stop in order for the relationship to continue. The ongoing level of danger is low due to the couple's good impulse control and their mutual ability to set interpersonal limits. Environmental support systems (such as police, medical personnel, family, and psychotherapeutic services) are actively utilized by the couple and serve to reinforce these internal and interpersonal controls.

Precipitant to the Violence

The violence occurs at a particular juncture within the relationship and is reflective of a failure to master a developmental stage confronting the couple (such as the birth of a child, a marital separation, or a divorce) or of overwhelming external life stressors (such as an unexpected job loss, death, life-threatening illness, bankruptcy, or the process of immigration).

Affective and Interactional Nature of the Relationship

Both the man and woman are consciously aware of the dysphoria within the relationship and report feelings of depression and anxiety. They are able to distinguish their feelings about the crisis within their lives from their reaction to the battering itself. Both assume that the responsibility for the violence is the man's, although both recognize that it is in response to the relationship and/or environmental distress. The man is consciously able to tolerate and describe uncomfortable feelings of guilt, embarrassment, or shame about the fact that he has injured another human being—particularly his spouse. The woman is able to express feelings of outrage about the fact that she has been assaulted and unequivocally communicates that this behavior is unacceptable and intolerable. She also readily acknowledges her fear during the episodes of violence and is not likely to repress this affect over time.

The partners often request couples therapy although one partner will seek therapy even if the other is unwilling. When couples are seen conjointly, they congruently describe the violent episode(s). The vividness of the battering episode, and each individual's recall of his or her accompanying feelings (such as outrage, shame, or fear) do not diminish over time. The couple can interact appropriately during the session, sharing the time and the responsibility for presenting their individual and collective histories.

Each partner is reasonably well informed about the family and life history of the other. The partners are able to cognitively and affectively recall the quality of their relationships with their families of origin. If the childhood of either was characterized by severe discipline or physical and/or emotional abuse, he or she is able to perceive the parental behavior as inappropriate, and respond with appropriate affect and without rationalization.

Their mutual marital choice was made on the basis of a relatively realistic perception of the qualities of the other person and neither used the relationship as an avenue of precipitous escape from a dysfunctional family. As individuals they are psychologically differentiated and not enmeshed. The relationship is characterized by a clear sense of interpersonal boundaries. There are no unrealistic expectations that one partner can or should know or anticipate the feeling states and needs of the other. Each partner has the ability to enjoy individual pursuits and has the capacity to be alone without feeling a loss of the relationship. Each partner can tolerate the emotional and/or physical withdrawal of the other partner. Each partner can consciously maintain ambivalent feelings about the other without rapid shifts from idealization to devaluation.

Effects on the Children

The woman in particular expresses concern about the impact on the children of witnessing the violent episode(s) but may be uneducated about recognizing signs of childhood distress. The parents, however, do not turn to the children for psychological support and thus do not triangulate the children into the violence. If the mother acts to protect the children from future violent events by psychologically and/or physically separating from the man, he respects these limits and does not breach them in spite of his emotional distress.

Clinical Impressions

Although psychologically often unsophisticated, the man and woman often have some capacity for psychological mindedness and have good ego functions. In the man, homicidal ideation and threats are absent, although depression and suicidal ideation may be present. The man has limited insight into what precipitated his violence, but his guilt, curiosity, and belief in the woman's determination to leave if he is repeatedly violent all serve to motivate him for therapy. The woman may suffer from acute anxiety, depression, or posttraumatic reactions due to situational stressors. She is not at risk for long-term emotional disorder subsequent to the violence because she is able to perceive the behavior as inappropriate, out of her control, and not attributable to her own behavior. She can experience a sense of appropriate outrage about having been physically assaulted and can set limits within the relationship. She clearly conveys that she has the intent and emotional capability of leaving if the violence continues.

Treatment Implications

The therapist's countertransference reactions must be monitored to prevent collusion with the couple's wish to disavow the violence. The violence should not be viewed solely as a symptom of temporary relationship dysfunction but rather as an event with physically and emotionally traumatic consequences in itself. Clinicians must guard against a tendency to focus on other aspects of the relationship in a misguided attempt to alleviate the man's compelling self-acknowledged culpability and self-punitive guilt.

Short-term (12-20 session) individual and/or couples therapy is appropriate. The "time out" technique can be utilized by this couple as a tool in the initial stages of treatment to defuse explosive interactions.

Children within the family who may have been traumatized by witnessing the violence can be assisted by educating parents to recognize symptoms of posttraumatic stress. Both parents are instructed not to deny the fact that violence has occurred or that it is traumatizing to the children. Parents are provided support for their role in buffering the children from the emotional trauma of the violence by correctly identifying the behavior as unacceptable and by encouraging children to share in an age appropriate fashion their affective reactions to the events. In the cases of more severely traumatized children who are not amenable solely to parental intervention, short-term individual play therapy or family therapy is helpful.

Type II: Repetitive Violent Rages in the Primary Relationship Manifesting the Man's Intolerable Internal Affective States

History and Type of Violence

This type of violence, occurring only within the context of the family, begins early on in the relationship, often during courtship or within the first year of marriage. Physical violence occurs in cyclical, repetitive patterns with gradually increasing frequency and severity and is accompanied by psychological, sexual, and/or property violence. The woman suffers increasingly severe physical injuries. The level of dangerousness increases as life threats and weapons become involved, and as the individuals become increasingly isolated from their own families, friends, and supportive networks. The violence is mutually dystonic to the couple who stay tenaciously attached to one another in spite of the violence, not because of it.

The woman's recall of her affective response to the violence will range from denial to terror depending on whether she is at that moment psychologically fused with, or estranged from, the man. The man's most common form of denial regarding the violence is faulty recollection; total amnesia for the violence is rare. He experiences temporary regret rather than true guilt. He is usually unaware of the traumatic emotional effects of his violence on the family. He has a limited ability to accept responsibility for his violence because he truly feels emotionally controlled and dominated by the woman.

Precipitants to the Violence

Repetitive violence results from the interplay of a constellation of factors: a chronically vulnerable psychological state of unconscious ambivalent fusion within the relationship; a preexisting characterlogical vulnerability on the part of the man; and the man's internal psychological experience of a real or imagined precipitating "insult" by the woman. Dysphoric affective states (ranging from depression, anxiety, rage, frustration, anger, jealousy, envy, fear, and/or shame) within the man precede, accompany, and follow episodes of physical battering. His attempt to alleviate an often unconscious intolerable affective state triggers a behavioral response to either withdraw from and abandon, or fuse with and control, the perceived stimulus, in other words, the woman. The man's violence is instrumental in that it attempts to coerce the woman into behaving or responding in a manner that will restore his elusive internal sense of well-being.

If violence results from the man's experience of the woman's withdrawal from him, this withdrawal may be either real or fantasied, manifesting itself in either behavior or affective attunement. The woman's withdrawal of affective attunement may be real and appropriate; for example, a pregnant woman may focus her psychological energy internally, toward her unborn child, and away from her partner. The woman's withdrawal may also be imagined by the man; for example, a woman whose pathologically jealous partner irrationally believes she is involved with other men. The man's experience of the woman's real or imagined withdrawal triggers his longstanding, unconscious fears of separation and abandonment against which he defends through the primitive mechanisms of splitting, projection, and projective identification. He splits off and projects his abandoned bad self—full of self-destructiveness, self-hate, and self-derision—into the woman, whom he then batters in a desperate attempt to reestablish psychological fusion within the relationship and to mitigate his abandonment fears. In a reversal of his childhood role, he becomes the external abusive object battering his denigrated, hateful bad self.

Violence may also express the rage resulting from the man's pathological belief that the woman has failed in her perceived role of shielding him from a terrorizing feeling of aloneness and consequent fears of psychological disintegration. He depends on her comforting, nurturing, and soothing functions to feel whole and good. He irrationally believes that she is intentionally withholding these functions. He batters her in a paradoxical attempt to "get her to stop withholding." The violent behavior is reinforced if, in fact, the battering results in a restoration of the woman's emotional attunement during the reconciliation stage of the repetitive cycle of violence.

A narcissistically vulnerable, shame-prone man is desperately dependent on empathic mirroring and affective attunement by the woman in order to maintain his self-esteem. Any real or anticipated departure from the idealizing fusion within the relationship is experienced by the man as a narcissistic injury and results in revengeful, sadistic rage devoid of empathy or compassion for the woman he batters (Adler, 1986; Kohut, 1972).

The woman also participates in projective identification (Ogden, 1982) by introjecting and identifying with the split-off projections of the battering man. She experiences herself as hateful and bad. She believes the man's false accusations that she has failed in her empathic role of adequately soothing him. She accepts the man's vilifications of her and attributes blame for the violence to her self—omnipotently and irrationally believing that the violence will stop if only she behaves differently.

The woman herself may also use splitting and projection in a futile effort to maintain the violence-free relationship state of idealized psychological fusion. Utilizing the defense of splitting, the woman maintains two different, contradictory views of the man that alternate over time with her two disconnected feeling states about him and herself in relation to him. When in the state of psychological fusion with the man, she experiences him as a loving, warm person whom she comforts during affective storms, soothes when narcissistically injured, and shields from the consequences of his actions. When the idealized psychological fusion, inevitably, is violently disrupted, he becomes the abusive, frightening, denigrating, insulting partner whom she hates and from whom she withdraws, recoils, or flees (Gilman, 1980).

As a consequence, the woman introjects and identifies with the man's projected hate and derision. She feels angry, ashamed, and embarrassed about the violence—but not outraged. Her anger, hurt, and confusion fade as the state of psychological fusion in the relationship is restored. Her denial serves as a defense against overwhelming fear and anxiety about remaining in, or returning to, a potentially life-threatening situation. Attributing omnipotent responsibility to herself for the man's violence serves as a defense against her reality based fear of being out of control of his violence. She is vulnerable to developing the battered woman's syndrome (Walker, 1984).

Affective and Interactional Nature of the Relationship

If the man and woman present as a couple in a state of psychological fusion, it is the woman who gives voice to the inner life of the couple and family, describing the man's poignant history of abuse and/or narcissistic injury as a child. She is empathically attuned to the man in spite of the battering.

If either partner appears individually in a state of temporary separation, his or her view of the spouse often alternates between states of idealization and devaluation. The man describes the woman as a "withholding, nagging bitch" whom he hates. The woman presents a picture of a man as an omnipotently destructive terrorizer from whom she needs protection.

Partner choice in this couple was most likely based on a quick, idealized romantic attachment. Psychological fusion and enmeshment characterizes the couple. Each expects primitive empathy from the other. One or both experience a threat to his or her self if the other separates physically or emotionally. The range of capacity for autonomous activity or decisionmaking is limited. The relationship is threatened if outside attachments or interests develop. There is little capacity for either to be alone (Wexler & Steidl, 1978). One or both partners alternate between a need for constant approval to a denial of dependence and vulnerability. The quality of attachment shifts from anxious clinging to avoidant distancing.

Such men and women typically have hostile dependent relationships as adults with their families of origin. The men often report histories of shame, humiliation, or violence in their families of origin. They were often the children who were most triangulated into their parents' violence. However, the men rarely perceive parental behavior as abuse and attempt to play down the consequences of childhood physical and emotional abuse by claiming it was "good for them" (Miller, 1983). The women who were raised in families in which abuse occurred are likely to be able to cognitively recall, but not affectively react to, the abuse (Reiker & Hilberman-Carmen, 1986). They often experience impaired judgment regarding the man's potential for violence when they are affectively flooded, and, as a result, fail to react in a self-protective manner.

The man and woman are likely to turn to their parents for support when separated from one another. Thus, the parents become triangulated into the marital conflict. The man may literally move back into his parent's home because of his inability to take care of his daily living needs. The man's mother (often a battered woman herself) may pressure the woman to drop legal charges and reunite with her son. The woman's parental family, often feeling "burnt out" by her numerous separations from the man, may eventually withdraw and no longer be available for support. The message is "you made your bed hard, you lie in it." It is not uncommon for the woman's father, if he is also a batterer, and the battering husband to band together in mutual support during times of marital discord.

Effects on the Children

The children witness repetitive cycles of battering. Although not primary targets of violence, they are often inadvertently injured. A particular child in the family may assume the role of a parentified child vis-a-vis the mother. This child will be intermittently triangulated into the cycles of violence and assume responsibilities such as calling the police or rounding up younger siblings into a bedroom to hide during an episode of violence. A triangulated child remains vulnerable during adolescence to a reenactment of the latent propensities for violence within the family system. A child who has identified with his or her aggressive father may batter, ignore, and devalue the mother or torment and abuse younger siblings or peers. A child who identified with the abused mother may experience abuse in his or her peer relationships.

Because the mother herself denies the emotional impact of the violence, she cannot function as a buffer or container for the child's overwhelming feelings. Due to the family's fluid psychological boundaries, the child experiences both the primitive nature of the father's self-absorbed rage, and also the mother's fear and helplessness, as intensely as do the parents. The child is intermittently flooded with overwhelming rage and terror. The child's internal psychological distress is never acknowledged. Because the parents decontextualize terrifying behavior, explain it away, and do not label it as abuse, denial and disavowal of the child's overwhelming affects occurs. The child does not develop an ability to identify and modulate internal affective responses and so may develop a dread of intense affective states (Stullman, Schoenenberger, & Hanks, 1987). Such children may manifest symptoms of school phobia, separation anxiety, learning disorders, enuresis, digestive disorders, major depression, and peer difficulties.

Given that family holidays may be particularly violent times, anniversary reactions to violent episodes are common. Posttraumatic stress disorder disturbances may become enduring features of the child's personality (Eth & Pynoos, 1985). The most severe effects occur in the child who is both witness to, and the intentional target of, parental violence.

Clinical Impressions

Such men who are violent have great difficulty with basic trust. Their capacity for psychological mindedness is impaired. Internal object relations are split, ego functions of judgment, memory, and affect regulation are impaired, and severe depressive states lead to intermittent suicidal or homicidal ideation. Narcissistic and borderline character disorders are prevalent.

These battered women also have difficulties with basic trust. Their capacity for psychological mindedness is undeveloped. Internal object relations may be whole or split, and ego functions of judgment and affect regulation are impaired. They suffer from severe and often debilitating anxiety and depression as a result of living in an intermittently violent, life-threatening atmosphere. Self-medication with alcohol and/ or prescription drugs is common.

Treatment Implications

The request for therapy often follows police involvement, arrest, and court referral of the man, or increasing fear and demoralization on the woman's part. Clients in these relationships may benefit particularly from participation in same sex group therapy in conjunction with individual or couples therapy, which can later be combined with family therapy for the children.

A woman's motivation for treatment may be high when she is estranged from the relationship, but difficult to sustain when she is reenmeshed in the relationship if the man is not also in therapy. The man's motivation for treatment often arises when he is separated from his wife, when he is arrested for spouse abuse, or when he himself reaches a point of despair and realizes that he cannot be in any intimate relationship nonviolently.

Several factors may contribute to the recurrence of physical violence during the course of treatment. The man's affective storms and violent rages have served as defenses against intolerable painful affects that he will inevitably reexperience during the course of treatment. He is at risk for ongoing physical violence because he habitually uses it as a form of affect regulation. Additionally, if the man stops behaving violently, the woman may feel unrealistically safe in venting her long pent-up anger. She may be angered by her often reality based perception that the man utilizes the anger management technique of "time outs" in a passive-aggressive fashion. She may be angered by his continued use of subtle but pernicious psychological violence. The man, in turn, may experience her anger as a narcissistic injury and respond violently. Likewise, the woman may experience the man's newfound restraint as emotional withdrawal and unwittingly precipitate an episode of violence in order to reinstate a state of psychological fusion.

Both the man and the woman must confront their disappointment that the relationship does not necessarily feel better just because the physically violent behavior has stopped. In fact, it may subjectively feel worse because painful affects are not being defended against by the use of violence. Both the man and the woman may be disappointed that the relationship does not provide the intimacy and psychological security they long to experience.

Men, if separated from their wives and their children, must mourn the loss of their family and previous life style without resorting to violence to ward off the loss. Likewise, women must also grieve the loss of the relationship if they do decide to leave (Turner, 1986) and not ameliorate their loneliness by reuniting with the batterer. They must also confront their anxiety about autonomy and individuation and must often be prepared to face the formidable task of constructing a single-parent lifestyle.

Children in these families are psychologically traumatized by the cumulative stress of witnessing repeated parental violence. The family's functioning as a unit has come to revolve around anticipating and enduring the episodes of marital violence. Issues of control, authority, and decisionmaking have often become interwoven with the violent behavior. Individual therapy for severely traumatized children is indicated. Family therapy is beneficial after the violence has been brought under control and while the parents participate in their own treatment (Stullman, Schoenenberger, & Hanks, 1987).

Type III: Habitual Violent Interpersonal Style in Multiple Relationships Used for Intimidation and Control

History and Type of Violence

The physical violence in this type of relationship is chronic, repetitive, and accompanied by psychological, sexual, and property violence toward family members and toward others outside the family. For the man, the violence is instrumental, that is, used as a means to an end, or as a method of intimidation and control. Physical violence occurs at all stages of the relationship. The level of danger is high with frequent life threats and the use of weapons. Alcohol and street drugs may be used by the man and, often, by the woman. Legal justice system involvement is high for criminal and violent behavior. The woman in this relationship is angered and frightened by the violence but does not consider it "out of character" for intimate relationships.

Affective and Interactional Nature of the Relationship

The man does not experience guilt, shame, remorse, or regret subsequent to his violence, although he may become enraged and retaliatory when confronted with the inconvenient consequences of his actions. The level of dangerousness is high due to the ego-syntonic nature of the violence and the man's psychological inability to be empathic with his victims. For example, as one man stated, "Violence is not a problem for the one who does it; it's only a problem for the recipient!" The man often consciously lies about the extent and frequency of violence, as well as about other details in his current and past history. He seeks treatment to enhance his case in a pending legal hearing, because he is ordered to do so by the court, or as a manifestation of his pathological, intrusive pursuit of the woman who might also be in therapy.

The woman, although angered and fearful subsequent to her battery, may also experience an inappropriate sense of fascination with, or apathetic resignation toward, the violence. She is often unable to realistically assess the man's level of dangerousness. For example, one woman who sought treatment only at the insistence of a friend, "wondered if [she] should be concerned about the guy" who was indeed clearly quite dangerous.

The woman describes in distressing detail the brutal and sometimes bizarre nature of her physical and sexual assaults. Violence has become embedded within the fabric of her emotionally depleted life. She alternates between states of omnipotent denial of the man's dangerousness and overwhelming terror. She may dramatically enlist the help of others in fleeing this dangerous man and then abruptly switch and defend him against attack by others. She is at risk for developing the battered woman's syndrome (Walker, 1984).

These relationships are characterized by pathological, tenacious attachment on the part of the man to the woman 'as an object within his life. There is little sense of authentic interpersonal relatedness. The man's history is replete with serial intense relationships in which battering and/or exploitation were common features.

Effects on the Children

Children are often direct targets of physical violence by either the man, the woman, or both. The woman is not only unable to buffer the child from the trauma of the man's violence but also is often the source of emotional and physical trauma herself. The violence is only one of a multitude of dysfunctional family dynamics with which these children have to cope.

Clinical Impressions

The man often has a sociopathic character disorder with paranoid features. He often abuses both drugs and alcohol. He has no capacity for psychological minded-ness or empathy. Countertransference reactions are characterized by initial and continuing dislike and, on occasion, reality based fear.

The woman may be competent in the work arena, yet her relationships are chronically chaotic, abusive, and exploitive. She commonly abuses drugs or alcohol and suffers from severe depression.

Treatment Implications

Couples therapy is not appropriate, as couples sessions are dominated by vituperative arguing and mutual blaming. In addition, the risk of postsession violence is high. Individual therapy is also inappropriate. The man's potential for dangerousness and paranoia is high. He lacks authentic motivation for change. Therapy is often used as a manipulative device in order to gain some leniency in a court disposition or to intrude into his female partner's attempts to separate. Drug and alcohol treatment programs are often useful, but abstinence will not necessarily eliminate the man's propensity to act violently.

A woman trapped in this type of relationship is best advised to utilize the protection of the legal justice system and battered women's shelters in order to protect herself and her children. Battered women's peer support groups are often helpful in conjunction with drug and alcohol treatment programs. Once the woman is in a safe environment, individual psychotherapy is useful in overcoming the effects of post-traumatic stress disorders subsequent to the multiple assaults the woman has experienced throughout her life, in assisting the woman in extricating herself from a life style of exploitation, and in supporting her in appropriately parenting her children.

Type IV: Repetitive or Acute Violent Behavior in Multiple Relationships Secondary to Severe Mental Disorder and/or Drug or Alcohol Addiction

History and Type of Violence

This type of man's physical violence occurs in multiple relationships and is a manifestation of a severe mental disorder (such as a manic depressive disorder or paranoid schizophrenia) or is secondary to a drug or alcohol addiction. The physical violence is not intentionally accompanied by other forms of violence. It is a manifestation of an underlying impulse control disorder and/or acute psychotic process. If the violence is secondary to an acute psychotic process, hallucinations, delusions, and/or paranoid ideation may be present. The violence does not emanate from the dynamics within the relationship but is directed randomly toward anyone within proximity. Hence, a spouse or another family member is most at risk due to their physical proximity.

Treatment Implications

Such cases are not appropriate for treatment in a psychotherapy program with the primary focus being on marital violence. For the chronically or acutely mentally ill person, traditional out-patient therapy combined with psychiatric evaluation, appropriate hospitalization, and/or medication is the treatment of choice (Binder & McNeil, 1988). Families of chronically mentally ill patients can benefit more from educational and supportive interventions than from psychotherapy (Swan & Lavitt, 1988).

In cases of violence secondary to drug and/or alcohol abuse, treatment of the drug addiction should be undertaken prior to, or concurrent with, treatment of the violence. The man's propensities toward violence within his relationships must be monitored as they may not necessarily abate as the drug abuse comes under control.

COUNTERTRANSFERENTIAL STRESS

Clinical work with violent families requires sophisticated clinical skill and significant emotional resilience. Therapists will invariably have strong induced and personal countertransferential reactions. Within their professional role, therapists must refrain from acting out countertransference feelings of retaliatory rage, disgust, contempt, anger, or frustration. They must be maximally available to their clients while simultaneously able to set emotional boundaries within their work and between their professional and personal lives. To minimize the stress of the work, therapists are best advised not to devote more than half of their clinical practice time to work with problems of family violence. Balancing caseloads with clinical work with both male batterers and battered women is essential in protecting the therapist from over-identification with either the battered woman or the battering man (Hanks, 1988).

Maintaining an Alliance

It is difficult to maintain a working alliance with a man who needs to speak in detail about his violent behavior (Haley, 1974). The therapist will need to contain temporarily the man's projected unconscious, intolerable, split-off bad self and its accompanying feelings of self-hatred. Through the mechanism of projective identification, the therapist will introject the man's feelings of self-hatred and also, in reality, experience these feelings of hatred toward the man (Ogden, 1982). The ever present tendency for the therapist to disavow the man's violence potential is often the therapist's own intrapsychic defense against the self-hatred the therapist must "carry" for the client while simultaneously struggling to contain his or her own impulses toward retaliatory rage. This is particularly taxing on the therapeutic alliance because a battering man will often devalue the person upon whom he depends—and he will devalue the therapist and the therapeutic process when unconsciously feeling most dependent, vulnerable, and in need of the most empathic response.

It is also difficult to maintain an empathic therapeutic alliance with a battered woman whose anxiety about autonomy and individuation and fear for her safety may not allow her to remain apart from the batterer. In order to continue a violent relationship, a woman must deny her anxiety about the level of danger. Through the defensive operation of projective identification, the therapist will experience this anxiety on behalf of the woman and may react by rejecting the woman because she makes the therapist anxious. Although the therapist must confront a battered woman's denial about the reality of the danger in the battering relationship, the battered woman must also be allowed to maintain her ambivalent attachment to the therapist and the therapeutic process. A battered woman should not be put in the untenable double bind of working with a therapist who insists she leave the batterer while concurrently living with a batterer who insists she leave the therapist.

Managing Ambivalence

The client's ambivalence about therapy presents a major difficulty for a therapist who works in the field of domestic violence. The therapist's capacity to adequately attach to clients may become gradually eroded due to the client's tendency to abruptly drop in and out of treatment. Without an adequate conceptual framework for predicting, understanding, and managing this client behavior, the therapist is at risk for becoming demoralized. The therapist may defend against this repeated abandonment and demoralization by emotionally withdrawing from the client(s), and, thus, inadvertently contributing to the client's ambivalence.

Countertransference difficulties will also inevitably manifest themselves within the context of the total treatment team. It is expected that the therapists working with different individuals within a given family will introject parts of that family's dynamic process and, in a parallel process manner, reenact family or couple dynamics within the treatment team. Clinical case conferences, individual and group supervision, and clinical consultation should be structured into any treatment program. A supportive collegial team process buffers individual therapists from feelings of clinical demoralization and mediates countertransferential acting out (Hanks, 1988).

INTEGRATING THEORY WITH PRACTICE

Staunch adherence to either political philosophies or rigid clinical paradigms does disservice to the men, women, and children who suffer the emotional and physical pain of domestic violence. Sociopolitical and clinical theories must be bridged creatively and adapted flexibly to meet the differing needs of differing individuals and families. Effective psychotherapeutic interventions must be developed and offered in a context that supports and respects other modes of sociocultural and environmental intervention. This most urgent social and psychological problem of violence within the family challenges clinicians to adapt their theories creatively to meet the needs of their clients and not to expect their clients to adapt to the theories of the clinicians.

BIBLIOGRAPHY

Adler, G. (1986). Psychotherapy of the narcissistic personality disorder patient: Two contrasting approaches. *American Journal of Psychiatry, 143*(4), 430–436.

Binder, R., & McNeil, D. (1988). Effects of diagnosis and context on dangerousness. *American Journal of Psychiatry, 145*(6), 728–732.

Bograd, M. (1982). Battered women, cultural myths, and clinical interventions: A feminist analysis. *Current Feminist Issues in Psychotherapy*, 69–77.

Bograd, M. (1984). Family systems approaches to wife battering: A feminist critique. *American Journal of Orthopsychiatry, 54*(4), 558–568.

Bowan, M. (1978). *Family therapy in clinical practice*. New York: Jason Aronson.

Bowlby, J. (1984). Violence in the family as a disorder of the attachment and caregiving systems. *American Journal of Psychoanalysis, 44*(1), 2–27.

Brennan, F. (1985). Political and psychosocial issues in psychotherapy for spouse abusers: Implications for treatment. *Psychotherapy, 22*(3), 653–654.

Breines, W., & Gordon, L. (1983). The new scholarship on family violence. *Signs: Journal of Women and Culture in Society, 8*(3), 490–531.

Carlson, B. (1977). Children's observations of interpersonal violence. In A. Roberts (Ed.), *Battered women and their families* (pp. 147–167). New York: Springer.

Ceasar, P. (1985). *The wife beater: Personality and psychosocial characteristics*. Unpublished doctoral dissertation, California School of Professional Psychology. Berkeley, CA.

Coleman, K. (1980). Conjugal violence: What 33 men report. *Journal of Marital and Family Therapy, 6*(2), 207–214.

Cook, D. R., & Frantz-Cook, A. (1984). A systemic treatment approach to wife battering. *Journal of Marital and Family Therapy, 10*(1), 83–92.

Dobash, R. E., & Dobash, R. (1979). *Violence against wives*. New York: Free Press.

Dutton, D., & Painter, S. (1981). Traumatic bonding: The development of emotional attachments in battered women and other relationships of intermittent abuse. *Victimology: An International Journal, 6*, 139–155.

Emory, R. (1989). Family violence. *American Psychologist, 44*(2), 321–328.

Eth, S., & Pynoos, R. (1985). *Post-traumatic stress disorders in children*. Washington, DC: American Psychiatric Press.

Fairbairn, W. (1952). *Psychoanalytic studies of the personality*. Boston: Routledge & Kegan Paul.

Fitch, F. (1983). Men who batter: Some pertinent characteristics. *Journal of Nervous and Mental Disease, 171*, 190–192.

Geller, J., & Wasserstrom, J. (1985). Conjoint therapy for the treatment of domestic violence. In A. Roberts (Ed.), *Battered women and their families* (pp. 33–48). New York: Springer.

Gelles, R. (1979). Determinants of violence in the family: Toward a theoretical integration. In W. Burr, R. Hill, F. Nye, & I. Reiss (Eds.), *Contemporary theories about the family* (pp. 549–581). New York: Free Press.

Gelles, R. (1982). Applying research on family violence to clinical practice. *Journal of Marriage and The Family, 2*, 9–20.

Gilman, I. (1980). An object relations approach to the phenomenon and treatment of battered women. *Psychiatry, 43*, 345–358.

Gondolf, E., & Russell, D. (1986). The case against anger control treatment programs for batterers. *Response, 9*(3), 2–5.

Greenberg, B. (1987). *A psychodynamic inquiry into violent relationships*. Unpublished doctoral dissertation, California School of Professional Psychology, Berkeley, CA.

Griswold, R. (1986). Sexual cruelty and the case for divorce in victorian America. *Signs: Journal of Women in Culture and Society, 11*(3), 529–541.

Guntrip, H. (1969). *Schizoid phenomenon, object-relations, and the self*. New York: International Press.

Haley, S. (1974). When the patient reports atrocities. *Archives of General Psychiatry, 30*, 191–196.

Hanks, S., & Rosenbaum, C. (1977). Battered women: A study of women who live with violent alcohol abusing men. *American Journal of Orthopsychiatry, 47*(2), 291–306.

Hanks, S. (July, 1984). The sexual revolution and violence against women: The boundary between liberation and exploitation. In J. Baum & J. Coleman (Eds.), *The sexual revolution (sexuality, religion, and society), Concilium: International Journal of Sociology and Religion, 193,* 41–49.

Hanks, S. (1988). *The therapist in context: The organization as a contextual holding environment for clinical work with violent families.* Unpublished manuscript.

Herman, J. (1986). Histories of violence in an outpatient population: An exploratory study. *American Journal of Orthopsychiatry, 65*(1), 137–141.

Hilberman, E. (1980). Overview: "The wife beater's wife" reconsidered. *American Journal of Psychiatry, 137*(11), 1336–1347.

Hilberman, E., & Munson, K. (1978). Sixty battered women. *Victimology: An International Journal, 2*(3–4), 460–470.

Hobbs, J. (1987). Violence—A personal and societal challenge. *Social Work, 32*(6), 467–468.

Hotaling, G., & Sugarman, D. (1987). An analysis of risk markers in husband to wife violence: The current state of knowledge. *Violence and Victims, 1*(2), 101–124.

Hughes, H., & Barad, S. (1983). Psychological functioning of children in a battered woman's shelter: A preliminary investigation. *American Journal of Orthopsychiatry, 53,* 525–531.

Jaffe, P., Wolfe, D., Wilson, S., & Zak, L. (1986a). Family violence and child adjustment: A comparative analysis of girls' and boys' behavioral symptoms. *American Journal of Psychiatry, 143*(1), 74–76.

Jaffe, P., Wolfe, D., Wilson, S., & Zak, L. (1986b). Similarities in behavioral and social maladjustment among child victims and witnesses to family violence. *American Journal of Orthopsychiatry, 56*(1), 142–146.

Jacobson, A., Koehler, J., & Jones-Brown, C. (1987). The failure of routine assessment to detect histories of assault experienced by psychiatric patients. *Hospital and Community Psychiatry, 38*(4), 386–389.

Kernberg, O. (1984). *Severe personality disorders.* New Haven, CT: Yale University Press.

Kaufman, J., & Zigler, E. (1987). Do abused children become abusive parents? *American Journal of Orthopsychiatry, 57*(2), 186–192.

Kohut, H. (1972). Thoughts on narcissism and narcissistic rage. *The Psychoanalytic Study of the Child, 27,* 360–400.

Miller, A. (1983). *For your own good: Hidden cruelty in child-rearing and the roots of violence.* New York: Farrar, Straus, Giroux.

Ogden, T. (1982). *Projective identification and psychotherapeutic technique.* New York: Jason Aronson.

Ogden, T. (1983). The concept of internal object relations. *International Journal of Psycho-Analysis, 64,* 227–241.

Pagelow, M. (1981). Factors affecting women's decisions to leave violent relationships. *Journal of Family Issues, 2*(4), 391–414.

Parnell, L. (1983). *Fusion, Differentiation of self and interpersonal perception in battering couples.* Unpublished doctoral dissertation, California School of Professional Psychology, Berkeley, CA.

Rieker, P., & Hilberman-Carmen, E. (1986). The victim-to-patient process: The disconfirmation and transformation of abuse. *American Journal of Orthopsychiatry, 56*(3), 360–370.

Rosenbaum, A., & O'Leary, K. D. (1981). Marital violence: Characteristics of abusive couples. *Journal of Consulting and Clinical Psychology, 49*(1), 63–71.

Rosenbaum, A., & O'Leary, K. D. (1986). The treatment of marital violence. In N. Jacobson & A. Gurman. (Eds.) *Clinical handbook of marital therapy* (pp. 385–405). New York; Guilford.

Scharff, D., & Scharff, J. (1987). *Object relations family therapy.* Northvale, New Jersey: Jason Aronson.

Slipp, S. (1984). *Object relations: A dynamic bridge between individual and family treatment.* New York: Jason Aronson.

Snyder, D., & Fruchtman, L. (1981). Differential patterns of wife abuse: A data based typology. *Journal of Consulting and Clinical Psychology, 49*(6), 878–885.

Sonkin, D., & Durphy, M. (1982). *Learning to live without violence.* San Francisco: Volcano Press.

Sonkin, D., Martin, D., & Walker, L. (1985). *The male batterer.* New York: Springer.

Stark, E., & Flitcraft, A. (1988). Women and children at risk: A feminist perspective on child abuse. *International Journal of Health Services, 18*(1), 97–118.

Stullman, M., Schoenenberger, A., & Hanks, S. (July, 1987). *Assessment and treatment of the child witness of marital violence.* Paper presented at the Third National Family Violence Researchers Conference, University of New Hampshire, Durham.

Straus, M. (1978). Wife beating: How common and why? *Victimology: An International Journal, 2,* 443–458.

Swan, R., & Lavitt, M. (1988). Patterns of adjustment to violence in families of the mentally ill. *Journal of Interpersonal Violence, 3*(1), 42–54.

Taubman, S. (1986). Beyond the bravado: Sex roles and the exploitive male. *Social Work, 31*(1), 12–18.

Turner, S. (1986). Battered women: Mourning the death of a relationship. *Social Work, 5,* 372–376.

Waldinger, R. (1987). Intensive psychodynamic therapy with borderline patients: An overview. *The American Journal of Psychiatry, 144*(3), 267–274.

Walker, L. (1979). *The battered woman.* New York: Harper & Row.

Walker, L. (1984). *The battered woman syndrome.* New York: Springer.

Walker, L. (1989). Psychology and violence against women. *American Psychologist, 44*(4), 695–702.

Wexler, J., & Steidl, J. (1978). Marriage and the capacity to be alone. *Psychiatry, 41*(2), 72–82.

Wolfe, D., Jaffe, P., Wilson, S., & Zak, L. (1985). Children of battered women: The relation of child behavior to family violence and maternal stress. *Journal of Consulting and Clinical Psychology, 53,* 657–665.

Wolfe, D., Zak, L., & Wilson, S. (1986). Child witness to violence between parents: Critical issues in behavior and social adjustment. *Journal of Abnormal Child Psychology, 14*(1), 95–102.

14

Woman Abuse Among Separated and Divorced Women: The Relevance of Social Support

Desmond Ellis
Department of Sociology, York University, North York, Ontario, Canada

INTRODUCTION

Separated and divorced women vary in the amount and seriousness of violence directed against them by the men they lived with formerly. These variations are a function of dependency, availability, and deterrence. Separated women provided with the type and timing of social support that increase their independence (making them unavailable to the men who beat them and making deterrence work more effectively), are less likely to be abused than are women exposed to forms of social support that do not work through these variables.

Many separated and divorced women include abuse by the men they lived with among the reasons for leaving them (MacLeod & Cadieux, 1980; Ellis & Ryan, 1987). Here, separation is seen as a solution to a number of marital problems including the problem of emotional and physical abuse (Dobash & Dobash, 1979, p. 173). As a solution to the problem of wife abuse, separation appears to have effects that are quite variable. Thus some women who were not beaten during the time they lived with their partners get beaten after they leave, some who were beaten prior to separation get beaten more seriously (but less frequently) afterwards, and others who were beaten before they separated report not being beaten after they had separated (Ellis & Wight, 1987).

These variations in post-separation women abuse raise an important theoretical question, one that also has nontrivial policy implications. A review of theory and research on wife abuse, separation/divorce, and marital conflict intervention, suggests that variations in the types and timing of social support make an important contribution toward understanding these variations. To describe the nature of this contribution is the primary objective of this chapter.

The author gratefully acknowledges the support provided by the LaMarsh Research Program on Violence and Conflict Resolution, York University.

Desmond Ellis is a professor in the Department of Sociology, York University. He is also on the Executive Committee of the LaMarsh Research Program on Violence and Conflict Resolution at York. He is the director of three research projects (in process), Marital Conflict Mediation and Post-Separation Woman Abuse, Traditional Iroquois "Law-Ways," the Criminal Justice System, and the Family Mediation Pilot Project.

POST-SEPARATION WOMAN ABUSE

For the specific purposes of this chapter, post-separation woman abuse refers to the emotional and/or physical harms that are intentionally inflicted on a woman by the man she lived with formerly in an intimate, heterosexual relationship and from whom she is separated physically. Findings from a variety of sources indicate that woman abuse among separated women is a more serious problem than is the abuse experienced by married women who are living with their husbands (Carlson, 1977; Ellis & Wight, 1987; Gaquin, 1978; Levinger, 1966; Long, Tauchen, & Witte, 1983; O'Brien, 1971; Russell, 1982; Schwartz, 1987; Solicitor General of Canada, 1985).

As is true of woman abuse generally, post-separation woman abuse is conceived of as a symptom of a wider problem, the problem of eliminating gender as a basis for the hierarchical ordering of relationships between men and women.[1] When power is associated with gender and masculine power is greater than feminine power, then intimate, heterosexual relationships can easily become traps, and woman abuse becomes one manifestation of entrapment. Many married women who anticipate their abuse cannot do much about it, even when they really try (Walker, 1979).[2] After they have been abused, pretty much the same situation obtains. The law, poverty, professional helpers and healers, agents of the state, the lack of child care, all contribute to their entrapment in abusive marital relationships (Dobash & Dobash, 1979; Stark, Flitcraft, & Frazier, 1979).

For an increasing number of women, marital separation represents an escape from this kind of relationship. However, many have discovered that the process of separation is also hazardous to their health. In addition to the existence of general societal conditions conducive to woman abuse, a number of specific conditions associated with or exacerbated by separation, markedly increase the likelihood of violence. These include stress (Chan, 1978; Schinke, 1986; Straus, 1980; Wallerstein & Kelly, 1980), anger induced by loss of attachment (Weiss, 1979, pp. 207–208), revenge, perceived betrayal, jealousy, challenges to male hegemony (Dobash & Dobash, 1979; Dobash, Dobash, & Cavanagh, 1985; Ellis & Ryan, 1987; Wallerstein & Kelly, 1980). Not infrequently, the same factor that inhibited violence during the marriage, for example, presence of children, becomes the occasion for conflicts resolved by male violence following the breakup of the marriage (Long et al., 1983).

Most of the specific factors identified here may be subsumed under three general classes of variable. These mediate the effects of patriarchal society factors on woman abuse in general and on post-separation woman abuse in particular. These mediating variables are dependency, availability, and deterrence. Taken together, their interrelations constitute a DAD model of woman abuse. If it is to reduce post-separation woman abuse, social support must work on these three variables.

SOCIAL SUPPORT

Conceptually defined, social support refers to the actions and reactions of another person or persons that result in the actual or perceived melioration or removal of

---

[1]For a more detailed treatment of this conception, see Breines and Gordon (1983), Dobash and Dobash (1979), Stark, Flitcraft, and Frazier (1979) and Walker (1979).

[2]Note however that Dobash, Dobash, and Cavanagh (1985) do not find abused wives to be as helpless as Walker (1979) implies.

aversive outcomes or experiences and/or, the actual or perceived attainment of desired outcomes or experiences.

A perusal of the literature on social support reveals the existence of three major conceptualizations of social support. These are gratification, equalization, and contextual threat reduction.[3] A well-known proponent of the gratification or needs satisfaction conception of social support is Thoits (1982). She defines social support as, "the degree to which a person's basic needs (socioemotional and instrumental/ material) are gratified through interaction with others" (1982, p. 147). Here, support is equated with the satisfaction of needs by others.

By way of contrast, Lazarus (1981) conceives of social support in resource equalization terms. Here, social support refers to social interactions with others that induce in individuals the perception that the resources they provide (emotional, cognitive, and material) are equal to or greater than the demands for them by individuals experiencing life-event stress. For Lazarus then, support means reducing the gap between perceived stress and available resources.

In the contextual threat reduction model (Brown, 1981), support is conceived of as mind-work. Cognitive appraisal, assumptions about the world, and beliefs are central to this conception. Stressful life events involving change threaten stable, contextual meanings. Social support refers to social interactions that inculcate in individuals stable meanings that help them readjust to major life transitions or changes. For Brown, social support is being provided when stable meanings are inculcated by others.

These three major conceptions of social support differ from each other in a number of ways (Cohen & Wills, 1985; Jacobson, 1986). Three of these differences are especially significant for understanding the relation between support and post-separation woman abuse. First, the needs-gratification and resource equalization conceptions assume that support works best when the type of support provided is appropriate to the type of need whose gratification is made problematic by life event stresses of different kinds. These typological conceptions also assume that the needs of the individual experiencing life-event stress remain relatively stable over time. In sum, the needs-gratification and resource equalization conceptions are typological and static.

By way of contrast, the contextual threat or cognitive conception is based on the assumptions that the stressed individual's needs for support change over time and because of this, the timing of support is as important to psychological and physical well-being as the matching of type of support to type of need. The cognitive conception model then, is a process one.

Finally, supporters of these three conceptions of social support differ in the degree to which they emphasize perceptions of support availability or the actual provision of support resources. Thus, Wethington and Kessler (1986) would favor the equalization and cognitive-contextual threat models because they emphasize perceptions. They believe that the actual provision of social support, the emphasis in the needs-

---

[3]These conceptualizations are implied by the needs, transactions, and transitions theories of stress, respectively. For a discussion of these, see Jacobson (1986). According to Breines and Gordon, stress research is important because it "represents a method of searching for mediations between the individual personality and family tensions and societal problems, and because it demonstrates that wife beating is a social problem, not just an individual one. Furthermore, stress research tends to produce progressive policy implications, underlining the need for good social (i.e., support) services" (1983, p. 513).

gratification model, is not as important for the health (or safety) of women as the perception that adequate social support is available.

The support provided by others who process separations or intervene in marital conflicts, may vary along a number of dimensions that are relevant to post-separation woman abuse. The first of these has to do with changing a separated woman's perceptions of the availability of support versus actually providing her with the material resources she needs. The second is support that focuses on the intimate/marital relationship versus support that emphasizes safety. The third source of variation has to do with support premised on the belief that woman abuse is a personal problem and one for which the woman is partly to blame, versus support based on the assumption that abused women are victims of violence used in the service of male domination. The final source of variation is between those who emphasize the timing of support versus those who are primarily concerned with matching the type of support to the type of stress.

Social Support: Perceptions Versus Provision

According to Wethington and Kessler (1986), the actual provision of social support is not as important for the health or safety of women as the *perception* that support is available. By extension, what generates fear in women living with men is not their actual victimization by them, but their perception that the men they live with are dangerous.

Wethington and Kessler may be correct. At the same time, perceptions are not entirely unrelated to behavior, if not the behavior of individual women, then to the behavior of women as a gender group. Thus, women's past experience with men in general certainly plays an important part in influencing the perceptions of individual women. In other words, if women perceive the world as fearful, this fear is, according to Hanmer and Saunders, "well founded" (1984). The same situation applies with perceptions of the availability and adequacy of social support provided to women by the lawyers, police officers, doctors, welfare workers, and so on, to whom separated women turn for help in a time of considerable stress. In short, there is a firm empirical basis for their perceptions of both abuse and support.

Evidence in support of this contention is provided, not only by Hanmer and Saunders (1984) and Stanko (1985), but also by Smith (1986). In a paper entitled "Women's Fear of Violent Crime: An Exploratory Test of a Feminist Hypothesis" (1986), Smith attempted to test the contention that women's fear of violent crime has an objective, experimental basis. If this is the case, then women's fear of crime should be greater among women who had actually been "physically abused by a husband, boyfriend, or other male intimate" than among those who had not. His findings offer tentative support for this hypothesis.

One important implication of insisting on the existence of an objective basis for women's fear of being abused is that it discourages, or should discourage, the provision of forms of social support based on the assumption that women are, as Smith puts it, "irrational" or, at least, "not objective." If it is not successfully challenged, this pejorative attribution will continue to undermine the credibility of abused women as genuine victims of male violence. After all, if women's fear of crime is perceptual rather than based on actual experiences, then their accounts of their actual abusive experiences may also be infected with a lack of objectivity. Perhaps this is one reason why intake workers in social agencies tend to believe the "objective" accounts of men, over the "perceived" accounts of women (Dobash & Dobash, 1979; Maynard, 1985).

To the extent that it is true, the social support provided by social agencies may be diverted away from providing those forms of support requested by women, forms that make them less available to be beaten (e.g., alternative housing) and/or, that deter the men who beat them (e.g., referring the matter to the police). In the extreme and in the absence of independent verification, these material forms of support may be provided only to those women whose abusers support their perceptions with their own objective accounts.

Social Support and Safety

Professionals who intervene in marital conflicts and/or who deal with its consequences are all participants in the safety business. At the same time, such professionals as lawyers, police officers, mediators, as well as others working in the area of woman abuse, vary in the significance they attach to safety as compared with the emphasis they place on factors that divert attention away from the physical safety concerns of separating or separated women (e.g., their professional standing, income, the law, the couple's relationship itself).

In this connection, consider the different emphases of Neidig (1984) and Pence (1983). Neidig is in private practice. His therapy business includes "the rehabilitation of couples involved in spouse abuse" (1984, p. 476). His method is "couples therapy." This method of therapy focuses on the couple's relationship. As spousal abuse, in Neidig's view, is caused by deficits in interpersonal skills, the support he provides takes the form of "skill building which attempts to change behaviors" (1984, p. 474). One result of his gender-integrated, skill-building approach is "a marked reduction of violent episodes" (1984, p. 474).

How does Neidig know this? Presumably, he has collected the requisite evaluation data. Unfortunately for the reader, he has not presented these data. Until he does, the alleged violence-reducing effect of the kind of support he provides remains just that, an allegation. Even if the requisite evidence were made available, Neidig's therapy would be unacceptable to some scholars because they believe it is unethical to continue to work with a couple when the male partner is still abusing the woman he lives with. Pence (1983) views couples therapy as both unethical and dangerous. Abused women who engage in the kind of therapy Neidig provides are, in her view, not less but more likely to be abused.

Instead of a gender-integrated, relationship oriented approach, Pence advocates a gender-segregated, safety-now orientation. For this reason she supports women's shelters. They aid abused women by providing immediate safety and security. Later, relationship matters can be addressed. For the same reason, she believes that the most effective way in which police officers can support abused women is to arrest the abuser, to separate him from his victim (Pence, 1984).

As was true of Neidig, Pence (1983) does not cite data that support her position. However, these data are available (Sherman & Berk, 1984; Burris & Harris, 1983; U.S. Department of Justice, 1986). In the Ellis and Wight study (1987), women who consulted lawyers advocating the decisive termination of the relationship reported fewer and less serious incidents of post-separation abuse than women who consulted lawyers who placed less emphasis on terminating the relationship.

These findings would not be surprising to feminist Lisa Lerman (1984). For some time now, she has contended that the support provided to abused women by lawyers is, compared with the support provided by mediators, less likely to be associated with post-separation abuse.[4] The primary reason for this is that mediators are less likely than lawyers to focus on battering as the issue, to clearly assign responsibility to the batterer, and to take legal steps to separate the batterer from his victim. Where lawyers see a victim and violent offender, mediators tend to view the same couple as interactants who make an equal contribution to the signing of a mediation agreement focusing on the future of the man, the woman, and the children.[5]

In some instances, these agreements may constitute a license to hit. Thus Lerman cites agreements in which the husband is required to stop beating his wife and the wife must not do things that provoke her husband. If she does violate the agreement by provoking her husband then, Lerman notes, " . . . he has been granted tacit permission to beat her again" (1984, p. 13). Here, the mediation agreement is a form of social support *for* woman abuse.

Support for woman abuse may also be provided inadvertently by mediators who adopt a neutral stance oriented toward the objective of achieving an agreement that is "best for the family," in other words, the husband, the wife, and the children. As the presence of children tends to markedly influence the actions and reactions of professionals who intervene in marital conflicts, mediators may undermine the resolve of women to leave abusive relationships or otherwise deal with them more effectively, by subtly and perhaps unintentionally playing on their guilt about breaking up the family or questioning the legitimacy of their claims and complaints about violence.

Mediators disagree among themselves regarding the effectiveness of the support mediation provides when the woman has been seriously hurt and is very frightened (Bethel & Singer, 1982). Cases such as this should be dealt with by lawyers and/or police officers. Presumably, women with less serious injuries are appropriate candidates for mediation. Yet, as Lerman asks, who is to judge the seriousness of injuries? (1984, p. 6). Members of a fledgling profession such as mediation have to compete with other professionals for clients. One consequence of this competitive state of affairs may be the temptation to scale down the seriousness of injuries in order to get clients. Where this occurs, mediators are providing abused women who want the violence stopped with a type of support that is inappropriate for them. The end result may be more serious injuries for women who initially entered mediation with less serious harms.

To conclude that the support provided by mediators does not reduce post-separation abuse is not to suggest, as Lerman appears to, that lawyers do a better job of ensuring the safety of their female clients. Compared with her critical analysis of the support provided abused women by mediators, her treatment of lawyers and lawyering is quite superficial and overly sanguine. Deeper analysis would reveal that not all lawyers are equally interested in the safety of the women they represent and

[4]Pearson and Thoennes define mediation as "a participatory and consensual process in which a third party—the mediator—encourages the disputants to find a mutually agreeable settlement by helping them to identify the issues, reduce misunderstandings, vent emotions, clarify priorities, find points of agreement, explore new areas of compromise, and ultimately negotiate an agreement" (1984, p. 249).

[5]A perusal of influential publications on mediation suggests that mediators assume either that woman abuse does not exist, or that where it does exist mediation can deal with it effectively. Thus, in the Folberg and Taylor (1984) text, neither violence nor abuse are mentioned in either the index or the chapter entitled "Family and Divorce Mediation." The same situation exists in Pearson and Thoennes (1984).

that the support they provide has quite variable effects on post-separation woman abuse.

In this specific connection, the findings of Ellis and Wight (1987) are relevant. They discovered that among women who experienced pre-separation abuse, those who consulted conciliatory lawyers were more likely to report post-separation abuse than were those who consulted adversarial lawyers. Women who did not experience pre-separation abuse but did report post-separation abuse, also reported that their lawyers had actually provoked their former mates by adopting a condescending, bullying, or threatening tone in telephone conversations with them. These allegedly provoked men (8 of 89), did not have lawyers and the Law Society permits family lawyers to deal with them directly. The consequences of this kind of professional conduct are sometimes felt by the lawyer (they are threatened, and on one occasion murdered), but more often by their female clients.

With respect to the motivation of family lawyers, there are probably many who are concerned with the safety of their female clients. At the same time, there appear to be some who are not. Here, an "atrocity tale" may be relevant.

A woman with a disabled child and still living with her husband from whom she has separated emotionally, goes to a lawyer to ask him if he could help remove the husband from their home or get him to provide the money that would enable her to move out temporarily. She also reported that her husband had struck her the previous night and that she was becoming fearful for her safety. After stating that he required a sum of money as a deposit, he ended the consultation by advising the woman to return to her husband and to come back when the wounds she received from him were more serious. Then he might be able to help her.

So long as primacy is given to income, the most seriously abused women will be least likely to obtain effective legal support at least partly because they are often those who are least able to afford the deposit their lawyers demand in order to act. Another option is to consult a Legal Aid lawyer. This can take days or weeks, depending on how long it takes for the lawyers to obtain a certificate indicating that the woman is eligible for legal aid. In the meantime, the perceived threat is immediate. Beyond this, so long as legal training and business concerns work in tandem to restrict the lawyer's role to purely legal-technical matters, he or she can process more clients in a smoother, less messy, and less personally burdensome manner.

Police officers, as was indicated earlier, are also in the safety business. However, they are also armed members of a fairly cohesive, secretive, and supportive work group, a group characterized by the rather emphatic espousal of masculine values (Faragher, 1985). Many police officers attending a "domestic dispute" in which the woman is hurt, bring their gender and occupationally induced biases with them to the scene. These tend to motivate police officers to intervene in a manner prejudicial to the safety of the woman. Hanmer and Saunders (1984) point out the irony of abused women seeking safety from male abuse from males who believe that "real" or criminal violence involving an innocent complainant and a guilty perpetrator often occurs among strangers but rarely among men and women who are living together.

If lawyers, mediators, and police officers do not always rank the safety of separating or separated women as an important priority, the same thing can be said of other agencies of the "generic state" (Burstyn, 1985; Ursel, 1986; Wilson, 1977). For example, the absence of subsidized housing literally traps women in abusive relationships (Pahl, 1985). They cannot afford to live elsewhere. In the meantime, they have to continue to live with men who beat them. Should they move out and live in a women's shelter or hostel, welfare will not provide financial support because shelters and hostels are not considered "fixed addresses." Yet, not being able to afford a private, fixed address (home, apartment, etc.) is precisely the reason why the women must remain in the dwellings in which they are beaten. In any case, for an abused woman to be required to leave her home and find another in a different town is to ask victims to bear the costs of their own victimization.

Compared with its obvious reluctance to provide the kind of material support—subsidized housing—that would help abused women separate themselves from the abusive men they live with and help ensure their greater safety afterwards, agents of the state are very keen on providing informational support via booklets, conferences, and television advertising. This kind of support, while not unhelpful, seems to be influenced more by the support it is thought to garner for the government providing it than by the actual support it provides to a bruised and beaten woman.

Political, Therapeutic, and Material Support

According to Schechter (1982), the kinds of social support provided by social agencies and shelters vary with the theories of women abuse they espouse.[6] The fundamental distinction is between those who view male violence against women as part of the oppression of women in general, in other words, "as a political and social issue" and those who view the same phenomenon as "a personal problem" (1982, p. 312). The relatively few social agencies and shelters in North America that fall into the first group link the provision of material support (e.g., money, accommodations) with a politic that challenges gender hierarchy as a desirable structural arrangement and coercion as a legitimate means of maintaining male hegemony. Politicized agencies and shelters provide a structure (non-hierarchical) and a process (democratic) based on a principle of self-determination that results in women choosing to become members of a gender group that challenges, rather than merely adjusts to, male domination. A politicized woman who is supported by her sisters is a woman with a restored sense of dignity, worth, and strength and therefore one who is strongly motivated to make herself unavailable to be beaten. She is also one who will take the steps necessary to effectively deter men who abused her in the past and/or may do so in the future.

The majority of agencies and shelters fall into the second group. Within this group, two subgroups exist. One group is influenced by feminist ideologies, but is also aware of the fact that the feminist movement " . . . cannot succeed if it divorces itself from the reality of the battered women's lives and minimizes the importance of providing essential services" (Schechter, 1982, p. 241). Food, housing, and clothing are essential services. These kinds of support do decrease the availability of women to their former abusers and, because of this, reduce post-separation women abuse. However, as neither emotional dependency nor deterrence are influenced by material support, the reduced likelihood of post-separation abuse is not as marked as it would be if support took the form of joining the provision of services with a politic of gender, a politic that deals simultaneously with all three of the mediating variables making up the dependency-availability-deterrence (DAD) model.

Shelters and social agencies that restrict the provision of support to providing

[6]These theories also imply a very different politics of victimization. See Elias (1986).

material forms of support are attending to highly salient needs (Spanier & Casto, 1979). At the same time, these groups are vulnerable to influences that undermine challenging feminist ideologies. They may also lead to the provision of forms of support that do little to reduce post-separation woman abuse. Major influences working in this direction are state funding conditions and professional mental health ideologies and therapies. Thus in the shelter studies by Ferraro (1983), the provision of services became contingent on enthusiastic participation in counseling sessions. The umbrella social work agency funding the shelter made its financial support contingent on "casework records." The relation of these records to reducing woman abuse seemed to be irrelevant to both the umbrella agency and those running the battered women's shelter.

Ferraro (1983) contends that most shelters in the United States are similar to the one she studied intensively. If this is so, it constitutes one reason for generalizing the critique of women's shelters co-opted by state funding agencies. Other reasons have to do with the nature of the support provided by professional counseling and the arrangements under which it is provided to battered women.

Although it need not be, casework counseling in practice seems to be supportive of the status quo, that is, of societal conditions that are conducive to the oppression of women in general and of post-separation woman abuse in particular. One reason for this is the assumption that woman abuse is either a personal problem or an outcome of marital interaction gone wrong due to deficits in various interactional skills.

The nature and direction of casework counseling in particular and social work support in general may be derived from studies of what these services actually do for and to battered women. According to Maynard (1985), the "support" they provide includes blaming the woman, not dealing directly with the violence itself and demonstrating a preoccupation with the welfare of the children (Maynard, 1985, p. 162). Pahl discovered "an emphasis on reconciliation rather than on providing escape routes" (1985, p. 169). Dobash, Dobash, and Cavanagh (1985) found that therapies provided by social workers were influenced by a professional commitment to three values that may actually be supportive of woman abuse. These are: protecting and caring for children, the maintenance of the family, and domestic privacy (1985, p. 160). If the first two values subordinate preventing or stopping woman abuse to the family as a unit—so long as the children are not abused and/or the abuse occurs without the knowledge of the children, and/or the children do not appear to be harmed by witnessing their mother being beaten up—woman abuse is an acceptable cost of keeping the family together. The third value, domestic privacy, enables woman abuse to continue without undue interference. The result may be that women are kept dependent and are made available to be beaten, while the men who beat them are not deterred effectively.

The societal context in which woman abuse occurs is characterized by male dominance, female dependence, and the use of coercion by males against females in the service of female subordination. Shelters and agencies committed to egalitarian relationships, self-determination, and cooperation and community provide an example of political and social processes that stand in marked contrast to those that obtain in the larger society. This in itself is a very important form of support: "Experiencing egalitarian relations, (battered women) begin to question hierarchical, authoritarian relations . . . (and see) a new vision of how people can relate to each other" (Schechter, 1982, p. 318). On the other hand, the therapies provided by mental health professionals seem to require hierarchical relations between experts and battered women and a politic geared to the continued existence of the shelter—a politic to which stopping violence against women does not seem to be central. In sum, a frequently encountered context for the provision of support via therapy makes unavailability (e.g., staying at the shelter) contingent on counseling, maintains dependency, and does little to make deterrence work.

The Timing of Support[7]

As was indicated earlier, the process of marital separation is associated with a number of factors that are themselves associated with violence. These include stress, loss of attachment, anger, revenge, zero-sum conflicts, and challenges to male hegemony.

Evidence from a number of sources suggests that the strength of instigation to violence against women who have separated from the men they lived with has two peaks. These are during the first few months after the separation and then again, between 18 and 24 months. These two peaks appear to be associated with the woman's explicit demonstration of independence of her former partner. The types of support that are most likely to effectively prevent or stop woman abuse are different during the two periods, however.

During the initial few months following separation, a period called the "crisis stage" by Weiss (1975) and the "adjusting to the dissolution stage" by Spanier and Casto (1979), stress, anger, sense of loss of attachment, and threats to the man's control over his partner are at their highest. At this point, providing support that makes the woman unavailable to be hurt (i.e., safe housing) is a most effective form of support.

During the second hazardous phase, 18 to 24 months later, challenges to male hegemony come not only from the fact of separation, but also from the changes-for-a-future-without-him, that the women themselves and with the support of others, have brought about. Thus, high school graduation, entering university, a job (or a new one), a new lover or boyfriend, and/or a separate residence may have occurred. These confirm the strength of the woman's commitment to be emotionally and (eventually) economically independent of her former partner. If separation meant rejecting his past behavior, these accomplishments represent a future that excludes him altogether. This is likely to instigate further violence. As the woman is already less available—she is living in her own residence and is no longer as dependent on her former partner—support should now take the form of motivating the woman to report threats and assaults by her former partner to the police. In other words, support that makes deterrence work should be emphasized during this stage.

Support that successfully attends to immediate safety concerns brings to the forefront emotional and material needs that, if not adequately attended to, may well result in battered women returning to their abusive husbands (Pahl, 1985). Guilt and self-deprecation seem to be assuaged by emotional support during the stage immediately following support that provides safety. Along with emotional support, information and assistance that help a woman obtain alternative housing, a job, legal advice, and so forth should also be provided. Following the provision of emotional and informational support that meets immediate psychological and material needs, informational

[7]For an excellent and more general discussion of the importance of the timing of social support, see Jacobson (1986).

support should become more politicized. A politicized woman—a woman aware of herself as a dignified member of a female gender class challenging the hegemony of the male gender class—is a woman who will seek out and use those resources that are most likely to make life safer for her over the long run.

To sum up, with the motivational strength of instigation to woman abuse held constant, the various instigators identified earlier are most likely to lead to actual violent behavior where the male is highly stressed and dependent on the woman, has an opportunity to harm the woman (she is present and available to be hurt), and perceives the likelihood and severity of punishment to be low. If they are appropriately timed, types of social support that simultaneously challenge male supremacy, provide salient material resources, and deal adequately with dependency, availability, and deterrence are most likely to prevent or stop post-separation woman abuse.

CONCLUSION

The first and most important conclusion to emerge from this article has to do with the effect of social support on post-separation abuse. Types of support that decrease the woman's dependency on her former partner, that provide alternative housing and so make her unavailable to be assaulted, that encourage the use of arrest by the police and so make deterrence work more effectively, are more likely to prevent or stop violence than types of support that do none of these things.

Second, the timing of support is as relevant to preventing or stopping woman abuse as is matching appropriate and adequate types of support to those specific and salient needs identified by battered women at a given point in time.

Third, forms of social support that deal directly with the safety of women should be given priority over other forms of support, especially during the initial phases of the separation process.

Fourth, appropriately matched and timed forms of emotional, informational, and material support are most likely to prevent or stop post-separation woman abuse when they are provided in a politicized context, one that challenges and provides an alternative to male domination and the use of coercion in its service.

The final conclusion has to do with major gaps in our knowledge concerning the interaction among separation, support, and post-separation abuse. For example, the evidence indicates that many abused women were beaten for years, the beatings often starting during their first year of marriage. Even after they eventually leave their partners, they return on a number of occasions to be beaten more severely. Is this because no support is available, or because the wrong kind of support is provided at the wrong time?

A second topic on which research is needed has to do with the question, why does support work? At the level of the battered woman, what mechanisms or transformations underly successful support, support that enables a separated woman to choose to do whatever is necessary to make post-separation life safer in the short and long run? Clues provided by Dobash and Dobash (1979) and Schechter (1982) are, in my estimation, very relevant.

BIBLIOGRAPHY

Bethel, J., & Singer, R. (1982). Mediation: A new remedy for cases of domestic violence. *Vermont Law Review, 16*, 47–59.

Breines, W., & Gordon, L. (1983). The new scholarship on family violence. *Signs: Journal of Women in Culture and Society, 8,* 490–531.

Brown, W.G. (1981). Contextual measures of life events. In B. S. Dohrenwend & B. D. Dohrenwend (Eds.), *Stressful life events and their contexts.* New Brunswick, NJ: Rutgers University Press.

Burris, A., & Harris, T. (1983, July). Wife abuse as a crime: The impact of police laying charges. *Canadian Journal of Criminology, 309*–318.

Burstyn, V. (1985). Masculine dominance and the state. In V. Burstyn & D. Smith (Eds.), *Women, class, family, and state* (pp. 45–89). Toronto: Garamond Press.

Carlson, B. (1977, November). Battered women and their assailants. *Social Work, 455*–460.

Chan, K. (1978). *Husband-wife violence in Toronto.* Doctoral dissertation, York University, Department of Sociology.

Cohen, S., & Wills, T. (1985). Stress, social support, and the buffering hypothesis. *Psychological Bulletin, 98,* 310–357.

Dobash, R. E., & Dobash, R. (1979). *Violence against wives: A case against the patriarchy.* New York: Free Press.

Dobash, R. E., Dobash, R., & Cavanagh, K. (1985). The contact between battered women and social and medical agencies. In J. Pahl (Ed.), *Private violence and public policy* (pp. 142–165). London: Routledge and Kegan Paul.

Elias, R. (1986). *The politics of victimization.* New York: Oxford University Press.

Ellis, D., & Ryan, J. (1987). *Lawyers and post-separation women abuse: The relevance of social support.* A report submitted to the Department of Justice (Ottawa) Canada and the Laidlaw Foundation.

Ellis, D., & Wight, L. (1987). Separation and woman abuse: The impact of lawyering style. *Victimology 12,* 27–36.

Faragher, T. (1985). The police response to violence against women in the home. In J. Pahl (Ed.), *Private violence and public policy* (pp. 110–124). London: Routledge and Kegan Paul.

Ferraro, K. (1983). Negotiating trouble in a battered women's shelter. *Urban Life, 12,* 287–306.

Folberg, J., & Taylor, A. (1984). *Mediation.* San Francisco, CA: Jossey-Bass.

Gaquin, D. (1978). Spouse abuse: Data from the National Crime Survey. *Victimology, 2,* 632–643.

Hanmer, J., & Saunders, S. (1984). *Well founded fear: A community study of violence to women.* London: Hutchinson.

Jacobson, D. (1986). Types and timing of social support. *Journal of Health and Social Behavior, 27,* 250–264.

Lazarus, R. S. (1981). The stress-coping paradigm. In C. Eisdorfer, D. Cohen, A. Kleinman, & P. Maxim (Eds.), *Models for clinical psychopathology.* Jamaica, NY: Spectrum.

Lerman, L. (1984). A feminist critique of wife abuse cases. *Response, 7,* 5–6, 12.

Levinger, G. (1966). Sources of marital dissatisfaction among applicants for divorce. *American Journal of Orthopsychiatry, 36,* 804–806.

Long, S., Tauchen, H., & Witte, A. (1983). *Violence and dominance within male-female relationships: An empirical study.* A report prepared for the National Institute of Mental Health, Washington, DC.

MacLeod, L., & Cadieux, A. (1980). *Wife battering in Canada: The vicious circle.* Ottawa: Ministry of Supply and Services.

Maynard, M. (1985). The response of social workers to domestic violence. In J. Pahl (Ed.), *Private violence and public policy* (pp. 125–141). London: Routledge and Kegan Paul.

Neidig, P. (1984). Women's shelters, men's collectives, and other issues in the field of spouse abuse. *Victimology, 9,* 464–476.

O'Brien, J. (1971). Violence in divorce-prone families. *Journal of Marriage and the Family, 33,* 692–698.

Pahl, J. (1985). Conclusion. In J. Pahl (Ed.), *Private violence and public policy* (pp. 189–193). London: Routledge and Kegan Paul.

Pearson, J., & Thoennes, N. (1984). Custody mediation in Denver: Short and longer term effects. In J. M. Eeklaar & S. Katz (Eds.), *The resolution of family conflicts,* (pp. 248–267). Toronto: Butterworths.

Pence, E. (1983). The Duluth domestic abuse intervention project. *Hamline Law Review, 6,* 247–275.

Pence, E. (1984). Response to Peter Neidig's article, "Women's shelters, men's collectives, and other issues in the field of spouse abuse." *Victimology, 9,* 477–482.

Russell, D. (1982). *Rape in marriage.* New York: Macmillan.

Schechter, S. (1982). *Women and male violence.* Boston: South End Press.

Schinke, S. P. (1986). Stress-management intervention to prevent family violence. *Journal of Family Violence, 1,* 74–83.

Schwartz, M. D. (1987, March). *Marital status and spousal violence theory.* Paper presented at the annual meetings of the Academy of Criminal Justice Sciences, St. Louis, MO.

Sherman, L., & Berk, R. (1984). The specific deterrence effects of arrest for domestic assault. *American Sociological Review, 49,* 261–272.
Smith, M. (1986). *Women's fear of violent crime: An exploratory test of a feminist hypothesis.* Unpublished manuscript.
Solicitor General of Canada. (1985). *Female victims of crime.* Ottawa: Canadian Urban Victimization Survey, Statistics Canada.
Spanier, G. B., & Casto, R. (1979). Adjustment to separation and divorce: A qualitative analysis. In G. Levinger & O. Moles (Eds.), *Divorce and separation.* (pp. 211–227). New York: Basic Books.
Stanko, R. (1985). *Intimate intrusions.* Toronto: Methuen.
Stark, E., Flitcraft, A., & Frazier, W. (1979). Medicine and patriarchal violence: The social construction of a private event. *International Journal of Health Services, 9,* 461–493.
Straus, M. (1980). Wife beating: How common and why? In M. Straus & G. Hotaling (Eds.), *The social causes of husband-wife violence.* Minneapolis, MN: University of Minnesota Press.
Thoits, P. (1982). Conceptual, methodological, and theoretical problems in studying social support as a buffer against life stress. *Journal of Health and Social Behavior, 23,* 145–149.
Ursel, J. (1986). The state and the maintenance of patriarchy: A case study of family, labor, and welfare legislation in Canada. In J. Dickinson and R. Russell (Eds.), *Family, economy, and state.* Toronto: Garamond Press.
U.S. Department of Justice. (1986). *Preventing domestic violence against women.* Bureau of Justice Statistics. Washington, DC.
Walker, L. (1979). *The battered women.* New York: Harper and Row.
Wallerstein, J., & Kelly, J. (1980). *Surviving the breakup.* New York: Basic Books.
Weiss, R. (1975). *Marital separation.* New York: Basic Books.
Weiss, R. (1979). The emotional impact of separation. In G. Levinger and O. Moles (Eds.), *Divorce and separation.* (pp. 201–210). New York: Basic Books.
Wethington, E., & Kessler, R. (1986). Perceived support, received support, and adjustment to stressful life events. *Journal of Health and Social Behavior, 27,* 78–89.
Wilson, E. (1977). *Women and the welfare state.* London: Tavistock.

15

Agency Response to Domestic Violence: Services Provided to Battered Women

Ida M. Johnson
Department of Criminal Justice, University of Alabama, Tuscaloosa

Joan Crowley
Department of Criminal Justice, University of New Mexico, Las Cruces

Robert T. Sigler
Department of Criminal Justice, University of Alabama, Tuscaloosa

INTRODUCTION

As primary resources for battered women, shelters play a vital role in providing the essential services needed to develop a sense of independence and autonomy in women so that they can freely choose whether they want to stay in the abusive relationship. Although the growth of the shelter movement has proliferated over the years, limited systematic research has evaluated the perception of shelter workers themselves. This research, based on a population of shelters in a southern state, attempts to describe the role of shelters in intervening in cases of domestic violence.

Domestic violence, especially wife abuse, has gained national recognition as a serious social, economic, and legal problem. The growing awareness of wife abuse

Ida M. Johnson is assistant professor of criminal justice at The University of Alabama. She teaches courses in criminological theory, criminal justice research, corrections, and female criminality. Her recent publications are in the areas of sexual harassment and domestic abuse. These publications include "A Log-Linear Analysis of Abused Wives' Decision to Call the Police" (1991), as well as articles in *Journal of Criminal Justice* and *Families in Society.*

Dr. Joan Crowley is an assistant professor in the Department of Criminal Justice at New Mexico State University. Her research interests include community criminal justice, coordination between social service and criminal justice agencies, substance abuse, and minorities issues in criminal justice. Publications in the area include "Educational Status and Driving Patterns: How Representative are College Students?" in the *Journal of Studies on Alcohol* (1991), as well as articles in the *Journal of Criminal Justice.*

Dr. Robert T. Sigler is professor of criminal justice at The University of Alabama. His research interests include delinquency and juvenile justice, volunteerism, corrections, theory, and research. He is the author of *Placing Domestic Violence in Context* (Lexington Press, 1989). He has written extensively on victimization (e.g., marital violence, domestic abuse), substance abuse and criminality, probation and parole, and police stress.

The authors express their appreciation to the Subcommittee on Domestic Violence of the Alabama State Attorney General's Task Force on Victims for its support of the research project reported here.

by academicians, criminal justice personnel, social service workers, and the public at large has led to efforts to uncover the economic, psychological, situational, and legal determinants of the phenomenon (Bowker, 1983; Gelles, 1976; Kalmuss & Straus, 1982; Okun, 1986; Pagelow, 1981; Pfouts, 1978; Synder & Frutchman, 1981; Star, 1980; Straus, 1975; Truninger, 1971; Walker, 1978; Weitzman & Dreen, 1982) and to provide workable solutions to the problem.

Wife abuse is not a new phenomenon. For centuries, the abuse of wives by their husbands has been approved covertly and supported by laws, societal views, and cultural attitudes (Eisenberg & Micklow, 1977; Paterson, 1979). Crisis-intervention services and publicly and privately funded shelters designed to provide needed services to victims and their children are a recent development in our society. The development of shelters was greatly influenced by the women's movement (Peltoniemi, 1980, 1981; Pleck, 1979). The seriousness and reoccurrence of wife abuse has led to an international movement dedicated to the development of shelters (Dobash & Dobash, 1979; Martin, 1976; Schechter, 1982). The United States alone has more than 1,500 shelters for battered women (Berk, Newton, & Berk, 1986). The fact that some shelters are filled to capacity daily indicates the seriousness of this ubiquitous problem (Martin, 1976).

Research on shelters for battered women has been incorporated into the broader framework of research that addresses the social, economic, psychological, and situational determinants of wife abuse; therefore, research on agency response to battered women is limited, despite the substantial growth of research in the area of family violence. Most studies on shelters have focused on the battered woman's perception of shelters and the impact that shelters have on domestic violence. This research, in contrast, reports the perceptions of shelter staff. Examination of shelter workers' perceptions and attitudes, goals, and operational procedures is needed to clarify the role of shelters in a society that continues to experience severe and frequently occurring acts of violence. When the ideology, goals, and practical aspects of shelters are distorted, the role of shelters in domestic violence will also be unclear.

REVIEW OF THE LITERATURE

Shelters offer a variety of services to women who seek refuge from violent relationships (Martin, 1976; Walker, 1979). Although shelters vary in the kinds of services offered (Lynch & Norris, 1978), they share the function of providing the victim with a temporary, safe environment. In his national survey of 89 emergency shelter programs for abused women, Roberts (1981) reported that in addition to providing the victim with a safe environment, shelters also provide important informational, referral, crisis-intervention, and advocacy services. Furthermore, Loseke and Berk (1982) stated that the misconception that the primary service of shelters is to provide refuge to battered women overshadows other important services provided by the shelters.

Some researchers have given shelters credit for providing a host of services and programs (Agranoff, 1977; Ferraro, 1981; Loseke, 1982; Pagelow, 1981; Pahl, 1979; Redington, 1978), while other observers have criticized shelters for being unresponsive to the needs of battered women (Bass & Rice, 1979; Dobash & Dobash, 1979; Paterson, 1979). The paucity of shelters to accommodate the thousands of women seeking shelter help each year affects the types and amount of services that shelters can offer. It is not unusual for community organizations such as shelters to find that the demands of battered women far exceed the services they can offer (Bass & Rice, 1979; Dobash & Dobash, 1979; Martin, 1976).

Funding of shelters is an important issue in the quality and quantity of services provided. Securing public and private funds for the continued operation of shelters is one of the most significant problems facing shelters today (Roberts, 1981). Many shelters have the desire and need to function in the community financially independent of the state (Peltoniemi, 1980). However, this perceived need for independence has limited the amount and kinds of funding available to shelters. The funding of shelters becomes even more difficult when funding sources have negative stereotypical views of shelters (Stone, 1984). Specifically, funding to shelters has been denied because of the belief that such agencies facilitate the destruction of the family by encouraging the victim to leave the abuser (Gardey, 1981). However, Stone (1984) suggests that when the shelter victim decides to divorce her abuser, the shelter does not play an important role in this decision. Regardless of the types of funding sources utilized by shelters, most shelter workers agree that the key variable in securing funds is the attainment of budgetary support on a continued basis (Roberts, 1984).

Shelters play a vital role in the response to wife abuse. Martin (1976) reports that the use of shelters is one of the most effective ways of dealing with the phenomenon of wife abuse. Although more than 700 battered women's shelters have been established in the United States as a consequence of the women's movement, the growth of the shelter movement has not been supported with systematic research on the role, operational procedures, and practical work of shelters. Although the existing literature on shelters has focused primarily on the need for effective services and how shelters should operate (Gentzler, 1977; Janes & Naples, 1978), few systematic and rigorous research efforts have been directed toward an understanding of how shelters actually operate (Loseke, 1982).

This descriptive study is designed to examine shelters' interaction with the community, services provided by the shelters, and the attitudes and perceptions of the shelters' staffs. Using a population of shelters in a southern state, this study attempts to describe the shelters' interaction with the community, services provided by shelters, and the attitudes and perceptions of the shelters' staffs by focusing on the following issues: (a) background characteristics of staff and clientele populations, (b) admission policy, (c) funding, (d) contacts with community agencies, (e) services and training, (f) barriers to improved services, (g) secrecy of the location of shelters, (h) frequency of warrants sworn and dropped by the victims, (i) perceived reasons for dropping charges against the abuser, (j) frequency of victims returning home to the abuser, and (k) perceived reasons for returning to the abusive relationship.

METHOD

Respondents

The data are taken from a questionnaire commissioned in 1987 by the Subcommittee on Child Abuse and Domestic Violence of the Alabama Attorney General's Task Force on Victims. The project surveyed six different agencies involved with domestic violence issues. These agencies included shelters for battered women, mental health centers, the Department of Human Resources (DHR) county offices, district attorneys, judges, and law enforcement officers. Included in this study are the 11 shelters established in the state to assist battered women.

Under the auspices of the Alabama Coalition Against Domestic Violence, questionnaires were mailed to the directors of each shelter, requesting that they or one of their staff directly involved with providing services to battered women respond to the mailed survey. Ten of the 11 shelters provided usable responses.

Instrument

The data for this study were collected from a statewide survey designed to measure system response to cases of domestic violence by social service and criminal justice agencies in the state of Alabama. The questionnaire was composed of two schedules of items. The first schedule was designed to elicit information on topics common to all respondents: the degree of training and education; perceptions of interagency and inter-resource cooperation; work load; attitudes toward definition, criminalization, and punishment of domestic violence; and perceived priorities. The second schedule varied from agency to agency and was designed to assess policies and attitudes specific to the respondent's agency. The items that addressed major issues in the staffing and operation of shelters were included in this study.

Data Collection and Analysis

The data for the study were collected from the population of shelters for battered women in the state of Alabama. Each shelter director was mailed a questionnaire. One follow-up letter was sent to each shelter to encourage responses.

The data for the study were analyzed using SPSS-X descriptive procedures (SPSS-X, 1988). The shelters in this study represent a population and not a sample in that all shelters in the state were asked to participate in the study. The very small sample size precludes any attempt at multivariate analysis.

FINDINGS

Shelters and Their Interaction with the Community

Characteristics of Shelters and Populations Served

Shelters are the only organizations in the state of Alabama that have primary responsibility for providing services to battered women. These shelters are coordinated by the Alabama Coalition Against Domestic Violence and serve multi-county areas. Although most of the shelters are located in the northern portion of the state, they have established service for the entire state. For the ten shelters that participated in this study, the average number of years of operation was five, with the oldest shelter having been in operation for nine years and the newest for one year.

Shelter directors in the state of Alabama are predominantly white (90%, $n = 9$) and female (100%, $n = 10$). The expertise of shelter workers in the area of domestic violence is reflected in their educational background. Shelter directors have at least a college or graduate degree (100%, $n = 10$) with 70% ($n = 7$) of the workers having a bachelor's degree and 30% ($n = 3$) having a master's degree.

Admission Policy

Shelters for battered women in the state of Alabama allow both the victim and her children to be admitted to the shelter. Although the majority of the shelters defined eligibility in terms of physical abuse (70%, $n = 7$), three shelters also included emotional harm as a criterion of eligibility. Interesting to note is the fact that no shelter defines eligibility in terms of sexual abuse. Of course, this might be reflected in the staff's lack of training in this area of spouse abuse or that shelters consider sexual abuse as a part of physical abuse. Several shelters also reported secondary factors as criteria for eligibility. For example, four of the shelters reported the victim's lack of a safe place to go as a criterion for eligibility, while two shelters specified the restrictions of no current alcohol or drug problems and the victim's ability to accept the program as offered.

The average maximum capacity of the shelters is 14, or an average of nine adults and five children at any given time. In terms of duration of the shelter stay, most shelters allow women and their children to stay up to four weeks. However, some shelters have provisions in their admissions policy that allow the staff to extend the duration of the shelter stay if the situation warrants.

Funding of Shelters

Half of the shelters (50%, $n = 5$) reported that they are funded by multiple sources (i.e., a combination of United Way, state grants, and voluntary contributions). The other five shelters are funded primarily by state grants (30%, $n = 3$) and United Way (20%, $n = 2$). All the shelters have paid full-time and part-time workers. The average number of paid full-time staff persons and part-time persons is four and three, respectively. Because the number of paid staff is so small, it is common for shelters to have more volunteers than paid staff. The average number of volunteers per shelter is 32. The mean, however, is affected by three shelters that have a larger number of volunteers. One shelter reported that it has more than 100 volunteers. The median for the number of volunteers per shelter is 21.

Concerning the clientele served by the shelters, the majority of the shelters (60%, $n = 6$) reported that they serve both rural and urban populations. Three of the 10 shelters studied reported that they served predominantly rural populations, and one shelter reported serving a predominantly urban population. The economic and racial compositions of the clientele served revealed that the majority of the shelters provide services primarily for the poor and working class (80%, $n = 8$) and an equal proportion of black and white clients (60%, $n = 6$). Only 20% ($n = 2$) of the shelters reported that they serve all socioeconomic classes.

Community Services Available in the Service Area of the Shelters

Each shelter staff was asked to describe the services available in their service area. All of the shelters are located in communities that offer a variety of services. Table 15-1 presents the data for the distribution of community services available in the service area of the shelters. In terms of the availability of services in the general geographical locations of the shelters, the majority of the shelters reported that the services of Alcoholics Anonymous (100%, $n = 10$), community mental health services (90%, $n = 9$), Parents Anonymous (80%, $n = 8$), a victim service officer (70%, $n = 7$), a family child specialist (70%, $n = 7$), and child emergency shelters (60%, $n = 6$) are available in their service area. Other less available services in-

Table 15-1 Types of community services available in the service area of the shelters (*N* = 10)

	Yes		No	
Community service	Number	Percent	Number	Percent
Alcoholics Anonymous	10	100	0	00
Community mental health center	9	90	1	10
Parents Anonymous	8	80	2	20
Victim service officer	7	70	3	30
Family/child specialist	7	70	3	30
Children's emergency shelter	6	60	4	40
Family counseling	5	50	5	50
Children's group home	4	40	6	60
Child advocacy center	4	40	6	60
Multidisciplinary team	4	40	6	60
Drop-in crisis center	3	30	7	70
In-home services	3	30	7	70
Respite day care	2	20	8	80
Safe home network	1	10	9	90
Sex offender program	1	10	9	90
Other spouse abuse programs	1	10	9	90

cluded child advocacy, group homes for children, and a multidisciplinary team to coordinate the services provided by social service and criminal justice agencies. The majority of the shelters (80%, *n* = 8) reported that they do not attend nor participate in the meetings of the multidisciplinary team. However, all shelters reported that the number of domestic violence cases handled in their service area had increased during the last year.

Services Offered by the Shelters

Training

Each shelter respondent was asked to describe the areas of domestic violence in which they have received training and to describe the services that they provide to battered women and their dependents. All of the shelter workers have had training in domestic violence (100%, *n* = 10), with 90% (*n* = 9) reporting that their most recent training session occurred during the past year. Most of the training that shelter workers have received is in the area of spouse abuse (100%, *n* = 10) and child abuse (50%, *n* = 5). The shelters are designed primarily to provide supportive services to abused women. Therefore, it is not surprising that shelter workers have received the least amount of training in the area of offender treatment (80%, *n* = 8). Although all shelter workers have received training in the areas of physical abuse and emotional abuse, 80% (*n* = 8) have not received specific training in the area of sexual abuse of women. When asked to identify areas of spouse abuse for which additional training was desired, 70% (*n* = 7) of the shelter workers reported that they would like to receive more training in the areas of sexual abuse of women and treatment of the offender (60%, *n* = 6).

Services Offered

The shelters offer a variety of services to the community and to victims of spouse abuse. All shelters reported that they have crisis line services (100%, $n = 10$) and that this service is usually staffed by shelter personnel (50%, $n = 5$) as opposed to some form of answering service (30%, $n = 3$) or a combination of personnel and answering services (20%, $n = 2$).

Table 15-2 provides a frequency distribution of the types of services offered by shelters. The six most frequent types of services offered by the shelters include linkage to other community agencies (100%, $n = 10$), training for community agencies (100%, $n = 10$), counseling for adult victims in the shelter (90%, $n = 9$), non-residential counseling (80%, $n = 8$), advocating for victims in coping with the criminal justice system (70%, $n = 7$), and counseling for children (60%, $n = 6$). Services that shelters are less likely to provide are third-party visitation services (i.e., providing a neutral observer for parental visits) (10%, $n = 1$) and counseling services for the abuser (20%, $n = 2$).

Barriers to Handling Cases of Domestic Violence

Although shelters offer a variety of services to battered women and their children, they do experience difficulty in handling cases of wife abuse. Shelters were asked to indicate the major barriers they encountered in working with victims of domestic violence. The five types of barriers that shelter workers face in handling wife abuse are inadequate legal response from the criminal justice system (30%, $n = 3$), lack of resources (20%, $n = 2$), the victim's attitude (20%, $n = 2$), poor coordination of services (20%, $n = 2$), and lack of societal concern about domestic violence (10%, $n = 1$).

Perceptions and Attitudes of the Shelter Staff

Secrecy of the Location of Shelters

Measures were taken of the shelter workers' attitudes toward keeping the location of the shelter secret. Respondents were given a list of arguments for and against such secrecy, and asked to indicate their degree of agreement. The results indicated that the majority of the shelters have a strict policy of secrecy and their staff would like to maintain that policy (90%, $n = 9$). When shelter workers were asked to rate their reactions to a number of advantages and disadvantages of disclosing or maintaining the secret location of their shelter, the mean rating ($\bar{x} = 9.750$) revealed that the majority of the shelter workers supported the argument for secrecy. The shelter workers felt that their secret location is important for the purpose of keeping the assailant away from the victim ($\bar{x} = 8.750$) and making her feel more secure in the shelter environment ($\bar{x} = 9.750$). These shelter workers feel that disclosure of the location of the shelter would interfere with the basic objective of providing the victim with a safe environment. The only highly rated advantage of making the location of the shelter public knowledge is that it increases the community's involvement in domestic violence.

Warrants

Shelter workers must work with the police in handling wife abuse cases. Shelter workers were asked whether they counseled their clients about warrants. The majority of the respondents reported that wife abuse should be treated as a crime. The majority of the respondents reported that they provide counseling to their adult shelter residents about warrants (90%, $n = 9$). Nine out of ten shelters reported that they prefer that their clients obtain warrants. The provision of counseling concerning warrants does not, in many cases, result in the victim's signing of a warrant. It is interesting to note that despite the shelter workers' preference for having the victim obtain the warrant, the shelters reported that only about one-fourth of the battered women actually obtain a warrant, and that almost one-half of these women eventually drop the charges for a variety of reasons.

The shelters were asked to rate the reasons for the victim's decision to drop the charges against the abuser on a scale from least important (1) to most important (10). The six most important reasons for dropping the warrants included giving the abuser one more chance ($\bar{x} = 9.200$), lack of support from the legal system ($\bar{x} = 8.800$), emotional dependency on the abuser ($\bar{x} = 8.500$), fear of the abuser ($\bar{x} = 8.100$), lack of financial resources ($\bar{x} = 7.6000$), and lack of housing ($\bar{x} = 7.1000$). As can be seen in Table 15-3, reasons related to the victim's relationship with the abuser (i.e., the victim's desire to give the abuser another chance and emotional dependency on the abuser) were important reasons for dropping charges against the abuser. The criminal justice system itself plays a vital role in the victim's decision to drop the charges. The lack of legal support received a relatively high rating.

Victims Returning Home to the Abusive Relationship

The existing literature indicates that battered women frequently return to their abusive partners for a variety of reasons. The data for this study revealed that a substantial portion of victims who seek help from shelters return home to the abusive relationship. Seventy percent ($n = 7$) of the shelters reported that more than half of their clients return home to their abusive relationship. Two of the shelters reported

Table 15-2   Frequency of the types of services provided by spouse abuse shelters ($N = 10$)

	Yes		No	
Service	Number	Percent	Number	Percent
Linkage to community agencies	10	100	0	00
Training for community agencies	10	100	0	00
Counseling for adults	9	90	1	10
Non-residential counseling	8	80	2	20
Advocate for victim through legal systems	7	70	3	30
Court escort for victim residents	3	30	7	70
Counseling for children	6	60	4	40
Contact with outside agencies for services	5	50	5	50
Day care for shelter residents	3	30	7	70
Counseling for abusers	2	20	8	80
Other	2	20	8	80
Third-party visitation	1	10	9	90

Table 15-3 Perceived reasons for dropping charges against the abuser
(N = 10)

Reasons	Mean
Give the abuser one more chance	9.2
Lack of support or follow-through by the legal system	8.8
Emotional dependency on the abuser	8.5
Fear that the abuser will find her and do her harm	8.1
Lack of financial resources	7.6
Lack of housing resources	7.1
Lack of support from other family members	6.9
Lack of job opportunities	6.2
Denial of a cycle of violence	6.4
Lack of transportation	5.6
Lack of child care resources	4.8
Fear that the abuser will kidnap the children	4.3
Fear that the abuser will get custody of the children	4.0
Children miss the absent parent	3.9
Lack of professional counseling for the abuser	3.9
Fear that the abuser will harm the children	3.6

that less than 35% of the victims returned home to their abuser, and one shelter did not respond to this question.

The current literature indicates that battered women return to their abusive partners for a variety of reasons. The shelter workers were asked to rate their perceptions of important reasons for the victim's decision to return to the abusive relationship on a scale from least important (1) to most important (10). The reasons for returning home to the abusive relationship were quite similar to the reasons for dropping charges against the abuser (see Table 15-4). The four most important reasons reported by the shelters as to why victims return to the abusive relationship are the victim's desire to give the abuser another chance ($\bar{x}$ = 10.000), lack of financial resources

Table 15-4 Perceived reasons for returning home to the abusive
relationship (N = 10)

Reasons	Mean
Give the abuser one more chance	10.0
Lack of financial resources	9.1
Emotional dependency on the abuser	9.0
Lack of housing resources	8.7
Lack of job opportunities	7.7
Denial of cycle of violence	7.6
Lack of support or follow-through by the legal system	7.6
Lack of child care resources	7.1
Lack of transportation	6.7
Fear that the abuser will find her and do her harm	6.7
Lack of support from other family members	6.6
Fear that he will get custody of the children	5.8
Fear that the abuser will kidnap the children	5.8
Children miss the absent parent	5.6
Lack of professional counseling	5.1
Fear that the abuser will harm the children	4.6

($\bar{x}$ = 9.100), emotional dependency on the abuser ($\bar{x}$ = 9.000), and the lack of housing resources ($\bar{x}$ = 8.700). The victim's desire to give the abuser another chance ranked as the most important reason for the victim's decision to drop charges against the abuser as well as to return home to the abusive relationship. The lack of professional counseling for the abuser and fear that he will harm the children ranked as the least important reasons for returning home to the abusive relationship.

DISCUSSION AND SUMMARY

This study describes the policies and operational procedures of shelters for battered women in a southern state. Spouse abuse shelters, as grass-roots organizations, are the primary community agencies that provide battered women with a temporary safe place to explore their options and alternatives to abusive relationships. In some geographical locations, shelters may be the only community resources available to battered women.

Shelter workers' ability to provide multiple services to a diverse client population is reflected in the types of services offered. As service providers, shelters see their primary role as providing counseling and support services to the battered woman who finds herself in a violent situation. The services provided by shelters range from educating the victim about domestic violence to providing referral services for obtaining job skills, housing, educational training, financial aid, and so forth, to victim advocacy services. Because battered women have diverse and multiple problems, it is important for community services to network and coordinate the services provided to victims of domestic violence. All of the shelters have linkages to other community agencies and provide domestic violence training to these agencies. One of the most important functions of shelters is training staff from other agencies in handling domestic violence cases. Such training increases the resources available to their clients.

Because shelter workers are involved in helping the battered woman identify alternatives to the violent relationship, two of the most consistent problems confronting shelter workers are the victim's decision to drop the charges against the abuser and her decision to return home to the abusive relationship. Shelters are concerned about the reasons why battered women return home to the abusive relationship. By being knowledgeable about the relationship decisions of battered women, the shelters can provide the appropriate services needed to help the victim make a rational decision. Shelter directors believe that it is vital for a portion of their counseling services to focus on educating the victim about domestic violence and the victimization process. This type of service is essential to women who believe that their spouse will stop being violent without seeking treatment. All of the shelters reported that battered women often return to the abusive relationship because of their desire to give the abuser one more chance. Without being knowledgeable about the characteristics of domestic violence, the victim can become trapped in a continuous cycle of violence. It has been substantiated in the domestic violence literature that battered women become trapped in a cycle of violence that is difficult to break without appropriate social and legal intervention (Walker, 1978, 1979).

Shelters workers' concern about the legal rights of battered women is reflected in their perception of domestic assaults as crimes. Shelter workers tend to view domestic violence as a crime that warrants legal intervention. The majority of the shelters surveyed in the study counsel their clients about warrants and encourage them to obtain warrants for the arrest of their abusers. However, only one-fourth of the victims actually obtain a warrant against their abuser and almost half of these later drop the charges. It has been well substantiated in the domestic violence literature that battered women do not receive adequate legal services from the criminal justice system. The majority of shelter workers reported that one of the primary reasons why battered women return home to the abusive relationship is the lack of adequate legal support from the criminal justice system. Although shelter workers can provide the victim with assertive skills, job training, financial support, and other services needed to help the victim minimize her emotional and financial dependence on the abuser, it is imperative that effective legal support be provided by the police, lawyers, and judges if the cases are to be handled successfully by the criminal justice system. Only when community agencies acknowledge domestic violence as an interdisciplinary problem and not a social or legal problem can meaningful solutions to wife abuse be found.

BIBLIOGRAPHY

Agranoff, R. (1977). Service integration. In W. Anderson, B. Frieden, & M. Murphy (Eds.), *Managing human services*. Washington, DC: International City Managers Association.

Bass, D., & Rice, J. (1979). Agency responses to the abused wife. *Social Casework, 60*, 338–342.

Berk, R. A., Newton, P. J., & Berk, S. F. (1986). What a difference a day makes: An empirical study of the impact of shelters for battered women. *Journal of Marriage and the Family, 48*, 481–490.

Bowker, L. (1983). *Beating wife beating*. Lexington, MA: Lexington Books.

Dobash, R., & Dobash, R. (1979). *Violence against wives*. New York: Free Press.

Eisenberg, S., & Micklow, P. (1977). The assaulted wife: Catch 22 revisited. *Women Rights Law Reporter, 3*, 138–161.

Ferraro, K. J. (1981). Processing battered women. *Journal of Family Issues, 2*, 415–438.

Gardey, K. (1981). Personal letter. In L. Stone, *Shelters for battered women: A temporary escape from danger or the first step toward divorce? Victimology: An International Journal, 9*, 284–289.

Gelles, R. (1976). Abused wives: Why do they stay? *Journal of Marriage and the Family, 38*, 659–668.

Gentzler, R. (1977). *Advocacy programs for abused victims*. Lancaster, PA: Pennsylvania Coalition Against Domestic Violence.

Janes, S., & Naples, S. (1978). *Establishing and operating a shelter for battered women: A how to book*. Orange County, CA: Women's Traditional Living Center.

Kalmuss, D., & Straus, M. (1982). Wife's marital dependency and wife abuse. *Journal of Marriage and the Family, 44*, 277–286.

Loseke, D. (1982). *Social movement theory in practice: A shelter for battered women*. Unpublished doctoral dissertation, University of California, Santa Barbara.

Loseke, D., & Berk, S. (1982). The work of shelters: Battered women and initial calls for help. *Victimology: An International Journal, 1*, 35–48.

Lynch, C., & Norris, T. (1978). Service for battered women: Looking for a perspective. *Victimology: An International Journal, 2*, 553–562.

Martin, D. (1976). Battered wives. San Francisco, CA: Glide.

Okun, L. (1986). *Women abuse: Facts replacing myths*. New York: State University of New York Press.

Pahl, J. (1979). Refuges for battered women: Social provision or social movement. *Journal of Voluntary Action Research, 8*, 25–35.

Pagelow, M. (1981). *Women and crime*. New York: Macmillan.

Paterson, E. (1979). How the legal system responds to battered women. In D. Moore (Ed.), *Battered women*. Beverly Hills: Sage.

Peltoniemi, T. (August, 1980). Family violence: The first six months of Finnish shelters. Paper presented at the Violence: An International Psychoanalytic and Interdisciplinary Conference, Haikko, Finland.

Peltoniemi, T. (1981). The first 12 months of the Finnish shelter. *Victimology: An International Journal, 6*, 198–211.

Pfouts, J. (1978). Violent families: Coping responses of abused wives. *Child Welfare, 57*, 101–111.

Pleck, E. (1979). Wife beating in Nineteenth-Century America. *Victimology: An International Journal, 4*, 60–74.

Redington, J. (1978). The tradition process: A feminist environment as reconstitutive milieu. *Victimology: An International Journal, 2,* 563–575.

Roberts, A. (1981). *Sheltering battered women: A national study and service guide.* New York: Springer.

Roberts, A. (1984). *Battered women and their families: Intervention strategies and treatment programs.* New York: Springer.

Schechter, S. (1982). *Women and male violence: The visions and struggles of the battered women's movement.* Boston, MA: South End Press.

Synder, D., & Frutchman, L. (1981). Differential patterns of wife abuse: A data-based typology. *Journal of Consulting and Clinical Psychology, 49,* 878–885.

Star, B. (1980). Comparing battered and non-battered women. *Victimology: An International Journal, 5,* 32–44.

SPSS-X User's Guide. (1988). Chicago, IL: SPSS-X.

Stone, L. (1984). Shelters for battered women: A temporary escape from danger or the first step toward divorce? *Victimology: An International Journal, 9,* 284–290.

Straus, M. (1976). Sexual inequality, cultural norm and wife beating. *Victimology: An International Journal, 1,* 54–76.

Truninger, E. (1971). Marital violence: The legal solutions. *Hastings Law Review, 13,* 159–176.

Walker, L. (1978). Battered women and learned helplessness. *Victimology: An International Journal, 2,* 525–534.

Walker, L. (1979). *The Battered Woman.* New York: Harper & Row.

Weitzman, J., & Dreen, K. (1982). Wife-beating: A view of the marital dyad. *Social Casework, 63,* 386–397.

16

Educating the Professional to Aid Abuse Victims in Achieving Human Rights

Irma MacKay
Department of Social Work, Health Sciences Center, Winnipeg,
Manitoba, Canada

INTRODUCTION

Her inner pain only deepened as she left the emergency department that night, but in many ways she was relieved that her family life had remained private. She deserved it, didn't she? And the hope of any change seemed so remote. The professionals with whom she had an encounter that day did not ask the question. Was it because they did not want to know or, maybe, they did not know what to say when she would reply "yes" to the question? This scenario occurs many times across the country as battered wives leave hospitals.

This chapter examines the education of professionals to enable them to assist in the empowerment process of domestic violence victims. Professional groups include nurses, doctors, social workers, teachers, clergy, lawyers, and police. Education within Canada is examined at both the preservice and inservice level. A sociological approach is taken to explain the prevalence of domestic violence. The education is evaluated in its ability to challenge the values of students, to provide information on barriers to the empowerment process, and to provide skills for intervention, including an interdisciplinary approach. The chapter proposes that most education available for professionals is optional, if available at all. Some professional groups such as the clergy need to make a major value shift. Therefore, most professionals in Canada have limited, if any, skills in intervening with domestic violence victims. An overview is given of curriculum material and inservice programs available in Canada, although most have not been researched for effectiveness. Professional educators are challenged to address this issue.

Professionals in the health care, social service, and justice systems are called on to

Irma MacKay was Director of Social Work at the Misericordia General Hospital, Winnipeg, Canada, when this chapter was written. She has provided interdisciplinary inservice programs on domestic violence in her own hospital as well as to other professionals in the community. In 1985 and 1986, Ms. MacKay was President of the Canadian Association of Social Work Administrators in Health Facilities. During this term, she coordinated a Health and Welfare Canada grant resulting in the publication of *Domestic Violence Protocol Manual For Social Workers in Health Facilities (1985)*. In 1987, she received an award of recognition from C.A.S.W.A.H.F. for outstanding contribution in the development of social work administration in health care.

intervene in domestic situations when domestic problems have been identified or have already reached crisis proportions. However, teachers and clergy are key professionals in the education of the members of our society and can prevent, at times, the occurrence of domestic violence. Thus, this chapter will examine the preparation of professionals for their roles in prevention and intervention, allowing them to contribute effectively to the resolution of an existing problem.

In North America, the reality of domestic violence was acknowledged in the legislation of mandatory reporting of child abuse in the 1960s (Wachtel, 1989). Awareness of the extent of the violence, and acknowledgement of society's responsibility to intervene, is more recent. Concern about abuse in intimate male-female relationships was first raised in Canada as recently as in the 1970s (Hilton, 1988).

On May 12, 1982, when a study of wife battering was raised in the House of Commons, laughter could be heard throughout the House. The study by the Canadian Advisory Counsel on the Status of Women (MacLeod, 1980), estimated that one in every ten women involved in a male-female relationship is battered each year. This was felt to be a conservative statistic. Horror and disbelief at the reaction of the elected representatives rippled through the country. Since that time, political attention to the problems of domestic violence has increased. Wife battering was identified as a priority concern in two Throne speeches. Just prior to the last federal election, the federal government announced $40 million worth of funding for new programs to address the needs of battered women and their children.

In 1984, the Report of the Committee on Sexual Offences Against Children and Youths was released. Again, the pervasiveness of the problem was astounding as the study reported that "at some time during their lives, about one in two females and one in three males has been a victim of one or more unwanted sexual acts—about four in five of these unwanted sexual acts have been first committed when they were children or youths" (Committee on Sexual Offences Against Children and Youths, 1984).

The acknowledgement of elder abuse is a more recent phenomenon. A major study carried out in Manitoba in 1982 estimated that 2.2% of the province's elder population suffered abuse. Podnieks (1988) states that other studies confirm the existence—but not the extent—of the problem. No one is dealing with elder abuse in an organized, effective manner at the present time.

The personal anguish and sense of helplessness experienced by the victims have become more evident. The human rights of these citizens are badly violated. In a country that prides itself on providing social justice to its citizens, the question "why?" is asked frequently. A psychological rationale is not sufficient to explain such a prevalent problem. Domestic violence is not caused primarily by mental illness, alcoholism, pathological marriage relationship, status imbalance, or stress (MacLeod, 1980).

Family violence is best understood from a cultural perspective. Canadian culture has emerged from the European roots of the early explorers and settlers. They brought with them a tradition of the patriarchal nuclear family (Martin, 1981). Men were considered to own their wives and children who, in return, were to obey the men with unquestioned obedience and loyalty. Women were to conform to the ideals of self-denial, hard work, and endurance.

Because European culture was most dominant, the Native family styles and culture have suffered. Prior to the European influence, Native Indian culture depended on the balance to be achieved through the efforts of each member of the group. A woman, because of her gender, was given respect automatically (Wolk, 1982). The fur traders who would deal only with Native men and the missionaries who taught patriarchal family values to the "pagan" natives (Martens, 1988) contributed to the serious disintegration of Native culture.

The institution of the patriarchal, nuclear family is well entrenched in all aspects of today's society. Martin (1981) writes about the benefits of this structure to capitalism, which thrives on competition. If women remain in the home, the labor market is diminished greatly and competition for jobs, money, and power is reduced proportionately. The judicial, religious, educational, and social service institutions continue to perpetuate these values. Professionals trained to fulfill the rules, regulations, professional ethics, and expectations within these institutions inevitably promote their traditional, cultural values.

Hope for the abused woman and societal awareness of the problem commenced within the sheltering movement during the 1970s (Gilman, 1985). Women who had been battered extended hope and safety to other women through the provision of safe homes and transition houses. Victims looked to other women who understood their plight to support and guide them to greater freedom.

Women who left the authoritarian relationships within their homes were exposed to democratic decisionmaking within the transition homes. They experienced women, who like them, had left the victimization and were now able to make their own decisions about housing, child rearing, and jobs. Frequently, financial security was abandoned for a poverty level existence that did not involve abuse. The need for better, low cost housing, higher wages for women, and improved, accessible day-care emerged. Women were able to lobby collectively for themselves. Through this process of mutual problem-solving and support, victims of family violence became empowered to claim the human rights that were rightly due to them.

Children, unfortunately, have not had the same opportunity to experience empowerment. Canadian law assumes the family to be a safe and nurturing environment for a child and provides parents with full rights over the child (Ayim, 1986). Parents' rights over the child are only compromised if blatant physical or sexual abuse occurs. Neglect and emotional abuse are often tolerated by society. Therefore, all children are not guaranteed the right to live in safe, kind, and nurturing families.

When society removes the rights of parents over their children, the victims are placed into the hands of other adults such as foster parents or legal guardians. Children's input into this process is often minimal and, too frequently, they continue to be victimized. Instances of physical and sexual abuse in foster care are not uncommon. The empowerment of all children to achieve full human rights in Canada has not occurred.

Professionals, particularly social workers, have been the primary caregivers and intervenors on behalf of abused children. In most instances, an authoritarian approach has been taken, replacing the authority of the father in the family. Mutual decisionmaking, to the extent possible with the child's understanding and age, has rarely occurred. In as much as this same professional approach is used with victims of spousal and elderly abuse, the victimization process will continue. Mutual respect and decisionmaking with the victims are essential if empowerment is to occur.

METHOD

For the purpose of this chapter, education is defined broadly. The preservice or basic training, which is the most common method of training professionals, is examined for all seven professional groups. Inservice and protocols in the work-place are essential. Because the awareness of societal responsibility for domestic violence is a recent phenomenon, many human service professionals will have graduated from school prior to the inclusion of domestic violence material at the preservice level.

Professional associations at both the national and provincial levels are often leaders at the voluntary education level. Frequent vehicles used for education are journals, protocols, and educational conferences.

For this study, a representative sample of education material was obtained from across Canada. An exhaustive exploration was not possible, but an attempt was made to find material that could be seen as most effective within Canada.

The newsletter of the National Clearinghouse on Domestic Violence, *Vis-A-Vis,* was an important source of information. Staff of National Health and Welfare were helpful, as were faculty, government, and inservice staff within the Provinces of Manitoba and Ontario. Each person contacted was asked to direct the author to any other source that was perceived to be effective in their profession in the education of domestic violence in Canada.

Each education program was reviewed in its ability to address the societal values regarding domestic violence; address difficulties encountered by victims in attempting to break out of the violence, including the cycles of violence; provide strategies and skills to intervene with and on behalf of the victims; acknowledge the importance of working with other appropriate disciplines and agencies; provide supervised case experience; and evaluate the effectiveness of the learning process.

FINDINGS

A high probability exists that 1989 graduates from the human service professional schools within Canada will have no skills in identifying or assisting victims of domestic violence. If courses are offered on either child abuse or wife abuse, they will have been electives and, in some schools, offered only at the postgraduate level.

A common curriculum approach for those faculties addressing the domestic violence issue is to provide a three- to eight-hour overview. Police academies address this subject within the crisis intervention course. Medicine and nursing may address it in a community or preventive health course. Films or guest lecturers who specialize in the field are often used, along with a bibliography and a sample protocol or guideline for intervention. Guest lecturers indicate that their primary goal is to impress on the students the reality of the problem. Techniques used are the review of statistics, graphic and concise definitions of abuse, and vivid illustrative case studies.

The process of victimization is covered, including the cycle of violence. Most overviews also touch on the importance of working with members of other disciplines such as lawyers, police, and social welfare staff. Strategies and skills to intervene and supervised case experience are usually not provided.

The Canadian Police College provides standards and references for each of the sessions in the crisis intervention curriculum. The college uses these standards to educate trainers from academies across the country. Case experience is provided through the use of actors who simulate typical domestic disputes. The trainers' intervention is videotaped for further discussion and supervision. Similar training is provided by the trainers to cadets across the country.

Effective curriculum material to train professionals in intervention with domestic violence victims is being developed. Taylor, at the School of Social Work, University of Toronto, has received a grant from the Ontario Ministry of Community and Social Services to develop a curriculum on violence in relationships. A format being considered is to videotape specialists in the field and provide a guide for teaching, so the package would be readily transferable to other postsecondary settings. Dr. Lero, from the University of Guelph, developed interdisciplinary curriculum material on child abuse for early childhood educators in 1980. The curriculum was evaluated in 1985 and revised in 1987. It is widely used in community colleges across the province of Ontario.

The George Brown College of Applied Arts and Technology in Toronto is offering a four-semester program for the assaulted women's and children's counselor/advocate. It presents a feminist and child-centered focus, and prepares students for work in transition houses, sexual assault centers, and other settings designed to assist survivors. Structured field experience is included in the program. Thomleson (1983) and Barber and Burns (1986), have also recommended curriculum material for child abuse and prevention of child abuse in preservice training. In February 1989, Judith Myers-Avis, from the University of Guelph, received a Health and Welfare Canada grant to research and prepare training material for professionals who treat victims of child sexual abuse (National Health and Welfare, 1989, 1990).

Protocols and guidelines are readily available on both child and wife abuse. Elder abuse protocols are not as available. Protocols typically define the terms used for physical, sexual, and emotional abuse. Indicators for each type of abuse are provided, along with appropriate action and resources to which victims can be referred. Canadian Association of Social Work Administrators in Health Facilities (1985) also include an audit procedure. The Ontario Medical Association published an emergency department protocol for wife assault in the association's journal.

Because interaction with victims requires a multidisciplinary approach, interdisciplinary protocols are available. The Province of British Columbia (1985) has developed such a handbook for child abuse. Guidelines are provided for the ministries of Human Resources, Attorney General, and Health and Education. The appendices include guidelines for interviewing child victims of sexual abuse and signals of possible abuse. Health and Welfare Canada is in the process of developing program guidelines for sexual and physical assault treatment services in institutions. Administrators will be encouraged to initiate and approve appropriate guidelines within their facilities. This is an important step, as professionals have encountered difficulty in gaining approval from administrators for guidelines and supporting inservices.

Protocols are effective only when understood and used. Too frequently, protocols have stayed on the shelves. The Province of British Columbia is planning a major inservice with the distribution of the revised Handbook on Child Abuse (1985). The observation, after the first printing, was that the guide was not used extensively. The Ottawa General Hospital provided a four-step compulsory inservice with the distribution of its protocol. The identification of victims in their emergency department rose 1500% from 1984 to 1986. A similar inservice is now planned for psychiatry, family medicine, and obstetrical staff.

Inservices on domestic violence, if done at all, are usually voluntary for staff. A common approach in Winnipeg hospitals has been an awareness week when speakers and films are made available for staff. Although the sessions have been well attended, no significant increase has occurred in the number of identified cases. Inservice should be compulsory and convenient for staff.

Key components of inservices are similar to the overview provided in curriculums. Educators stress the need to describe the abuse vividly so that participants may accept the reality of the problem. Guidelines are essential for staff to gain comfort in identifying victims. Comprehensive training material is available to train professionals to identify and assist abused children (Falconer & Swift, 1983), battered women (Sinclair, 1985; Province of Saskatchewan, 1985), and the batterer (Currie, 1988).

Professional associations have contributed significantly to the inservice process. The Ontario Medical Association has established a Committee on Wife Assault. Articles from its journal have been reprinted in a booklet (Ontario Medical Association, 1988) that provides a medical perspective on wife assault and approaches to treatment for male batterers. An emergency department protocol is given, along with a selective bibliography. More recently, the association has published another article (Bain, 1989) providing guidelines for physicians to work effectively within the criminal justice system. The article provides clear guidelines to its members and provides a list of resources for male batterers. The interface with the justice system is covered comprehensively. Pamphlets that provide information for identification of victims, intervention strategies, and local resources are made available to its membership. Inservices have been provided by the association on the interface with the justice system and the emergency department response. Most recently, the association has initiated communication with the Province's medical schools to address the issue of pre-service education.

Other associations have provided education, but in a less comprehensive and organized approach. The journal *The Canadian Nurse* published a series of articles on battered women, elder abuse, incest, and sexual abuse in 1985. The value base is not clearly a sociological one. Although the statement is made that a woman is not responsible for her husband's violence (Delgaty, 1985), in a later article on incest, in the same series, a psychological approach is taken to understand the abuse. The authors state "most types of incest are a reflection of disturbed familial relationships" (McCay, Bater, & Arthur, 1985, p. 27).

The Canadian Association of Social Work provided a policy statement in 1983 on domestic violence, which offers a clear sociological cause for abuse. A subsequent article (Hepworth, 1985) on child abuse registers in the *Social Worker* states, "it is important to believe that many of the perpetrators are not as much victims of society as are the children" (p. 163). The effectiveness of education is seriously thwarted if the message is not clear. Are these associations telling their members to see domestic violence as primarily being caused by pathological family dynamics in which the victim assumes some responsibility for the violence? Other professionals (Adams, 1986; Bagard, 1984; Williams, 1985) would adamantly dispute this approach. If the value base is not clear for professionals, identification and intervention strategies can not be clearly formulated, let alone taught.

The legal profession is affected directly in the limitations of the Canadian law as it addresses the issue of domestic violence. Bissett-Johnson (1986) and McGillivray (1987) identify the legal issues that interfere with a concise sociological approach. The Canadian justice system reflects the sanctity and the privacy of the family, allowing the parents' right to use corporal punishment, not allowing young children to give sworn evidence and, too frequently, hearing family violence matters in family courts rather than criminal courts.

A brief comment on the clergy will be made as the profession is organized significantly differently from the other professions. Christian theology and teaching have been based on the patriarchal family system, granting males the right to control and chastise women and children. Some churches, such as the Anglican Church of Canada and the United Church of Canada, are providing resource material for the church workers to rethink this theological stance and to formulate one that is more inclusive and egalitarian.

An ecumenical resource (Morris, 1988) has just been released to train pastoral care workers to both prevent and intervene with victims of violence. The challenge for the clergy will be to make a major value shift and perceive women as equal members of society. Voluntary inservices are being initiated, but are too recent to be evaluated for attendance and effectiveness.

Two other approaches to education are training through private institutes and workbooks that the professional can use with the victim. The Institute for the Prevention of Child Abuse, formed in Toronto in 1987, is committed to the prevention of all forms of child abuse. It provides three- to five-day training sessions for new, frontline child protection staff as well as for interdisciplinary teams working in the field. Advanced study is provided to a limited number of senior child protection staff at the institute's expense.

The Province of Saskatchewan (1987) has prepared a kit for battered women about family law. The kit is to be given to the victim both to aid her in giving the appropriate information to the justice professionals, as well as to guide her in her own problem-solving. This approach can be most effective in the empowerment process and ensures that each victim is given standard, pertinent information. If she is unable to read, the kit will guide a counselor through the appropriate steps during the counseling process. Because education for professionals is lagging, this approach does ensure that identified victims have the information needed to begin the empowerment process.

DISCUSSION

A wide chasm exists within Canada as issues of family violence are addressed. On the one hand, government initiatives have been numerous in the last five years. Millions of dollars have been designated for health and welfare projects, research and evaluation, education, justice, and housing (Government of Canada, 1988). On the other hand, the Canadian legal system reflects an understanding of the family as patriarchal, sacred, and private from the law. Child abuse definitions are left open to judgment as reasonable corporal punishment is excluded from the definition of abuse. How should professionals be taught to interpret reasonable discipline? In the justice system, judges have been faced with victims of domestic violence who refused to testify and were, in turn, prosecuted for their refusal. Major changes are needed within Canada's justice system to provide human rights to all citizens, including women and children.

Educational resource material is available in Canada on both child and spousal abuse. Much of this material is recent and has not been evaluated for effectiveness. The National Clearinghouse on Domestic Violence is an effective vehicle for the distribution of the material. It also minimizes duplication of effort. Much of the material meets the essential criteria identified earlier in the paper by acknowledging a clear sociological value base, offering theories of victimization, and providing identification skills and multidisciplinary intervention strategies. However, in most instances, training is voluntary. Furthermore, most preservice teaching faculties are not providing sufficient education to train new graduates to intervene effectively with victims. Perhaps incentives, such as significant grants, are needed for faculties of Canadian professional schools to encourage those academicians to teach domestic violence courses to their students.

The value base that most professionals bring to the domestic violence issue requires a review. If empowerment of victims is to take place, means to reach full human potential must be provided to all citizens. Professions such as teachers, clergy, nurses, and doctors have the opportunity to influence citizens through the entire life cycle. Children can be taught respect for each other, regardless of sex, violent-free conflict resolution, and encouraged to make decisions within their own capacity. Couples can be taught joint decisionmaking. Parents can be encouraged to take equal responsibility for the emotional nurturance of children. A change in professional education curriculum is needed if professionals are to facilitate the process of empowerment. Courses such as human behavior, family dynamics, and human growth and development require an update to reflect a shift from the patriarchal family value base to one of equality. At this time, little evidence exists that professional schools have an awareness of their responsibility in contributing to a major empowerment process for the victims of domestic violence.

CONCLUSION

An examination has been conducted of the education of human service professionals to acquire skills and knowledge that are needed to address issues of intimate and domestic violence. Serious questions have been raised about the will or even awareness of preservice educators to address this most serious social problem. Each year, new professional graduates are contributing to continued victimization in their daily roles by not having the awareness and skills to identify victims of domestic abuse. Educators and clergy are continuing to teach values in which family matters are seen as sacred and private from the law, and males are given sanction to control other family members, by force if necessary.

Exciting programs are offered in the inservice field and useful material is available. However, in most instances, inservice is voluntary and much of this material is not utilized extensively. Many human service professionals continue to condone violence through their silence while victims are struggling, not only to free themselves from their own personal violence, but also to develop essential services for themselves and others like them. It is time for professionals to take a mighty leap to support all members of the family and of society in enjoying equality and achieving full human rights.

BIBLIOGRAPHY

Adams, D. (1986, May). *Counselling men who batter: A profeminist analysis of five treatment models.* Presented at the annual meeting of the American Psychiatric Association, New York.
Ayim, M. (1986). The need for legal protection of children's rights in Canada. *Canadian Journal of Education, 11*(3), 338–352.
Bain, J. (1989, January). Spousal assault: The criminal justice system and the role of the physician. *Ontario Medical Review, 56*(1), 2–28.

Barber, P., & Burns, G. (1986, Spring). An alternative approach to the prevention of child abuse: Pre-service training. *Education Canada, 26*(1), 18–23.

Bissett-Johnson, A. (1986). Domestic violence: A plethora of problems and precious few solutions. *Canadian Journal of Family Law, 5,* 253–276.

Bograd, M. (1984). Family systems approaches to wife battering: A feminist critique. *American Journal of Orthopsychiatry, 54*(4), 558–567.

Canadian Association of Social Work Administrators in Health Facilities. (1985). *Domestic violence protocol manual.* Ottawa: Author.

Committee on Sexual Offences Against Children and Youths. (1984). *Sexual offences against children in Canada.* Hull, Quebec: Canada Government Publishing Centre.

Currie, D. (1988). *The abusive husband.* Ottawa: Health and Welfare Canada.

Delgaty, K. (1985, February). Battered women: The issues for nursing. *The Canadian Nurse, 85*(2), 21–23.

Falconer, N. E., & Swift, K. (1983). *Preparing for practice.* Toronto: Children's Aid Society of Metropolitan Toronto.

Gilman, S. T. (1985). A history of the sheltering movement for battered women in Canada. *Canadian Journal of Community Mental Health, 7*(2), 9–21.

Government of Canada. (1988). *Federal government announces new family violence initiatives.* Ottawa: Government of Canada.

Hepworth, H. P. (1985). Hundreds and thousands: Putting child abuse in context. *The Social Worker, 53*(4), 160–163.

Hilton, N. Z. (1989). One in ten: The struggle and disempowerment of the battered women's movement. *Canadian Journal of Family Law, 7,* 313–335.

McCay, E., Bater, E., & Arthur, H. M. (1985, February). Incest: A violation of trust. *The Canadian Nurse, 81*(2), 26–28.

McGillvray, A. (1987). Battered women: Definition models and prosecutorial policy. *Canadian Journal of Family Law, 6,* 15–45.

MacLeod, L. (1987). *Battered but not beaten—preventing wife battering in Canada.* Ottawa: Canadian Advisory Council on the Status of Women.

MacLeod, L. (1980). *Wife battering in Canada: The vicious circle.* Hull, Quebec: Canada Government Publishing Centre.

Martens, T. (1988). *The spirit weeps.* Edmonton: Nechi Institute.

Martin, D. (1981). *Battered wives.* San Francisco: Volcano Press.

Morris, R. (1988). *Ending violence in families.* Ottawa: National Clearinghouse on Domestic Violence.

National Health and Welfare (1989, 1990). *National Welfare Grants.* Ottawa: Government of Canada.

Ontario Medical Association. (1988). *Reports on wife assault.* Ottawa: Health and Welfare Canada.

Podnieks, E. (1988). Understanding the dimensions of elder abuse. *Vis-A-Vis, 6*(3), 1–8.

Province of British Columbia. (1985). *Inter-ministry child abuse handbook* (2nd ed.). Victoria: Queens Printer.

Province of Saskatchewan. (1987). *A place to start: A kit for battered women about family law.* Regina: Author.

Province of Saskatchewan. (1985). *Core knowledge training program on wife battering.* Regina: Author.

Sinclair, D. (1985). *Understanding wife assault.* Toronto: Ontario Government.

Status of Women, Canada. (1986). *Implementation report on the 1984 federal/provincial/territorial report on wife battering: Federal section.* Hull, Quebec: Canada Government Publishing Centre.

The Taskforce Report to General Synod (1986) of the Anglican Church of Canada. (1987). *Violence against women.* Toronto: Anglican Book Centre.

Thomleson, B. (1983). A proposed curriculum for child abuse content in social work education. *Canadian Social Work Review, 1,* 235–243.

Wachtel, A. (1989). Discussion paper: Child abuse. Prepared for 1989 National Forum on Family Violence. Ottawa: Government of Canada.

Williams, T. (1985). Family violence. A debate treatment or social control? *Canadian Social Work Review, 3,* 301–304.

Winnipeg Presbytery Working Group on Family Violence. (1988). *No fear in love.* Winnipeg United Church.

Wolk, L. E. (1982). *Minnesota's American Indian battered women: The cycle of oppression.* Minnesota: St. Paul Indian Center.

17

Domestic Violence Legislation in the United States: A Survey of the States

James E. Hendricks
Department of Criminal Justice, Ball State University, Muncie, Indiana

INTRODUCTION

In the past decade, increased attention has been focused on domestic violence legislation. During this time, 39 states have enacted new domestic violence statutes. A central focus of this legislation has been on probable cause warrantless arrests. This aspect of the legislation as well as other legislative elements has provided the police with an increase in their sworn powers as well as allowing the victim to gain assistance during the time of crisis. This national study examines specific elements of the new legislation while comparing and contrasting differing state statutes.

Prior to the 1980s, few states had laws that focused on reducing or preventing domestic violence. A battered mate had few options available through the legal protection avenue. Protective orders for married couples offered limited assistance though penalties for violation were not sanctioned or provided.

During the late 1970s and early 1980s, states began passing legislation aimed specially at protecting the battered mate. These provisions included civil and criminal penalties for violating protective orders, record keeping on family violence for those agencies interfacing with abusive families, and funding for shelters, as well as other services for violent families. This legislation provided for increased assistance to victims of abuse.

During the past ten years, most states have enacted legislation governing police powers of arrest in domestic violence cases. Prior to this time, the police were reluctant interveners. That is, they generally avoided domestic calls and when they did intervene, their assistance was minimal, at best. Some police officers did offer quality crisis intervention, but their sworn powers of arrest were limited to only those cases of the most severe nature, for example, serious bodily injury. As a consequence of recent domestic violence legislation, police officers in many states may now arrest for misdemeanor battery. In fact, they may arrest based on probable cause without the use of a warrant.

Dr. James E. Hendricks is professor of criminal justice and criminology at Ball State University. For three years he was a county police officer in Indiana, and during that time he served as Chief Deputy of the Delaware County Police Department. Previously, he served as a counselor in the Illinois Department of Corrections and worked in psychiatric hospitals in Washington, DC, and Chicago, Illinois. He has published two books on crisis intervention.

The purpose of this chapter is twofold. One, to identify those states with and without probable cause warrantless arrest statutes and two, to review other elements of the domestic violence legislation in the 50 states. A probable cause warrantless arrest is defined as an arrest without a warrant for a misdemeanor (e.g., misdemeanor battery) when a police officer has probable cause to believe that the crime has occurred.

BACKGROUND

The rapid development of recent domestic violence statutes in the United States is a consequence of a myriad of local, state, and federal individuals and groups who saw a need and attempted to meet the needs of families in crisis. Although the new legislation cannot by itself fully impact the responses of the police or the courts, it does place more responsibility on them to provide a more effective response and to provide better services to victims and their families.

It is important to note that not all "domestic cases" involve domestic violence. In domestic cases, mediation and referral may resolve the crisis. Arrest may not be an appropriate and viable option. Police who use understanding and compassion with quality crisis intervention skills can assist the family in resolution of the crisis, decrease repeat calls, and help ensure a level of community safety. The problem begins when the criminal justice system handles domestic violence cases as domestic quarrels. This traditional approach is inadequate and the system begins to face liability judgments that, unfortunately, may be necessary to effect adequate policy and procedural changes in the criminal justice system. The social costs of domestic violence touch on every aspect of society. Therefore, mediation is no longer an acceptable option in domestic violence cases.

STUDY DESIGN

Three major sources of information were used in the present study, which was conducted during calendar year 1987 and the first half of 1988. A letter was mailed to each of the 50 state coalitions against domestic violence with a follow-up letter mailed 90 days later. Both of these letters requested a copy of the individual state's domestic violence laws and/or proposed legislation. Second, telephone interviews were conducted with supervisors of a few coalitions and with legislative counsel offices. This was conducted in order to clarify some of the data collected. Reviews of each state's legislation were also conducted. This information was gained from several law libraries. This third step was taken to collect additional information not collected elsewhere and also to substantiate data collected previously. Data from all sources yielded information on all 50 states.

FINDINGS

Warrantless Arrest: Status of the Fifty States

Figure 17-1 shows the status of the 50 states in relation to three possible outcomes regarding domestic violence probable cause warrantless arrest legislation.

As of June 1988, 11 states have not legislated probable cause warrantless arrests.

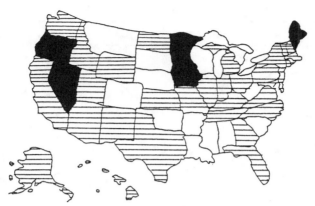

Figure 17-1   Domestic violence arrest legislation: Status of the states. □ no warrantless legislation; ▤ warrantless arrests; ■ mandatory arrests.

These states are Alabama, Arkansas, Colorado, Mississippi, Montana, Nebraska, Oklahoma, South Carolina, South Dakota, West Virginia, and Wisconsin. Five states have enacted probable cause mandatory arrest statutes. These states are Iowa, Maine, Minnesota, Nevada, and Oregon. Thirty-four states have enacted discretionary probable cause warrantless arrest statutes. In effect, 39 states have one form or the other of either mandatory arrest or allow the officer more discretion in effecting an arrest of a batterer. The specifics of these two legislative options are discussed in more detail in Table 17-1.

Table 17-1 may be used to compare and contrast domestic violence legislation within the United States. Further, the table may be used by those involved in drafting new state domestic violence legislation so as to examine the provisions that might be included. The table allows the reader to examine the year of effective legislation. State statutes may be consulted for a more detailed explanation of relief that might be available to an individual. Hence, a list of citations of the statutes is included in the reference section.

An asterisk in the table indicates that a statute contains language comparable to that listed on the table. It is helpful to remember that statutory language varies widely and as such only an approximation of the common language is made. In some cases, language related directly to specific domestic violence legislation is not to be found. However, other statutes that speak to domestic violence appear in the state code.

Definition of Abuse

The 39 statutes were passed between 1978 and 1987, beginning with New York and ending with Connecticut and Wyoming. Because later statutes were modeled on earlier efforts, their definitions and wording were somewhat similar. However, key terms used, such as abuse, were unstandardized and vague. Thus it follows that each state has somewhat different definitions of domestic violence due to key word differential. This wide variety of definitions makes it difficult to selectively place definitions into precise categories. Further, the lack of uniformity in statutes also makes it difficult or impossible to offer a general definition of abuse in domestic violence situations. Five states do not offer a definition of abuse. These states that lack a

Table 17-1   United States domestic violence legislation

	AL	AK	AZ	AR	CA	CO	CT	DE	FL	GA
Definition of abuse		*	*		*		*	*	*	*
Eligibility:										
Spouse relationship										
presently/formerly		*	*		*		*	*	*	*
Living as a spouse										
presently/formerly		*	*		*		*	*	*	*
Same-sex relationships					*				*	
Blood relationships		*	*		*		*	*	*	*
Warrantless arrest	+	1981	1980		1983		1987	1984	1979	1981
Permitted if misdemeanor										
was committed		*	*		*		*	*	*	*
Permitted if protection										
order was violated									*	
Arrest mandatory										
Arrest discretionary		*	*		*		*		*	*
Abuse need not occur										
in presence of the police		*	*		*			*	*	
Police must										
Prepare a written report					*		*			
Maintain statistical reports										
Police department must/may										
Create D.V. teams										
Develope and implement										
D.V. training		*			*		*			
Police officer must/may										
Transport victim to hospital					*					
Transport victim to shelter					*					
Inform victim of legal rights		*	*		*		*		*	
Stay until victim is no										
longer in danger							*			
Supervise the return home										
for personal property					*					*
Police immune from civil										
liability for good faith			*				*		*	

D.V. = domestic violence; + = year of legislation.

definition of abuse are Alabama, Arkansas, Colorado, Montana, and Wisconsin. The states that do have a definition differ as to the severity of the abuse committed with regard to the probability of arrest. A few states, such as Connecticut, define family violence as verbal abuse that is likely to lead to physical violence.

States that do not offer a definition of abuse should investigate the states that do have a definition. Then they should draft legislation to make the needed inclusions. Indiana treats bodily injury domestic violence abuse cases as a misdemeanor battery. Perhaps other states should examine the potential of treating their violence cases in the same vein. Clearly, every state needs to incorporate the violence as a crime as 39 states have done so already.

Eligibility: Who Is Covered?

The majority of the state statutes list who is covered under the legislation, with a description of the victim. An inclusive definition of a victim, with exceptions noted in

HI	ID	IL	IN	IA	KS	KY	LA	ME	MD	MI	MN	MS	MO
*	*	*	*	*	*	*	*	*	*	*	*	*	*
*		*	*	*	*	*	*	*	*	*	*	*	*
		*	*	*	*	*							
*		*		*									
		*		*		*	*	*	*		*	*	*
1980	1979	1980	1985	1986	1985	1980	1985	1979	1986	1980	1982		1980
*		*	*	*	*	*	*	*	*	*	*		
		*						*		*			*
		*						*			*		
*	*	*	*		*	*			*	*			*
*	*	*	*	*		*	*	*	*	*	*		*
*		*	*			*	*				*		
		*								*			
											*		*
		*		*	*		*				*		
*		*	*		*	*	*						
		*				*	*						
		*	*		*	*	*			*	*		*
			*		*		*						
*		*		*									
		*		*			*		*		*	*	

Table 17-1, is that a victim is a spouse or former spouse of the respondent, a parent, grandparent, child, or grandchild of the respondent, or a member of the social unit comprised of those living together in the same dwelling as the respondent but who previously lived in a spousal relationship with the respondent. In 37 states, blood relationships are considered to be covered under domestic violence legislation. In some states such as California, Florida, Illinois, Iowa, New York, and Oregon, coverage is extended to same-sex relationships which treat the relationship as a family unit. In 38 states, marriage is not required in order for the parties to be covered under the definition of abuse. In six states, marriage is required by law in order for the disputants to be covered under the abuse statute. In six states, a definition of who is covered under domestic violence legislation does not exist. These six states need to define the persons covered. Without such a definition, citizens in those states cannot know who is protected and who is not protected under the current statute.

Table 17-1 United States domestic violence legislation (*Continued*)

	MT	NB	NV	NH	NJ	NM	NY	NC	ND	OH
Definition of abuse		*	*	*	*	*	*	*	*	*
Eligibility:										
Spouse relationship presently/formally		*	*	*	*	*	*	*	*	*
Living as a spouse presently/formally		*		*	*	*	*		*	*
Same-sex relationships						*				
Blood relationships		*	*	*	*		*			*
Warrantless arrest	+		1985	1979	1981	1979	1978	1979	1981	1980
Permitted if misdemeanor was committed			*	*	*	*	*	*	*	*
Permitted if protection order was violated			*					*		
Arrest mandatory							*			
Arrest discretionary			*	*	*			*	*	*
Abuse need not occur in presence of the police			*	*	*	*		*	*	*
Police must										
Prepare a written report	*		*	*					*	*
Maintain statistical reports			*							*
Police department must/may										
Create D.V. teams				*				*		
Develope and implement D.V. training		*	*		*					
Police officer must/may										
Transport victim to hospital				*		*		*	*	
Transport victim to shelter						*		*		
Inform victim of legal rights				*	*		*			*
Stay until victim is no longer in danger						*				
Supervise the return home for personal property						*		*	*	*
Police immune from civil liability for good faith				*	*	*		*	*	

D.V. = domestic violence; + = year of legislation.

Warrantless Arrest

Thirty-nine of the recent statutes on domestic violence expand police power to arrest in domestic violence cases. In 37 states, warrantless arrest is permitted if probable cause exists that a misdemeanor or offense was committed. Probable cause warrantless arrest means that an officer may effect an arrest without a warrant if the officer's observations of the situation, including any remarks made by the parties involved or witnesses, that lead the officer to believe that to the best of his or her judgment, an assault did take place and was committed by the person to be arrested.

In 15 states, police may arrest without a warrant if they have probable cause to believe that a person has violated a protection order. Fourteen states allow probable cause warrantless arrest if a protection order was violated and an associated misdemeanor was committed. Clearly, this requires more investigation by the police. However, it does add more weight to the prosecutor's case.

OK	OR	PA	RI	SC	SD	TN	TX	UT	VT	VA	WA	WVA	WI	WY
*	*	*	*	*	*	*	*	*	*	*	*	*		*
*	*	*	*	*	*	*	*	*	*	*	*	*		*
*	*	*	*		*	*		*	*	*	*	*		*
*	*	*	*	*	*	*	*	*	*	*	*	*		*
	1985	1979	1980			1981	1980	1979	1982	1984	1981			1987
	*	*				*	*	*	*	*	*			*
	*	*				*	*				*			*
	*													
		*	*			*			*	*	*			*
	*	*	*			*		*	*	*	*			*
	*	*				*			*	*	*	*		*
	*	*				*				*	*	*		*
										*	*		*	*
		*	*		*	*					*			
			*		*	*					*			
*	*	*	*			*	*	*			*			*
		*	*							*				
	*				*									
	*				*					*		*		*

Mandatory arrest laws impose a duty on the police to make warrantless arrests in domestic violence cases for violations of protective orders, provided the requisite probable cause to make the arrest exists. This law states that the police officer shall make an arrest rather than affording the officer more discretionary arrest power. However, officers still have discretion even here. Failure to make an arrest generally involves writing up a report or filling out a checklist explaining why the arrest was not made.

More states should follow the lead of those states with mandatory arrest. Although officer discretion is limited, it still exists. The paperwork involved in making an arrest or not effecting an arrest is similar. This helps deter those officers who simply do not arrest in order to avoid paperwork. Further, the responsibility for the arrest remains primarily within the criminal justice system where it belongs. Domestic violence abuse/battery is a crime like any other crime. To treat it differently only reinforces the abuser's belief that his or her behavior is acceptable.

Reporting Provisions

The majority of states list a wide variety of health care, social service, and police agencies that are required reporters of domestic abuse. Many states also mandate law enforcement officers and other institutions serving domestic abuse victims to report cases to a centralized statewide registry for maintaining information on case reports and dispositions. Police reports generally include the victim's statements as to the frequency and severity of prior incidences of abuse by the same family member as well as the number of prior calls for police assistance to prevent such abuse. The police report oftentimes is the only piece of information that the prosecutor has at the time of arraignment.

In 20 states, police must prepare a written report for all domestic violence cases. In nine states, police must maintain statistical reports on domestic violence cases. Reports should be written for every incident, whether or not there is an arrest. A report should be made whenever a victim alleges an assault or when an officer has reasonable suspicion to believe an assault has occurred although probable cause may not exist.

Police Department Must/May

It has long been recommended that training for police officers be increased and maintained. In addition to training, attitudes that impact on the stereotypical view of women and their role in the family must change. More training geared toward attitudinal change and crisis intervention and investigation would aid the police when confronted with a domestic abuse situation.

In 15 states, the police department must develop, implement, and maintain domestic violence training. States such as Minnesota, Missouri, New Jersey, and North Dakota require the police department to establish domestic violence teams. On the whole, this is seen as a positive step, simply because domestic violence cases are given the priority needed for effective intervention.

Police Officer Must/May

A law enforcement officer has certain responsibilities with regard to domestic cases. Officers should use all reasonable means to prevent abuse or further abuse. This would include providing transportation for the abused victim to a hospital for treatment of injuries or transportation to a nearby shelter. In 16 states, police must transport abused victims to a nearby hospital or medical facility. With this statute provision, victims will be able to receive the necessary medical assistance for their well-being. Further, a medical report can aid in the investigation of abuse as well as provide more data necessary for prosecution.

Informing the victim of legal rights is an important part of a law enforcement officer's duties. In 27 states, police must inform the victims of their legal rights. In most of these states, the police must read or present a written statement of victim rights. For example, in Minnesota, police shall advise the victim of the following items: availability of a shelter, other services in the community, and legal rights and remedies available. Many of these legal rights are contained in a written statement that must be read to the victim, similarly as *Miranda* is read to offenders. With this information, victims may then be informed of choices regarding the action taken against the abuser.

The police, if requested or if they deem necessary, must remain at the domestic scene as long as there is danger to an abused person's safety. This includes, but is not limited to staying in the household unit, or if unable to remain on the scene, the officer must assist the abused victim in leaving the scene. In eight states, the police must stay on the scene until the victim is no longer in danger. For example, in Connecticut, the police shall remain on the scene for a reasonable time until in the reasonable judgment of the officer the likelihood of further imminent violence has been eliminated. Also, in these eight states, the police shall supervise the eviction of the abuser to maintain the safety of the victim or for the return home of the victim to obtain personal property. The police may accompany the victim to the victim's residence to remove the victim's clothing as well as those personal effects required for immediate needs. In 11 states, police are able to provide this type of supervision for eviction of the abuser or the removal of personal property.

Good Faith Clause

The police are hesitant, in some domestic cases, to act for fear of being sued for false arrest. Some states have a limited liability clause for any act of omission or commission by any law enforcement officer acting in good faith and without malice in rendering emergency assistance. This act must not be a result of willful or wanton misconduct. In 19 states, the police are immune from civil liability for good-faith enforcement. For example, in Oregon, if an officer acting in good faith arrests someone who it turns out should not have been arrested, the statute insulates the officer from liability. This provision of the statute helps alleviate fears, perhaps unfounded in some cases, of law enforcement officers who fear retaliation for arresting the abuser when the victim refuses to cooperate in the prosecution.

CONCLUSION

The police response to domestic violence is crucial to subsequent efforts at preventing and reducing family abuse. Battered mates who want help generally turn to the police first. As such, the police act as gatekeepers to the criminal justice/social service systems. Their attitudes and actions reflect on the systems as a whole and may be the determining factor as to whether the victim and the abuser seek or are referred for additional assistance.

The police must feel they are supported by the prosecutor and the courts, especially if they effect a warrantless arrest. Too often, police have been reluctant to use their full sworn police powers due to lack of support, even though the law clearly states that they can or should make such an arrest. Failure to support the police in their fight against domestic violence also reflects unfavorably on the whole criminal justice system.

Police departments should implement policies that support arrest if conditions warrant it. Several arguments favor such a policy. By increasing the number of persons arrested for violence against their mates, a clear signal is sent to the abuser that violent behavior will not be tolerated by our society. Further, arrest places the burden on the prosecutor and the courts to initiate further action including initiating cooperation from the victim and the police. Also, courts cannot assess the problem of domestic violence unless it is brought to their attention.

Arrest also helps prevent further injury and offers abusers time to decrease their hostility level. By effecting an arrest, the abuser realizes that family violence is a crime, and that the criminal justice system will take steps to stop the abuse. The abuser realizes that serious consequences will result from such inappropriate behavior.

Arrest (or the possibility of it) of the abuser may prove to be an effective tool that the criminal justice system can use to deter violence. Domestic violence will still continue, though hopefully at a lower incidence rate. True equality of the sexes is another avenue to pursue in decreasing the violence rate. However, this is difficult to achieve because inequality is built into the fabric of our society and into our beliefs, values, and behavioral repertoire. Elimination of all domestic violence depends on elimination of this inequality. It appears that this is not soon forthcoming. Consequently, steps such as probable cause warrantless arrest, as well as other factors, will help alter the system of violence on which so much of our society rests.

CITATIONS

Act. No. 81-476, 1981 Ala. Acts (1981)

ALASKA STAT. Sect. 18.65.510 (1980)
ALASKA STAT. Sect. 18.65.520 (1982)
ALASKA STAT. Sect. 25.35.010 (1985)
ALASKA STAT. Sect. 25.35.060 (1985)

ARIZ. REV. STAT. Sect. 13-3601 (1986)
ARIZ. REV. STAT. Sect. 13-3602 (1987)

ARK. STAT. ANN. Sect. 41-1653 to 41-1659 (1979)

CAL. PENAL CODE Sect. 273 (1983)
CAL. S.B. CODE Sect. 1472 (1985)
CAL. PENAL CODE Sect. 273.5 (1983)
CAL. PENAL CODE Sect. 13700 (1980)

COLO. REV. STAT. Sect. 13-6-104 (1973)

Pub. Act No. 87-567 1987 Conn. Legis. Serv. p. 346 (1987)

DEL. CODE tit. 11 Sect. 1904 (1984)
DEL. CODE tit. 16 Sect. 1001 (1970)

FLA. STAT. ANN. Sect. 741.29 (1984)
FLA. STAT. ANN. Sect. 741.30 (1986)
FLA. STAT. ANN. Sect. 901.15 (1983)
FLA. STAT. ANN. Sect. 943.085 (1986)

GA. CODE ANN Sect. 17-4-20 (1986)
GA. CODE ANN Sect. 19-13-20 (1985)

HAW. REV. STAT. Sect. 586-1 (1982)
HAW. REV. STAT. Sect. 586-10 (1982)
HAW. REV. STAT. Sect. 709-906 (1986)

IDAHO CODE Sect. 19-603 (1979)

ILL. ANN. STAT. Sect. 103 of Public Act 84-1305 (1986)

ILL. ANN. STAT. Sect. 301 of Public Act 84-1305 (1986)
ILL. ANN. STAT. Sect. 302 of Public Act 84-1305 (1986)
ILL. ANN. STAT. Sect. 303 of Public Act 84-1305 (1986)
ILL. ANN. STAT. Sect. 304 of Public Act 84-1305 (1986)

IND. CODE ANN. Sect. 35-33-1-1 (1985)
IND. CODE ANN. Sect. 35-42-2-1 (1976)
IND. CODE ANN. Sect. 35-41-1-4 (1985)

IOWA CODE ANN. Sect. 236-11 (1980)
IOWA CODE ANN. Sect. 236-9 & 236-10 (1980)

KAN. CIV. PRO. STAT. ANN. Sect. 60-3101 to 60-3111 (1980)
KAN. CIV. PRO. STAT. ANN. Sect. 1607 (1979)

KY. REV. STAT. Sect. 431.005 (1984)
KY. REV. STAT. Sect. 403.720 (1984)
KY. REV. STAT. Sect. 403.785 (1984)

LA. REV. STAT. ANN. Sect. 46:2132 (1982)
LA. REV. STAT. ANN. Sect. 46:2140 (1986)
LA. REV. STAT. ANN. Sect. 46:2141 (1985)
LA. REV. STAT. ANN. Sect. 46:2142 (1985)

ME. REV. STAT. ANN. tit. 19 Sect. 762 (1979)
ME. REV. STAT. ANN. tit. 19 Sect. 769 (1979)
ME. REV. STAT. ANN. tit. 19 Sect. 770 (1979)

MD. ANN. CODE Sect. 4-513 (1984)
MD. ANN. CODE Sect. 4-501 (1987)
MD. ANN. CODE art. 27 Sect. 11F (1980)
MD. HOUSE JOINT RESOLUTION NO. 32 (1977)

MASS. GEN. LAWS ANN. ch. 209A Sect. 1 (1988)
MASS. GEN. LAWS ANN. ch. 209A Sect. 6 (1979)

MICH. COMP. LAWS ANN. Sect. 600.2950 (1983)
MICH. COMP. LAWS ANN. Sect. 764.15a (1980)
MICH. COMP. LAWS ANN. Sect. 28.257 (1978)
MICH. COMP. LAWS ANN. Sect. 780.751 (1985)

MINN. STAT. ANN. Sect. 518B.01 (1979)
MINN. STAT. ANN. Sect. 241.61 (1977)
MINN. STAT. ANN. Sect. 241.66 (1977)
MINN. STAT. ANN. Sect. 629.341 (1982)

MISS. SUPP. Sect. 93-21-1 (1981)
MISS. SUPP. Sect. 93-21-27 (1981)
MISS. SUPP. Sect. 93-21-25 (1981)

MO. ANN. STAT. tit. 30 Sect. 455.010 (1986)
MO. ANN. STAT. tit. 30 Sect. 455.080 (1986)
MO. ANN. STAT. tit. 32 Sect. 544.216 (1983)

MONT. CODE ANN. Sect. 40-2-402 (1979)

NEB. REV. STAT. Sect. 42-903 (1978)
NEB. REV. STAT. Sect. 42-927 (1978)

NEV. REV. STAT. Sect. 171.137 (1985)
NEV. REV. STAT. Sect. 33.018 (1985)
NEV. REV. STAT. Sect. 171.147 (1981)

N.H. REV. STAT. Sect. 594:10 (1981)
N.H. REV. STAT. Sect. 173-B:1 (1979)
N.H. REV. STAT. Sect. 173-B:9 (1979)
N.H. REV. STAT. Sect. 173-B:10 (1979)
N.H. REV. STAT. Sect. 173-B:4 (1981)

N.J. STAT. ANN. Sect. 2C:25-1 (1981)
N.J. STAT. ANN. Sect. 2C:25-3 (1981)
N.J. STAT. ANN. Sect. 2C:25-4 (1981)
N.J. STAT. ANN. Sect. 2C:25-5 (1981)
N.J. STAT. ANN. Sect. 2C:25-6 (1981)
N.J. STAT. ANN. Sect. 2C:25-7 (1981)
N.J. STAT. ANN. Sect. 2C:25-8 (1981)

N.M. STAT. ANN. Sect. 31-1-7 (1979)
N.M. STAT. ANN. Sect. 40-13-7 (1987)

N.Y. DOM. REL. LAWS Sect. 240(2) (McKinney Supp. 1980-1981)
N.Y. FAM. CT. ACT Sect. 155 (McKinney 1975 and Supp. 1976-1980)
N.Y. JUD. LAW. Sect. 216 & 751 (1) (1980-1981)
N.Y. EXEC ORDER NO. (Hugh L. Carey, Gov., May 17, 1979) 9NYCRR Sect. 3.90

N.C. GEN. STAT. Sect. 50B-1 (1979)
N.C. GEN. STAT. Sect. 50B-4 (1979)
N.C. GEN. STAT. Sect. 50B-5 (1979)
N.C. GEN. STAT. Sect. 15A-401 (1979)

N.D. CENT. CODE Sect. 14-07.2-02 (1981)
N.D. CENT. CODE Sect. 29.06-15G (1981)

OHIO REV. CODE ANN. Sect. 3113.13 (1980)
OHIO REV. CODE ANN. Sect. 2919.25 (1978)
OHIO REV. CODE ANN. Sect. 2935.03 (1980)
OHIO REV. CODE ANN. Sect. 109.73 (1981)

OKLA. STA. ANN. tit. 22 Sect. 40 (1982)
OKLA. STA. ANN. tit. 22 Sect. 40.2 (1982)
OKLA. STA. ANN. tit. 22 Sect. 60.1 (1982)

OR. REV. STAT. Sect. 133.055 (1985)
OR. REV. STAT. Sect. 133.315 (1985)
OR. REV. STAT. Sect. 107.705 (1985)

35 PA. CONS. STAT. ANN. Sect. 10182 (1976)
29 PA. CONS. STAT. ANN. Sect. 2711 (1986)
42 PA. STAT. ANN. Sect. 1901 (1977)

R.I. GEN. LAWS Sect. 15-15-1 (1980)
R.I. GEN. LAWS Sect. 15-15-5 (1982)
R.I. GEN. LAWS Sect. 12-7-3 (1980)
R.I. GEN. LAWS Sect. 8-8.1-5 (1987)

S.C. CODE Sect. 20-4-20 (1984)
S.C. CODE Sect. 20-4-100 (1984)
S.C. CODE Sect. 20-4-110 (1984)

S.D. CODIFIED LAWS ANN. Sect. 25-10-1 (1981)

TENN. CODE ANN. Sect. 40-7-103 (1981)
TENN. CODE ANN. Sect. 36-3-601 (1979)
TENN. CODE ANN. Sect. 39-2-101 (1977)

TEX. PENAL CODE ANN. tit. 5,22.02 and 22.02 (Supp. Vernon 1984)
TEX. PENAL CODE ANN. tit. 1,1.07 (a) (7) (Vernon 1974)
TEX. FAM. CODE ANN. tit. 2,34.01-.08 (Vernon 1980)
TEX. HUMAN RESOURCES CODE ANN. tit. 2,48.001-48.084 (Vernon 1980)
TEX. FAM. CODE ANN. tit. 4,71.01 (a) (2) (Vernon 1980)
TEX. PENAL CODE ART. 1.07 (a) (14), 12.32, 12.33, 12.34 (Vernon 1974)
TEX. PENAL CODE ART. 1.07 (a) (21), 12.21, 12.22, 12.23 (Vernon 1974)

UTAH CODE ANN. Sect. 30-6-1 (1979)
UTAH CODE ANN. Sect. 30-6-8 (1979)
UTAH CODE ANN. Sect. 76-5-108 (Supp. 1979)

VT. STAT. ANN. tit. 15 Sect. 1101-1109 (1979)
VT. RULES OF CIV. Pro., Rule 3 (1983)
VT. RULES OF CIV., Pro., Rule 4 (6) (1984)

VA. HOUSE JOINT RESOLUTION 27 (1982)
VA. CODE Sect. 20-103 (1980)

WASH. REV. CODE ANN. Sect. 10.31.100 (1980)
WASH. REV. CODE ANN. Sect. 26.50.010 (1984)
WASH. REV. CODE ANN. Sect. 26.50.140 (1984)
WASH. REV. CODE ANN. Sect. 10.99.030 (1979)

W.VA. CODE Sect. 48-2A-9 (1979)
W.VA. CODE Sect. 48-2A-2 (1979)

W.S. STAT. ANN Sect. 165.85 (4) (b) (1974)

WYO. STAT. ANN. Sect. 7-2-103 (1987)
WYO. STAT. ANN. Sect. 35-21-102 (1982)
WYO. STAT. ANN. Sect. 7-20-102 (1987)
WYO. STAT. ANN. Sect. 7-20-104 (1987)
WYO. STAT. ANN. Sect. 7-20-105 (1988)
WYO. STAT. ANN. Sect. 7-20-106 (1987)
WYO. STAT. ANN. Sect. 7-20-107 (1987)

PART VII

COMPARATIVE PERSPECTIVES

18

Attitudes Toward Wife Abuse in a Cross-Cultural Context: A Comparison of Colombian and American Human Service Students

Liane V. Davis
School of Social Welfare, University of Kansas, Lawrence

Despite the fact that much of the recent literature on wife abuse emphasizes the sociocultural determinants of the problem, there has been little cross-cultural research on the topic. This chapter presents data from a small-scale study that compares attitudes toward abused women among Colombian and American students preparing for careers in human service. Attitudes toward abused wives and abusing husbands were affected by nationality, gender, and attitudes toward the role of women. As expected, Colombians held more traditional attitudes toward violence against women. This was reflected in their holding both partners equally responsible for wife abuse. Men's and women's attitudes reflected a tendency to identify with their same-sex counterpart. A surprising finding was that the most liberal of Colombian women tended to blame the victim most. It is suggested that this may reflect the need for these women to defend themselves psychologically against the threat of abuse.

INTRODUCTION

Despite the fact that recent literature on wife abuse has been strongly dominated by a theoretical view emphasizing the sociocultural determinants of the problem (Dobash & Dobash, 1979; Steinmetz & Straus, 1974; Straus, 1976; Straus & Hotaling, 1980), there has been surprisingly little cross-cultural research on the topic. This chapter describes a small-scale study of attitudes toward abused women among Colombian and American students preparing for careers in human service.

The author thanks Marguerite Lemmerman, without whose assistance this project would neither have been attempted nor completed.

Liane V. Davis is associate professor, School of Social Welfare, University of Kansas. She received her Ph.D. in social psychology from the University of North Carolina at Chapel Hill and an M.S.W. from Adelphi University. She is presently conducting research on what enables abused women to escape from violence, writing a book on social work practice with abused women, and working with a group of ex-offenders to provide a spectrum of services to reduce the violence in their lives.

SOCIOCULTURAL DETERMINANTS OF WIFE ABUSE

There is almost no research on attitudes toward wife abuse. There is, however, a substantial literature on abuse against wives. Because most of this literature assumes that a primary determinant of wife abuse is the social norms that place men in positions of dominance over women, it can easily be argued that the same conditions create and facilitate both abusive behaviors toward women and tolerant attitudes toward such behaviors by persons who, themselves, might not engage in abusive acts. For this reason, I begin by reviewing the literature on the sociocultural determinants of wife abuse.

Most of the empirical research on wife abuse has come from a group of sociologists in the United States who have systematically built up an impressive body of knowledge (Steinmetz, 1977; Steinmetz & Straus, 1974; Straus & Gelles, 1990; Straus & Hotaling, 1980). Although they have certainly acknowledged the important role that intrapersonal and interpersonal factors play in specific incidents of wife abuse, they have been very strong exponents of the view that the widespread acceptability and incidence of wife abuse in the Western world can best be attributed to the sexist nature of the family and society. (See also Dobash & Dobash, 1979, for a similar, if somewhat more radical, perspective on wife abuse.) This is reflected in the following quote from Murray Straus:

> Perhaps the most pervasive sets of factors bringing about wife-beating are those connected with the sexist social structure of the family and society. In fact, to a considerable extent, the cultural norms and values permitting and sometimes encouraging husband-to-wife violence reflect the hierarchical and male-dominant type of society that characterizes the Western world. (1980, p. 221)

Although Straus (1976) has identified nine specific ways in which the male-dominant social structure contributes to the high level of violence against women, two of these, the defense of male authority and economic constraints and discrimination, have the most clear-cut implications for cross-cultural research. Furthermore, as I argue later, the different rates of social change in American and Latin cultures directly affect both the need for men to defend their authority and the economic opportunities available to women. This may result in differential acceptability of wife abuse within these two countries.

Defense of Male Authority

Variants of exchange and resource theory of marital power have long suggested that men have historically been granted higher status and greater authority within the family because they have contributed more highly valued resources than have women (see Blood & Wolfe, 1960, for an early statement of resource theory of family power). Both William Goode (1971) and Murray Straus (1974) have suggested that men may resort to the "ultimate resource," their physical power, to defend their authority when the other resources they contribute to the marriage (e.g., income, education, and occupation) fail to justify the superior status and authority they have been socialized to expect for themselves. Empirical support for this "status inconsistency effect" comes from studies demonstrating increased rates of violence against women in families in which the husband's absolute resources are seriously deficient or he contributes relatively fewer resources to the marriage than does his wife (Allen & Straus, 1980).

The following, taped in a working-class bar in the United States, captures this phenomenon:

> *I'm a plumber and I make pretty good money and . . . me and my wife, we've been married for a couple of years. And you see I only got a high school education and she like graduated from college, you know, and she sort of holds that over my head like I'm supposed to be stupid and everything. I make the money around this place and . . . I'm the one that controls here and what I say kind of goes. I hit her on occasion, but what the heck . . . I'm sure I'm not the only guy that once in a while when his wife gets out of control slaps her up the side of the head. . . . I don't mean to hurt her or anything. Hell, I love her. But sometime she gives me problems and I just got to put her in her place a little bit.*

Economic Constraints and Discrimination

Economic constraints and discrimination against women in the marketplace contribute to abuse against wives by providing them with few alternatives to staying in an abusive relationship. Discrimination also provides affirmation that women are less valuable to society than are men. Evidence in support of the role of economic constraints comes from studies demonstrating that (1) women who are dependent on their husbands experience more and more violent forms of physical abuse than do women who are not so dependent (Kalmuss & Straus, 1982; Strube & Barbour, 1983), and (2) abused women are more likely to seek outside intervention when they are employed (Gelles, 1976).

RODMAN'S THEORY OF RESOURCES WITHIN A CULTURAL CONTEXT

Hyman Rodman's (1972) theory of resources within a cultural context provides a basis for understanding the role of resources in determining marital power in different cultures. By extension, it can help explain cultural differences in (1) men's use of violence as the "ultimate resource" and (2) the acceptability of violence against wives as a means of maintaining the status quo.

Finding traditional resource theory of marital power inadequate to explain who wielded the power in different cultures, Rodman theorized that power within the family depends on two factors: (1) the relative resources of husband and wife, and (2) the cultural norms that define valued resources and legitimate authority. In some societies there are unambiguous, widely accepted social norms about family power. In other societies the norms that legitimize the exercise of power are ambiguous, weak, and/or in transition. It is only in these latter societies in which norms are less crystallized that valued resources contribute to determining who wields family power. Furthermore, it is only in these societies that men may need to resort to physical violence to defend their authority (Rodman, 1972).

Rodman classified societies into four ideal types (or stages) based on the nature of the norms about the allocation of power and the extent to which various strata of society accepted them. He then analyzed the relationship between actual marital power and relative resources for countries that conformed to these ideal types.

In Stage I societies, characterized by India, where male authority is unambiguously sanctioned by the prevailing norms, and in Stage IV societies, characterized by Sweden, where egalitarian norms about the distribution of authority are sanctioned unambiguously, Rodman found little relationship between resources and allocation of marital power. In each of these cases, the widespread acceptability of norms sanction-ing legitimate authority minimized the role of resources.

In Stage III societies, represented by the United States, in which egalitarian norms are replacing patriarchal norms throughout all social strata, Rodman found a direct relationship between marital power and resources. As Rodman (1972) suggested, "the situation in these societies can be characterized as a 'power struggle' in which additional resources bring additional power" (p. 64). Furthermore, as Rodman him-self recognized, it is when authority must be earned that men who are unable to contribute sufficiently valued resources may resort to physical violence to win the power struggle.

Stage II societies, characterized by Greece, are somewhat more complex. In the society as a whole, power is ascribed to men. However, the most educated are likely to have adopted the norms of Stage III societies. Under these circumstances, re-sources are insignificant for determining marital power for the society as a whole, but become significant among the upper strata. In support of this hypothesis, Rodman found an inverse relationship between resources and marital power in these societies. By extension, physical violence should be needed to defend male authority only among the more educated. Because these men are voluntarily adopting egalitarian norms, however, it seems unlikely that they will then turn around to use, or even tolerate the use of, violence to assert male authority.

Other studies support Rodman's contention that cultural variations in the norma-tive prescriptions about sex roles affect the relationship between resources and family power (Burr, Ahern, & Knowles, 1977; Cooney, Rogler, Hurrell, & Ortiz, 1982; Richmond, 1976). In a study whose results are directly applicable to differences between Colombians and Americans, Cooney et al. (1982) compared the relationship between resources, marital power, and adherence to traditional versus egalitarian norms in two generations of Puerto Ricans living in the United States. In the parent generation, in which there was greater adherence to the patriarchal norms of the Puerto Rican culture, they found the expected inverse relationship between husband's education and his decisionmaking power. Among their married children, where there was greater adherence to the transitional egalitarian norms, they found the expected positive relationship between husband's education and his decisionmaking power.

Some Implications of Rodman's Theory for Wife Abuse

Rodman's theory provides a theoretical anchor for the study to be presented. Colombia and the United States represent Stage II and Stage III societies, respec-tively. If we consider only the relationship between "defense of male authority" and violence against women, it suggests there may be no difference in attitudes toward wife abuse among students in these two countries because the Colombian students are from the class in Colombian society that is expected to have voluntarily accepted the same egalitarian norms prevalent in American society.

There is an alternative possibility. It seems safe to assume that men, in general, will feel threatened when their historically ascribed positions of authority are chal-lenged. In Stage III societies, there may be less ambivalence about giving up male power because of the increasing legal sanction for egalitarian norms than in the upper strata of a Stage II society in which only the more educated are voluntarily sharing their authority because it is the "intelligent, progressive" thing to do.

There is ample evidence that, while there has been some modification of patriarchal norms in Latin American countries, male domination is still firmly entrenched (Castro, 1983; Cromwell & Cromwell, 1978; Fitzpatrick, 1976; Mojica & Rodriguez, 1983; Richmond, 1976). Under these circumstances, while giving intellectual lip service to egalitarian norms, even the more educated men may feel a heightened sense of threat as well as strong tacit support to behaviorally maintain the patriarchal domination. There is some empirical support in American samples for the "well-meaning liberal man" who verbally espouses liberal attitudes toward women but behaves no differently, on average, than men with conservative attitudes (Gackenbach, 1978; Gackenbach & Auerbach, 1975; Steinman & Fox, 1966). It seems even more likely that such a phenomenon would exist in a society in which acceptance of egalitarian norms is a choice that exists in a society that is still strongly patriarchal. This suggests that there may be greater tolerance of abuse against wives in Colombia than in the United States, especially among the men. As William Goode (1971) has argued, one of the major reasons for the acceptance and sanctioning of violence within the family is to maintain order within both the family and society. In a society such as Colombia, in which order in the family is threatened for some, and normative change is not widely sanctioned, violence may be strongly, albeit oftentimes covertly, sanctioned.

ATTRIBUTION THEORY AND THE EFFECT
OF OTHER CULTURAL INFLUENCES

Ample evidence exists that persons are held more responsible for negative outcomes that are attributed to internal rather than external factors (see Shaver, 1975, for a review). This recurrent finding from attribution theory provides a second theoretical basis for exploring some of the potential cultural differences in attitudes toward wife abuse. It leads, for example, to the hypothesis that persons who believe that women contribute to their own abuse will blame the victim more than persons who believe in the sociocultural determinants of abuse.

Until recently, the most widespread explanation of why women remain in abusive relationships has been that of female masochism (see Deutsch, 1930, for a classic statement of the masochistic personality; see Waites, 1977–1978, for a critique of this view). It has only been in the past few years that serious attention has been given to the central role that such external factors as economic dependency play in keeping women in abusive relationships (Kalmuss & Straus, 1982). Because personality factors are internal to the abused woman, those persons who ascribe to a personality defect model should blame the victim more and feel less sympathy toward her than persons who identify the external factors of economic discrimination or sexist norms as significant contributors.

Because economic opportunity is more circumscribed for women in Colombia than in the United States (Mojica & Rodriguez, 1983), it is possible that Colombians, especially women, will focus more strongly on these economic barriers and be less likely to blame the victim than will Americans. On the other hand, the generally higher level of "feminist consciousness" in the United States implies that persons in the United States may be more aware of the role of economic discrimination. This may result in less victim blaming among Americans, especially women, than among Colombians.

Gender Differences in Attributions About Women as Victims

There is substantial evidence to suggest that attributions are influenced by the similarity between the person making the judgment and the person being judged (Chaiken & Darley, 1973; Lerner & Miller, 1978; Shaver, 1975; Walster, 1966). There is inconsistency as to the nature of the attributions that will be made, however. Shaver (1975) suggests that persons will protect their own egos by not blaming a victim if they anticipate being in a similar situation where they, too, may be blamed. Walster (1966) and Lerner and Miller (1978) both suggest that observers will blame a victim with whom they identify to (1) avoid confronting their own vulnerability (Walster, 1966) and (2) to maintain their belief in a just world where suffering occurs only to those who deserve it (Lerner & Miller, 1978).

In a study of attitudes toward rape victims using a methodology similar to that of the present study, Coates, Wortman, and Abbey (1979) found that women empathized more with a rape victim but held her more responsible for her victimization than did men. They concluded that persons who believe themselves vulnerable to similar victimization reduce their threat by blaming the victim. Other research supports their finding that women blame rape victims more than do men (Krulewitz, Nash, & Payne, 1977; Nash, 1977).

There has been little research that directly assesses attitudes toward wife abuse. The two studies that have been published used similar vignette methodologies and assessed attributions that persons make about abused women and abusing men. In her study of a sample of the general population, Kalmuss (1979) found that almost 25% of both men and women held the husband and wife equally responsible for a wife's abuse. She also found that women's judgments of abusers were moderated when the abuse was justified, while those of men were not. This led her to speculate that women who identify with a victim, cognizant of their own economic dependency on their husbands, may justify abuse to allow themselves to remain in a marriage should they experience similar abuse.

In the second study, Davis and Carlson (1981) found that factors irrelevant to the specific acts of violence, such as the socioeconomic class of the depicted couple, influenced attributions about wife abuse among a diverse group of service providers. They, also, found evidence of substantial victim-blaming, but surprisingly, found no significant sex differences. This, however, may have been due to the extremely small numbers of men in many of the service provider groups.

SOME HYPOTHESES

Although the study is exploratory in nature, the literature reviewed suggests that three major factors are likely to influence attitudes toward wife abuse: (1) nationality/culture, (2) gender, and (3) adherence to a male-dominant versus egalitarian social structure (referred to for simplicity as "attitudes toward women"). Clearly these are not independent factors.

First, we expect Colombians and men to be more tolerant of wife abuse than will Americans and women. Second, we expect that Americans and women will be most liberal in their attitudes toward women. Third, if wife abuse is significantly influenced by societal norms about sex roles, attitudes toward women should be a moderating variable that explains much of the nationality and gender differences. Fourth, those women who identify most strongly with the victim should defend against their own vulnerability by focusing attention on factors internal to the victim and, as a result, hold her more responsible for her own abuse. We expect that it is among Colombian women, who are living in the most patriarchal society, that there should be the greatest tendency to engage in such defensive attributions.

METHOD

Overview

After reading one of two vignettes describing a woman being beaten by her husband, respondents completed two questionnaires. The first was an instrument to assess attitudes toward wife abuse adapted from prior research (Davis, 1984; Davis & Carlson, 1981) in which respondents rated the importance of nine factors in causing the incident. They also allocated responsibility for the abuse and indicated how much sympathy they felt toward each partner as well as rating how likely such an incident was to occur. Seven-point scales were used for each of these questions. The Spanish version was an identical translation.

The second instrument was the 15-item version of the Attitudes toward Women Scale (Spence & Helmreich, 1978). The scale consists of statements describing the roles, responsibilities, and rights of women in society. Respondents indicated their agreement-disagreement with each item on a four-point scale. High scores are indicative of liberal or egalitarian attitudes, low scores of conservative or traditional attitudes. Most of the statements were literally translated into Spanish. In a few instances, the words were changed to maintain the sense of the item, while accommodating to different sociocultural norms.

Data were also obtained on their actual experience with abused women, how knowledgeable they considered themselves to be on the subject, as well as relevant demographic variables.

Questionnaires were completed in classrooms. All students were told of the purpose of the research and advised that their participation was completely voluntary. All students agreed to and completed questionnaires.

Characteristics of the Samples

The Colombian sample consisted of 145 women and 27 men enrolled in their fifth year of a psychology program at five different Colombian universities. The United States sample consisted of 73 women and 29 men enrolled in their first year of a master's program in social work. Students in both countries were participating in field practica in the human services.

The two samples were comparable on a number of dimensions. They came from similar socioeconomic classes, with the fathers, on average, being managers, small business owners, technicians, and semiprofessionals. The majority of students in both countries had no professional experience with domestic violence, but had done at least some reading on the subject. Eighty-eight percent of the U.S. sample and 82% of the Colombian sample reported exposure to some literature on family violence. A majority of students in both countries had known a woman who was abused in an intimate relationship (60% of the U.S. sample and 65% of the Colombian sample). Students in both countries also shared the belief that wife abuse was a serious problem in their respective countries (the average rating for the seriousness of the problem was 6.1 on a seven-point scale, with no significant differences either as a function of nationality or gender).

The only demographic difference that appeared was that United States students were, on average, 6 years older than the Colombian students. The average age of the Colombian students was 25.6 and the average age of the United States students was 31.6.

RESULTS

Differences in the Major Dependent Variables as a Function of Nationality and Gender

Attitudes Toward Women

As had been hypothesized, Colombian students were significantly more conservative in their attitudes toward women than were the U.S. students [$F(1,266) = 11.81$, $p = .001$] and men were significantly more conservative in their attitudes than were women [$F(1,266) = 14.27$, $p = .001$]. (See Table 18-1 for means.)

Attributions About Violence

As the attributional dependent variables were not strongly intercorrelated, the data were analyzed by univariate ANOVAs with gender and nationality as independent variables. Table 18-2 presents the attributional measures by country and gender of respondent. Again the significant differences reflected main effects for gender and nationality. As the data in Table 18-2 indicate, however, these differences appear more explicable in terms of gender differences within countries. Colombian students believed that the wife's personality, socialization, and marital problems were more important determinants of the incident than did the U.S. students. The table suggests that Colombian women thought that the wife's personality and her socialization were more important factors, whereas American women minimized the importance of marital problems. This is consistent with our hypothesis that Colombian women would be most likely to make defensive attributions. Colombian students also believed that the husband's personality, socialization, and stress he had recently experienced at work were less important determinants of the incident than did students in the United States. In the case of attributions to husband's personality and stress, the significant nationality differences appear uniquely due to lower ratings by the Colombian women. There were no differences in the importance attributed to societal norms that define men as dominant and women as submissive in relationships.

Overall, women believed that the wife's personality and her socialization were

Table 18-1 Mean attitudes toward women as a function of nationality and gender

	Women	Men	
Colombia	38.33	35.59	X = 37.90
United States	40.64	37.55	X = 39.72
	X = 39.07	X = 36.61	

Table 18-2 Attributions about violence as a function of nationality and gender[a]

	Colombia		United States	
Attribution	Men	Women	Men	Women
H's personality*	5.00	4.60	5.11	5.05
W's personality***,****	3.33	4.17	2.79	3.14
H's socialization*	4.26	4.48	4.96	5.00
W's socialization*,****	3.56	4.19	3.21	3.64
H's stress***,*****	3.56	2.41	3.93	3.55
W's stress	2.11	1.89	2.18	1.88
Marital problems*	4.59	4.89	4.79	4.26
Male norms	4.07	4.04	4.29	4.36
Female norms	4.19	4.10	4.04	4.30

All responses were made on seven-point scales where 1 = very unimportant and 7 = very important. Therefore, the larger the number, the more important the factor.
*Differences between Colombian and U.S. samples significant at the .05 level.
**Differences between Colombian and U.S. samples significant at the .005 level.
***Differences between Colombian and U.S. samples significant at the .001 level.
****Differences between men and women significant at the .05 level.
*****Differences between men and women significant at the .005 level.
[a]Although the significant differences reflect main effects for gender and nationality, it was decided to present the means for gender within each country to allow the reader to see these differences.

more important factors than did men, while men thought that something stressful that had happened to the husband at work was more important.

As can be seen in Table 18-3, Colombian students held the husband less responsible and the wife more responsible for the abuse than did the American students. In fact, the Colombian students held both partners nearly equally responsible, while the U.S. students believed the husband to be more responsible than the wife. The Colombian students also were less sympathetic toward both wife and husband than were the U.S. students. Although it is reasonable to assume that persons would be less sympathetic toward a victim they believed responsible for her own abuse, this was found true only among the American students. This was reflected in a significant negative correlation between sympathy and responsibility among the Americans $(r(102) =$

Table 18-3 Perceptions of responsibility and sympathy as a function of nationality and gender

	Colombia		United States	
	Men	Women	Men	Women
H's responsibility*,**	4.19	4.94	5.56	6.35
W's responsibility*,**	3.63	4.70	2.96	3.42
Sympathy for H*,***	2.74	2.15	3.59	3.06
Sympathy for W*	4.00	3.39	6.19	6.14

All responses were made on seven-point scales where the greater the number, the more sympathy or responsibility.
*Differences between Colombian and U.S. samples significant at the .001 level.
**Differences between men and women significant at the .01 level.
***Differences between men and women significant at the .05 level.

$- .41, p = .001$), while among the Colombians there was no relationship ($r(170) = - .04, p = .30$).

Women held both partners more responsible for the abuse than did men and men were more sympathetic toward the husband than were women.

It had been hypothesized that persons who believed in a personality defect theory of wife abuse would believe the wife to be more responsible and feel less sympathy toward her, while those who focused more on external factors would hold the wife less responsible and feel more sympathy toward her. Among the Americans, this was reflected in a positive correlation between attributions to the wife's personality and holding her responsible ($r(101) = + .45, p = .001$), a negative correlation between her personality and feeling sympathy toward her ($r(101) = - .35, p = .001$), and a positive correlation between belief in sexist norms and sympathy toward her ($r(101) = .21, p = .02$ and $r(101) = .22, p = .02$ for male norms and female norms, respectively). Belief in the importance of sexist norms was unrelated, however, to attributions of responsibility. Among the Colombian students, attribution to the wife's personality was unrelated to holding her responsible, although it was negatively related to feeling sympathetic toward her ($r(169) = - .22, p = .002$). Beliefs in the importance of sexist norms were only marginally correlated with holding the wife responsible ($r(171) = .13, p = .051$ and $r(171) = .12, p = .064$ for male and female norms, respectively).

Attitudes Toward Women and Attributional Measures

Because it was hypothesized that normative change would influence attitudes toward violence against women, the attributional data were reanalyzed by gender and nationality, with AWS as a covariate. Contrary to expectation, there was little change in results when AWS was covaried out. This suggested that attitudes toward women contributed independently to attitudes toward wife abuse. To explore this further, respondents within each country were divided at the median in terms of their attitudes toward women, and similar analyses of variance were performed with this as a third independent variable. There were few statistically and logically meaningful differences in the attributions to personality, socialization, and stress as a function of AWS. However, as can be seen in Table 18-4, in both countries, those with liberal attitudes toward women believed that the norms prescribing male and female behaviors were more important determinants of the incident, held the husband more responsible for the abuse, and believed that the incident described was more likely to have occurred than did those with more conservative attitudes.

As can be seen in Table 18-5, there were also some more complex effects involving interactions between nationality and AWS. Colombians with more liberal attitudes held the wife more responsible and felt less sympathy for her than did Colombians with conservative attitudes. Americans with liberal attitudes held the woman less responsible and felt more sympathy for her than did Americans with conservative attitudes.

To further explore the relationship between AWS and attitudes toward abuse, Pearson r's were computed between AWS and those attitudinal variables for which there had been significant differences as a function of nationality and gender. These were norms about men and women, responsibility of and sympathy for the partners, and the likelihood of the incident occurring. Separate correlations were computed for men and women of each country. There was no relationship between AWS and any of the variables for the Colombian men. The only significant relationships for the American

Table 18-4 Differences as a function of attitudes toward women

	Colombia		United States	
	Conservative	Liberal	Conservative	Liberal
Male norms*	3.80	4.40	3.96	4.69
Female norms*	3.86	4.48	3.86	4.58
H's responsibility**	4.48	5.25	6.02	6.27
Likelihood**	4.38	4.87	4.43	4.77

*Differences between conservatives and liberals significant at the .005 level.
**Differences between conservatives and liberals significant at the .05 level.

men was a positive correlation between AWS and belief in the role of male norms and sympathy for the victim. Among the U.S. women, AWS was positively correlated only with sympathy toward the victim. Among the Colombian women, however, the more liberal the woman, the more likely she was to believe in the role of male and female norms, and hold the husband responsible for the abuse. AWS was also marginally positively correlated with holding the wife responsible and marginally negatively related to sympathy for the victim.

DISCUSSION

Three factors were found to relate to attitudes toward abuse against women: nationality, gender, and attitudes toward women. As had been expected, Colombian men and women held more traditional attitudes toward violence against women than did the Americans. They held both husband and wife almost equally responsible for the abusive incident. They were also less sympathetic toward both partners than were their American counterparts. Surprisingly, feelings of sympathy were unrelated to beliefs about responsibility among the Colombians. Colombians, especially the women, believed that factors within the wife were more important determinants of the abuse than did the Americans. The students in the United States, on the other hand, were more "modern" in their attitudes toward wife abuse, considering factors in the husband to be more important determinants of the abuse, and believing him to be more responsible than the wife. Furthermore, Americans were more sympathetic when they believed the wife was not responsible for her own abuse. The gender differences that were found appear to reflect a tendency for men and women to have identified with their same-sex counterpart. Among the men, such identification re-

Table 18-5 Perception of wife's responsibility and sympathy toward her as a function of nationality and AWS

	Colombia		United States	
	Conservative	Liberal	Conservative	Liberal
Responsibility*	4.42	4.88	3.72	2.92
Sympathy	3.72	3.21	5.72	6.53

*Interaction between AWS and nationality significant at the .001 level.

sulted in giving more weight to the importance of a stressful precipitating incident, holding the husband less responsible for the abuse, and being more sympathetic toward him. The tendency for the women to blame the victim more than did the men is consistent with prior research that has demonstrated that women blame a victim with whose plight they identify in order to feel less vulnerable. This defensive attributional style was especially salient among the Colombian women who gave greatest weight to the wife's personality and socialization. They were also the least sympathetic toward the victim. The finding that Colombian women who were most liberal in their attitudes toward women tended to hold the abused woman more responsible for her abuse and feel less sympathy for her than those with conservative attitudes was consistent with the need of women to defend themselves psychologically against the threat of abuse. In a country in which sexist norms are still strongly entrenched, it is the nontraditional women who may find themselves most at risk of abuse and most in need of defending themselves against this threat.

As had been expected, Colombians were more conservative in their attitudes toward women than were the Americans, and men were more conservative than were women. However, attributions about wife abuse were not mediated by attitudes toward women as we had expected. Instead, the two variables contributed independently toward attitudes toward wife abuse. Clearly, attitudes toward abuse against women are influenced by multiple factors. Attitudes toward women, at least as assessed by a paper and pencil instrument, may play only a small role in determining attitudes toward abuse against wives.

There has been little cross-cultural research on wife abuse. The data that we have presented suggest that this is a rich area for exploration. The finding that we think warrants most urgent attention pertains to "feminist" Colombian women who blamed the victim most for her own abuse. This contrasted with the United States, where those women with the most liberal attitudes were the least likely to blame the victim. Other research has demonstrated that one of the important factors in helping women stop the cycle of violence is for them to externalize blame (Frieze, 1979). In the United States, those who work closest with battered women are least likely to blame the victim, and, therefore, are in the best position to help them break out of the cycle of violence (Davis & Carlson, 1981). The students in our study were future service providers. If these data can be generalized, then holding liberal attitudes toward women may be a necessary but not sufficient condition for believing that abused women are not responsible for their own abuse. This would suggest that a more specific form of "consciousness raising" may be necessary if battered women are to be helped in different countries throughout the world.

BIBLIOGRAPHY

Allen, C. M., & Straus, M. A. (1980). Resources, power, and husband-wife violence. In M. A. Straus & G. T. Hotaling (Eds.), *The social causes of husband-wife violence.* (pp. 188–210). Minneapolis, MN: University of Minnesota Press.

Blood, R. O., & Wolfe, D. M. (1960). *Husbands and wives: The dynamics of married living.* New York: Free Press.

Burr, W. R., Ahern, L., & Knowles, E. M. (1977). An empirical test of Rodman's theory of resources in cultural context. *Journal of Marriage and the Family, 39*(3), 505–514.

Castro, M. L. (1983). Problemas de la Transicion Familia Colombiana. (Problems of the Colombian family transition). *Foro Distrital Sobre Familia.* Bogota.

Chaiken, A. L., & Darley, Jr., J. M. (1973). Victim or perpetrator: Defensive attribution of responsibility and the need for order and justice. *Journal of Personality and Social Psychology, 25*(2), 268–275.

Coates, D., Wortman, C. B., & Abbey, A. (1979). Reactions to victims. In I. H. Frieze, D. Bar-Tal, & J. S. Carroll (Eds.), *New approaches to social problems.* (pp. 21–52). San Francisco, CA: Jossey-Bass.

Cooney, R. S., Rogler, L. H., Hurrell, R., & Ortiz, V. (1982). Decision making in intergenerational Puerto Rican families. *Journal of Marriage and the Family, 44*(3), 621–631.

Cromwell, V. L., & Cromwell, R. E. (1978). Perceived dominance in decision-making and conflict resolution among Anglo, black and Chicano couples. *Journal of Marriage and the Family, 40*(4), 749–759.

Davis, L. V. (1984). Beliefs of service providers about abused women and abusing men. *Social Work, 29*(3), 243–251.

Davis, L. V., & Carlson, B. E. (1981). Attitudes of service providers toward domestic violence. *Social Work Research and Abstracts, 17*(4), 34–39.

Deutsch, H. (1930). The significance of masochism in the mental life of women. *International Journal of Psychoanalysis, 11,* 48–60.

Dobash, R. E., & Dobash, R. (1979). *Violence against wives: A case against the patriarchy.* New York: Free Press.

Fitzpatrick, J. P. (1976). The Puerto Rican family. In C. H. Mindel & R. W. Habenstein (Eds.), *Ethnic families in America: Patterns and variations* (pp. 192–217). New York: Elsevier.

Frieze, I. H. (1979). Perceptions of battered wives. In I. H. Frieze, D. Bar-Tal, & J. S. Carroll (Eds.), *New approaches to social problems* (pp. 79–108). San Francisco: Jossey-Bass.

Gackenbach, J. I. (1978). A perceptual defense approach to the study of gender sex related traits, stereotypes, and attitudes. *Journal of Personality, 46*(4), 645–676.

Gackenbach, J. I., & Auerbach, S. M. (1975). Empirical evidence for the phenomenon of the "well-meaning liberal male." *Journal of Clinical Psychology, 31*(4), 632–635.

Gelles, R. J. (1976). Abused wives: Why do they stay? *Journal of Marriage and the Family, 38*(4), 659–668.

Goode, W. J. (1971). Force and violence in the family. *Journal of Marriage and the Family, 33*(4), 624–636.

Kalmuss, D. (1979). The attribution of responsibility in a wife-abuse context. *Victimology, 2*(2), 284–291.

Kalmuss, D., & Straus, M. A. (1982). Wife's marital dependency and wife abuse. *Journal of Marriage and the Family, 44*(2), 277–286.

Krulewitz, J. E., Nash, J., & Payne, E. (August, 1977). Sex differences in attributions about rape, rapists, and rape victims. Paper presented at the 85th annual meeting of the American Psychological Association, San Francisco.

Lerner, M. J., & Miller, D. T. (1978). Just world research and the attribution process: Looking back and ahead. *Psychological Bulletin, 85*(5), 1030–1051.

Mojica, C., & Rodriguez, C. (1983). Consideraciones generales sobre la Familia en Bogota. (General considerations about the family in Bogota). *Foro Distrital Sobre Familia.* Bogota.

Nash, J. E. (1977). Attributions about rape victim resistance. Paper presented at the 85th annual meeting of the American Psychological Association, San Francisco.

Richmond, M. L. (1976). Beyond resource theory: Another look at factors enabling women to affect family interaction. *Journal of Marriage and the Family, 38*(2), 257–266.

Rodman, H. (1972). Marital power and the theory of resources in a cultural context. *Journal of Comparative Family Studies, 3*(1), 50–69.

Shaver, K. G. (1975). *An introduction to attribution processes.* Cambridge, MA: Winthrop.

Spence, J. T., & Helmreich, R. L. (1978). *Masculinity and feminity: Their psychological dimensions, correlates, and antecedents.* Austin, TX: University of Texas.

Steinman, A., & Fox, D. J. (1966). Male-female perceptions of the female role in the United States. *Journal of Personality, 64*(2), 265–276.

Steinmetz, S. K. (1977). *The cycle of violence: Assertive, aggressive, and abusive family interaction.* New York: Praeger.

Steinmetz, S. K., & Straus, M. A. (Eds.). (1974). *Violence in the family.* New York: Harper & Row.

Straus, M. A. (1974). Cultural and social organizational influences on violence between family members. In R. Prince & D. Barrier (Eds.), *Configurations: Biological and cultural factors in sexuality and family life.* (pp. 53–69). Lexington, MA: Lexington Books.

Straus, M. A. (1976). Sexual inequality, cultural norms, and wife-beating. *Victimology, 1*(1), 54–70.

Straus, M. A. (1980). A sociological perspective on the prevention of wife-beating. In M. A. Straus & G. T. Hotaling (Eds.), *The social causes of husband-wife violence* (pp. 211–232). Minneapolis, MN: University of Minnesota Press.

Straus, M. A., & Gelles, R. J. (1990). *Physical violence in American families: Risk factors and adaptations to violence in 8,145 families.* New Brunswick, N.J.: Transaction Publishers.

Straus, M. A., & Hotaling, G. T. (Eds.). (1980). *The social causes of husband-wife violence.* Minneapolis, MN: University of Minnesota Press.

Strube, M. J., & Barbour, L. S. (1983). The decision to leave an abusive relationship: Economic dependence and psychological commitment. *Journal of Marriage and the Family, 45*(4), 758–783.

Waites, E. A. (1977–78). Female masochism and the enforced restriction of choice. *Victimology, 2*(3–4), 535–544.

Walster, E. (1966). Assignment of responsibility for an accident. *Journal of Personality and Social Psychology, 3*(1), 73–79.

19

Domestic Violence in Austria: The Institutional Response

Cheryl Benard
Edit Schlaffer
Ludwig Boltzmann Forschungsstelle für Politik
Vienna, Austria

INTRODUCTION

This chapter reviews the response of the justice system to the problem of domestic violence in Austria. It reports the results of a study of 1,200 cases of police intervention in cases of domestic violence, 500 court decisions, and other data. In particular, the study focused on the predominant philosophies concerning the problem of wife abuse and the social programs and responses resulting from them.

Austria is a predominantly Catholic country with social values still molded by traditional thinking. At the same time, it is part of the modern industrial milieu and has a government that considers itself to be socially progressive. For these reasons, it provides a case study for transitional problems within a modern industrial environment, and for the barriers reformers may expect to encounter in such a setting.

In Austria, as in most western European countries, the issue of domestic violence has, in recent years, been given considerable attention by the media. The United Nations Decade for Women and the desire of the ruling socialist government to introduce progressive reforms have given rise to a number of legal changes and to some pilot programs. The legal reforms in the marriage and divorce laws have included such things as equalizing the status of children born in and outside of marriage, giving mothers and fathers equal status as the legal representatives of minor children, introducing "no-fault" divorce, and so forth. However, these reforms remain incomplete in that, for example, rape laws still specifically exclude married women (rape is defined as coercive extra-marital sex) and prosecution of a man for assault is contingent on the consent of the victim (thus making the victim vulnerable to threats and pressure intended to force her to withhold that consent).

The pilot programs in Austria are generally adopted from other countries, most commonly Germany, the reasoning being that Austria, as a small state with limited

Dr. Cheryl Benard and **Dr. Edit Schlaffer** direct the Ludwig Boltzmann-Forschungsstelle für Politik und wischenmenschliche Beziehungen (Vienna). Their numerous works on the relations between the sexes and the situation of women include Liebesgeschichten aus dem Patriarchat: Von der übermäßigen Bereitschaft der Frauen, sich mit dem Vorhandenen zu arrangieren (1981), Im Dschungel der Gefühle: Expedition in die Niederungen der Leidenschaft (1987) and Männer: Eine Gebrauchsanweisung for Frauen (1988), published with the German publishing house Rowohlt.

resources, needs to benefit from the research and experience of its more prosperous neighbors.

The two main programs in the area of domestic violence have been the institution of women's refuges as safe shelters for abused women, and the so-called "contact officer" program of the police, which trains a select group of police officers to be especially informed about and sensitive to the specifics of domestic violence.

In the following sections, the institutional response to the problem of domestic violence in Austria, and some of its remaining deficiencies, will be reviewed. In Austria, two factors were responsible for the heightened awareness of the problem of domestic violence: the attention drawn to this problem by the information and studies generated during the United Nations Decade of Women, and improved crime statistics that dramatically outlined the dimensions of this problem. Although prior to 1984 crime statistics were not collected to reflect the relationship between victim and assailant, and in some cases did not even reflect the gender, after 1984 this "oversight" was remedied and some rather frightening facts emerged. Crime statistics for 1985 showed that 54% of all murders in Austria were committed within the family, with women and children making up nearly 90% of the victims.

A THREE-YEAR STUDY ON DOMESTIC VIOLENCE AGAINST WOMEN IN AUSTRIA BY THE LUDWIG BOLTZMANN INSTITUTE OF POLITICS

The study was carried out under a grant from the Austrian National Bank and the Austrian Ministry of the Interior. In the course of this study, we were able to evaluate 1,200 cases of police intervention in cases of domestic violence; 500 court decisions where such cases came to trial; 30 case studies of women living in a battered women's shelter; and 25 case studies of men convicted and under jail sentence for wife abuse. With the exception of the murder cases, our data concerned Vienna only. In the case of capital crimes, prisoners serve their sentences in Austria's only high-security facility near Vienna, the prison Stein.

As is known from other countries, only a fraction of women who experience abuse ever report this to the police, and only a minority of these cases ever come to trial. In order to get a better perspective on unreported cases, we supplemented our survey with an analysis of 1,500 divorce cases (as Austria has no-fault divorce, violence was not cited as grounds for divorce; thus it is likely that its incidence was not "invented" or exaggerated for purposes of gaining the divorce), and with a sample of 200 interviews drawn from women attending adult education courses in public school facilities (pottery and handicrafts, languages, literature, and basic social studies courses frequently attended, in Vienna, by housewives).

In this study, we were interested in qualitative information, in other words, in the qualitative role played by abuse and potential abuse and the social valuation of this abuse to the behavior of men and women within the marriage relationship and to the condition of family life. We were particularly interested in evaluating the impact of predominant philosophies concerning the problem of wife abuse, and the social programs and responses resulting from these philosophies.

However, our research also produced some quantitative results that are outlined briefly as follows:

• Nineteen percent of the 200 women attending adult education classes had personally experienced domestic violence within the previous year. This figure rose when unmarried women and women not currently living in a steady relationship were eliminated. Twenty-one percent of married women and 23% of women living with a man had experienced violence within the previous year.

• Seventy-nine percent of all the women who took part in the study knew of a case of domestic violence in their immediate environment, defined as their close relatives, close friends, and neighbors living in their apartment house.

• Sixty-two percent knew of several cases.

• Forty-three percent remembered incidents of violence between their parents when they were children. This was an open question, and elicited articulate and painful descriptions of the distress these experiences had caused them in their childhood.

• Fifty-nine percent of the 1,500 divorce cases cited domestic violence against the wife as a contributing factor to the breakdown of the marriage. We would like to emphasize that mention of this violence did not affect the outcome of the divorce hearing, did not benefit the woman, and was not prominent in the case, but was merely mentioned at some point in the file or the proceedings. Divided by class, 38% of working-class women, 13% of middle-class women, and 4% of upper-class women of these 59%, called the police at some point during their marriages in response to battering.

Of the 1,200 cases of police intervention, the woman victim had herself summoned the police in 45% of the cases. Neighbors of the women had called the police in another 43% (duplication possible, i.e., sometimes both the woman herself and the neighbors called the police independent of each other). Children had called or summoned the police in 9% of the cases. In 30% of the cases, the police were called after the woman had left home, and the call was made by her or her friends or relatives after she reached "safety."

The woman had visible injuries in 40% of the cases. A threat of murder was involved in 25% of the cases. Weapons were present in 30% of the cases (we include in our definition of weapons any object that can be used as a weapon, such as an umbrella, a broken bottle, etc.).

Of those women who were calling the police for the first time, 51% said this was not the first incidence of violence in this particular relationship. Seven percent specifically said it was the first incident. In the remaining cases no pertinent statement was made.

The most common reaction for women in this situation was still to leave their homes. Of these, 30% went to a close relative's house, 22% went to a female friend, 9% went to a hotel, and 17% went to a women's refuge. Two such refuges exist in Vienna.

Of those cases referred by the police to the district attorney, the district attorney evaluated the case as less serious and less dangerous than had been the judgment of the police in 55% of the cases. This was a particularly disappointing finding, because it may be assumed that the police, having witnessed the setting, seen the interaction between the couple, and formed an on-site opinion of the man, should be in a better position to judge the situation and the potential danger to the woman than the district attorney.

In court cases, the tendency to downplay domestic violence against women on the part of the judiciary also came to light. In trials concerning domestic assault, a prison sentence was given only in conjunction with some other crime for which the man was also being tried. None of the men jailed for wife battering were servicing sentences exclusively for that offense; all of them were serving much longer sentences for unrelated crimes, such as theft. In other words, judges are prepared to extend the sentence of a man they view as a criminal if he has also assaulted his wife, but they will not do so if he has only assaulted his wife—a clear reflection of the low priority and exceptional status they assign this offense. Far more frequent was a monetary fine, which, in effect, if the couple remains together, penalizes the entire family.

Of those women who brought their aggressors to trial (this is "voluntary" in Austria because the victim may, when the assailant is a relative, spouse, or common-law spouse, withdraw the complaint at any time), 67% had called the police at least once prior to the incident that led to the trial, and 40% had called the police more than once. This indicates that the police intervention was seen by these women to be of some benefit to their situation (or they would not have repeated it) or that they were desperate and could not think of any other source of help. In either case, we see this as a clear confirmation of the view emerging in other western industrial countries, that the police have a potentially significant role to play in intervening in the problem of domestic violence.

THE POLICE

In cases of more severe domestic disputes, it is fairly common for the police to be called in, either by the female victim or by neighbors. Because Austrian crime statistics show neither the relationship between offender and victim, nor in some cases even the gender, it is not possible to say exactly how frequent such interventions are. However, a review of police records for a nine-month period showed somewhat more than 2,000 such interventions for the city of Vienna alone.

Police intervention is not unproblematic. Often, it has been found, the police tend to be sympathetic to the man and willing to subscribe to the "provocation theory," in other words, to the theory that while men may be stronger than women, women are verbally and otherwise more articulate and can drive a man to despair and violence by their behavior. It has also been surmised by some that the police, generally holding an authoritarian view, tend to identify with the stronger party, in this case the man. However, in our various interviews with police officers, we did not find this to be true generally. If there was an authoritarian attitude, it was more likely to lead the police officer to do what his superiors instructed, namely to take down every complaint as thoroughly as possible and to suspend personal judgment on whether the act was justified.

A pilot program that trained a group of so-called "contact officers" to be especially informed about and sensitive to family problems has shown definite success. However, general training of all police officers does not yet adequately include instruction on this particular issue, and so one great problem remains: ignorance of many police officers regarding the proper procedures to be followed in such cases, and a consequent inability to counsel the woman correctly on her available options. For example, a woman desiring to leave her home in order to escape from a battering husband is required, if she also wishes to get a divorce, to register her new address (everyone in Austria must be registered at his or her domicile) according to a certain procedure. Otherwise, her departure from the marital home may, at the divorce trial, be interpreted as constituting desertion. This lack of information, which could have been provided by the police, has caused many women great difficulties.

Contact officers were sensitive to the dynamics of family conflict, but other officers often did not consider the weight that a random comment may have. Many women bitterly quoted statements by police officers that had reflected crass insensitivity or partiality for the husband. One woman was dismayed to hear a police officer commiserate with her boyfriend, who had just given her a concussion and broken her nose, over the fact that because he was not her husband, he could be thrown out of her apartment without a court order.

In general, however, it was found that the police responded to domestic calls promptly and recorded the statements of all parties without prejudice. Although there were cases in which the officer displayed partiality toward the man, there were at least an equal number of cases in which partiality toward the victim was shown, sometimes to the point of giving the man a personal lecture about his behavior. This was explained by the police officers to be a carryover from the "old days," in which a battering husband was often taken to the police station and given a dressing-down, sometimes even a beating, by the police officers.

THE DISTRICT ATTORNEYS

It was through the complaints of police officers that our attention was first directed to the fact that district attorneys were much less efficient in enforcing domestic peace than the police.

The procedure in Austria in cases of domestic disputes is as follows: after the police have taken down the complaint, and in cases in which a weapon has been used, the woman has a visible injury, or the man has threatened to kill her, the office of the district attorney is contacted because it must decide whether the man is to be held. In making this decision, it was found that class prejudice, as well as sexism, played a significant role. In other words, district attorneys showed a propensity both to believe that family violence (and the attendant problems of alcoholism and unemployment) were typical of the lower middle-class lifestyle, and as such were regarded as "normal" by those involved. Therefore, intervention was considered useless as it was assumed that this behavior would occur again, and there was the prevailing belief that the woman was ultimately to blame for the situation, whatever the circumstances.

Ironically enough, the classic tradition-minded police officer who felt it shameful for a man to hit a woman, particularly a "good" woman and mother, could in practice turn out to be more helpful to the victim than the district attorney, who as a member of the modern milieu theoretically held egalitarian views, but in practice often manipulated these egalitarian tenets to the disadvantage of the woman. Often disdainful toward all members of the lower middle class and suspicious of the woman's motives vis-à-vis her husband, such members of the legal profession often acted against the woman by a simple but effective trick, namely the trick of pretending that women should be treated as if perfect equality had already been achieved. Such individuals apply the law as if every woman were educated, employed, independent, and childless, capable of always deciding and acting as a free agent and clearly being manipulative, or masochistic, if she does not.

In the decisions made by many district attorneys, the basic underlying premise seemed to be that the woman is always wrong. For example, if a woman went to the police immediately after the violent act and reported it, this was taken to show that she had acted out of anger and had undoubtedly exaggerated in order to get revenge on her husband. However, if she reported the incident on the following day or even later, it was taken as evidence that she did not really feel endangered and had not really been injured—otherwise, she would not have waited.

If the woman giving the statement appeared calm and self-possessed, this indicated again that she was not frightened but was probably playing some kind of vindictive game. If she was visibly upset, it improved her credibility somewhat but also indicated that she was probably hysterical and not a reliable witness.

If the woman filed a complaint against her husband but did not initiate divorce proceedings, this was seen to show that violence was part of the neurotic nature of that particular relationship, and that the woman was probably masochistic and needed it, or at least recognized that she was at least half to blame. If, however, she did file for divorce at the same time as filing the complaint, the district attorney would often imply that she had invented or provoked the violent incident in order to obtain a more favorable settlement at the divorce trial.

Being uninformed about her rights indicated to the district attorney that the woman came from a social class in which violence was not the exception but the rule, and as such not a "problem"; if she was informed, then it was assumed that a devious lawyer had instructed her in order to trick her husband and maneuver him into a position of guilt.

In the view of the police, the tendency of the district attorney's office to trivialize domestic violence was a great problem because this often removed the one remaining barrier to serious abuse. If the husband realized that even if the police did come nothing would happen to him, then even the wife's threat to call the police would lose its efficacy.

Some illustrations of the district attorney's attitudes follow: a 38-year-old unemployed mechanic, whose girlfriend had left him, was harassing her in an attempt to get her to change her mind. He lurked about in front of her apartment waiting for her to appear so he could pressure her to come back to him. On this particular day, he rang her doorbell so long that she finally opened the door. When she did, he stormed inside and began beating her. At the same time, he shouted, "If you don't come back to me, that will be the end of you." Neighbors called the police. On their arrival, the woman stated that she felt endangered, that she considered the man capable of killing her, and that she was afraid to leave her apartment. Even the arrival of the police did not immediately calm the man down, who continued, in their presence, to beat her with an umbrella until he was restrained forcibly.

The district attorney decided that because the man was under the influence of alcohol at the time, his behavior should be viewed as "reflective of his social class." The sentence "that will be the end of you" could be interpreted as a threat, but it also allows for other interpretations, and the real meaning is open for conjecture.

Besides illustrating the class-specific arrogance of many district attorneys, this example also evidences an even bigger problem: the tendency to consider acts of violence between a man and woman differently if they have once had a personal relationship. Thus, even a woman who has long since ended a relationship—and even a woman who ended it as soon as she saw that it was destructive—may find herself bound to the man in the eyes of officialdom.

The law provides no objective basis for such a view, but it is pervasive enough to distort the application of the law. The tendency to trivialize the complaint, as it has occurred within the family, is clearly evident in cases were broken teeth, a dislocated jaw, and an injury to the lip requiring several stitches were arbitrarily dismissed by the district attorney as "injuries of an insufficiently serious nature" to warrant prosecution.

It is clear that such decisions are arbitrary, and the arbitrariness of the district attorneys is a major obstacle to the better handling of domestic violence cases in Austria. In one case, a woman with a dislocated shoulder, a concussion, and numerous bruises was considered to be insufficiently credible by the district attorney when she asserted that her husband had also prevented her forcibly from calling the police and had threatened to kill her. In her case, she was not believed until she produced two witnesses who had heard his threats.

In another case, however, a woman with cigarette marks on both arms was informed that her husband, who was drunk at the time, may have inflicted these numerous burns accidentally. When she produced two neighbors who had been told by her husband that he intended to kill her, the district attorney in this case judged that the threat was less, rather than more credible, for having been uttered in front of witnesses.

The arbitrary nature of these decisions is further underscored by the fact that district attorneys at times make decisions clearly contradictory to the law. For example, by law, charges for personal injuries can be filed up to one year after the incident. However, district attorneys routinely dismiss the complaints of women who have waited as little as three or four days before filing their charges.

THE COURTS

The courts are confronted with cases of domestic violence in two situations: as a criminal charge against the husband, and in connection with divorce proceedings. After our experiences with the district attorneys, we had expected judges to display a similar bias. However, this expectation was not confirmed. Judges, with few exceptions, showed a tendency to be sympathetic to the victim and disapproving of male violence in the family. Problems encountered by women in courts were due more to the inadequacies of the judicial and penal systems in dealing with domestic violence.

One reason for this is that no distinctions are made among the couples appearing before the judge. The differences in their situations and in their expectations are, however, of great significance and must be taken into account if effective responses are to be found.

In regard to the female victims, we must distinguish the following categories:

1. The woman wants to leave the violent man, but is unable to do so for material reasons (no education, no job possibilities, small children, etc.).
2. The woman wants to leave the violent man, but is unable to do so for subjective reasons (emotional dependence, a religion that does not accept divorce, fear of social stigma, etc.).
3. The woman wants to leave the violent man, but is afraid to do so (because he has threatened to kill her if she leaves, or similar reasons).
4. The couple's relationship is essentially over, but they remain together for practical reasons (too difficult to divide shared property, they want to wait until the children are grown up, etc.).
5. The woman wishes to maintain the relationship, but wants the man to stop his abusive behavior, while the man (a) also wishes to uphold the relationship, but thinks

his behavior is justified (expression of husbandly authority, understandable response to stress, etc.), or (b) also wishes to maintain the relationship and agrees that his behavior is wrong, but can't or won't change it.

Clearly, cases coming before the court make sense only against the backdrop of the specifics of the individuals involved. A woman appearing as a witness against a husband or boyfriend charged with assaulting or battering her may do so out of different motives and with different personal expectations and assessments. The relationship may have been finished before the violent incident, and the violence may have been part of a program of harassment on the part of a man who did not accept the separation. In that case, the woman may expect that court action will make it clear to him that she really has no intention of ever resuming their relationship, and that she wants him to leave her alone.

Alternatively, the woman may be seeking redress for the violence committed against her and regard the assailant as someone who has abused a relationship of trust and intimacy and who receives the same legal treatment as anyone else. Finally, the woman may regard the man's violence as the one intolerable aspect of a relationship she would otherwise very much wish to maintain. Such a woman will hope that the court will accomplish that which she has been unable to achieve, namely, to demonstrate to the man the incorrectness and gravity of his behavior, and her own refusal to tolerate it any longer.

In the cases we reviewed, the distribution of these three viewpoints was as follows: the woman desires a court decision to free her of the undesired attentions of a former partner (15%); the woman seeks redress for violence she has suffered (20%); the woman wants the court to change the partner's behavior (60%); and other (5%).

Here we have a direct conflict between the expectations of the clients and the attitude of the legal professionals. In the view of the legal professionals, the partners of an ongoing relationship do not belong in a courtroom. As long as they continue to live together, attorneys, district attorneys, and many judges tend to feel they should not be filing court complaints against each other. This view is supported by the law, which is full of provisions exempting family members from ordinary legal treatment in the case of internal disputes and offenses. Some of these provisions are that married people need not testify against each other, that an accidental injury committed by one relative (spouse, parent, child, sibling) against another is not prosecutable.

The courtroom is not considered the place to negotiate disputes or right wrongs committed in a family or marital context. This view has changed somewhat in recent decades as various liberal movements have pointed out that while the intent may be to guard the private sphere against state intervention, the effect often is to further benefit the stronger against the weaker by robbing the weaker of public support and legal redress.

Women and children have been the two groups around whom this discussion has mostly revolved, as such formerly private issues such as incest, child abuse, wife beating, and marital rape have begun to be unearthed from the taboo against their discussion and integrated into the sphere of public intervention. However, the former attitude lingers on, both in the laws and in the minds of those who enforce the laws.

Therefore, when a case of assault, battery, or other such violent crime between a husband and wife, or between cohabiting couples, comes to trial, the court is more likely to be sympathetic and understanding when the individuals in question have separated or are in the process of separating. However, the majority of cases are different (for the simple reasons that, due to new Austrian divorce laws, most couples who intended to get a divorce anyway will not want the added burdens of another court case for assault). To the legal professionals, in whose own social class it would be almost unthinkable for a couple to go through the scandal of such a court case (divorce trials, which are closed to the public, are a different matter), the spectacle of a wife testifying to the violence of her husband and then going home with him again after the trial is evidence of a neurotic relationship.

Although sympathy still tends to be with the woman as the clearly injured party, many judges also display a very obvious feeling that both individuals involved are hopeless and will never lead a different life from the one that has just been described in all its unsavory and graphic details.

The viewpoint of the couples involved, especially the woman's, is quite different. Typically, this is a woman who does not want to consider divorce for a variety of emotional and practical reasons: the children are very young, the couple is heavily in debt, she still loves her husband, and so forth. However, she is determined that the abusive behavior must stop, and she is at a loss as to how to stop it. Usually, she has tried everything she can think of: she has explained to the man how she feels and he has promised to change but the promises have not lasted more than a few days or weeks. She has demonstratively left him to stay with a girlfriend or relative. She has threatened repeatedly to call the police. Finally, at her wit's end, or alarmed because his violence has escalated and she feels he may injure her seriously, she makes good her threat. She feels that her husband has not taken her seriously so far and that he beats her because he knows he can get away with it and knows she does not really want to leave him. She wants some outside authority to tell him that he should stop abusing her, and the only authority she can think of is the judge.

A smaller percentage of women call the police the very first time their partners become violent, believing that if they do not, they will be setting a precedent and the men will conclude that the women are prepared to tolerate their behavior. In fact, the fears of these women are borne out by numerous empirical studies: a battering husband does tend to be the kind of person who tests the limits very early in the relationship and will treat the woman exactly as she and the environment allow her to be treated.

It seems obvious that there is a clear need here for some kind of outside support for marriages suffering from the problem of violence. If such assistance is not forthcoming, the woman only has two choices: she can remain in the abusive relationship, accepting treatment that endangers her health, her emotional well-being, and certainly the well-being of her children; or she can get a divorce, which may not be the most desirable outcome either societally or personally.

Finally, it should be pointed out that violent relationships do not often remain stable, but usually deteriorate further until the violence escalates, extends to include the children, and destroys whatever positive elements may have remained in that relationship.

In our interviews, 85% of the men convicted for killing their wives (seven of them had also killed a small child in an overall explosion of rage, or because the child had accidentally witnessed the killing of its mother) had a long history of battery before the final incident. All of the women convicted for killing their husband or a child had committed this act to set a concluding point to a violent relationship they had not otherwise been able to escape from.

Women see—and their husbands often accept—the courts as the voice of authority that will affirm to the husband what the wife has not otherwise been able to convince him of, namely, that it is not permissible for him to go on abusing his wife. It was interesting to note that husbands often accepted this "didactic measure." Waiting to be called into the courtroom, they sat placidly next to the wives who were about to testify against them. Often, some kind of internal trade-off had been made by the couple, with the wife agreeing to withdraw a more serious charge in return for the husband "taking his medicine" on a lesser one. Of the husbands we interviewed, more than half actually viewed their wife's decision to follow up on the charges in a positive light and accepted the blame for "going too far."

However, these results are somewhat distorted by the fact that those men who are absolutely opposed to a courtroom appearance can generally force their wife by threats or by further violence to drop the charges or, where the district attorney is prosecuting, to withdraw her testimony. Therefore, those couples who actually appear in court tend to be those whose relationship is still in a more hopeful state. The man has some degree of guilt for his behavior and the wife is determined to take desperate measures to save the marriage. Thus, it is all the more unfortunate that the courts cannot provide the kind of response that might help these individuals. For cases not involving the use of a dangerous weapon and not involving graver charges, the usual sentence is a fine. In the case of lower-middle-class couples, who most often end up taking such a case to court, this fine is fairly high, usually amounting to at least a month's salary. Not only does this penalize the wife just as much as the husband, it also increases the strain within the family, because financial problems often touch off the domestic fight in the first place.

For these cases—and they represent the majority of all domestic violence cases that come before the courts—it would seem advisable to adopt what Austria already does in the case of juvenile drug offenses, and what other western countries are experimenting with in the case of domestic violence, namely to provide an alternative between a fine or prison sentence on the one hand and participation in a special therapy program on the other. Because domestic violence often appears in conjunction with alcoholism, a program designed to address these cases specifically would be advisable as well.

Even if this could be accomplished, other problematic situations remain. One group requiring attention are those women who are unable to get police protection or to testify in court because of intimidation by their victimizer. Although reliable figures are not possible, interviews and police observations indicate that there are many such cases. These women are in the worst possible situation, unable to leave and unable to get help because a man of proven violence threatens to kill them if they do. Not uncommonly, this threat is issued in the presence of police officers who have arrived at the summons of a neighbor. In such cases, or in cases in which the man has a criminal record for violence, a past record of wife abuse, or the woman has a visible injury, there should be special procedures to provide for the protection of the women and the children. These procedures would include the issuing of an immediate restraining order in the above situations.

Another group is composed of those women whose former partners refuse to accept the separation. These cases include women who ended a very brief association (sometimes just a few days) with a man upon discovering his violent or otherwise abnormal predisposition, women who have been divorced for many years, and even women being pursued by someone who has unilaterally taken an interest in them without ever receiving any encouragement whatsoever from the women. There is still an inclination on the part of legal professionals to treat such cases as "personal matters" on the outer fringes of the law. Clearly, such women are entitled to the same legal protection as any other citizen, and legal professionals should be educated to respond accordingly.

Austrian criminal statistics show that such women are in fact in very clear and present danger of being seriously injured and even killed by these men, and it is not justified to dismiss these cases as private romantic excesses. In one typical case, a disturbed man had singled out a woman living in his neighborhood. Unbeknownst to her, he spied on her when she walked to work, to the supermarket, and so forth. When he began appearing at her doorstep, she became alarmed and notified the police, who took no interest and dismissed her complaint. A few weeks later, he broke into the house and assaulted the woman, and when she resisted, he killed her and her mother. Here, an earlier intervention might have prevented this outcome, protecting the victim and providing her assailant with obviously needed psychiatric help.

In another typical case, a woman who had been divorced for two years was tormented by her former husband, who persistently broke into her house, hid in her bedroom, smashed the windows of her car, and so forth, in an effort to persuade and intimidate her into returning to him. The district attorney chose to view this "couple"—though they were no longer a couple—as a joint annoyance instead of trying to assist the woman. In such cases, providing counseling and therapy would help the couple in coping with the separation at the time of the divorce, preventing such later problems.

In spite of the theme of the problem of family violence, there is still a tendency to regard it as something personal. However, intervention is necessary. Nonintervention leaves the victim alone with the problem, and does not discourage the attacker from repeating violent behavior. Even a successful individual solution—to leave the violent man—is not really a satisfactory social conclusion, because the man may well go on to form another abusive relationship.

BIBLIOGRAPHY

Benard, C., & Schlaffer, E. (1986). Im Dschungel der Gefühle. Reinbek: Rowohlt-Verlag.

Benard, C., & Schlaffer, E. (1985). Viel Erlebt und Nichts Begriffen. Reinbek: Rowohlt-Verlag.

Benard, C., & Schlaffer, E. (1985). Police intervention in domestic assault cases. Report for the Austrian Ministry of the Interior.

Benard, C., & Schlaffer, E. (1984). Die Grenzen des Geschlechts. Reinbek: Rowohlt-Verlag.

Bruckner, M. (1983). Die Liebe der Frauen. Uber Weiblichkeit und Misshandlung. Berlin: Fischer-Verlag.

Burgard, R. (1985). Misshandelte Frauen: Verstrickung und Befreiung. Berlin: Fischer-Verlag.

Haffner, S. (1979). Gewalt in der Ehe. Berlin: Wagenbachs Taschenbücherei.

Komitee für Grundrechte und Demokratie. (1985). Sexuelle Gewalt. Bonn: Herder-Verlag.

Pletscher, M. (1985). Weggehen is Nicht so Einfach. Zürich: Schweizer Verbgshaus.

20

Violence Against Women in Australia's Capital City

Rosemary A. Knight
Australian Capital Territory Board of Health

Suzanne E. Hatty
Department of Social Work, University of New South Wales, Australia

INTRODUCTION

Violence against a female sexual partner ("domestic violence") incurs serious and long-term costs for both the victims and society. Such violence is as prevalent in Australia as elsewhere. The present study examined the main features of intersexual violence as reported by 120 women in Australia's capital city. Information was elicited through telephone interviews with victims following mass media advertising. In analyzing the data, specific emphasis was given to the factors implicated in the termination of abusive relationships. Three models (the attitudinal, behavioral, and sociodemographic accounts of violence) were fitted using logistic regression analysis. The following factors emerged as critical: type of violence experienced, intervention of medical and police personnel, and marital status. Victims' difficulties in extricating themselves from abusive relationships were discussed.

Violence perpetrated by a male against a female sexual partner, usually labeled "domestic violence," particularly if it occurs in the private domain, has been described as "a crime of momentous proportion" (Ellis, 1984, p. 56). Indeed, the

Dr. Rosemary A. Knight is director of research and statistics at the Australian Capital Territory Board of Health. She has been involved with legislative, policy, and planning decisions concerning "domestic violence" training workshops, with special emphasis on the role of health care personnel.

Dr. Suzanne E. Hatty is a senior lecturer in the Department of Social Work at the University of New South Wales. She was previously a research psychologist at the Australian Institute of Criminology. Her research interests focus on violence against women and children. She has been involved in a comprehensive examination of the Australian criminal justice system's responses to "family disputes," particularly police policy, training, and practice. Dr. Hatty has also conducted a survey of women's experiences with violent relationships, the first attempt to establish a national database for Australia.

Each author contributed equally to the preparation of this chapter. Correspondence and reprint requests should be addressed to Dr. R. Knight, Research Section, A.C.T.H.A., GPO Box 825, Canberra City, A.C.T. 2601, Australia.

We acknowledge the assistance of the following: The women who responded to our questionnaire, some of whom have survived the violence and some of whom continue to suffer; Ross Cunningham, for advice on regression analyses; Karen Fogarty, Paul Faithfull, and Betty Tyerman for computing; Anne-Marie Slattery, for clerical duties; the anonymous interviewers and coders; the Office of the Status of Women, for training interviewers and assisting with media coverage; the Australian Law Reform Commission for financial support for coding; and the ACTHA, for the use of its computing facilities.

social cost of this physical abuse is exorbitant: serious injury, and sometimes, death to the woman; psychological disturbance in children raised in the culture of violence (Hughes & Barad, 1982); and the allocation of a significant proportion of policy, judicial, and medical resources in an attempt to intervene, prosecute, or heal (Goldberg & Tomlanovich, 1984; Parnas, 1967).

It can be asserted that the structural inequalities inherent in society promote the use of intersexual violence. Indeed, the systematic use of violence against women may be viewed as a form of social control (Black, 1984; Dobash & Dobash, 1979). Leidig (1981) claims that all men accrue benefits from the violent activities of their male counterparts: women's lives are regulated and insubordination is averted.

It is well documented that the police appear to believe that violence in the private domain is qualitatively different from the aggressive acts of a stranger (Parnas, 1971), and they consequently exhibit a reluctance to intervene (Berk & Loseke, 1981; Cannings, 1984; Field & Field, 1973). The logical outcome of this attitude toward male-female relations is the formulation of a policy of non-arrest except in cases of severe injury (Thorman, 1980). Ellis (1984) reports that members of the judiciary manifest a similar reticence to process violent offenders who commit violent acts against a female partner, especially if the latter is a spouse.

There are significant difficulties in estimating the incidence of violent male assaults against a female partner (Straus et al., 1980; Walker, 1983). Despite the methodological difficulties, it is important to recognize that such violence should not be conceptualized as distinct from physical aggression inflicted by a male beyond the sphere of the family, that is, by a male not currently in an intimate relationship with the victim. The issues discussed above are of special relevance to factors involved in the termination of abusive relationships.

TERMINATING THE ABUSIVE RELATIONSHIP

Although the decision to quit an abusive relationship has received some research attention (Martin, 1979; Pagelow, 1981), few studies have attempted to delineate this circumstance in terms of the economic and emotional realities involved (Loseke & Berk, 1982). Frequently, the decision to leave or remain is informed by the success or failure of victims' previous help-seeking behavior: the neglect of victims by social service agencies in this decisionmaking process results in a distortion of the psychological position of the woman concerned. In order to extricate herself from a violent relationship, a woman must overcome substantial emotional and social barriers. Even if a semblance of independence is accomplished, there are no guarantees that this autonomy will persist (Johnson, 1981; Healy, 1984). Commenting on the findings of a survey of women who sought refuge in seven shelters in Adelaide, Australia, Healy (1984, p. 58) stated: "Over half the women continued to be threatened by their ex-husbands after leaving the shelter, and some were bashed. Leaving an abusive partner does not necessarily put an end to fear, harassment and violence."

Further light may be shed on the factors affecting termination of abusive relationships through an examination of three models predominant in the literature. These models may be sequentially described as the attitudinal, behavioral, and sociodemographic accounts. They may, on occasion, be implicit in the literature; also, they are not necessarily mutually exclusive.

The Attitudinal Model of Domiciliary Intersexual Abuse

This model focuses on the psychological characteristics of the male aggressor and the female victim as interpreted within the pattern of violence displayed, for example, the involvement of mental abuse, physical abuse, or both. Hofeller (1982) notes that violent men often display a need to totally dominate their female partner—indeed, a compulsive masculinity. The latter attitude is extended to a dictatorial control over the deployment of women's sexuality. Hofeller believes that this stance of domination may reflect an adherence to the rigidly defined male role. Moreover, the research conducted by Hofeller has revealed that the level of dominance exhibited by the male within the relationship is directly related to the severity of the violence inflicted upon the female partner.

In studying the dynamics underlying the violent interaction between sexual partners, Dobash and Dobash (1984, p. 282) isolated a predictable pattern of events culminating in violence: "[The incidents] begin with verbal confrontations, usually of short duration and *often perceived as challenges to the man's authority*. This is followed by attempts on the part of the woman to avoid or avert violence, and then proceeds to the physical attack" (Author's emphasis).

With respect to the psychological characteristics of the female partner, it has been reported that abused women often exhibit an adherence to the stereotyped feminine role (Davidson, 1978), with its attendant low self-esteem. Of course, this attitude may be at least partially induced by the endurance of sustained violence. Consequently, there may be a relationship between low self-esteem and guilt or depression (Hilberman, 1980). Stube and Barbour (1983) found that women who were experimentally defined as psychologically committed to the maintenance of the existing relationship were more tolerant of the abuse and were less likely to leave the violent partner. In contrast, women who do not adhere to a rigid feminine stereotype appear to quit a violent relationship after a relatively short time (Hofeller, 1982). Moreover, female economic dependence is associated with higher rates of severe violence within a relationship (Kalmuss & Straus, 1982); a woman is more likely to sever a relationship if she is employed (Stube & Barbour, 1983).

The Behavioral Model of Domiciliary Intersexual Abuse

A second theoretical model evident in the literature on domiciliary violence focuses on the behavior of the participants. Of particular interest is the response of the female to this situation.

Ferraro (1983) examined the defense mechanisms employed by women who suffered violence at the hands of their male partners and yet attempted to maintain the existing relationship. Applying the schema developed to describe the "techniques of neutralization" used by delinquents, Ferraro (1983) reported that women who lived with violence resorted to six strategies in order to cope with their emotional response to the violence: appeal to the salvation ethic (a belief that they can reform the male partner); denial of the victimizer (responsibility for behavior is not attributed to the violent male); denial of injury (there is an avoidance of the acknowledgement of violent acts); denial of victimization (responsibility for violence is attributed to the woman); denial of options (a belief that there are no practical or emotional alternatives); and appeal to higher loyalties (a commitment to moral principles such as the ideal of the everlasting marriage).

The Sociodemographic Model of Domiciliary Intersexual Abuse

A third model evident in the literature emphasizes the importance of sociodemo-graphic variables. Gelles (1972) developed the social structural theory, in which it is claimed that certain structural or situational stresses predispose toward violence. Members of the lower socioeconomic classes are assumed to be less equipped to cope adequately with these stresses and, consequently, are more likely to resort to violence as an aid to stress reduction. Similarly, Parker and Schumaker (1977) assert that violent men are more likely to be less educated than nonviolent men. Straus, Gelles, and Steinmetz (1980) also found that violent abuse of a female partner varies between socioeconomic groupings.

Australian data on this matter appear to be more ambiguous. The evidence indicates that working-class women avail themselves more frequently of services such as shelters (O'Donnell & Craney, 1982). However, this may reflect the fact that middle-class women have more resources at their disposal or perhaps attempt to deal with the violence in a different way. Indeed, Johnson (1981, p. 10) notes the need to challenge the assumption that "wife bashing is a lower-class pastime apart from the occasional middle-class psychopath."

OBJECTIVES OF THE PRESENT STUDY

The present study set out to examine the main features of intersexual violence in the private domain as experienced in Australia's capital city. In particular, the factors associated with leaving a relationship were assessed within the general framework of the three models outlined above.

Method

The methodology employed in this research was victim-initiated telephone inter-viewing following media advertising. The interviews were conducted over a seven-day period, from 9.00 A.M. to 9.00 P.M. Trained interviewers were rostered through the week, and respondents were assured of anonymity. Media exposure, prior to and during the salient period, was ensured by wide radio, television, and newspaper coverage.

A detailed questionnaire was constructed to gather as much information as possible about the violence. The victims were asked to describe their relationships, with par-ticular reference to the last violent incident. This strategy was assumed to yield higher reliability than exclusive focus on a description of typical violence or the worst incident endured. Information elicited included the type of violence inflicted (mental or physical abuse), the way in which it was enacted (involvement of weapons or character of physical assault), type of injury sustained, and the date of the last violent incident.

Victims were questioned about the extent to which they sought police intervention, medical treatment, and support and counseling from other community agencies. In addition, the degree to which these services were helpful or judgmental was assessed.

Women gave information regarding their response to the violent incident (for ex-ample, leaving the scene, fighting back), and their psychological reaction (for exam-ple, guilt, shame, shock).

Furthermore, victims were asked to describe the general features of the violence they typically experienced, such as the duration and frequency of the violence, and the time of its initiation. Sociodemographic features of the victim and perpetrator (e.g., age, marital status, number and sex of children, occupation, and education) were also sought.

RESULTS

The total number of interviews conducted throughout the week was 120, which represents 0.05% of the Australian Capital Territory (ACT) adult population.

General Features of the Sample

Detailed information about the respondents and reported patterns of violence is given in Hatty and Knight (1985). However, a broad description of the sample is as follows: most victims were female (98%), and husbands were the main perpetrators of the violence (71%). Regarding marital status, 54% were currently married and 29% were separated or divorced. The remainder were "never married." Most commonly, both victims and perpetrators were within the 30–34-year-old age range. The mean age of the first child ranged from 10 to 14 years. The general level of educational attainment was high (29% of victims and 27% of perpetrators had completed tertiary education).

Table 20-1 shows that, contrary to popular myth, the violent males were not characterized by unemployment or low-status occupations. Few were unemployed and a substantial proportion were in professional, managerial, or senior administrative positions. In contrast, the majority of the victims were not employed outside the home. If in paid employment, they typically occupied secretarial or sales positions, but many victims were in professional or top administrative jobs. Of the women who were employed, approximately half claimed to have control of their earnings, or to possess their own money.

For the majority of victims, the violence occurred with a marked regularity (once per week for 24% and daily for 16% of victims). In a quarter of the sample, the violence had been going on for 15 to 20 years or longer, and for 37% of women, the violence had continued for 5 to 10 years. In over half the reported incidents, there was evidence of both mental and physical abuse. Mental abuse was defined as constant verbal abuse, harassment, denigration, excessive possessiveness, and deprivation of physical and economic resources. Physical abuse was most often inflicted through punching, kicking, or hitting (43%), attempted strangulation/smothering

Table 20-1 Occupational distribution of respondents and A.C.T. population

	Males		Females	
	Respondents	A.C.T.	Respondents	A.C.T.
Professional/Administrative	37.8%	26.9%	19.7%	13.8%
Clerical/Sales	8.2%	18.0%	27.9%	28.1%
Trade/Manual	34.4%	20.7%	0%	2.0%
Other	6.5%	12.8%	9.9%	7.9%
Unemployed	4.9%	4.0%	3.3%	2.9%
Not in labor force	8.2%	17.6%	39.3%	45.3%

(18%), or use of a weapon (15%). Sexual assault was the main form of abuse for 4% of women, verbal abuse only was experienced in 8% of cases, and 11% of victims did not report the type of abuse.

Consistent with the assertions of Dobash and Dobash (1984), many of the respondents commented on the exaggerated nature of the perpetrator's behavior. The victim's actions were often perceived as a challenge to masculine authority. For example, one woman reported, "I wasn't allowed to disagree on anything, or I was bashed"; another stated, "He didn't want me to work. Violence started after I actively sought work."

In addition, another form of constraint reported in this study concerned male sexual jealousy or possessiveness. The phenomenon is illustrated by the following comment: "I was kept isolated from my parents and my friends. I was literally locked in when he went to work. He still constantly accused me of having affairs, of doing the most terrible things. He'd wake me up at night by punching me; then he'd violently rape me."

The victims responded to the violence in a number of ways; one-third of the women reported that they were unable to fight back, leave, or do anything to end the violence. Following the cessation of the violent incident, the majority of victims consulted medical personnel and/or community agencies. Doctors were most often consulted (43%), followed by friends (30%), social workers or psychologists (8%), and parents (8%). Friends were typically reported to be most supportive. The data on reported injuries showed, however, that many women who required medical treatment did not seek it. In some cases, the perpetrator actively prevented the victim from seeking help. For instance, one woman reported, "He said he'd kill the baby if I went to the hospital."

Only one-third of victims sought police intervention. The figures for arrest show that the perpetrator was arrested in 31% of cases, although 75% of victims had wanted arrest. In no case was the perpetrator arrested against the victim's wish, indicating that ACT police decisionmaking regarding arrest is not solely based on violations of the law. Women's reasons for not seeking police intervention varied. Some victims reported feeling guilt or shame, others were cynical about police effectiveness. One woman commented, "I was told they would not come unless my life was in jeopardy."

Terminating the Abusive Relationship

Logistic regression analysis[1] was applied to the data to test what features distinguish those victims who are currently in a violent relationship from the victims who are reporting on violence that has occurred in the past and has now ceased.

The three models outlined in the introduction were fitted in every possible permutation on a priori theoretical grounds. The sample was divided into those victims who had recently experienced violence (less than 12 months ago: $n = 60$) and those who had experienced violence in the past (more than 2 years ago and not since: $n = 52$). It

---

[1]The logistic regression model is a particular example of a statistical model, used when the dependent variable (or response variable of interest) is binary, and the technique has certain advantages. First, this approach allows a unified framework for testing hypotheses. Second, the fitted model, as well as providing a concise summary of the relationship between the response and the concomitant variables, can also be used to estimate and predict responses for new individuals. The computer package GENSTAT was used in this study.

is important to recognize here that the three models are not mutually exclusive, but represent alternative theoretical accounts of intersexual violence, and as such, are investigated independently.

The Effects of the Attitudinal Model

The attitudinal model can be operationalized through an examination of the patterns of violence experienced by the women reporting on their relationships. That is, the probability of the violence being recent may be a function of the kind of violence experienced (i.e., mental abuse, physical abuse, or both); or the average frequency of the violence (i.e., once or more a week or once a month/intermittent violence); or the length of the violence (i.e., less than 2 years, or 5–15 years or more).

If p represents the probability that a victim experienced violence recently, then the logistic regression model can be formulated as: for mental abuse, $p = 0.8$; for physical abuse, $p = 0.3$; and for mental and physical abuse, $p = 0.56$, such that victims are more likely to have experienced recent violence if they are subject to mental violence only, than if they suffer physical violence only, or both mental and physical violence. In other words, the presence of physical violence means that it is more likely that the violence experienced was in the past—the victims have presumably instigated some action to end the violence, or the violence has stopped for other reasons.

It is important to note that the length and frequency of violence are not salient factors; they do not add further to the explanatory power of the model. Regardless of how the model is set up, only the type of violence is critical. Clearly, the presence of physical violence is the strong factor that accounts for the occurrence of past violence.

The Effects of the Behavioral Model

As argued earlier (cf. Ferraro, 1983), the experience of violence may be associated with the employment of certain defense mechanisms by the victim, such as denial of injury or denial of victimization. Such strategies involve behavioral passivity on the part of the victim. It was postulated that any victim action, such as calling the police (i.e., yes or no), seeking medical treatment (i.e., yes or no), or consulting community agencies (i.e., yes or no) would be positively related to the cessation of the violence. These three forms of seeking external intervention were investigated.

If p represents the probability that a victim experienced violence recently, then the logistic regression model can be formulated as:

		Police intervention sought	
		Yes	No
Medical treatment sought	Yes	$p = 0.29$	$p = 0.55$
	No	$p = 0.20$	$p = 0.78$

such that victims who have experienced recent violence are likely to have sought external intervention with a probability of only 0.29. The victims who are reporting on past violence are thus more likely to have sought medical treatment and to have called the police at the time of the violence $(1 - p = 0.71)$. The victim's use of community agencies does not add anything to the regression model, even when alternative orders of fit were attempted.

The behavioral model indicates the significance of the victim's active seeking of both police intervention and medical treatment. Such strategies may be tantamount to a public disclosure of the violence and an explicit avoidance of denial.

The Effects of the Sociodemographic Model

The following sociodemographic variables were used in a logistic regression model to test the critical factors in recent versus past violence: marital status (i.e., living together or separated); education of victim and perpetrator (tertiary education or high school education only); occupation of victim and perpetrator (high-status occupation or low-status occupation); age of first child (child < 10 years, adolescent 11–19 years, adult 20+ years). Many permutations were possible for this model and all were tried. The only significant effect however was status, such that victims of recent violence were more likely to be married or in a de facto situation than victims of past violence, who were more likely to be separated or divorced.

If p represents the probability that a victim experienced violence recently, then the logistic regression model can be formulated as: for married victims, $p = 0.74$; and for separated victims, $p = 0.22$.

It is highly significant that the remaining sociodemographic variables are unimportant in predicting whether or not victims have experienced recent violence. The present data clearly demonstrate that victims with tertiary education and employed in high status positions are no less susceptible to recent violence than their less-educated, possibly unemployed counterparts.

DISCUSSION AND CONCLUSIONS

The results of this study have shown that violence against women in the private domain is remarkably similar across international samples. For instance, violence in Australia's capital city is clearly not confined to any particular sociodemographic grouping, but is distributed throughout the community. Similarly, the type and frequency of violence experienced is comparable with overseas findings from other studies.

With respect to the termination of the abusive relationship, it was found in this sample that several factors were critical: the occurrence of physical violence, marital status, and the active seeking of intervention from legal or medical agencies. One issue that emerged as especially important was the degree to which victims sought intervention and the response which they received. Future research needs to examine whether these factors are crucial in a different sample. Because the role of intervention agencies appears to be pivotal (Borkowski, Murch, & Walker, 1983), victims' attitudes toward such services could be assessed in more detail. Correspondingly, the attitude of the service providers themselves could be further explored.

Despite the empirical relationships demonstrated in the present study, leaving a violent situation is, nevertheless, complex. For instance, many women described a process of accommodating to the violence, despite the serious and long-term consequences of maintaining such a relationship. Attempts to endure the violence may incur both physical and psychological injury on the part of the victim; resolving to terminate the relationship also poses extraordinary difficulties. Statements by some of the women attested to the dilemma: "I wish people would realize that the pain does not end on parting. Even now, I have nightmares. I am afraid of the dark. I know I have low self-esteem."

BIBLIOGRAPHY

Berk, S. F., & Loseke, D. R. (1981). Handling family violence: Situational determinants of police arrest in domestic disturbances. *Law and Society Review, 15,* 351–364.

Black, D. (1984). Crime as a social control. In D. Black (Ed.), *Toward a general theory of social control* (pp. 1–27). Orlando, FL: Academic Press.

Borkowski, M., Murch, M., & Walker, V. (1983). *Marital violence.* London: Tavistock.

Cannings, D. M. (1984). Myths and stereotypes—Obstacles to effective police intervention in domestic disputes involving a battered woman. *The Police Journal, 57*(1), 43–56.

Davidson, T. (1978). *Conjugal crime—Understanding and changing the wifebeating patterns.* New York: Hawthorn.

Dobash, R. E., & Dobash, R. P. (1979). *Violence against wives: A case against the patriarchy.* New York: Free Press.

Dobash, R. E., & Dobash, R. P. (1984). The nature and antecedents of violent events. *British Journal of Criminology, 24*(3), 269–288.

Ellis, J. W. (1984). Prosecutorial discretion to charge in cases of spousal assault: A dialogue. *Journal of Criminal Law and Criminology, 75*(1), 56–102.

Ferraro, K. J. (1983). Rationalising violence: How battered women stay. *Victimology, 8*(3–4), 203–212.

Field, M. A., & Field, H. F. (1973). Marital violence and the criminal process: Neither justice nor peace. *Social Service Review, 47*(2), 221–240.

Gelles, R. J. (1972). *The violent home—A study of physical aggression between husbands and wives.* Beverly Hills: Sage.

Goldberg, W. G., & Tomlanovich, M. C. (1984). Domestic violence victims in the emergency department. *Journal of the American Medical Association, 251*(24), 3259–3264.

Hatty, S., & Knight, R. (1985). Capital punishment: The privatisation of violence against women in Canberra. Australian Law Reform Commission. Domestic Violence Reference Research Paper. In press.

Healy, J. (1984). *After the refuge: A study of battered wives in Adelaide.* Adelaide: Department for Community Welfare.

Hilberman, E. (1980). Overview: The "wife-beater's wife" reconsidered. *American Journal of Psychiatry, 137,* 1336–1347.

Hofeller, K. H. (1982). *Social, psychological, and situational factors in wife abuse.* California: R. and E. Research Associates.

Hughes, H. M., & Barad, S. J. (1982). Changes in the psychological functioning of children in a battered women's shelter: A pilot study. *Victimology,* (1–4), 60–68.

Johnson, V. (1981). *The last resort: A women's refuge.* Ringwood: Victoria.

Kalmuss, D. S., & Straus, M. A. (1982). Wife's marital dependency and wife abuse. *Journal of Marriage and the Family, 44,* 277–286.

Leidig, M. W. (1981). Violence against women: A feminist-psychological analysis. In S. Cox (Ed.), *Female psychology: The emerging self* (pp. 190–205). New York: St. Martin's.

Loseke, D. R., & Berk, S. F. (1982). The work of shelters: Battered women and initial calls for help. *Victimology, 7*(1–4), 35–48.

Martin, D. (1979). What keeps a woman captive in a violent relationship? The social context of battering. In D. M. Moore (Ed.), *Battered women* (pp. 33–58). Beverly Hills: Sage.

O'Donnell, C., & Craney, J. (Eds.). (1982). *Family violence in Australia.* Melbourne: Longman Cheshire.

Pagelow, M. D. (1981). Factors affecting women's decisions to leave violent relationships. *Journal of Family Issues, 4,* 391–415.

Parker, E., & Schumaker, D. (1977). The battered wife syndrome and violence in the nuclear family of origin: A controlled pilot study. *American Journal of Public Health, 67,* 760–761.

Parnas, R. E. (1967). The police response to the domestic disturbance. *Wisconsin Law Review,* (4), 914–960.

Parnas, R. I. (1971). Police discretion and diversion of incidents of intrafamilial violence. *Law and Contemporary Problems, 36*(4), 539–565.

Straus, M. A., Gelles, R. J., & Steinmetz, S. K. (1980). *Behind closed doors: Violence in the American family.* New York: Doubleday.

Stube, M. J., & Barbour, L. S. (1983). The decision to leave an abusive relationship: Economic dependence and psychological commitment. *Journal of Marriage and the Family, 45*(4), 785–793.

Thorman, G. (1980). *Family violence.* Springfield, IL: Charles C Thomas.

Walker, L. E. (1983). Victimology and the psychological perspectives of battered women. *Victimology, 8*(1–2), 82–104.

21

Dowry and Women's Status: A Study of Court Cases in Dhaka and Delhi

Ishrat Shamim
University of Dhaka

INTRODUCTION

This chapter analyzes the dynamics of the dowry phenomenon in India and Bangladesh and its negative impact on women's position and status in the marital household. It identifies the various social and economic forces that have given shape and strengthened the demand element of dowry in contemporary Bangladesh and India. It presents a brief account of women's status in those patriarchical societies, of legal measures introduced by the government to control this phenomenon, and of some court cases of women victims. The chapter also aims at developing a specific perspective and providing a better understanding of dowry as a social compulsion in the two countries.

The subordinate position of women in society is a worldwide phenomenon. Sex discrimination starts soon after birth because the differences, both physically and stereotypically, between male and female, are clearly demarcated and practiced. Diverse cultural factors do support and encourage accentuating sex differences and discrimination. However, physiological differences are exaggerated in a patriarchal and unequal society like ours, in which husbands literally own the women.

Bangladesh and India are the world's most densely populated countries where most women play traditional roles. Traditional values, both societal and religious, have limited women's access to certain types of employment, educational attainment, and health services, thus inhibiting them from obtaining greater prominence in social and political life. Poverty, illiteracy, purdah, religious sanctions, taboos, and lack of earning opportunities have forced women to be trapped and depend on the male members of their family. Dependence breeds subordination and a vulnerable position that is further reinforced by the patriarchal and patrilineal kinship system. Before marriage, a woman is dependent on her parents; after marriage on her husband; in separation, divorce, or widowhood, she is dependent again on her parents, brothers, or her

Ishrat Shamim is an associate professor in the Department of Sociology of the University of Dhaka, Bangladesh. She has researched and written extensively on women's issues, giving particular attention to trafficking of Asian women, prostitution, sexual exploitation, and reproductive rights. She has also done fieldwork for UNICEF, and is currently working on environmental issues.

children. Her status is, therefore, one of subordination. She never gains economic security and independence.

The status of women can be described in terms of the level of women's income, employment, education, health, and fertility, as well as of the roles they play within the family, community, and society. What women do—their work in agriculture or industrial production, government, administration or affairs of state, their contribution to the family income, household maintenance, community organization, and development and their roles in the bearing and rearing of children in family functioning—contributes to their status and position in society. Women's status in a traditional social structure may be conceptualized as a hybrid, "multifaceted construct" whereby status is not only related to the rights and duties exercised by a woman, but also to the degree of her subordination at home, her education, the number of sons she has, and her role in decisionmaking (Chaudhury & Ahmed, 1980).

A woman is assigned the role to be performed within the household. As a wife, she has to serve and obey her husband; as a mother, she has to bear and rear the children. These various roles ultimately determine her position and status in the family, which is never equal to that of the male household head. The domination of men over women, the power structure that is socially accepted, is extended in the control of the father over the daughter, the husband over the wife, and the son over the mother in her old age. Within the family, there exists a hierarchical relationship between husband and wife—the husband as the authority figure and the wife as the obedient subordinate. This repressed and oppressed position of women is further reinforced by norms, customs, and religious beliefs that invariably uphold male domination, male control, and aggression to be the "daily normal" behavior of the figurehead, whether it is the father, husband, or son.

The family is the cornerstone of the patriarchal society. Patriarchy has two elements: structure and ideology. The structure aspect becomes manifest in the nature of the hierarchical organization of social relations, while the ideology ensures that internal controls regulate the complaints of the subordinates. When the ideology legitimizes the order, it is met with acceptance rather than rejection, and with compliance rather than defiance (Dobash & Dobash, 1979).

Thus, violence is inherent in the patriarchal family's structure that institutionalizes power and gender relations. It has been said that women's vulnerability and their victim-prone role within the family are mostly contributed by the female reproductive role. The extension of women as child-bearers to women as child-rearers is the heart of female-defined work (United Nations, 1985). In the traditional society of Bangladesh, an infertile woman is looked down on and believed to bring misfortune to her husband's household. A woman's social position becomes secured only after bearing a male child (Shamim, 1986).

The sociocultural heritage reflecting the dominant ethos and attitudes may be responsible for the multiple social disadvantages of women. These are again aggravated in the transitional socioeconomic system of ours where inequality is rampant. Usually, a woman is considered to be a "commodity" that is to be disposed of by her parents as early as possible after she attains puberty. She is to be possessed, transferred from one man (father) to another (husband), and a liability to be looked after. Without "accompanying assets," that is a dowry, she usually does not have much value. The phenomenon of dowry reveals the inferior status and position of women in a patriarchal societal with patrilocal residence. The daughter in marriage becomes a mere object to be given away by her parents to another family. After marriage, her life is no longer her parents' responsibility. The social norms and values compel her to adjust to the new mode of life in her in-laws' household. The social milieu thus aids and perpetuates the oppression and violation of social behavior, which is the result of unjust dowry demands.

The practice of dowry has to be looked at in the context of marriage. A set of values connected with marriage appears to have aided dowry to assume its present form. Marriage is universal, as is the custom of giving presents at the time of marriage. Parents give material goods to their daughters because they believe that this will contribute toward safeguarding their daughters' interests and enhance their status and position in their husbands' households. But when parents are compelled by others to provide and fulfill demands for cash or kind beyond their capacity, then the harmful effects of such a system become evident. Thus, the dowry reveals the inferior status and position of women in a patriarchal society with patrilocal residence. Marriage among the Muslims of Bangladesh is not a sacrament, but a civil contract between the parties that can be subject to dissolution for good cause. One of the essential part of Muslim marriage is "mehr" or dower paid or promised to be paid by the husband to the wife. Dower is the sum of money or other property that the wife is entitled to receive from the husband in consideration of marriage.

In India, among the Hindus, marriage is said to be the only religious sacrament for a woman. It is the underlying spirit of Hinduism, unlike in Islam, which creates an indissoluble tie between the husband and the wife. It is thought inauspicious for a woman to be or remain unmarried. In modern times, the most prevalent is the Brahma form of marriage, which is known as *kanyadan*, or gift of the virgin daughter form of hypergamous marriage. At one time it was followed by the ritual of *varadakshina*, the nominal token payment decided unilaterally by the bride's father according to his financial position. Presently, the groom or the groom's kin demand *varadakshina* by right. Thus, it takes the form of dowry. The *kanyadan* marriage is between two asymmetrical kin groups and is fundamentally a product of the development of private property, along with a new Brahmanic ideology to strengthen the patriarchal social order. Thus *stridhan* (marriage wealth of a woman) became a vital aspect of marriage. A woman's *stridhan* gifted to her at the time of marriage by her father was considered as a "part of the sacred cultural concept of *kanyadan* marriage" (Khare, 1970) and was given by her parents and other kin to provide her the economic security for any eventuality in her life. In its present form, dowry has become a perversion of this traditional custom of *stridhan*, which was essentially deemed as postmortem inheritance. Furthermore, the woman has no control over her own wealth, which is the manifestation of a lower status of woman in modern society.

A woman has been viewed solely in terms of male-related roles like daughter, wife, mother, and widow with corresponding duties and obligations to her husband, as well as his kin. While the Muslim law has made provision for "mehr," the societal system has made the provision of dowry. Dowry demands from the bridegroom's side is a custom not included in religious ideology of Islam and is obviously borrowed from non-Muslim traditions.

To summarize, dowry usually refers to the property that a woman receives from her parents and other kin as a part of her marriage settlement. Although dowry connotes the wealth in cash or kind given to the daughter at the time of marriage, in recent times, its focus is on the gifts in kind and cash transferred to the bridegroom and his kin not only at the time of marriage, but also perpetuated after the wedding ceremony. An implicit and explicit element of coercion has gradually crept into the social transaction of dowry. It is becoming a "social evil" for parents who cannot afford to comply with the social compulsion. The daughter in marriage becomes a mere "object" to be given away by the parents to her affinial household after wedding rites.

METHOD

The present study analyzes the dynamics of the dowry phenomenon and its negative impact on the woman's position and status in her marital household. Its objective is to identify the various social and economic forces that have given shape and strengthened the demand element of dowry and to correlate these forces that have helped to sustain and augment the phenomenon in contemporary Bangladesh and Indian societies in general, and in the cities in particular. The purpose of this chapter is to present a brief account of women's status and patriarchy and of the legal measures initiated by the government, followed by court cases of women victimized by the evil effects of the dowry system. It is also meant to develop a specific perspective and to provide a better understanding and analysis of dowry as a social compulsion in the highly urbanized social milieu of the two countries.

The comparative study of the dowry phenomenon is urban based. Two metropolitan cities, Dhaka and Delhi, capital cities of Bangladesh and India respectively, were selected for the study, which attempts to understand and analyze the following:

- Concept of dowry;
- Size, content, and form of payment of dowry;
- When demand for dowry was made, whether at the time of marriage or after marriage;
- Mode of mental and physical harassment, its extent, and severity due to nonfulfillment of dowry demands;
- Legislative provisions and measures taken against dowry and other related exploitation of women; and,
- Nature of the social support system to assist and support those who are living under such pressures and oppression.

For an in-depth study on the incidents that followed due to payment, partial payment, or nonpayment of dowry, ten cases were selected from the Family Courts of Dhaka and ten from the trial courts of Delhi. Court proceedings were recorded to reveal the gaps in the legal system itself and to focus on the implementation of the Dowry Prohibition Acts of the two countries. Also, some 200 dowry cases covered in the press and information collected by non-governmental organizations (NGO's) working for women and development were used.

LEGAL PROVISIONS AND GOVERNMENT MEASURES RELATED TO DOWRY

Dowry as a social phenomenon has aroused much public concern in contemporary Bangladesh and India, especially due to its compulsions and harmful effects. Efforts have begun at the governmental level and by others in society to eradicate this system. The Dowry Prohibition Act 1961 of India and subsequently the Dowry Prohibition Act 1980 of Bangladesh were steps in this direction.

In India, the Dowry Prohibition Act was passed in 1961 to "prohibit the giving and taking of dowry." However, it has become increasingly apparent that the act has failed to check the practice of dowry and the related crimes. The reported cases of "dowry victims" have more than doubled during the last few years in India. Dowry victims are married women who are victims of violence, including killing, because of the nonfulfillment of dowry promised by the parents of the bride. Such breach of promise may be real, perceived, or contrived by her husband and in-laws. Reported cases of dowry victims increased from 68 in 1984, to 146 in 1985, and to 172 in 1986 (Indian Express, 1987).

During the last ten years, female activists and politicians have urged the government of Bangladesh to take up the issue of violence against women seriously and to take necessary steps toward its redress. Bangladesh Mohila Parishad, a leading nongovernment organization of female activists, has continuously put pressure to bring about far-reaching changes in the existing legal system. In June 1980, they organized an anti-dowry campaign that collected signatures from 17,000 women. The same year, the Dowry Prohibition Act of 1980, prohibiting the taking or giving of dowry in marriages, was enacted. In 1983, the Cruelty to Women (Deterrent Punishment) Ordinance was promulgated by the government of Bangladesh to provide for deterrent punishment for all types of cruelty to women and for matters connected therewith. Section 6 of the Ordinance states the penalty for causing death or grievous injuries for dowry (Government of Bangladesh, 1983). The most recent measure was setting up the Family Courts. The Family Court Ordinance of 1985 was enacted to deal with matters related to dissolution of marriage, restitution of conjugal rights, dowry, maintenance, guardianship, and custody of children.

Apart from the laws to deal with dowry atrocities, the Delhi Police headquarters in India has a "crime against women" unit. They help female victims of dowry related crimes. The squad is performing its role commendably by counseling through a reconciliation-cum-guidance program. Similarly in Bangladesh, due to the increasing incidence of cases being reported to the Department of Women's Affairs in Dhaka, a step has been taken by the ministry to set up a legal aid unit. It started functioning in March 1986. Mostly, it provides legal counseling in cases of violence against women and other family related matters. It acts more as a counseling unit, giving advice to the victims about what to do and where to seek redress, rather than as a litigator of their cases in the Family Courts.

DOWRY CASE STUDIES IN DHAKA

The case studies show that almost all those women in Dhaka became victims of mental and physical torture, including murder, on account of dowry. Most of them could not bear the tortures and had to leave their marital homes to rely and depend on their parents for shelter and support. Those who have appealed to the Family Courts of Dhaka are mostly housewives, illiterate and without any means of livelihood. Two such cases are given here to reveal the distressed condition of these women.

Nilufer Begum's marriage was solemnized when she was 18 years of age, and "mehr" or dowry money was fixed at Taka 20,001, a good deal of money, of which half was prompt dowry to be paid during the marriage ceremony. Her monthly living allowance was assessed at Taka 1,000 per month, according to the present living standards. In December 1982, after more than a year and a half of married life, the husband started demanding money. Moklesur, the husband, indulged both in wine and women. He started torturing Nilufer both mentally and physically to extract money from her father. As a result, she requested her father to give some money as a loan. Nilufer's father, seeing the situation of his daughter, gave Taka 10,000 and a cassette recorder worth another Taka 7,000 as dowry, which was later sold by the son-in-law. In addition, he gave Taka 30,000 as a loan to be repaid. However, the son-in-law never repaid the money.

On the first of December 1985, Moklesur, along with his friend, came home at about midnight, after drinking heavily. They both raped the maid servant Rashida, who subsequently told Nilufer about the incident. Rashida complained to the police and until now the case is pending for trial under the Cruelty to Women (Deterrent Punishment) Ordinance of 1983. When Nilufer protested against the inhumane and intolerable behavior of her husband, she was severely assaulted and forcibly driven out of the house, along with her minor sons, on the same day. From that time on, she had been staying at her father's house with her children. On March 27, 1986, she filed a suit at the Family Court. The suit was for the recovery of the "mehr" money, maintenance for herself and her sons, guardianship and custody of the children, and restitution of conjugal rights. Nilufer not only filed suit against her husband, but also against his brothers and others who were equally responsible for such unjust demands and mistreatment. Salma, who was known to be the mistress of Nilufer's husband and had maintained an illicit relationship with him, was also one of the accused. Three months after the suit, which amounted to Taka 68,001, was filed, the Family Court started issuing summonses to both parties to appear for a hearing. Nine such summonses were issued but no one ever appeared before the court, nor was any cause given for the nonappearance of the parties concerned. The judge dismissed the case for default on November 26, 1986 (The Family Court, 1986a).

Sayeda's marriage was arranged by her parents. After marriage, her husband Safi Mia stayed in his in-law's house, without having to bear household expenses. According to the marriage contract, Taka 30,001 was fixed as "mehr," half of which was prompt dowry. Safi earned his livelihood by doing different types of odd jobs and earned about Taka 2,000 per month. Although he stayed with his in-laws, he still demanded dowry in kind, namely a cassette player and a wristwatch. Claiming that his demands were not met, he abandoned his wife for a period of eight months. At first, Sayeda issued a legal notice as a warning to her husband. But the notice did not serve any purpose because her husband remained indifferent. On such grounds, she filed a suit with the Family Court, valued at Taka 21,400 on January 28, 1986, which included her prompt dowry and maintenance. During the three-month trial, Sayeda appeared only once. Afterwards she did not take steps to contest the case. The court issued seven summonses but all were in vain. The suit was dismissed for default (The Family Court, 1986b).

DOWRY CASE STUDIES IN DELHI

The case studies of Delhi show similar patterns. They are mostly housewives who filed divorce petitions because living with their husbands was intolerable. Some of them were working women. Still, they faced ill treatment by their husbands and in-laws due to dowry. For example, it was through a newspaper advertisement that

Usha's marriage was arranged. She was highly educated and worked in a government organization at Dehradun as a scientific assistant. Before marriage, her husband Ramesh claimed to be an engineer in the merchant navy in Bombay. But after the wedding it was found that he had only studied up to the intermediate level and that he was working as a fitter in Bombay. During the marriage, her parents gave a very large amount, Rs 50,000 in cash and kind, as dowry to the groom's parents. It was agreed before marriage that she should leave her job and stay with her in-laws in Delhi, even though her husband would continue working in Bombay. However, she continued working in Dehradun and living with her parents. She used to visit her in-laws every now and then, whenever she got leave. She used to give her monthly salary to her mother-in-law after keeping a part of it for her personal expenses. Problems started when she learned that her husband was a fitter and not an engineer. Then she stopped giving money to her mother-in-law. The in-laws further demanded a refrigerator, a television, and other household items. They started abusing her physically when their demands were not met.

Finally, after one and a half years of marriage, on July 25, 1981, she complained to her parents about all that happened. On October 27 of the same year, she was practically thrown out from the in-law's house while she was visiting them. Since then, she had been living with her parents. She wanted to get back the dowry with the help of the police and live a separate life of her own. All of this was kept secret by her parents because of the social stigma and their desire to protect the reputation of the family. Later she learned that her husband had remarried. With adequate police help, she did retrieve all her dowry items and filed a divorce suit on the ground of cruelty. The court decreed her divorce in 1983 (Session Court, 1982).

Geetha belonged to a poor family. Her mother earned her livelihood by working as a maid. Geetha's marriage was arranged by her mother at the age of 18, with a tailor who also was illiterate. Before marriage, she used to make envelopes to supplement her mother's income. After the marriage, her husband became unemployed due to ill health. Her father-in-law, who earned Rs 2,000 per month, gave them financial support. During the marriage, Geetha's mother gave a large amount, Rs 25,000, as dowry to the groom's family. She had arranged this money by taking loans from others and from her personal savings. A month after the marriage had taken place, there was a further demand of dowry by her husband and in-laws. They demanded a bicycle, a gold chain, and Rs 5,000 in cash in order to renovate their house. Her husband, who was an alcoholic, occasionally used pressure to obtain money to meet his needs. But Geetha was in no position to bring any more dowry, as her mother was very poor and still had two more unmarried daughters. As a consequence, she was abused and battered physically. Her in-laws even attempted to burn her by pouring kerosene on her body. Initially, her mother told her to bear the physical torture and be patient. She felt insulted and helpless as her in-laws made every attempt to force her to bring more dowry money. On the night of March 12, 1985, her husband and in-laws beat her severely and attempted to kill her. However, she managed to escape and went back to her mother's house. She left behind everything in her marital home and since then has lived with her mother. In June 1985, she filed suit in the Session Court for dissolution of marriage and for the recovery of dowry amounting to Rs 25,000 in cash and kind. Her husband did not appear in court. In the end, after issuing a dozen summonses, the court gave the ex-parte decree that the marital ties be dissolved (Session Court, 1985).

Case studies have clearly demonstrated that the courts are not very effective in bringing about a just solution. However well-formulated and defensive the laws may be, it must be recognized that there is overwhelming resistance to their implementation in the courts. Dowry related cases that occur in the home, and particularly between husband and wife, are seen as lesser offenses. It is even more so when the victim is a woman, while the lawyers and judges are mostly men.

SOCIOECONOMIC DIMENSIONS OF THE PROBLEM

The problem of dowry giving and taking has other dimensions that are socioeconomical. When marriages are arranged, it is not just the groom's family who makes sure that the bride's family is well-to-do and well-connected so that they can give their daughter a large sum of money. The bride's family too judges the future son-in-law by his education, job, income, future prospects, and social status. Thus, we find large amounts of "mehr" or dower money in case of Muslim marriages paid by the bride's parents to act as a measure of the social status of both the bride's and groom's families as well as for the economic security of the bride. In addition, there is a belief that higher dower will prevent the husband from divorcing his wife. Still we find cases like Asma, Mahmuda, and Hasina, all of whose "mehr" money exceeded Taka 50,000, which is quite a large amount. However, this hardly prevented their husbands from deserting them and ultimately divorcing them, even without paying the "mehr" as stipulated in the marriage contract.

The Family Courts of Dhaka dismiss many cases for default, mainly because the contesting parties do not appear. But why does the long-suffering wife, who has appealed for justice, not come for the hearing?

One could say that women contribute to the courts' inefficiency by not cooperating and that they undermine their only source of empowerment. Although the law and the courts may be a source of empowerment, one must also question for whom and for which class. The cases dealt with here are from the lower and lower-middle classes. These women do not have sufficient funds or influence to pursue a case. Women's organizations, however, have been successful in using the legal system to fight for justice. The women's failure to appear is sometimes also due to fear, threats, love, desire to protect the matrimonial home, family ties of children, and social prestige. Women who have no formal education or a job have to fully depend on male members of their household for the decisionmaking that affects their lives. Before marriage, they are under the guidance of their fathers or other male kin. Marriages are usually arranged and ultimately decided by male members. At marriage, this power and authority to control and make decisions affecting their lives is transferred to the husband. Thus, women are not accustomed to making decisions and taking charge of their lives.

Therefore, when they are separated from their husbands, they return back to depending economically on their parents or brothers. For them, the natal home is the only source of moral and economic support. In most cases, the parents try to reach a compromise with the son-in-law, knowing fully well that the daughter has suffered mental abuse and physical beatings for demands not being fulfilled. Disputes may be settled for the time being, like in the case of Nigar Sultana, who was sent back to her violent marital home. However, this did not solve the problem. The result was even worse, when her minor son was forcibly taken away from her and she was driven out of the house by her husband. Again, Nigar had to return to her parents' house for food and shelter.

In other times, parents advise their daughters to be tolerant and patient, like in the cases of Geetha and Raj Rani. But even they could not stay for long in their violent marital homes, and were forced to go back to their natal homes. Many women are threatened with death by the husbands and in-laws. They are often driven out, leaving behind whatever little dowry they brought from their natal home or was given them after marriage as gifts. On her return, a woman's character and conduct are closely scrutinized by parents and elders of the family. Women are perceived as victims of their own faults and blamed for what happened.

Dowry that is not demanded at the time of marriage, later becomes an issue for marital disagreements and quarrels, followed by physical violence and even death. Demands are made without any consideration for the economic conditions of the in-laws, who are not always in a position to satisfy the demands of their son-in-law (even if they try hard) and especially when the amounts demanded are extremely high. Moreover, sons-in-law sometimes stay in their in-laws' house without having to bear any expenses. Even in such situations, demands are made in cash and kind. For example, the husbands of Dewelara and Sayeda did not set up their own households, but rather stayed as long as they wished in their in-laws' house. When demands were not met, they abandoned their wives.

CONCLUSION

In every marriage, some amount of cash, jewelry, and household goods has always changed hands. To that extent, dowry is not a new practice; the difference is only in degree. Presently, there has been an enormous rise in the quantum of dowry items, and this despicable give-and-take enjoys wide social acceptance. It is more or less prevalent in all communities. There are dowry murders and other brutal forms of abuse of young wives by their in-laws, who often try to extract more money from the bride's parents and sometimes wish to arrange a second marriage for their son so as to secure a second dowry. The demands of dowry by the groom's family have increased in the past two decades both among the Hindus and the Muslims. Cases of women being burned to death have also been increasing in Delhi. In Bangladesh, many deaths of poor rural women that are being passed off as suicides or accidents are in fact murders (Akanda & Shamim, 1985).

The victims' parents are not fully ready to help their daughters once they are given away in marriage. There is a saying that once a daughter is married off, she cannot be taken back alive by her parents.

It is like the warning on a cash receipt, "goods once sold cannot be taken back." Battered or not, women dislike to come out of their dependent and protected existence and face the world. They prefer economic "security" and do not like to take risks. Moreover, employment opportunities are meager and women often do not qualify for lack of education and skills. If supported by parents and other relatives, only then may they muster enough courage to come out of their marital homes. But in our Asian societies, the conception of marriage is the "be all and end all" for women. More-over, the glorification of the image of the ideal woman drives her to suffer in silence at the feet of her husband. This has enslaved and banished her from the idea of equality. In this cultural setting and conditioning, she is unable to save herself from abuse, humiliation, and oppression. She perceives it as her fate and believes that nothing can undo it. Even after repeated tortures have been inflicted on her, she refuses to implicate her husband and her in-laws. In some ways, parents contribute in perpetuating her subordination as she is being brought up as someone else's property and has to be married off as soon as possible to the first "eligible" man.

Most parents are quite aware that their daughters are being abused, threatened, or persecuted. Many of these battered women come to their parents' homes in desperation several times before they are either killed or driven to suicide. Parents advise them to adjust and be tolerant. Most of the time, they are again sent back against their wills to be reconciled with their husbands. When a woman undergoes stress and violence in the marital home, there is a persistent demand from her parents to adjust with the in-laws, and there is no shelter. The only alternative left to her is to commit suicide. On the other hand, unable to satisfy the demand for dowry, many parents cannot get their daughters married. Unmarried daughters are considered economic liabilities and are socially despised. Thus, socioeconomic and cultural conspiracies have encouraged parents to perpetuate the dowry system to accentuate their status by subordinating women's position. Thus, unless the whole social system, along with the concept and attitudes of men, is thoroughly overhauled and a society based on socioeconomic equality of men and women is developed, the practice of dowry and its related violence against women will continue and spread in some form or another.

Some stringent legal sanctions have been enacted against dowry. However, very few culprits have ever been arrested and tried in court. The anti-dowry movement can only claim some cases of convictions for crimes resultant from dowry demands. Parents continue to pay dowry to the groom's family because the biggest loophole in the Dowry Prohibition Acts of Bangladesh and India is the vague distinction made between gifts and dowry. Another clause is that the giver and taker of dowry are equally punishable. This surely stops the father of the bride from lodging a complaint. In many cases, the daughter wants her parents to transfer valuable assets to her marital home. Even educated youth appear to perpetuate this custom.

The police are usually known for their indifferent attitude toward dowry victims. One Indian Judge remarked, "No judge can be unmindful of the kind of havoc the police can play when it comes to investigate crimes against the weak, unorganized, and backward classes." He also stated that the process of legal redress is lengthy, cumbersome, and expensive. Sometimes the justice sought is not done due to the lack of evidence (Government of India, 1982). The same is true for Bangladesh.

Very few women's organizations in Dhaka and Delhi have come forward to provide social support systems like legal aid, medical help, counseling and guidance, and programs for meeting and reconciliation between the aggravated parties. Some of them run shelter homes, but they are constantly facing economic crises.

The law as a remedial measure alone cannot be implemented properly unless society as a whole is aware of the situation. There is a need for a major change in our social values, considering that the despicable practice of dowry enjoys social acceptance and is even glorified as a status symbol.

BIBLIOGRAPHY

Akanda, L., & Shamim, I. (1985). *Women and violence: A comparative study of rural and urban violence against women in Bangladesh*. Dhaka: Women for Women.

Chaudhury, R. H., & Ahmed, N. R. (1980). *Female status in Bangladesh*. Dhaka: Institute of Development Studies.

Dobash, R. E., & Dobash, R. P. (1979). Love, honor and obey: Institutional ideologies and the struggle for battered women. *Women's International Network News, 5*(4).

Family Court. (1986a). Nilufer Begum v. Md. Moklesur Dahman and others. F.T.S. No. 10. Dhaka.

Family Court. (1986b). Sayeda Khatoon v. Md. Safi Mia. M.S. No. 5. Dhaka.
Government of India. (1982). Report of the Joint Committee of the Houses to Examine the Question of Dowry Prohibition Act of 1961. New Delhi.
Government of Bangladesh. (1983). The Cruelty to Women (Deterrent Punishment) Ordinance No. IX of 1984. Dhaka.
Indian Express. (1987, May 24). New Delhi.
Khare, R. S. (1970). *The changing Brahmans*. Chicago: University of Chicago Press.
Session Court. (1982). Usha Rani Choudhury v. Sekhar Choudhury. M.S. No. 57. New Delhi.
Session Court. (1985). Geetha Rani v. Mohan Ram. C.S. No. 29. New Delhi.
Shamim, I. (1986). Cultural tradition and women's position in Bangladesh. *Bangladesh Sociological Review, 1,* 137–147.
United Nations. (1985). Seventh United Nations Congress on the Prevention of Crime and the Treatment of Offenders. New York: United Nations.

22

Epidemiological Survey of Spousal Abuse in Korea

Kwang-iel Kim
Youn-gyu Cho
School of Medicine, Hanyang University, Seoul, Korea

INTRODUCTION

This chapter presents nationwide epidemiological findings of spousal violence in Korea. Samples were selected by the three-stage stratified random sampling. Among available samples, there were 1,316 persons who had lived a married life at least for the last two years. By face-to-face interview, respondents were asked whether they had any experience of being battered by their spouses for the last year. If they stated to have experience, they were asked to rate the severity according to Straus's Conflict Resolution Technique Scale. In spite of stereotypes, experience rates of spousal violence are definitely high. The overall experience rate of being battered by spouses was 30.9%: 37.5% in women and 23.2% in men. Experience rate of being seriously battered was 8.4%: 12.4% in women and 3.7% in men. The rate was higher in the lower social strata and in the younger couples.

Epidemiological survey of spousal violence is prerequisite for understanding the nature of the problem and for providing a relevant plan for management and prevention. The epidemiological finding, however, is scarcely documented in literature as far as spousal violence is concerned, presumably due to considerable difficulties in assessment of violent behavior, lack of objective criteria such as severity and frequency, and respondents' tendency to conceal the fact.

In Korea, several epidemiological surveys of wife battering were carried out (Korea Gallup Survey Polls, 1983; Sohn, 1983; Kim, 1985; Shim, 1988). But these surveys are insufficient because of a small sample size and lack of sophisticated criteria. Thus, the authors carried out a nationwide epidemiological survey of wife battering and husband battering.

An earlier version of this chapter received the First Prize of the Wyeth-Ayerst Award for Distinction in Psychiatry, conferred at the VIII World Congress of Psychiatry, Athens, Greece, October, 1989.

Kwang-iel Kim, M.D., Ph.D., is professor and chairperson in the Department of Neuropsychiatry, School of Medicine and the Mental Health Research Institute, Hanyang University, Seoul, Korea.

Youn-gyu Cho, M.D., is a senior student in the Ph.D. course, Department of Neuropsychiatry, The Graduate School, Hanyang University, Seoul, Korea.

METHOD

The available sample size was 1,316 persons (707 women and 609 men) who had lived a married life at least for two years. The sample was selected by the three-stage stratified sampling over the whole country. Sample error is 2.7%. Thirty professional interviewers were trained for two days for this survey. The survey was done by face-to-face interview using questionnaire form.

Each respondent was asked, "During the last year, have you had any experience of being battered by your spouse?" If the subjects stated to have experience, they were asked to rate the severity of being battered according to Straus's Conflict Resolution Technique Scale (Straus, 1974). For proving the interviewers' reliability, 10% of the sample were interviewed again by two other interviewers. This survey was done during the period of March 17–21, 1989.

Demographic data of the sample are found in Table 22-1.

Table 22-1 Demographic data of the sample (total sample, 1,316 cases, 100.0%)

Characteristics	Case	Percent
Sex		
Female	707	53.7
Male	609	46.3
Age		
Twenties	167	12.7
Thirties	427	32.5
Fourties	339	25.8
Fifties and over	382	29.0
Education		
Elementary	435	33.1
Middle	327	24.9
High	403	30.6
College and above	150	11.4
Occupation		
Farmer/fisherman	253	19.2
Self-supporting*	176	13.4
Blue collar	156	11.8
White collar	162	12.3
Housewife	505	38.4
Student	2	0.2
Unemployed or other	62	4.7
Urban-rural		
Big urban	539	44.0
Middle and small urban	290	22.0
Rural	487	37.0
Economic level**		
Upper	357	27.1
Middle	534	40.6
Lower	424	32.3

*Merchant, small factory owner, and so on.
**Higher income, US $800 and above; Middle, US $450-799; Lower, US $449 and under. These figures represent monthly disposable income, excluding savings.

Table 22-2   Spousal violence rates

| | Incidence rate | | |
CTR violence item[a]	Total	Wife	Husband
Experience rate of being seriously battered (N to R)	8.4	12.4	3.7
Overall experience rate of being battered (K to R)	30.9	37.5	23.2
K. Threw something at spouse	19.8	24.9	13.9
L. Pushed, grabbed, shoved spouse	19.2	22.7	15.3
M. Slapped spouse	13.5	19.0	7.2
N. Kicked, bit, or hit with fist	6.1	9.0	2.8
O. Hit or tried to hit with something	4.7	7.2	1.7
P. Beat up spouse	2.9	4.2	1.3
Q. Threatened with a knife or gun	0.5	0.7	0.3
R. Used a knife or gun	0.3	0.5	0.2

[a]Straus's Conflict Resolution Technique Scale (1974).

RESULTS

Overall experience rate of being battered (K to R in CRT) for the last year was 30.9%: 37.5% in women and 23.2% in men. The experience rate of being seriously battered (N to R in CRT) was 8.4%: 12.4% in women and 3.7% in men. Both rates were significantly higher in women (Table 22-2). Rate of the seriously battered to the overall experience rate was 33.1% in women and 16.0% in men.

Both the overall experience rate and the rate of being battered seriously were higher in the younger persons (twenties) and lower in the elderly (fifties) (Table 22-3). The overall experience rate was higher in the lower economic strata and lower in the higher strata. But the experience rate of being seriously battered revealed no significant difference among the economic strata (Table 22-4). In the college graduated group, there is a tendency of a low experience rate of being battered seriously (Table 22-5).

No significant difference of experience rate of being battered, mildly or seriously, could be evaluated in other demographic factors such as occupational status and geographical distribution.

DISCUSSION

This survey of spousal violence is the first nationwide epidemiological study in Korea. However, there are several weak points. The frequency of violence could not be surveyed because of respondents' difficulty to recall the correct frequency of episodes. And causes of violence were not inquired because of poor objectiveness in response.

The first problem to be discussed is the experience rate of spousal violence in this finding. In Korea, only the wives' experience rates of being battered are available among the previous data. The rates, since their marriage, were 42% in Seoul and Suwon (Shim, 1988), 49% in the slum area of Seoul (Sohn, 1983), and 61% over the country (Korea Gallup Survey Polls, 1983). But these data are not applicable for

Table 22-3 Spousal violence rates by age groups

Experience rates (%)	Twenties	Thirties	Fourties	Fifties & over
Overall experience rate of being battered (K to R*)	43.8	30.2	33.7	23.3
Experience rate of being seriously battered (N to R*)	13.4	7.5	10.4	5.4

*Straus's Conflict Resolution Technique Scale (1974).

comparison with our finding because these data were collected from life experience "since their marriage," whereas ours from the experience of "the last one year." Only one finding that 14% of 708 wives had been battered by their husbands for the last year (Shim, 1988) is available for direct comparison. The wives' one-year experience rate of being battered was 37.5% in our study, which is definitely higher than 14% in Shim's report (1988). This discrepancy can be attributed to the different methods of survey. Shim's survey was conducted by distributing a questionnaire to easily available persons in the two cities, Seoul and Suwon, without statistical controls such as strategy in sampling and proving respondents' reliability. Our survey was conducted with a face-to-face interview after three-stage stratified sampling over the country was selected for minimizing concealed response and uneven distribution of the sample. It was followed by a 10% re-interview for proving interviewers' reliability. Furthermore, we carried out the same survey again five months later. The results were similar.

In comparison with American findings (Straus, 1977), Korean findings manifested in this survey revealed an apparently higher experience rate of spousal violence. This comparison is appropriate because both surveys used the same methodology. In America, the overall experience rate of being battered for the last year was 11.6% in wives and 12.1% in husbands, whereas in Korea it was 37.5% in wives and 23.2% in husbands. The wives' experience rate of being seriously battered was 4.6% in America and 12.4% in Korea. The husband's experience rate of being seriously battered was similar in both countries: 3.8% in America and 3.7% in Korea.

Reasons for the higher rate of spousal violence in Korea have been suggested. Family's cohesion and excessive attachment to blood-relatedness, patriarchical headship and dominance of men over women, public prejudice toward divorce, public ignorance and toleration of spousal violence, and lack of legal support and commu-

Table 22-4 Spousal violence rates by economic status

Experience rates (%)	Upper[a]	Middle[a]	Lower[a]
Overall experience rate of being battered (K to R[b])	26.3	32.1	33.2
Experience rate of being seriously battered (N to R[b])	8.4	7.8	9.2

[a]Higher income, US $800 and above; Middle, US $450-799; Lower, US $449 and under. These figures represent monthly disposable income, excluding savings.
[b]Straus's Conflict Resolution Technique Scale (1974).

Table 22-5 Spousal violence rates by education levels

Experience rates (%)	Elementary	Middle	High	College
Overall experience rate of being battered (K to R[a])	28.6	38.1	28.8	27.5
Experience rate of being seriously battered (N to R[a])	8.8	11.9	7.0	3.3

[a]Straus's Conflict Resolution Technique Scale (1974).

nity networks can be considered factors facilitating domestic violence in Korea (Kim & Kim, 1985; Kim, 1990).

Another interesting finding that arose from this study is the husbands' high experience rate of being battered by their wives, in spite of the stereotype that the victims of family violence are the wife and the child. American findings also show this (Straus, 1977). It seems to be important to reevaluate whether the wives' violent behavior toward their husbands really exists at such a high rate, or the husband's overreporting has influenced the high rate. One clinical report showed that 18% of mothers of wife-beaters battered their husbands (Kim, 1987). But further clarification would be necessary to understand the nature of this finding.

Also to be discussed is the demographic difference in the rate of spousal violence. In Korea, wife battering was reported to be more prevalent in the lower social strata such as lower-income groups and unskilled workers; affecting spouses from economically poorer families with unbalanced and unequal power between parents; and spouses that had a marked discrepancy in educational levels and a shorter duration of dating before marriage (Kim, 1985).

There is considerable agreement that the most violent wives and husbands come from violent and broken families (Rounsaville, 1978). Spousal violence occurs in almost any social class (Pizzey, 1974; Dobash & Dobash, 1979). But most Korean epidemiological findings, including this report, support the fact that family violence such as spousal battering and child abuse are more prevalent in the lower social strata (Kim, 1985; Kim & Ko, 1990). In this study, it was noticed that younger couples are more violent and elderly couples are less violent. It is uncertain whether violent couples become less violent by aging or the younger generation is simply more violent than the older generation. Hopefully, this question will be resolved in future studies.

BIBLIOGRAPHY

Dobash, E., & Dobash, R. (1978). Wives: The "appropriate" victims of marital violence. *Victimology, 2*, 426–442.

Kim, J. O. (1985). A study on the conflict resolution techniques of urban spouses: On the basis of conjugal violence behavior. *Journal of Family Study* (Seoul), *23*(2), 91–101.

Kim, K. C., & Kim, K. I. (1985). Korean attitude toward wife beating. *Mental Health Research* (Seoul) *6*, 218–234.

Kim, K. I. (1987). Seventy battered wives in Korea: Clinical manifestations and problems in Korea. *International Journal of Family Psychiatry, 8*, 387–416.

Kim, K. I. (1990). Spousal violence in Korea: Present status and problem. *Mental Health Research* (Seoul), *9*, 121–130.

Kim, K. I., & Ko, B. J. (1990). An incidence survey of battered child in the two elementary schools of Seoul. *Child Abuse & Neglect, 14*, 273–276.

Korea Gallup Survey Polls. (1983). Family life and child rearing in Korea. Seoul: Korea Gallup Survey Polls.

Pizzey, E. (1974). *Scream quietly or the neighbours will hear.* London: If Books.

Rounsaville, B. J. (1978). Theories of marital violence: Evidence from a study of battered women. *Victimology, 3,* 11–31.

Shim, J. K. (1988). Family violence and aggression. In K. I. Kim (Ed.), *Family violence: The fact and management* (pp. 67–98). Seoul: Tamgudang.

Sohn, D. S. (1983). Women abuse in a slum area. In Korean Christian Academy for the Social Issues (Ed.), *Deprived women in Korea* (pp. 48–65). Seoul: Minjungsa.

Straus, M. A. (1974). Levelty, civility, and violence in the family. *Journal of Marriage and the Family, 36,* 13–29.

Straus, M. A. (1977). Wife beating: How common and why? *Victimology, 2,* 443–458.

Name Index

Subject Index